I0878671

Ham Radio License Manual

All 1500+ Questions

30 Practice Tests for the ARRL® Technician, General, and Extra Class Exams

Mometrix
TEST PREPARATION

Written and edited by Matthew Bowling

This paper meets the requirements of ANSI/NISO Z39.48-1992 (Permanence of Paper).

ISBN 13: 978-1-5167-2130-6
ISBN 10: 1-5167-2130-6

TABLE OF CONTENTS

Introduction

The FCC (Federal Communications Commission) has **three levels of licensure**: Technician class, General class, and Extra class. Each class provides further permissions. The Technician class allows for basic amateur radio use. The General class allows for a greater amount of freedom in amateur radio use, such as the ability to take part in world-wide communications. The Extra class allows for the greatest freedom of amateur radio use.

To aid in the process of studying, the FCC releases the full question pool for each exam. The question pools for the Technician and General class exams are made up of **35 topics** each. The Extra class question pool has **50 topics**. Each test will contain one question from each topic. The question pools contain enough questions to provide for at least 10 unique tests per class.

Because this guide contains the full question pool and 10 practice tests for each class, it is possible to familiarize yourself with the questions to a point where you can pass the exams on rote memory alone. However, to do so would be to miss out on a great opportunity to discover what knowledge gaps you have in the field of amateur radio and address them. We recommend that you **study for memory and comprehension simultaneously**. One possible strategy is outlined below:

1. Read through the question bank once to understand the full scope of the topics.
2. Address any obvious knowledge gaps with supplemental research.
3. Take a practice test and score yourself.
4. Examine each question you answered incorrectly and research its topic until you feel confident with that content.
5. Reread the question bank.
6. Repeat steps 3-5 until you comprehend each topic and its questions.

Of course, you should optimize any study plan for your individual strengths. No matter what study plan you follow, if you study diligently, you can be prepared and confident on your test day.

Technician Question Pool

T1 – FCC Rules

T1A – Purpose and permissible use of the Amateur Radio Service; Operator/primary station license grant; Meanings of basic terms used in FCC rules; Interference; RACES rules; Phonetics; Frequency Coordinator; Beacon

T1A01. Which of the following is part of the Basis and Purpose of the Amateur Radio Service?

A. Providing personal radio communications for as many citizens as possible
B. Providing communications for international contesting
C. Advancing skills in the technical and communication phases of the radio art
D. All these choices are correct

C: As stated in the FCC rules, advancing skills in the technical and communication phases of the radio art is a purpose of the Amateur Radio Service

T1A02. Which agency regulates and enforces the rules for the Amateur Radio Service in the United States?

A. ARRL
B. Homeland Security
C. The FCC
D. All these choices are correct

C: The Federal Communications Commission (FCC) is the agency that regulates and enforces the rules for the Amateur Radio Service in the United States.

T1A03. What do the FCC rules state regarding the use of a phonetic alphabet for station identification in the Amateur Radio Service?

A. It is required when transmitting emergency messages
B. It is encouraged when using phone emissions
C. It is required when in contact with foreign stations
D. All these choices are correct

B: By a phone emission in the English language. Use of a phonetic alphabet as an aid for correct station identification is encouraged.

T1A04. How do you receive official notification of your new license and call sign after passing the exam?

A. Email from the FCC with a link to download the license grant
B. USPS First-Class Mail from the FCC
C. Email from the lead volunteer examiner
D. USPS First-Class Mail from the lead volunteer examiner

A: Official notification of new licensure and call signs after passing the exam are received by email from the FCC with a link to download the license grant.

T1A05. What proves that the FCC has issued an operator/primary license grant?

A. A printed copy of the certificate of successful completion of examination
B. An email notification from the NCVEC granting the license
C. The license appears in the FCC ULS database
D. All these choices are correct

C: When transmitting, each amateur station must have a control operator. The control operator must be a person:

(a) For whom an amateur operator/primary station license grant appears on the ULS consolidated licensee database, or

(b) Who is authorized for alien reciprocal operation by § 97.107 of this part.

T1A06. On which of the following HF frequencies can automatically controlled amateur propagation beacons be found?

A. Anywhere in the Technician portion of 10 meters
B. Anywhere, if they are registered with the FCC
C. In a specific portion of each of the HF Technician bands
D. On ten meters, between 28.200 MHz and 28.300 MHz

D: Automatically controlled amateur propagation beacons can be found on ten meters between 28.200 MHz and 28.300 MHz.

T1A07. What is the FCC Part 97 definition of a space station?

A. Any satellite orbiting Earth
B. A manned satellite orbiting Earth
C. An amateur station located more than 50 km above Earth's surface
D. An amateur station using amateur radio satellites for relay of signals

C: A space station is an amateur station located more than 50 km above the Earth's surface.

T1A08. Who recommends transmit/receive channels for repeater and auxiliary stations?

A. A Frequency Spectrum Manager appointed by the FCC
B. A Volunteer Frequency Coordinator recognized by local amateurs
C. An FCC Regional Field Office
D. The International Telecommunication Union

B: A frequency coordinator recommends transmit/receive channels and other parameters for auxiliary and repeater stations. A frequency coordinator is a person or group of people who advise users of the appropriate repeater frequencies, with the intention of diminishing interference between repeaters who are operating in roughly the same frequency in the same geographical area.

T1A09. Who selects a Frequency Coordinator?

A. The FCC Office of Spectrum Management and Coordination Policy
B. The local chapter of the Office of National Council of Independent Frequency Coordinators
C. Amateur operators in a local or regional area whose stations are eligible to be repeater or auxiliary stations
D. The FCC Regional Field Office

C: Amateur operators in a local or regional area whose stations are eligible to be auxiliary or repeater stations may select a frequency coordinator. [97.3(a)(22)]

T1A10. Besides an FCC-issued amateur operator license, what is required to be the control operator of a Radio Amateur Civil Emergency Service (RACES) Station?

A. A written recommendation by the local ARRL Emergency Coordinator
B. Membership in the Amateur Radio Emergency Service (ARES)
C. Certification of current enrollment by a civil defense organization
D. Nothing

C: Certification of current enrollment by a civil defense organization is required, in addition to an FCC-issued amateur operator license, to be the control operator of a RACES station. [97.407(a)]

T1A11. Which of the following is prohibited?

A. International communications on VHF bands and higher frequencies
B. Willful or malicious interference
C. Third-party traffic using digital modes
D. All these choices are correct

B: Willful or malicious interference is prohibited.

T1B – Frequency allocations; Emission modes; Spectrum sharing; Transmissions near band edges; Contacting the International Space Station; Power output

T1B01. Which of the following frequency ranges are available for phone operation by Technician licensees?

A. 28.050 MHz to 28.150 MHz
B. 28.100 MHz to 28.300 MHz
C. 28.300 MHz to 28.500 MHz
D. 28.500 MHz to 28.600 MHz

C: Frequencies in the 28.300 MHz to 28.500 MHz range are available for phone operation by Technician licensees. [97.301(e)]

T1B02. Which of the following U.S. amateur radio operators are allowed to contact the International Space Station (ISS) on VHF bands?

A. Only amateurs with a General class or higher license
B. Any amateur with a Technician class or higher license
C. Only amateurs with a General class or higher license, and NASA approval
D. Any amateurs with a Technician class or higher license, and NASA approval

B: For a station having a control operator who has been granted a Technician, General, Advanced, or Amateur Extra Class operator license or who holds a CEPT radio-amateur license or IARP of any class. The following frequency bands and segments are authorized to space stations:

(1) The 17 m, 15 m, 12 m, and 10 m bands, 6 mm, 4 mm, 2 mm and 1 mm bands; and

(2) The 7.0-7.1 MHz, 14.00-14.25 MHz, 144-146 MHz, 435-438 MHz, 2400-2450 MHz, 3.40-3.41 GHz, 5.83-5.85 GHz, 10.45-10.50 GHz, and 24.00-24.05 GHz segments.

[97.301, 97.207(c)]

T1B03. Which frequency is in the 6-meter amateur band?

A. 49.00 MHz
B. 52.525 MHz
C. 28.50 MHz
D. 222.15 MHz

B: 52.525 MHz is within the 6-meter band. [97.301(a)]

T1B04. Which amateur band includes 146.52 MHz?

A. 6 meters
B. 20 meters
C. 70 centimeters
D. 2 meters

D: If your station is transmitting on 146.52 MHz, it is using the 2-meter amateur band. [97.301(a)]

T1B05. Which of the following bands include frequencies where Technicians are authorized to use digital modes such as FT8?

A. 10 meters
B. 6 meters
C. 2 meters
D. All these choices are correct

D: All of the provided choices are correct. [97.301, 97.305]

T1B06. On which HF bands does a Technician class operator have phone privileges?

A. None
B. 10-meter band only
C. 80-meter, 40-meter, 15-meter, and 10-meter bands
D. 30-meter band only

B: A Technician Class control operator can use 80, 40, 15, and 10m wavelengths, but only the 10m for phone privileges. [97.301(e), 97.305]

T1B07. Which of the following VHF/UHF band segments are limited to CW only?

A. 50.0 MHz to 50.1 MHz and 144.0 MHz to 144.1 MHz
B. 219 MHz to 220 MHz and 420.0 MHz to 420.1 MHz
C. 902.0 MHz to 902.1 MHz
D. All these choices are correct

A: 50.0 MHz to 50.1 MHz and 144.0 MHz to 144.1 MHz are the only ranges in VHF/UHF that are for CW only. [97.305(a), (c)]

T1B08. How are US amateurs restricted in segments of bands where the Amateur Radio Service is secondary?

A. U.S. amateurs may find non-amateur stations in those segments, and must avoid interfering with them
B. U.S. amateurs must give foreign amateur stations priority in those segments
C. International communications are not permitted in those segments
D. Digital transmissions are not permitted in those segments

A: The amateur service is secondary in some portions of the 70 cm band because U.S. amateurs may find non-amateur stations in the bands and must avoid interfering with them. [97.303]

T1B09. Why should you not set your transmit frequency to be exactly at the edge of an amateur band or sub-band?

A. To allow for calibration error in the transmitter frequency display
B. So that modulation sidebands do not extend beyond the band edge
C. To allow for transmitter frequency drift
D. All these choices are correct

D: There are several reasons why an operator should not set the transmit frequency to be exactly at the edge of an amateur band or sub-band. To begin with, this allows for calibration error in the transmitter frequency display. It also ensures that modulation sidebands do not extend beyond the band edge. Finally, it allows for transmitter frequency drift. [97.101(a), 97.301(a-e)]

T1B10. Where may SSB phone be used in amateur bands above 50 MHz?

A. Only in sub-bands allocated to General class or higher licensees
B. Only on repeaters
C. In at least some segment of all these bands
D. On any band if the power is limited to 25 watts

C: There is some part of all the amateur bands above 50 MHz that is available for SSB. [97.305(c)]

T1B11. What is the maximum peak envelope power output for Technician class operators in their HF band segments?

A. 200 watts
B. 100 watts
C. 50 watts
D. 10 watts

A: No station may transmit with a transmitter power output exceeding 200 W PEP:

(1) On the 10.10-10.15 MHz segment;

(2) On the 3.525-3.60 MHz, 7.025-7.125 MHz, 21.025-21.20 MHz, and 28.0-28.5 MHz segment when the control operator is a Novice Class operator or a Technician Class operator; or

(3) The 7.050-7.075 MHz segment when the station is within ITU Regions 1 or 3. [97.313]

T1B12. Except for some specific restrictions, what is the maximum peak envelope power output for Technician class operators using frequencies above 30 MHz?

A. 50 watts
B. 100 watts
C. 500 watts
D. 1500 watts

D: No station may transmit with a transmitter power exceeding 1.5 kW PEP. [97.313(b)]

T1C – Licensing: Classes, Sequential and Vanity Call Sign Systems, Places Where the Amateur Radio Service Is Regulated by the FCC, Name and Address on FCC License Database, Term, Renewal, Grace Period, Maintaining Mailing Address; International Communications

T1C01. For which classes of amateur radio licenses does the FCC currently issue new licenses?

A. Novice, Technician, General, Amateur Extra
B. Technician, Technician Plus, General, Amateur Extra
C. Novice, Technician Plus, General, Advanced
D. Technician, General, Amateur Extra

D: The classes of amateur operator license grants are: Technician, General, and Amateur Extra. The person named in the operator license grant is authorized to be the control operator of an amateur station with the privileges authorized to the operator class specified on the license grant. [97.9(a), 97.17(a)]

T1C02. Who may select a desired call sign under the vanity call sign rules?

A. Only a licensed amateur with a General or Amateur Extra Class license
B. Only a licensed amateur with an Amateur Extra Class license
C. Only a licensed amateur who has been licensed continuously for more than 10 years
D. Any licensed amateur

D: The person named in an operator/primary station license grant or in a club station license grant is eligible to make application for modification of the license grant, or the renewal thereof, to show a call sign selected by the vanity call sign system. [97.19]

T1C03. What types of international communications are FCC-licensed amateur radio stations permitted to make?

A. Communications incidental to the purposes of the Amateur Radio Service and remarks of a personal character
B. Communications incidental to conducting business or remarks of a personal nature
C. Only communications incidental to contest exchanges; all other communications are prohibited
D. Any communications that would be permitted by an international broadcast station

A: FCC-licensed amateur stations are permitted to make international communications incidental to the purposes of the amateur service and remarks of a personal character. [97.117]

T1C04. What may happen if the FCC is unable to reach you by email?

A. Fine and suspension of operator license
B. Revocation of the station license or suspension of the operator license
C. Revocation of access to the license record in the FCC system
D. Nothing; there is no such requirement

B: If the FCC is unable to reach you by email, then your station license may be revoked or your operator license may be suspended. [97.23]

T1C05. Which of the following is a valid Group D call sign format for Technician class?

A. KF1XXX
B. KA1X
C. W1XX
D. All these choices are correct

A: Of the choices listed, only the KF1XXX series of call signs is available to technician class amateur operators. The other two series listed are available only to extra class amateur operators.

T1C06. Which of the following statements is true about using your amateur radio license when operating aboard a vessel or craft in international waters?

A. Amateur operation is prohibited in international waters
B. You may only operate during maritime emergencies
C. You need special FCC authorization for maritime mobile operation
D. You may operate from a US-documented vessel with the master's permission

D: You may operate in international waters from a US-documented vessel with the master's permission. [97.5(a)(2), 97.11(a)]

T1C07. How long before the expiration date may an amateur radio license renewal be requested?

A. 30 days
B. 90 days
C. 6 months
D. 1 year

B: An amateur radio license renewal may be requested 90 days before the expiration date. [97.21, 1.949]

T1C08. What is the normal term for an FCC-issued amateur radio license?

A. Five years
B. Eight years
C. Ten years
D. Life

C: The normal term for an FCC-issued primary station/operator license grant is 10 years. [97.25]

T1C09. What is the grace period for renewal if an amateur license expires?

A. Two years
B. Three years
C. Five years
D. Ten years

A: The grace period following the expiration of an amateur license, within which the license may be renewed, is two years. [97.21(a)(b)]

T1C10. How soon after passing the examination for your first amateur radio license may you transmit on the amateur radio bands?

A. Immediately on receiving your Certificate of Successful Completion of Examination (CSCE)
B. As soon as your operator/station license grant appears on the ARRL website
C. As soon as your operator/station license grant appears in the FCC's license database
D. As soon as you receive your license in the mail from the FCC

C: After you pass the examination required for your first amateur radio license, you may operate a transmitter on an amateur service frequency as soon as your name and call sign appear in the FCC's ULS database. [97.5a]

T1C11. If your license has expired and is still within the allowable grace period, may you continue to transmit on the amateur radio bands?

A. Yes, for up to two years
B. Yes, as soon as you apply for renewal
C. Yes, for up to one year
D. No, you must wait until the license has been renewed

D: An operator whose license has expired but who is still within the allowable grace period may not continue to operate a transmitter on amateur service frequencies until the ULS database shows that the license has been renewed. [97.21(b)]

T1D – Authorized and Prohibited Transmissions; Sale of Equipment

T1D01. With which countries are FCC-licensed amateur radio stations prohibited from exchanging communications?

A. Any country whose administration has notified the International Telecommunication Union (ITU) that it objects to such communications
B. Any country whose administration has notified the American Radio Relay League (ARRL) that it objects to such communications
C. Any country banned from such communications by the International Amateur Radio Union (IARU)
D. Any country banned from making such communications by the American Radio Relay League (ARRL)

A: FCC-licensed amateur stations are prohibited from exchanging communications with any country whose administration has notified the ITU that it objects to such communications. [97.111(a)(1)]

T1D02. Under which of the following circumstances are one-way transmissions by an amateur station prohibited?

A. Announcements of upcoming ham radio operating events
B. Broadcasting
C. International Morse Code Practice
D. Telecommand or transmissions of telemetry

B: While an amateur station is broadcasting, one-way transmissions are prohibited. [97.113(b), 97.111(b)]

T1D03. When is it permissible to transmit messages encoded to obscure their meaning?

A. Only when using a remote station during a contest
B. Only when transmitting certain approved digital codes
C. Only when transmitting control commands to space stations or model craft
D. Never

C: An amateur station is allowed to hide the meaning of a transmitted message with codes or ciphers only when transmitting control commands to space stations or radio control craft. [97.211(b), 97.215(b), 97.113(a)(4)]

T1D04. Under what conditions is an amateur station authorized to transmit music using a phone emission?

A. When incidental to an authorized retransmission of manned spacecraft communications
B. When the music produces no spurious emissions
C. When transmissions are limited to less than three minutes per hour
D. When the music is transmitted above 1280 MHz

A: The only time an amateur station is authorized to transmit music is when it is incidental to authorized retransmission of manned spacecraft communications. [97.113(a)(4), 97.113(c)]

T1D05. When may amateur radio operators use their stations to notify other amateurs of the availability of equipment for sale or trade?

A. Never
B. When the equipment is not the personal property of either the station licensee, or the control operator, or their close relatives
C. When no profit is made on the sale
D. When selling amateur radio equipment and not on a regular basis

D: Amateur radio operators may use their stations to notify other amateurs of the availability of equipment for sale or trade when the equipment is normally used in an amateur station and such activity is not conducted on a regular basis. [97.113(a)(3)(ii)]

T1D06. What, if any, are the restrictions concerning transmission of language that may be considered indecent or obscene?

A. The FCC maintains a list of words that are not permitted to be used on amateur frequencies
B. Any such language is prohibited
C. The International Telecommunications Union (ITU) maintains a list of words that are not permitted to be used on amateur frequencies
D. There is no such prohibition

B: As stated by the FCC, no amateur station shall transmit obscene or indecent words or language. [97.113(a)(4)]

T1D07. Which of the following is an example of an auxiliary station?

A. A station sending one-way transmissions between a remote repeater receiver and the main repeater transmitter
B. A backup radio for emergency use in case the main station radio fails
C. A station used in the Military Auxiliary Radio System for linking government and amateur stations in a digital network
D. A second station utilized in multi-operator contest stations

A: A station sending one-way transmissions between a remote repeater receiver and the main repeater transmitter is an example of an auxiliary station. [97.113(d), 97.201(e)]

T1D08. In which of the following circumstances may the control operator of an amateur station receive compensation for operating that station?

A. When the communication is related to the sale of amateur equipment by the control operator's employer
B. When the communication is a part of classroom instruction at an educational institution
C. When the communication is made to obtain emergency information for a local broadcast station
D. All these choices are correct

B: The control operator of an amateur station may receive compensation for operating the station when the communication is incidental to classroom instruction at an educational institution. [97.113(a)(3)(iii)]

T1D09. When may amateur stations transmit information in support of broadcasting, program production, or news gathering, assuming no other means is available?

A. When such communications are directly related to the immediate safety of human life or protection of property
B. When broadcasting communications to or from the space shuttle
C. Where non-commercial programming is gathered and supplied exclusively to the National Public Radio network
D. Never

A: Assuming no other means is available, amateur stations are authorized to transmit signals related to broadcasting, program production, or news gathering only where such communications directly relate to the immediate safety of human life or protection of property. [97.113(5)(b)]

T1D10. How does the FCC define broadcasting for the Amateur Radio Service?

A. Two-way transmissions by amateur stations
B. Any transmission made by the licensed station
C. Transmission of messages directed only to amateur operators
D. Transmissions intended for reception by the general public

D: In the FCC rules for the amateur services, broadcasting refers to transmissions intended for reception by the general public. Broadcasting refers to transmissions that are meant to be received by the general public, either on relay or directly. [97.3(a)(10)]

T1D11. When may an amateur station transmit without identifying on the air?

A. When the transmissions are of a brief nature to make station adjustments
B. When the transmissions are unmodulated
C. When the transmitted power level is below 0.1 watt
D. When transmitting signals to control model craft

D: The station identification procedure is not required for an amateur station's transmissions directed only to the model craft, provided that a label indicating the station call sign and the station licensee's name and address is affixed to the station transmitter. [97.215]

T1D12. Which of the following is required when making on-the-air test transmissions?

A. Identify the transmitting station
B. Conduct tests only between 10 p.m. and 6 a.m. local time
C. Notify the FCC of the transmissions
D. All these choices are correct

A: Identify the transmitting station when making on-the-air test transmissions. [97.119(a)]

T1E – Control operator: eligibility, designating, privileges, duties, location, required; Control point; Control types: automatic, remote

T1E01. When may an amateur station transmit without a control operator?

A. When using automatic control, such as in the case of a repeater
B. When the station licensee is away and another licensed amateur is using the station
C. When the transmitting station is an auxiliary station
D. Never

D: When transmitting, each amateur station must have a control operator. [97.7(a)]

T1E02. Who may be the control operator of a station communicating through an amateur satellite or space station?

A. Only an Amateur Extra Class operator
B. A General class or higher licensee with a satellite operator certification
C. Only an Amateur Extra Class operator who is also an AMSAT member
D. Any amateur allowed to transmit on the satellite uplink frequency

D: Any amateur station may be a space station. A holder of any class operator license may be the control operator of a space station, subject to the privileges of the class of operator license held by the control operator. [97.301, 97.207(c)]

T1E03. Who must designate the station control operator?

A. The station licensee
B. The FCC
C. The frequency coordinator
D. Any licensed operator

A: The station licensee must designate the station control operator. [97.103(b)]

T1E04. What determines the transmitting frequency privileges of an amateur station?

A. The frequency authorized by the frequency coordinator
B. The frequencies printed on the license grant
C. The highest class of operator license held by anyone on the premises
D. The class of operator license held by the control operator

D: The transmitting privileges of an amateur station are determined by the class of operator license held by the control operator. [97.103(b)]

T1E05. What is an amateur station's control point?

A. The location of the station's transmitting antenna
B. The location of the station's transmitting apparatus
C. The location at which the control operator function is performed
D. The mailing address of the station licensee

C: An amateur station control point is the location at which the control operator function is performed. The control point is the set of locations at which the control operator functions are carried out. [97.3(a)(14)]

T1E06. When, other than during an emergency, may a Technician class licensee be the control operator of a station operating in an Amateur Extra Class band segment?

A. At no time
B. When designated as the control operator by an Amateur Extra Class licensee
C. As part of a multi-operator contest team
D. When using a club station whose trustee holds an Amateur Extra Class license

A: Each class of license allows the licensee to operate only within the allotted frequencies at their level or below. [97.301]

T1E07. When the control operator is not the station licensee, who is responsible for the proper operation of the station?

A. All licensed amateurs who are present at the operation
B. Only the station licensee
C. Only the control operator
D. The control operator and the station licensee

D: When the control operator is not the station licensee, the control operator and the station licensee are both responsible for the proper operation of the station. [97.103(a)]

T1E08. Which of the following is an example of automatic control?

A. Repeater operation
B. Controlling a station over the internet
C. Using a computer or other device to send CW automatically
D. Using a computer or other device to identify automatically

A: A repeater operation may be automatically controlled. [97.3(a)(6), 97.205(d)]

T1E09. Which amateur stations may be remotely controlled?

A. Only repeater stations
B. Only automatically controlled stations
C. Only digital stations
D. Any station

D: Any amateur stations may be remotely controlled. [97.109(c)]

T1E10. Which of the following is an example of remote control as defined in Part 97?

A. A software defined radio (SDR)
B. Operating the station over the internet
C. Controlling a model aircraft, boat, or car by amateur radio
D. Earth-Moon-Earth (EME) communication

B: Operating the station over the internet is an example of remote control. [97.3(a)(39)]

T1E11. What is a control operator as defined in Part 97?

A. The person speaking or otherwise communicating messages over an amateur station
B. The person who is the licensee of an amateur station
C. An amateur operator identified in the FCC database as responsible for transmissions and FCC rules compliance at a station license location
D. An amateur operator designated by the licensee of a station to be responsible for transmissions and FCC rules compliance at that station

D: An amateur operator designated by the licensee of a station to be responsible for transmissions and FCC rules compliance at that station is the control operator as defined in Part 97. [97.3(a)(13)]

T1F – Station identification; Repeaters; Third-party communications; Club stations; FCC inspection

T1F01. When must the station licensee make the station and the station records available for inspection?

A. At any time ten days after notification by the FCC of such an inspection
B. At any time upon request by an FCC representative
C. At any time after a written notification by the FCC of such inspection
D. Only when presented with a valid warrant by an FCC official or government agent

B: The station licensee must make the station and the station records available for inspection upon request by an FCC representative. [97.103(c)]

T1F02. How often must you identify with your FCC-assigned call sign when using tactical call signs such as "Race Headquarters"?

A. Never, the tactical call is sufficient
B. Once every hour
C. At least every 10 minutes during and at the end of a communication
D. At the end of every transmission

C: When using tactical identifiers, a station must transmit its FCC-assigned call sign every 10 minutes. [97.119(a)]

T1F03. When are you required to transmit your assigned call sign?

A. At the beginning of each contact, and every 10 minutes thereafter
B. At least once during each transmission
C. At least every 15 minutes during and at the end of a communication
D. At least every 10 minutes during and at the end of a communication

D: An amateur station is required to transmit its assigned call sign at least every 10 minutes during and at the end of a communication. [97.119(a)]

T1F04. What language must you use for identification when using a phone emission?

A. Any language recognized by the United Nations
B. Any language recognized by the ITU
C. English
D. English, French, or Spanish

C: English is the acceptable language for station identification use when operating in a phone sub-band. [97.119(b)(2)]

T1F05. What method of call sign identification is required for a station transmitting phone signals?

A. Send the call sign followed by the indicator RPT
B. Send the call sign using a CW or phone emission
C. Send the call sign followed by the indicator R
D. Send the call sign using only a phone emission

B: When a station is transmitting phone signals, it should use the call sign identification system of sending the call sign using CW or phone emission. [97.119(b)(2)]

T1F06. Which of the following self-assigned indicators are acceptable when using a phone transmission?

A. KL7CC stroke W3
B. KL7CC slant W3
C. KL7CC slash W3
D. All these choices are correct

D: For identification during a phone transmission, KL7CC stroke W3, KL7CC slant W3, and KL7CC slash W3 would all be acceptable formats for a self-assigned indicator. [97.119(c)]

T1F07. Which of the following restrictions apply when a non-licensed person speaks to a foreign amateur radio station via a station under the control of an FCC-licensed amateur radio operator?

A. The person must be a U.S. citizen
B. The foreign station must be in a country with which the U.S. has a third-party agreement
C. The licensed control operator must do the station identification
D. All these choices are correct

B: An amateur station may transmit messages for a third party to any station within the jurisdiction of any foreign government when transmitting emergency or disaster relief communications and any station within the jurisdiction of any foreign government whose administration has made arrangements with the United States to allow amateur stations to be used for transmitting international communications on behalf of third parties. No station shall transmit messages for a third party to any station within the jurisdiction of any foreign government whose administration has not made such an arrangement. [97.115(a)(2)]

T1F08. What is the definition of third-party communications?

A. A message from a control operator to another amateur station control operator on behalf of another person
B. Amateur radio communications where three stations are in communications with one another
C. Operation when the transmitting equipment is licensed to a person other than the control operator
D. Temporary authorization for an unlicensed person to transmit on the amateur bands for technical experiments

A: Third-party communications are any message from the control operator (first party) of an amateur station to another amateur station control operator (second party) on behalf of another person (third party). [97.3(a)(47)]

T1F09. What type of amateur station simultaneously retransmits the signal of another amateur station on a different channel or channels?

A. Beacon station
B. Remote control station
C. Repeater station
D. Message forwarding station

C: A repeater station is an amateur station that simultaneously retransmits the signal of another amateur station on a different channel or channels. [97.3(a)(40)]

T1F10. Who is accountable if a repeater inadvertently retransmits communications that violate the FCC rules?

A. The control operator of the originating station
B. The control operator of the repeater
C. The owner of the repeater
D. Both the originating station and the repeater owner

A: If a repeater inadvertently retransmits communications that violate the FCC rules, the control operator of the originating station is accountable. [97.205(g)]

T1F11. Which of the following is a requirement for the issuance of a club station license grant?

A. The trustee must have an Amateur Extra Class operator license grant
B. The club must have at least four members
C. The club must be registered with the American Radio Relay League (ARRL)
D. All these choices are correct

B: A club station license grant may be held only by the person who is the license trustee designated by an officer of the club. The trustee must be a person who holds an operator/primary station license grant. The club must be composed of at least four persons and must have a name, a document of organization, management, and a primary purpose devoted to amateur service activities consistent with this part. [97.5(b)(2)]

T2 – Operating Procedures

T2A – Station Operation: Choosing an Operating Frequency, Calling Another Station, Test Transmissions; Band Plans: Calling Frequencies, Repeater Offsets

T2A01. What is a common repeater frequency offset in the 2-meter band?

A. Plus or minus 5 MHz
B. Plus or minus 600 kHz
C. Plus or minus 500 kHz
D. Plus or minus 1 MHz

B: The most common repeater frequency offset in the 2-meter band is plus or minus 600 kHz.

T2A02. What is the national calling frequency for FM simplex operations in the 2-meter band?

A. 146.520 MHz
B. 145.000 MHz
C. 432.100 MHz
D. 446.000 MHz

A: 146.520 and 446.000 are both simplex frequencies, but only 146.520 is in the 2m band.

T2A03. What is a common repeater frequency offset in the 70-centimeter band?

A. Plus or minus 5 MHz
B. Plus or minus 600 kHz
C. Plus or minus 500 kHz
D. Plus or minus 1 MHz

A: A common repeater frequency offset in the 70 cm band is plus or minus 5 MHz.

T2A04. What is an appropriate way to call another station on a repeater if you know the other station's call sign?

A. Say "break, break," then the other station's call sign, followed by your call sign
B. Say the station's call sign, then identify with your call sign
C. Say "CQ" three times, then the other station's call sign, followed by your call sign
D. Wait for the station to call CQ, then answer with your call sign

B: An appropriate way to call another station on a repeater if you know the other station's call sign is to say the station's call sign and then identify with your call sign.

T2A05. How should you respond to a station calling CQ?

A. Transmit "CQ" followed by the other station's call sign
B. Transmit your call sign followed by the other station's call sign
C. Transmit the other station's call sign followed by your call sign
D. Transmit a signal report followed by your call sign

C: When responding to a call of CQ, you should transmit the other station's call sign followed by your call sign.

T2A06. What is an effective way to seek a call from any phone station when not using a repeater?

A. Sign your call sign once, followed by the words "listening for a call;" if there is no answer, change the frequency and repeat
B. Say "QTC," followed by "this is" and your call sign; if there is no answer, change the frequency and repeat
C. Transmit an unmodulated carrier for approximately 10 seconds, followed by "this is" and your call sign, and pause to listen; repeat as necessary
D. Repeat "CQ" a few times, followed by "this is," and your call sign, then pause to listen; repeat as necessary

D: Repeating "CQ" a few times, followed by "this is," and your call sign, then pausing to listen is an effective way to seek a call from any phone station when not using a repeater.

T2A07. What does the term "repeater offset" mean?

A. The difference between a repeater's transmit and receive frequencies
B. The repeater has a time delay to prevent interference
C. The approximately half-second delay to allow for the "squelch tail" to be removed
D. The fee charged by the repeater owner or club to provide for maintenance

A: Repeater offset is the difference between the received and transmitted frequencies of a repeater station.

T2A08. What is the meaning of the procedural signal "CQ"?

A. A shortened form of the term "Contest QSO"
B. "Communication Quality," used to indicate transmitted audio clarity
C. Only the called station should transmit
D. Calling any station

D: The meaning of the procedural signal CQ is "calling any station."

T2A09. Which of the following is a customary way to indicate a station is listening on a repeater and looking for a contact?

A. "CQ CQ" followed by the repeater's call sign
B. The station's call sign followed by the word "listening"
C. The repeater's call sign followed by the station's call sign
D. "QSY" followed by your call sign

B: A call sign followed by the word "listening" is often used in place of CQ to indicate that you are listening on a repeater.

T2A10. What is a band plan, beyond the privileges established by the FCC?

A. A voluntary guideline for using different modes or activities within an amateur band
B. A list of operating schedules
C. A list of available net frequencies
D. A plan devised by a club to indicate frequency band usage

A: A band plan, beyond the privileges established by the FCC, is a voluntary guideline for using different modes or activities within an amateur band.

T2A11. What term describes an amateur station that is transmitting and receiving on the same frequency?

A. Full duplex
B. Diplex
C. Simplex
D. Multiplex

C: Receiving and transmitting on the same frequency is always referred to as 'simplex.'

T2B – VHF/UHF Operating Practices: FM Repeater, Simplex, Reverse Splits; Access Tones: CTCSS, DTMF; DMR Operation; Resolving Operational Problems; Q Signals

T2B01. What is the purpose of the reverse function on a VHF/UHF transceiver?

A. To reduce power output
B. To increase power output
C. To listen on a repeater's input frequency
D. To listen on a repeater's output frequency

C: A VHF/UHF transceiver's "reverse" function is used to listen on a repeater's input frequency.

T2B02. What term describes the use of a sub-audible tone transmitted along with normal voice audio to open the squelch of a receiver?

A. Carrier squelch
B. Tone burst
C. DTMF
D. CTCSS

D: CTCSS is the use of a sub-audible tone transmitted with normal voice audio to open the squelch of the receiver.

T2B03. Which of the following describes a linked repeater network?

A. A network of repeaters in which signals received by one repeater are transmitted by all the repeaters in the network
B. A single repeater with more than one receiver
C. Multiple repeaters with the same control operator
D. A system of repeaters linked by APRS

A: A linked repeater network is a network of repeaters that are all repeating the signal received by one repeater of the network.

T2B04. Which of the following could be the reason you are unable to access a repeater whose output you can hear?

A. Improper transceiver offset
B. You are using the wrong CTCSS tone
C. You are using the wrong DCS code
D. All these choices are correct

D: There are several common problems that might cause you to be able to hear but not access a repeater even when transmitting with the proper offset. This may occur when the repeater receiver requires audio tone burst, a CTCSS tone, or a DCS tone sequence for access.

T2B05. Which of the following would cause your FM transmission audio to drop out on voice peaks?

A. Your repeater offset is inverted
B. Your FM deviation is too low
C. You are talking too loudly
D. Your transmit power is too high

C: Speaking too loudly is the most common cause of audio distortions on voice peaks.

T2B06. What type of signaling to a repeater uses two simultaneous audio tones?

A. DTMF
B. CTCSS
C. GMRS
D. D-STAR

A: DTMF signals use pairs of audio tones.

T2B07. How can you join a digital repeater's "talkgroup"?

A. Register with the local Frequency Coordinator
B. Register with the digital repeater control operator
C. Program your radio with the group's ID or code
D. Program your radio with the DTMF tone used by the talkgroup

C: Once you have identified the talkgroup you wish to join, all you need is the group's ID or code in order to receive and transmit on their channel.

T2B08. Which of the following applies when two stations transmitting on the same frequency interfere with each other?

A. The stations should negotiate continued use of the frequency
B. Both stations should choose another frequency to avoid conflict
C. Whichever station was on the frequency first has preemptive rights to the frequency
D. Use subaudible tones so both stations can share the frequency

A: If two stations transmitting on the same frequency begin to interfere with one another, it is up to the participants to resolve the issue. There is no absolute right to any amateur frequency, so operators are encouraged to remain courteous and work out a solution.

T2B09. Why are simplex channels designated in the VHF/UHF band plans?

A. So stations within range of each other can communicate without tying up a repeater
B. For contest operation
C. For working DX only
D. So stations with simple transmitters can access the repeater without automated offset

A: The main purpose of designating simplex channels is to allow communication directly between sender and receiver and not tie up a repeater.

T2B10. Which Q signal indicates that you are receiving interference from other stations?

A. QRM
B. QRN
C. QTH
D. QSB

A: The Q signal used to indicate that you are receiving interference from other stations is QRM. Q signals are useful methods for accelerating communication. A Q signal may be issued as a question or as a response. For example, QRG may mean "What is my exact frequency?" or "Your exact frequency is."

T2B11. Which Q signal indicates that you are changing frequency?

A. QRU
B. QSY
C. QSL
D. QRZ

B: The Q signal used to indicate that you're changing frequency is QSY. This Q signal can also be used to request a shift to another frequency.

T2B12. What is the digital color code used on DMR repeater systems?

A. An access code which must be programmed into a DMR transmitter to access a specific repeater
B. A code which automatically programs the repeater offset to a frequency chosen by the user
C. A code which identifies the specific CODEC being used so that the repeater can properly decode the audio
D. A code transmitted by the repeater to indicate health and status of the equipment

A: The digital color code on DMR repeater systems is an access code that must be programmed into a DMR transmitter to access a specific repeater.

T2B13. What is the purpose of a squelch function?

A. Reduce a CW transmitter's key clicks
B. Mute the receiver audio when a signal is not present
C. Eliminate parasitic oscillations in an RF amplifier
D. Reduce interference from impulse noise

B: A squelch function is intended to mute the receiver audio when a signal is not present.

T2B14. Which of the following is a "talkgroup"?

A. A group of amateur radio operators who share email on a specific amateur radio topic
B. An identifier used by DMR to organize radio traffic so that those who want to hear the group aren't bothered by other radio traffic
C. The members of a net organized for amateur radio operators with a specific common interest
D. A method of automatically alerting all group members to the frequency where any member is transmitting

B: A talkgroup is an identifier used by DMR to organize radio traffic so that those who want to hear the group aren't bothered by other radio traffic.

T2C – Public Service: Emergency Operations, Applicability of FCC Rules, RACES and ARES, Net and Traffic Procedures, Operating Restrictions During Emergencies, Use of Phonetics in Message Handling

T2C01. When do the FCC Part 97 Amateur Radio Service rules NOT apply to the operation of an amateur station?

A. When operating under RACES rules
B. When operating under FEMA rules
C. When operating under ARES rules
D. FCC rules always apply

D: FCC rules always apply to the operation of an amateur station. [97.103(a)]

T2C02. Which of the following are typical duties of a Net Control Station?

A. Choose the regular net meeting time and frequency
B. Ensure that all stations checking into the net are properly licensed for operation on the net frequency
C. Call the net to order and direct communications between stations checking in
D. All these choices are correct

C: A typical duty of a Net Control Station is to call the net to order and direct communications between stations checking in. The Net Control Station helps maintain order and manages the flow of traffic on the net.

T2C03. What technique is used to ensure that voice messages containing unusual words are received correctly?

A. Send the words by voice and Morse code
B. Use the Q-code "QSR" to ask the receiving station to repeat the words back
C. Spell the words using a standard phonetic alphabet
D. All these choices are correct

C: To ensure that any proper names and unusual words are copied correctly by the receiving station, it is good practice to spell them out using a standard phonetic alphabet.

T2C04. What is RACES?

A. An emergency organization combining amateur radio and citizens band operators and frequencies
B. An international radio experimentation society
C. A radio contest held in a short period, sometimes called a "sprint"
D. An FCC Part 97 amateur radio service for civil defense communications during national emergencies

D: RACES is the Radio Amateur Civil Emergency Service, an FCC Part 97 amateur radio service for civil defense communications during national emergencies. It is a specific emergency communications service defined by FCC rules.

T2C05. What does the term "traffic" refer to in net operation?

A. Formal messages exchanged by net stations
B. The number of stations checking in and out of a net
C. Operation by mobile or portable stations
D. A count of the number of activations of the net each month

A: Traffic is a special term for messages on a network.

T2C06. What is the Amateur Radio Emergency Service (ARES)?

A. A group of licensed amateurs who have voluntarily registered their qualifications and equipment for communications duty in the public service
B. A group of licensed amateurs who are members of the military and who voluntarily agreed to provide message handling services in the case of an emergency
C. A training program that provides licensing courses for those interested in obtaining an amateur license to use during emergencies
D. A training program that certifies amateur operators for membership in the Radio Amateur Civil Emergency Service

A: Amateur Radio Emergency Service (ARES) are licensed amateurs who have voluntarily registered their qualifications and equipment for communications duty in the public service

T2C07. Which of the following is standard practice when you participate in a net?

A. When first responding to the net control station, transmit your call sign, name, and address as in the FCC database
B. Record the time of each of your transmissions
C. Unless you are reporting an emergency, transmit only when directed by the net control station
D. All these choices are correct

C: To minimize disruptions to an emergency traffic net once you have checked in, do not transmit on the net frequency until asked to do so by the net control station.

T2C08. Which of the following relays messages using email addresses based on amateur callsigns?

A. Winlink
B. FT8
C. PSK31
D. AMTOR

A: Winlink relays messages using email addresses based on amateur callsigns.

T2C09. Are amateur station control operators ever permitted to operate outside the frequency privileges of their license class?

A. No
B. Yes, but only when part of a FEMA emergency plan
C. Yes, but only when part of a RACES emergency plan
D. Yes, but only in situations involving the immediate safety of human life or protection of property

D: Amateur station control operators are permitted to operate outside the frequency privileges of their license class only if necessary in situations involving the immediate safety of human life or protection of property

T2C10. What information is contained in the preamble of a formal traffic message?

A. The email address of the originating station
B. The address of the intended recipient
C. The telephone number of the addressee
D. Information needed to track the message

D: The preamble in a formal traffic message is information needed to track the message as it passes through the amateur radio traffic handling system. The preamble is the first part of a radiogram. It identifies the source and some basic information about the message.

T2C11. What is meant by "check" in a radiogram header?

A. The number of words or word equivalents in the text portion of the message
B. The call sign of the originating station
C. A list of stations that have relayed the message
D. A box on the message form that indicates that the message was received and/or relayed

A: The term "check," in reference to a radiogram header, is a count of the number of words or word equivalents in the text portion of the message. It is important to confirm the word count with the receiving station, as an incorrect word count will suggest to relaying stations that there is an error in the message.

T2C12. Which of the following requires certification by a civil defense agency?

A. ARES
B. RACES
C. MARS
D. SKYWARN

B: RACES requires certification by a civil defense agency.

T3 – Radio Wave Propagation

T3A – Radio wave characteristics: how a radio signal travels, fading, multipath, polarization, wavelength vs absorption; Antenna orientation

T3A01. Why do VHF signal strengths sometimes vary greatly when the antenna is moved only a few feet?

A. The signal path encounters different concentrations of water vapor
B. VHF ionospheric propagation is very sensitive to path length
C. Multipath propagation cancels or reinforces signals
D. The Doppler effect causes slight frequency shifts which result in changes in signal strength

C: If a signal is experiencing multipath propagation, it can easily cancel itself out or reinforce itself over a distance of a few feet.

T3A02. How does vegetation affect UHF and microwave signals?

A. Causes knife-edge diffraction, distorting voice peaks
B. Absorbs signals, leading to poor reception of weak signals
C. Amplifies signals, improving reception of weak signals
D. Has no effect

B: Vegetation can absorb UHF and microwave signals, significantly weakening them in areas with dense vegetation.

T3A03. What antenna polarization is normally used for long-distance CW and SSB contacts on the VHF and UHF bands?

A. Right-hand circular
B. Left-hand circular
C. Horizontal
D. Vertical

C: A horizontal antenna polarization is normally used for long-distance weak-signal CW and SSB contacts using the VHF and UHF bands.

T3A04. What is the effect of antenna cross-polarization over a line-of-sight VHF or UHF path?

A. Modulation sidebands might become inverted
B. Received signal strength is reduced
C. Signals have an echo effect
D. Nothing significant will happen

B: If the antennas at opposite ends of a VHF or UHF line of sight radio link are not using the same polarization, the signals could be significantly weaker.

T3A05. When using a directional antenna, how might your station be able to communicate with a distant repeater if buildings or obstructions are blocking the direct line of sight path?

A. Change from vertical to horizontal polarization
B. Try to find a path that reflects signals to the repeater
C. Try the long path
D. Increase the antenna SWR

B: When using a directional antenna, a station might be able to access a distant repeater if buildings or obstructions are blocking the direct line of sight path by trying to find a path that reflects signals to the repeater.

T3A06. What is the meaning of the term "picket fencing"?

A. Alternating transmissions during a net operation
B. Rapid flutter on mobile signals due to multipath propagation
C. A type of ground system used with vertical antennas
D. Interference from cable TV in the form of carriers at fixed intervals across the band

B: Picket fencing is a term used to describe the rapid fluttering sound sometimes heard from mobile stations that are moving while transmitting.

T3A07. What weather condition might decrease range at microwave frequencies?

A. High winds
B. Low barometric pressure
C. Precipitation
D. Colder temperatures

C: Precipitation can decrease the effective range of microwave frequencies.

T3A08. What is a likely cause of irregular fading of signals propagated by the ionosphere?

A. Frequency shift due to Faraday rotation
B. Interference from thunderstorms
C. Intermodulation distortion
D. Random combining of signals arriving via different paths

D: The cause of irregular fading of signals from distant stations during times of generally good reception is the random combining of signals arriving via different path lengths.

T3A09. Which of the following results from the fact that signals propagated by the ionosphere are elliptically polarized?

A. Digital modes are unusable
B. Either vertically or horizontally polarized antennas may be used for transmission or reception
C. FM voice is unusable
D. Both the transmitting and receiving antennas must be of the same polarization

B: Because signals propagated by the ionosphere are elliptically polarized, either vertically or horizontally polarized antennas can be used to transmit and receive them.

T3A10. What effect does multi-path propagation have on data transmissions?

A. Transmission rates must be increased by a factor equal to the number of separate paths observed
B. Transmission rates must be decreased by a factor equal to the number of separate paths observed
C. No significant changes will occur if the signals are transmitted using FM
D. Error rates are likely to increase

D: If the data signals propagate over multiple paths, error rates are likely to increase.

T3A11. Which region of the atmosphere can reflect HF radio waves?

A. The stratosphere
B. The troposphere
C. The ionosphere
D. The electrosphere

C: The ionosphere is the region of the atmosphere that can reflect HF radio waves.

T3A12. What effect does fog or rain have on 10-meter and 6-meter band signals?

A. Absorption
B. Little effect
C. Deflection
D. Increased range

B: Fog or rain has little effect on 10-meter and 6-meter band signals.

T3B – Electromagnetic wave properties: wavelength vs frequency, nature and velocity of electromagnetic waves, relationship of wavelength and frequency; Electromagnetic spectrum definitions: UHF, VHF, HF

T3B01. What is the relationship between the electric and magnetic fields of an electromagnetic wave?

A. They travel at different speeds
B. They are in parallel
C. They revolve in opposite directions
D. They are at right angles

D: The electric and magnetic fields of electromagnetic waves are at right angles (perpendicular) to each other.

T3B02. What property of a radio wave defines its polarization?

A. The orientation of the electric field
B. The orientation of the magnetic field
C. The ratio of the energy in the magnetic field to the energy in the electric field
D. The ratio of the velocity to the wavelength

A: The orientation of a radio wave's electric field determines its polarization.

T3B03. What are the two components of a radio wave?

A. Impedance and reactance
B. Voltage and current
C. Electric and magnetic fields
D. Ionizing and non-ionizing radiation

C: The two components of a radio wave are electric and magnetic fields. This is because a radio wave is an electromagnetic wave.

T3B04. What is the velocity of a radio wave traveling through free space?

A. Speed of light
B. Speed of sound
C. 0.86 times the speed of light
D. 1.86 times the speed of sound

A: A radio wave travels through free space at the speed of light. This is approximately 300,000,000 meters per second.

T3B05. What is the relationship between wavelength and frequency?

A. Wavelength gets longer as frequency increases
B. Wavelength gets shorter as frequency increases
C. Wavelength is constant at all frequencies
D. Wavelength and frequency increase as path length increases

B: The wavelength of a radio wave gets shorter as the frequency increases. That is, these two characteristics are inversely proportional. If the wavelength grows longer, the frequency will decrease.

T3B06. What is the formula for converting frequency to approximate wavelength in meters?

A. Wavelength in meters equals frequency in hertz multiplied by 300
B. Wavelength in meters equals frequency in hertz divided by 300
C. Wavelength in meters equals frequency in megahertz divided by 300
D. Wavelength in meters equals 300 divided by frequency in megahertz

D: The formula for converting frequency to wavelength in meters is wavelength equals 300 divided by frequency in megahertz.

T3B07. In addition to frequency, which of the following is used to identify amateur radio bands?

A. The approximate wavelength in meters
B. Traditional letter/number designators
C. Channel numbers
D. All these choices are correct

A: The approximate wavelength (in meters) of radio waves is often used to identify the different frequency bands.

T3B08. What frequency range is referred to as VHF?

A. 30 kHz to 300 kHz
B. 30 MHz to 300 MHz
C. 300 kHz to 3000 kHz
D. 300 MHz to 3000 MHz

B: The frequency limits of the VHF spectrum are 30 to 300 MHz.

T3B09. What frequency range is referred to as UHF?

A. 30 to 300 kHz
B. 30 to 300 MHz
C. 300 to 3000 kHz
D. 300 to 3000 MHz

D: The UHF spectrum is from 300 to 3000 MHz.

T3B10. What frequency range is referred to as HF?

A. 300 to 3000 MHz
B. 30 to 300 MHz
C. 3 to 30 MHz
D. 300 to 3000 kHz

C: The frequency range of 3 to 30 MHz is referred to as HF.

T3B11. What is the approximate velocity of a radio wave in free space?

A. 150,000,000 meters per second
B. 300,000,000 meters per second
C. 300,000,000 miles per hour
D. 150,000,000 miles per hour

B: The approximate velocity of a radio wave as it travels through free space is 300,000,000 m/s.

T3B12. Which of these frequencies travels at the highest velocity in free space?

A. Microwaves
B. UHF
C. VHF
D. All radio frequencies travel at the same velocity

D: All radio frequencies travel at the same velocity in free space.

T3C – Propagation Modes: Sporadic E, Meteor Scatter, Auroral Propagation, Tropospheric Ducting; F Region Skip; Line of Sight and Radio Horizon

T3C01. Why are simplex UHF signals rarely heard beyond their radio horizon?

A. They are too weak to go very far
B. FCC regulations prohibit them from going more than 50 miles
C. UHF signals are usually not propagated by the ionosphere
D. UHF signals are absorbed by the ionospheric D region

C: Simplex (that is, not by means of a repeater) UHF signals are rarely heard from stations outside the local coverage area because UHF signals are usually not reflected by the ionosphere.

T3C02. What is a characteristic of HF communication compared with communications on VHF and higher frequencies?

A. HF antennas are generally smaller
B. HF accommodates wider bandwidth signals
C. Long-distance ionospheric propagation is far more common on HF
D. There is less atmospheric interference (static) on HF

C: The main benefit to HF radio waves is that they typically bounce off the ionosphere and therefore can have a much greater range. Higher frequencies penetrate the ionosphere and therefore aren't propagated.

T3C03. What is one characteristic of VHF signals received via auroral backscatter?

A. They are often received from 10,000 miles or more
B. They are distorted, with a characteristic raspy sound
C. They occur only during winter nighttime hours
D. They are generally strongest when your antenna is aimed west

B: A characteristic of VHF signals received via auroral backscatter is that the signals exhibit rapid fluctuations of strength and often sound distorted.

T3C04. Which of the following types of propagation is most commonly associated with occasional strong signals on the 10-, 6-, and 2-meter bands from beyond the radio horizon?

A. Backscatter
B. Sporadic E
C. D region absorption
D. Gray-line propagation

B: The sporadic E propagation type is most commonly associated with occasional strong signals on the 10, 6, and 2 meter bands.

T3C05. Which of the following effects may allow radio signals to travel beyond obstructions between the transmitting and receiving stations?

A. Knife-edge diffraction
B. Faraday rotation
C. Quantum tunneling
D. Doppler shift

A: A knife-edge diffraction might allow radio signals to be heard despite obstructions between the transmitting and receiving systems.

T3C06. What type of propagation is responsible for allowing over-the-horizon VHF and UHF communications to ranges of approximately 300 miles on a regular basis?

A. Tropospheric ducting
B. D region refraction
C. F2 region refraction
D. Faraday rotation

A: Tropospheric ducting is the type of propagation that regularly allows VHF and UHF signals to travel well beyond the horizon for distances of about 300 miles. It is caused by atmospheric conditions, often involving temperature inversions.

T3C07. What band is best suited for communicating via meteor scatter?

A. 33 centimeters
B. 6 meters
C. 2 meters
D. 70 centimeters

B: The 6-meter band is best suited to communicating via meteor scatter.

T3C08. What causes tropospheric ducting?

A. Discharges of lightning during electrical storms
B. Sunspots and solar flares
C. Updrafts from hurricanes and tornadoes
D. Temperature inversions in the atmosphere

D: Tropospheric ducting is caused by temperature inversions in the atmosphere. This is a type of very high frequency propagation that occurs when warm air passes over cold air.

T3C09. What is generally the best time for long-distance 10-meter band propagation via the F region?

A. From dawn to shortly after sunset during periods of high sunspot activity
B. From shortly after sunset to dawn during periods of high sunspot activity
C. From dawn to shortly after sunset during periods of low sunspot activity
D. From shortly after sunset to dawn during periods of low sunspot activity

A: Long-distance 10-meter band propagation via the F region is best conducted between dawn and shortly after sunset during periods of high sunspot activity.

T3C10. Which of the following bands may provide long-distance communications via the ionosphere's F region during the peak of the sunspot cycle?

A. 6 and 10 meters
B. 23 centimeters
C. 70 centimeters and 1.25 meters
D. All these choices are correct

A: During periods of high sunspot activity, the 6 meter and 10 meter bands may be used for long-distance communication.

T3C11. Why is the radio horizon for VHF and UHF signals more distant than the visual horizon?

A. Radio signals move somewhat faster than the speed of light
B. Radio waves are not blocked by dust particles
C. The atmosphere refracts radio waves slightly
D. Radio waves are blocked by dust particles

C: VHF and UHF radio signals usually travel somewhat farther than the visual line of sight distance between two stations because the atmosphere refracts radio waves slightly.

T4 – Amateur Radio Practices

T4A – Station setup: connecting a microphone, RF power meter, a power source, a computer, digital equipment, an SWR meter; RF grounding; Mobile radio installation

T4A01. Which of the following is an appropriate power supply rating for a typical 50-watt output mobile FM transceiver?

A. 24.0 volts at 4 amperes
B. 13.8 volts at 4 amperes
C. 24.0 volts at 12 amperes
D. 13.8 volts at 12 amperes

D: For a typical 50 watt output mobile FM transceiver, 13.8 volts at 12 amperes would be an appropriate power supply rating.

T4A02. Which of the following should be considered when selecting an accessory SWR meter?

A. The frequency and power level at which the measurements will be made
B. The distance that the meter will be located from the antenna
C. The maximum SWR anticipated on the transmission line
D. The ability of the meter to compensate for a poor transmission line match to the antenna

A: The frequency and power level at which the measurements will be made should be considered when selecting an accessory SWR meter.

T4A03. Why are short, heavy-gauge wires used for a transceiver's DC power connection?

A. To minimize voltage drop when transmitting
B. To provide a close match to the power supply output impedance
C. To avoid RF interference
D. To minimize radiative losses in the power cable

A: Heavier gauge wire and short lengths will reduce the resistance as much as possible, thus maintaining sufficient voltage for peak performance.

T4A04. How are the audio input and output of a transceiver connected in a station configured to operate using FT8?

A. To a computer running a terminal program and connected to a terminal node controller unit
B. To the audio output and input of a computer running FT8 software
C. To an FT8 conversion unit, a keyboard, and a computer monitor
D. To a computer connected to the FT8converter.com website

B: In a station configured to operate using FT8, the transceiver audio input and output are connected to the audio input and output of a computer running WSJT-X software.

T4A05. Where should an RF power meter be installed?

A. In the feed line, between the transmitter and antenna
B. At the power supply output
C. In parallel with the push-to-talk line and the antenna
D. In the power supply cable, as close as possible to the radio

A: An RF power meter should be installed in the feed line, between the transmitter and antenna.

T4A06. What signals are used in a computer-radio interface for digital mode operation?

A. Receive and transmit mode, status, and location
B. Antenna and RF power
C. Receive audio, transmit audio, and transmitter keying
D. NMEA GPS location and DC power

C: The connections needed are sending and receiving audio in conjunction with transmitter keying in order to allow the computer to trigger the transmitter automatically.

T4A07. Which of the following is one of the connections required between a computer and a transceiver to operate digital modes?

A. Computer "line out" to transceiver push-to-talk
B. Computer "line in" to transceiver push-to-talk
C. Computer "line in" to transceiver speaker connector
D. Computer "line out" to transceiver speaker connector

C: Connecting the computer "line in" to transceiver speaker connector enables operation of digital modes.

T4A08. Which of the following conductors is preferred for bonding at RF?

A. Copper braid removed from coaxial cable
B. Copper-clad steel wire
C. Twisted-pair cable
D. Flat copper strap

D: A flat strap conductor is the best to use for RF grounding. Most ham radio systems have a special terminal for grounding. Copper strap is most often used for grounding.

T4A09. How can you determine the length of time that equipment can be powered from a battery?

A. Divide the watt-hour rating of the battery by the peak power consumption of the equipment
B. Divide the battery ampere-hour rating by the average current draw of the equipment
C. Multiply the watts per hour consumed by the equipment by the battery power rating
D. Multiply the square of the current rating of the battery by the input resistance of the equipment

B: To determine how long equipment can be powered from a battery, divide the battery's ampere-hour rating by the average current draw of the equipment. This gives the approximate operating time in hours.

T4A10. What function does a digital mode hotspot perform for nearby transceivers?

A. Communication with a digital voice or data network
B. FT8 digital communications via AFSK using a smartphone connected to the internet
C. RTTY encoding and decoding without a computer
D. High-speed digital communications for meteor scatter

A: Communication using digital voice or data systems via the internet is performed with a transceiver and a digital mode hot spot.

T4A11. Where should the negative power return of a mobile transceiver be connected in a vehicle?

A. At the 12-volt battery chassis ground
B. At the antenna mount
C. To any metal part of the vehicle
D. Through the transceiver's mounting bracket

A: A mobile transceiver's power negative connection should be made at the 12 volt battery chassis ground.

T4A12. What is an electronic keyer?

A. A device for switching antennas from transmit to receive
B. A device for voice activated switching from receive to transmit
C. A device that assists in manual sending of Morse code
D. An interlock to prevent unauthorized use of a radio

C: An electronic keyer automatically generates the dits and dahs of Morse code. This is a key component of some CW/data setups.

T4B – Operating Controls: Frequency Tuning, Use of Filters, Squelch Function, AGC, Memory Channels, Noise Blanker, Microphone Gain, Receiver Incremental Tuning (RIT), Bandwidth Selection, Scanning Function; Digital Transceiver Configuration; DMR Code Plugs and Talk Groups

T4B01. What is the effect of excessive microphone gain on SSB transmissions?

A. Frequency instability
B. Distorted transmitted audio
C. Increased SWR
D. Sideband inversion

B: If a transmitter is operated with the microphone gain set too high, the output signal might become distorted.

T4B02. Which of the following can be used to enter a transceiver's operating frequency?

A. The keypad or VFO knob
B. The CTCSS or DTMF encoder
C. The Automatic Frequency Control
D. All these choices are correct

A: The keypad or the VFO knob can be used to enter the operating frequency on a modern transceiver. A transceiver is a single unit that contains both a radio transmitter and receiver.

T4B03. How is squelch adjusted so that a weak FM signal can be heard?

A. Set the squelch threshold so that receiver output audio is on all the time
B. Turn up the audio level until it overcomes the squelch threshold
C. Turn on the anti-squelch function
D. Enable squelch enhancement

A: Setting the squelch threshold so that receiver output audio is on all the time will help a weak FM signal be heard.

T4B04. What does an FM signal sound like when received slightly off frequency?

A. The audio increases in pitch
B. The audio decrease in pitch
C. There is no effect except for reduction in amplitude
D. The audio becomes distorted

D: An FM signal sounds distorted when it is received slightly off frequency.

T4B05. What does the scanning function of an FM transceiver do?

A. Checks incoming signal deviation
B. Prevents interference to nearby repeaters
C. Tunes through a range of frequencies to check for activity
D. Tunes through a range of frequencies to determine the antenna's resonant frequency

C: The scanning function of an FM transceiver tunes through a range of frequencies to check for activity.

T4B06. Which of the following controls could be used if the voice pitch of a single-sideband signal returning to your CQ call seems too high or low?

A. The AGC or limiter
B. The bandwidth selection
C. The tone squelch
D. The RIT or Clarifier

D: The RIT or clarifier controls could be used if the voice pitch of a single-sideband signal seems too high or low. Receiver incremental tuning allows the receiver to be tuned up to 3 kilohertz on either side of the transmitter frequency.

T4B07. What is a DMR "code plug"?

A. An adapter cable used to connect a DMR radio to a computer for internet access
B. Configuration data loaded onto your radio to access repeaters and talkgroups
C. An upgrade to DMR programming software provided by the radio manufacturer to accommodate new radio models
D. A Coder-Decoder (CODEC) that converts analog voice data to DMR digital data and vice versa

B: A DMR "code plug" contains configuration data loaded onto your radio to access repeaters and talkgroups.

T4B08. What is the advantage of having a choice of receiver filter bandwidths in a multimode transceiver?

A. Permits monitoring several modes simultaneously by selecting a separate filter for each mode
B. Permits noise or interference reduction by selecting a bandwidth matching the mode
C. Increases the number of frequencies that can be stored in memory
D. Increases the amount of offset between receive and transmit frequencies

B: The advantage of having a choice of receiver filter bandwidths in a multimode transceiver is that it permits noise or interference reduction by selecting a bandwidth that matches the mode being used. Narrower or wider filters can improve reception depending on the signal type.

T4B09. How is a specific group of stations selected on a DMR digital voice transceiver?

A. By retrieving the frequencies from transceiver memory
B. By enabling the group's CTCSS tone
C. By entering the group's identification code
D. By inserting a five-pin, pre-programmed code plug

C: A specific group of stations is selected on a digital voice transceiver by entering the group's identification code.

T4B10. Which of the following receiver filter bandwidths provides the best signal-to-noise ratio for SSB reception?

A. 500 Hz
B. 1000 Hz
C. 2400 Hz
D. 5000 Hz

C: 2400 Hz is an appropriate receive filter to select in order to provide the best signal-to-noise ratio for SSB reception.

T4B11. Which of the following must be programmed into a D-STAR digital transceiver before transmitting?

A. Your call sign
B. Your output power
C. The codec type being used
D. All these choices are correct

A: Your call sign must be programmed into a D-STAR digital transceiver before transmitting.

T5 – Electrical Principles

T5A – Current and Voltage: Terminology and Units, Conductors and Insulators, Alternating and Direct Current

T5A01. Electrical current is measured in which of the following units?

A. Volts
B. Watts
C. Ohms
D. Amperes

D: Electrical current is measured in amperes, usually referred to as amps. Current is the amount of electrons flowing through a circuit.

T5A02. Electrical power is measured in which of the following units?

A. Volts
B. Watts
C. Watt-hours
D. Amperes

B: Electrical power is measured in watts. Electrical power is the rate at which electricity can be converted into other types of energy. It is calculated by multiplying the current and the voltage drop. A watt is equal to one joule per second.

T5A03. What is the term for the flow of electrons in an electric circuit?

A. Voltage
B. Amperes per second
C. Volts per second
D. Current

D: The flow of electrons in an electric circuit is the current. Current is measured in amperes, also known as amps.

T5A04. What term describes the number of times per second that an alternating current makes a complete cycle?

A. Pulse rate
B. Wave number
C. Frequency
D. Wavelength

C: Frequency describes the number of times per second that an alternating current makes a complete cycle.

T5A05. A difference in which of the following causes electron flow?

A. Voltage
B. Ampere-hours
C. Capacitance
D. Inductance

A: The electrical term for the electromotive force (EMF) that causes electron flow is voltage. It is useful to think of voltage as the electrical equivalent of water pressure.

T5A06. What is the unit of frequency?

A. Hertz
B. Henry
C. Farad
D. Epicycles per second

A: Hertz is the unit of frequency.

T5A07. Why are metals generally good conductors of electricity?

A. They have relatively high density
B. They have many free electrons
C. They have many free protons
D. They have relatively high Young's modulus values

B: Metals generally good conductors of electricity because they have many free electrons. This phenomenon of the free electrons is also called the "sea of electrons."

T5A08. Which of the following is a good electrical insulator?

A. Sea water
B. Glass
C. Stainless steel
D. Graphite

B: Glass is a good electrical insulator.

T5A09. Which of the following describes alternating current?

A. Current that alternates between a positive direction and zero
B. Current that alternates between a negative direction and zero
C. Current that alternates between positive and negative directions
D. All these answers are correct

C: As the name implies, alternating current (AC) is current that alternates between positive and negative directions.

T5A10. Which term describes the rate at which electrical energy is used?

A. Resistance
B. Current
C. Power
D. Voltage

C: The rate at which electrical energy is used is power.

T5A11. What type of current flow is opposed by resistance?

A. Direct current
B. Alternating current
C. RF current
D. All these choices are correct

D: All current flow is opposed by resistance.

T5B – Math for Electronics: Conversion of Electrical Units, Decibels

T5B01. How many milliamperes is 1.5 amperes?

A. 0.0000015 milliamperes
B. 0.0015 milliamperes
C. 1500 milliamperes
D. 1,500,000 milliamperes

C: 1.5 amperes is equivalent to 1500 mA. The prefix milli- means thousandth, so a milliampere is a thousandth of an ampere. Therefore, 1.5 amperes can be converted to milliamperes by multiplying by a thousand: 1.5 x 1000 = 1500.

T5B02. Which is equal to 1,500,000 hertz?

A. 1500 kHz
B. 1500 MHz
C. 15 GHz
D. 150 kHz

A: Another way to specify a radio signal frequency of 1,500,000 Hz is 1500 kHz. In the metric system, the prefix kilo- means thousand, so a kilohertz is equal to 1000 hertz. Therefore, 1,500,000 Hz can be converted to kHz by dividing by a thousand: 1,500,000/1000 = 1500 kHz.

T5B03. Which is equal to one kilovolt?

A. One one-thousandth of a volt
B. One hundred volts
C. One thousand volts
D. One million volts

C: 1000 V is equal to 1 kV. The metric prefix kilo- means thousand, so a thousand volts is the same as one kilovolt. Therefore, V can be converted to kV by dividing by a thousand: 1000/1000 = 1.

T5B04. Which is equal to one microvolt?

A. One one-millionth of a volt
B. One million volts
C. One thousand kilovolts
D. One one-thousandth of a volt

A: 1/1,000,000 of a volt is equal to 1 μV. The metric prefix micro- means millionth, so 1,000,000 microvolts is equal to one volt. Volts can be converted to microvolts by dividing by a million: 1/1,000,000 = 1 μV.

T5B05. Which is equal to 500 milliwatts?

A. 5 watts
B. 0.5 watts
C. 500,000 watts
D. 500,000,000 watts

B: 0.5 W is equivalent to 500 mW. The metric prefix milli- means thousandth, so 1000 mW is the same as 1 W. This conversion can be accomplished by multiplying by a thousand: 0.5 x 1000 = 500.

T5B06. Which is equal to 3000 milliamperes?

A. 0.003 amperes
B. 0.3 amperes
C. 3,000,000 amperes
D. 3 amperes

D: A 3000-milliampere current is equivalent to 3 amperes. The metric prefix milli- means thousandth, so milliamperes can be converted to amperes by dividing by a thousand. An ammeter is an instrument used to measure electric current.

T5B07. Which is equal to 3.525 MHz?

A. 0.003525 kHz
B. 35.25 kHz
C. 3525 kHz
D. 3,525,000 kHz

C: A frequency of 3.525 MHz is equivalent to 3525 kilohertz. The metric prefix mega- means millions, and the prefix kilo- means thousands. Millions are the same as 10^6, while thousands are equal to 10^3. Megahertz can be converted into kilohertz, then, by multiplying by 10^3, or a thousand: 3.525 MHz x 1000 = 3525.

T5B08. Which is equal to 1,000,000 picofarads?

A. 0.001 microfarads
B. 1 microfarad
C. 1000 microfarads
D. 1,000,000,000 microfarads

B: 1,000,000 picofarads is equivalent to 1 microfarad. The metric prefix pico- means trillionths (10^{-12}), while the prefix micro-means millionths (10^{-6}). Picofarads can be converted to microfarads, then, by dividing by 10^6, or one million: 1,000,000/1,000,000 = 1.

T5B09. Which decibel value most closely represents a power increase from 5 watts to 10 watts?

A. 2 dB
B. 3 dB
C. 5 dB
D. 10 dB

B: A power increase from 5 to 10 watts creates approximately 3 dB of change. The relationship between power increases and changes in decibel levels is complex. Whenever the power is doubled, however, the decibel level will rise by three. If the power is quadrupled, the decibel level rises by 6. If the power increases by ten times, the decibel level also rises by ten.

T5B10. Which decibel value most closely represents a power decrease from 12 watts to 3 watts?

A. -1 dB
B. -3 dB
C. -6 dB
D. -9 dB

C: A power decrease from 12 watts to 3 watts would result in approximately 6 dB of change. Just as a quadrupling of power would result in an extra 6 dB, so will a quartering of power cause the decibel level to drop by 6.

T5B11. Which decibel value represents a power increase from 20 watts to 200 watts?

A. 10 dB
B. 12 dB
C. 18 dB
D. 28 dB

A: A power increase from 20 W to 200 W would result in approximately 10 dB of change. When the power increases by ten times, the result is 10 dB of change.

T5B12. Which is equal to 28400 kHz?

A. 28.400 kHz
B. 2.800 MHz
C. 284.00 MHz
D. 28.400 MHz

D: One megahertz (MHz) is equivalent to one thousand kilohertz (kHz), so to convert a frequency from kilohertz to megahertz, divide the kilohertz number by one thousand.

T5B13. Which is equal to 2425 MHz?

A. 0.002425 GHz
B. 24.25 GHz
C. 2.425 GHz
D. 242.5 GHz

C: 2425 MHz is equal to 2.425 GHz.

T5C – Capacitance and Inductance Terminology and Units; Radio Frequency Definition and Units; Impedance Definition and Units; Calculating Power

T5C01. What describes the ability to store energy in an electric field?

A. Inductance
B. Resistance
C. Frequency
D. Capacitance

D: The ability to store energy in an electric field is called capacitance. Capacitance can also be defined as the ratio of the electric charge that is shifted from one conductor to another to the resulting potential difference between them.

T5C02. What is the unit of capacitance?

A. Farad
B. Ohm
C. Volt
D. Henry

A: The basic unit of capacitance is the farad. One farad is equal to the capacitance of a capacitor that has an equal and opposite charge of 1 coulomb on each of its plates, and 1 V of potential difference between those plates.

T5C03. What describes the ability to store energy in a magnetic field?

A. Admittance
B. Capacitance
C. Resistance
D. Inductance

D: The ability to store energy in a magnetic field is called inductance. Inductance can also be defined as the characteristic of an electric circuit that enables electromagnetic force to be created in it through a varying magnetic flux.

T5C04. What is the unit of inductance?

A. Coulomb
B. Farad
C. Henry
D. Ohm

C: The basic unit of inductance is the henry.

T5C05. What is the unit of impedance?

A. Volt
B. Ampere
C. Coulomb
D. Ohm

D: The ohm is the unit of impedance.

T5C06. What is the abbreviation for kilohertz?

A. kHz
B. khz
C. KHz
D. KHZ

A: kHz is the abbreviation for kilohertz.

T5C07. What is the abbreviation for megahertz?

A. mHz
B. mHZ
C. Mhz
D. MHz

D: MHz is the abbreviation for megahertz.

T5C08. What formula is used to calculate electrical power (P) in a DC circuit?

A. P = I × E
B. P = E / I
C. P = I2 × E
D. P = I / E

A: The formula used to calculate electrical power in a DC circuit is power equals voltage multiplied by current.

T5C09. How much power is delivered by a voltage of 13.8 volts DC and a current of 10 amperes?

A. 138 watts
B. 0.7 watts
C. 23.8 watts
D. 3.8 watts

A: When the voltage is 13.8 volts DC and the current is 10 amperes, the power is 138 watts. Power is calculated by multiplying voltage by current: 13.8 × 10 = 138.

T5C10. How much power is delivered by a voltage of 12 volts DC and a current of 2.5 amperes?

A. 4.8 watts
B. 30 watts
C. 14.5 watts
D. 0.208 watts

B: When the applied voltage is 12 volts DC and the current is 2.5 amperes, 30 watts of power are generated. The power can be calculated by multiplying the voltage by the current: 12 x 2.5 = 30.

T5C11. How much current is required to deliver 120 watts at a voltage of 12 volts DC?

A. 0.1 amperes
B. 10 amperes
C. 12 amperes
D. 132 amperes

B: When the applied voltage is 12 volts DC and the load is 120 watts, 10 amperes are flowing in a circuit. The current can be calculated by dividing the load by the applied voltage: 120/12 = 10.

T5C12. What is impedance?

A. The opposition to AC current flow
B. The inverse of resistance
C. The inverse of reactance
D. The power handling capability of a component

A: Impedance is the opposition to AC current flow in a circuit. It is analogous to resistance in a DC circuit.

T5D – Ohm's Law; Series and parallel circuits

T5D01. What formula is used to calculate current in a circuit?

A. I = E × R
B. I = E / R
C. I = E2 × R
D. I = E2 / R

B: The formula for calculating current in a circuit is current equals voltage divided by resistance.

T5D02. What formula is used to calculate voltage in a circuit?

A. E = I × R
B. E = I / R
C. E = I2 × R
D. E = I2 / R

A: The formula for calculating voltage in a circuit is voltage equals current multiplied by resistance.

T5D03. What formula is used to calculate resistance in a circuit?

A. R = E × I
B. R = E / I
C. R = E + I
D. R = E - I

B: The formula for calculating resistance in a circuit is resistance (R) equals voltage (E) divided by current (I). Resistance is the opposition to the passage of current, the result of which is the conversion of electrical energy into heat or another type of energy.

T5D04. What is the resistance of a circuit in which a current of 3 amperes flows when connected to 90 volts?

A. 3 ohms
B. 30 ohms
C. 1/30 ohm
D. 270 ohms

B: The resistance of a circuit in which a current of 3 amperes flows when connected to 90 volts is 30 ohms. Resistance is calculated by dividing voltage by current. In this case, then, the resistance is found 90/3 = 30.

T5D05. What is the resistance of a circuit for which the applied voltage is 12 volts and the current flow is 1.5 amperes?

A. 18 ohms
B. 0.125 ohms
C. 8 ohms
D. 13.5 ohms

C: The resistance of a circuit with 12 volts applied and 1.5 amperes of current flow is 8 ohms. Resistance is calculated by dividing voltage by current: 12 ÷ 1.5 = 8.

T5D06. What is the resistance of a circuit that draws 4 amperes from a 12-volt source?

A. 3 ohms
B. 16 ohms
C. 48 ohms
D. 8 ohms

A: The resistance of a circuit that draws 4 amperes from a 12-volt source is 3 ohms. Resistance is calculated by dividing voltage by current: 12/4 = 3.

T5D07. What is the current in a circuit with an applied voltage of 120 volts and a resistance of 80 ohms?

A. 9600 amperes
B. 200 amperes
C. 0.667 amperes
D. 1.5 amperes

D: The current flow in a circuit with an applied voltage of 120 V and a resistance of 80 ohms is 1.5 amperes. The current flow can be found by dividing the voltage by the resistance: 120/80 = 1.5.

T5D08. What is the current through a 100-ohm resistor connected across 200 volts?

A. 20,000 amperes
B. 0.5 amperes
C. 2 amperes
D. 100 amperes

C: The current flowing through a 100-ohm resistor connected across 200 volts is 2 amperes. The current is found by dividing the voltage by the resistance: 200/100 = 2.

T5D09. What is the current through a 24-ohm resistor connected across 240 volts?

A. 2400 amperes
B. 0.1 amperes
C. 10 amperes
D. 5760 amperes

C: The current flowing through a 24-ohm resistor connected across 240 volts is 10 amperes. The current is found by dividing the voltage by the resistance: 240/24 = 10.

T5D10. What is the voltage across a 2-ohm resistor if a current of 0.5 amperes flows through it?

A. 1 volt
B. 0.25 volts
C. 2.5 volts
D. 1.5 volts

A: The voltage across a 2-ohm resistor if a current of 0.5 amperes flows through it is 1 volt. The voltage can be calculated by multiplying the current by the resistance: 2 x 0.5 = 1.

T5D11. What is the voltage across a 10-ohm resistor if a current of 1 ampere flows through it?

A. 1 volt
B. 10 volts
C. 11 volts
D. 9 volts

B: The voltage across a 10-ohm resistor if a current of 1 ampere flows through it is 10 volts. The voltage can be calculated by multiplying the current by the resistance: 10 x 1 = 10.

T5D12. What is the voltage across a 10-ohm resistor if a current of 2 amperes flows through it?

A. 8 volts
B. 0.2 volts
C. 12 volts
D. 20 volts

D: The voltage across a 10-ohm resistor if a current of 2 amperes flows through it is 20 volts. The voltage can be calculated by multiplying the current by the resistance: 10 x 2 = 20.

T5D13. In which type of circuit is DC current the same through all components?

A. Series
B. Parallel
C. Resonant
D. Branch

A: Components in series will have the same current flowing through them. However, the voltage will not be the same for each.

T5D14. In which type of circuit is the voltage always the same across all components?

A. Series
B. Parallel
C. Resonant
D. Branch

B: Components in parallel will have the same voltage across them. However, the current will not be the same for each.

T6 – Electronic and Electrical Components

T6A – Fixed and Variable Resistors; Capacitors; Inductors; Fuses; Switches; Batteries

T6A01. What electrical component opposes the flow of current in a DC circuit?

A. Inductor
B. Resistor
C. Inverter
D. Transformer

B: The electrical component used to oppose the flow of current in a DC circuit is a resistor. For ham radio technicians, the most commonly required resistors are quarter- and half-watt fixed value resistors and 100, 500, 1k, 5k, 10k, and 100k ohm variable resistors.

T6A02. What type of component is often used as an adjustable volume control?

A. Fixed resistor
B. Power resistor
C. Potentiometer
D. Transformer

C: A potentiometer is often used as an adjustable volume control. A potentiometer is an instrument that measures an unknown voltage by comparing it to a standard voltage.

T6A03. What electrical parameter is controlled by a potentiometer?

A. Inductance
B. Resistance
C. Capacitance
D. Field strength

B: Resistance is controlled by a potentiometer. A potentiometer will typically have a resistance element connected to the circuit with three terminals. Two of these are attached to the two input voltage conductors of the circuit, and the third is connected to the circuit output. The third terminal is typically able to move across the resistance element, which enables the magnitude of the input voltage to be adjusted.

T6A04. What electrical component stores energy in an electric field?

A. Resistor
B. Capacitor
C. Inductor
D. Diode

B: The capacitor is the electrical component that stores energy in an electric field. Typically, a capacitor is composed of two metallic plates that are separated and insulated from one another by a dielectric.

T6A05. What type of electrical component consists of conductive surfaces separated by an insulator?

A. Resistor
B. Potentiometer
C. Oscillator
D. Capacitor

D: A capacitor consists of two or more conductive surfaces separated by an insulator.

T6A06. What type of electrical component stores energy in a magnetic field?

A. Resistor
B. Capacitor
C. Inductor
D. Diode

C: An inductor stores energy in a magnetic field. Inductors are typically composed of at least one wire loop. An inductor may be fixed, adjustable, or variable, depending on whether the number of loops is able to be manipulated.

T6A07. What electrical component is typically constructed as a coil of wire?

A. Transistor
B. Capacitor
C. Diode
D. Inductor

D: An inductor is usually composed of a coil of wire.

T6A08. What is the function of an SPDT switch?

A. A single circuit is opened or closed
B. Two circuits are opened or closed
C. A single circuit is switched between one of two other circuits
D. Two circuits are each switched between one of two other circuits

C: An SPDT switch can toggle a single circuit between one of two other circuits. SPDT stands for Single Pole Double Throw, which means it has a single input and two possible outputs.

T6A09. What type of switch is represented by component 3 in figure T-2?

A. Single-pole single-throw
B. Single-pole double-throw
C. Double-pole single-throw
D. Double-pole double-throw

A: A single-pole single-throw switch is represented by component 3 in figure T-2.

T6A10. Which of the following battery chemistries is rechargeable?

A. Nickel-metal hydride
B. Lithium-ion
C. Lead-acid
D. All these choices are correct

D: There are many different types of batteries that may be recharged, including nickel-metal hydride (NiMH), lithium-ion (Li-ion), and lead-acid.

T6A11. Which of the following battery chemistries is not rechargeable?

A. Nickel-cadmium
B. Carbon-zinc
C. Lead-acid
D. Lithium-ion

B: The carbon-zinc battery is not rechargeable.

T6B – Semiconductors: Basic Principles and Applications of Solid-State Devices, Diodes and Transistors; Gain

T6B01. Which is true about forward voltage drop in a diode?

A. It is lower in some diode types than in others
B. It is proportional to peak inverse voltage
C. It indicates that the diode is defective
D. It has no impact on the voltage delivered to the load

A: Forward voltage drop is lower in some diode types than in others.

T6B02. What electronic component allows current to flow in only one direction?

A. Resistor
B. Fuse
C. Diode
D. Driven element

C: A diode allows current to flow in only one direction. A diode is an electronic device that includes two electrodes, an anode and a cathode. These devices can be used to convert an alternating current into a direct current.

T6B03. Which of these components can be used as an electronic switch?

A. Varistor
B. Potentiometer
C. Transistor
D. Thermistor

C: A transistor can be used as an electronic switch. It may also be used as a detector.

T6B04. Which of the following components can consist of three regions of semiconductor material?

A. Alternator
B. Transistor
C. Triode
D. Pentode

B: A transistor is made of three regions of semiconductor material.

T6B05. What type of transistor has a gate, drain, and source?

A. Varistor
B. Field-effect
C. Hall-effect
D. Bipolar junction

B: Field-effect transistors have three pins called gate, drain, and source.

T6B06. How is the cathode lead of a semiconductor diode often marked on the package?

A. With the word "cathode"
B. With a stripe
C. With the letter C
D. With the letter K

B: A semiconductor diode's cathode lead is usually identified with a stripe.

T6B07. What causes a light-emitting diode (LED) to emit light?

A. Forward current
B. Reverse current
C. Capacitively-coupled RF signal
D. Inductively-coupled RF signal

A: An LED is a semiconductor diode that, when a forward current passes through it, produces light in or near the visible range. Each diode is only capable of producing a single primary color, though diodes may be combined to produce any color.

T6B08. What does the abbreviation FET stand for?

A. Frequency Emission Transmitter
B. Fast Electron Transistor
C. Free Electron Transmitter
D. Field Effect Transistor

D: The abbreviation FET stands for Field Effect Transistor. In a field effect transistor, output current is controlled by a variable electric field.

T6B09. What are the names for the electrodes of a diode?

A. Plus and minus
B. Source and drain
C. Anode and cathode
D. Gate and base

C: The names of the two electrodes of a diode are the anode and cathode. Electrons leave a system through the anode and return through the cathode.

T6B10. Which of the following can provide power gain?

A. Transformer
B. Transistor
C. Reactor
D. Resistor

B: Transformers don't provide a gain. From the options provided, only a transistor provides a gain.

T6B11. What does the term gain mean in amplifiers?

A. The output signal voltage relative to the input signal voltage
B. The output signal current relative to the input signal current
C. The output signal power relative to the input signal power
D. All these choices are correct

D: In amplifiers, gain means the output signal relative to the input signal, whether measured as voltage, current, or power.

T6B12. What are the names of the electrodes of a bipolar junction transistor?

A. Signal, bias, power
B. Emitter, base, collector
C. Input, output, supply
D. Pole one, pole two, output

B: The three electrodes of a bipolar junction transistor are the emitter, the base, and the collector, often abbreviated E, B, and C, respectively.

T6C – CIRCUIT DIAGRAMS: USE OF TERM SCHEMATIC, BASIC STRUCTURE; SCHEMATIC SYMBOLS OF BASIC COMPONENTS

T6C01. What is an electrical diagram using standard component symbols called?

A. Connection chart
B. Instrumentation system
C. Schematic
D. Flow chart

C: An electrical diagram with standard wiring component symbols is called a schematic.

T6C02. What is component 1 in the figure below?

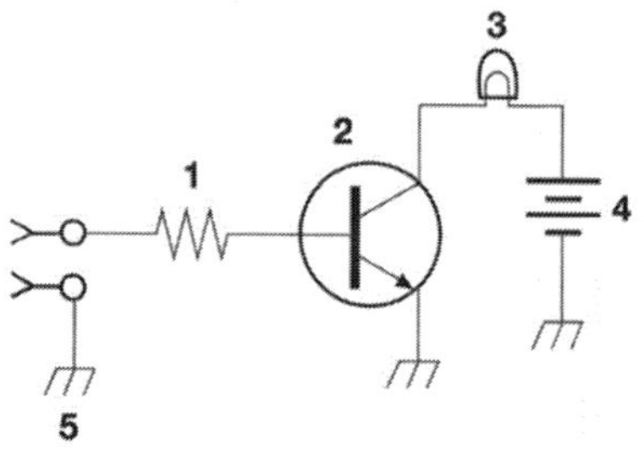

A. Resistor
B. Transistor
C. Battery
D. Connector

A: In the figure, component 1 is a resistor.

T6C03. What is component 2 in the figure below?

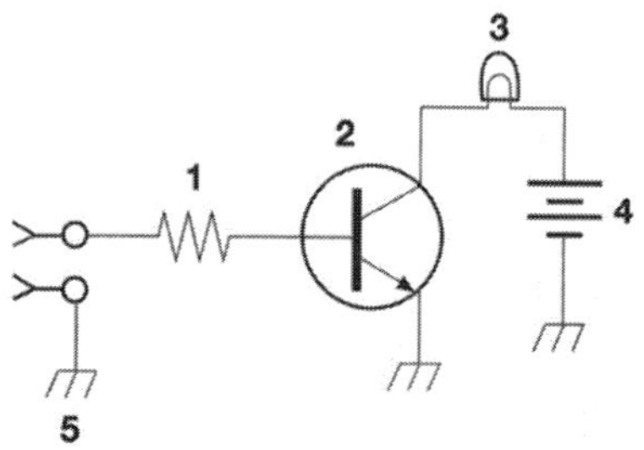

A. Resistor
B. Transistor
C. Indicator lamp
D. Connector

B: In the figure, component 2 is a transistor.

T6C04. What is component 3 in the figure below?

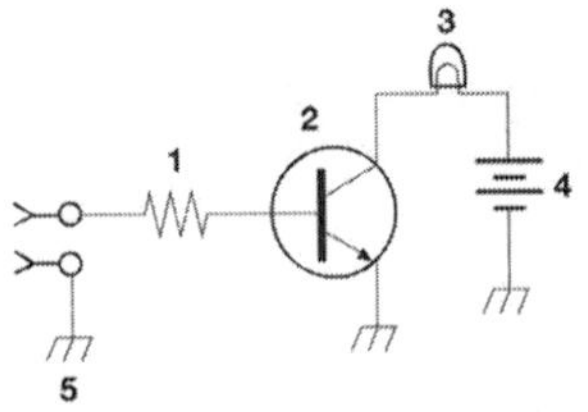

A. Resistor
B. Transistor
C. Lamp
D. Ground symbol

C: In the figure, component 3 is a lamp.

T6C05. What is component 4 in the figure below?

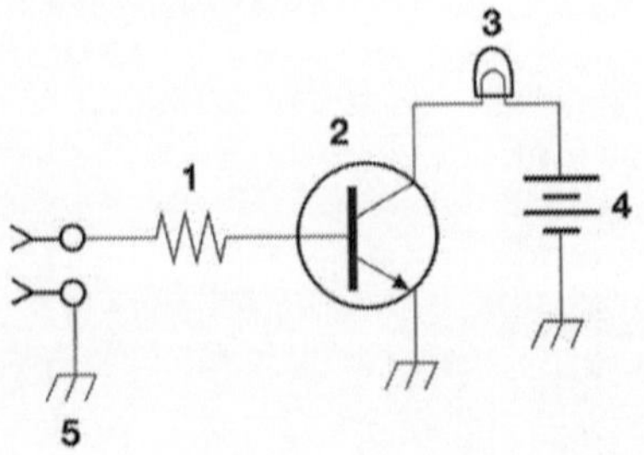

A. Resistor
B. Transistor
C. Ground symbol
D. Battery

D: In the figure, component 4 is a battery.

T6C06. What is component 6 in the figure below?

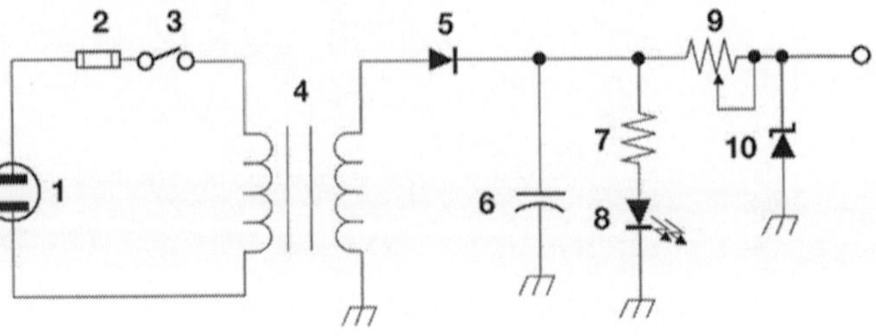

A. Resistor
B. Capacitor
C. Regulator IC
D. Transistor

B: In the figure, component 6 is a capacitor.

T6C07. What is component 8 in the figure below?

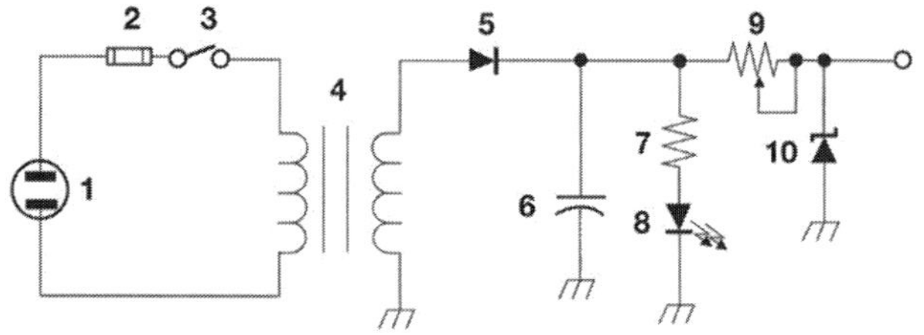

A. Resistor
B. Inductor
C. Regulator IC
D. Light emitting diode

D: In the figure, component 8 is a light emitting diode.

T6C08. What is component 9 in the figure below?

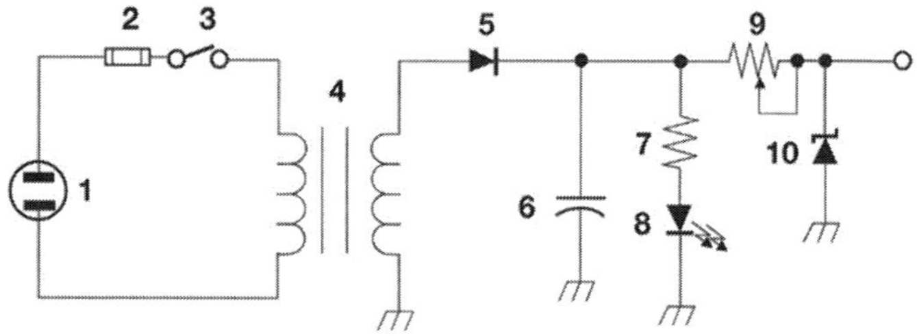

A. Variable capacitor
B. Variable inductor
C. Variable resistor
D. Variable transformer

C: In the figure, component 9 is a variable resistor.

T6C09. What is component 4 in the figure below?

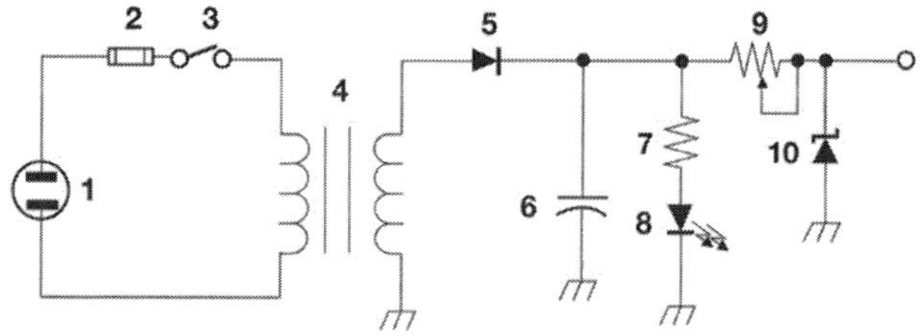

A. Variable inductor
B. Double-pole switch
C. Potentiometer
D. Transformer

D: In the figure, component 4 is a transformer.

T6C10. What is component 3 in the figure below?

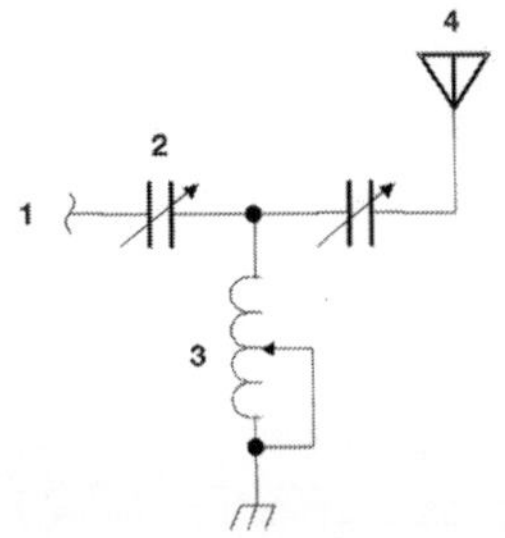

A. Connector
B. Meter
C. Variable capacitor
D. Variable inductor

D: In the figure, component 3 is a variable inductor.

T6C11. What is component 4 in the figure above?

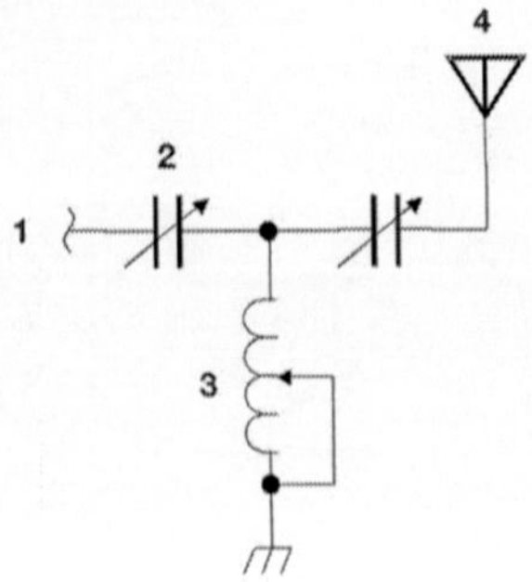

A. Antenna
B. Transmitter
C. Dummy load
D. Ground

A: In the figure, component 4 is an antenna.

T6C12. Which of the following is accurately represented in electrical schematics?

A. Wire lengths
B. Physical appearance of components
C. Component connections
D. All these choices are correct

C: The connections on an electrical circuit schematic diagram represent the actual connections of electrical components.

T6D – Component functions: rectifiers, relays, voltage regulators, meters, indicators, integrated circuits, transformers; Resonant circuit; Shielding

T6D01. Which of the following devices or circuits changes an alternating current into a varying direct current signal?

A. Transformer
B. Rectifier
C. Amplifier
D. Reflector

B: A rectifier changes an alternating current into a varying direct current signal. Specifically, it is a switch that blocks the current in one direction but permits it in the other.

T6D02. What is a relay?

A. An electrically-controlled switch
B. A current-controlled amplifier
C. An inverting amplifier
D. A pass transistor

A: A relay may best be described as a switch controlled by an electromagnet. When the device senses a miniscule voltage or current change, it activates a switch or another component in the electric circuit.

T6D03. Which of the following is a reason to use shielded wire?

A. To decrease the resistance of DC power connections
B. To increase the current carrying capability of the wire
C. To prevent coupling of unwanted signals to or from the wire
D. To reduce receiver overload

C: Shielding a wire is necessary to prevent coupling of unwanted signals to or from the wire.

T6D04. Which of the following displays an electrical quantity as a numeric value?

A. Potentiometer
B. Transistor
C. Meter
D. Relay

C: A meter is a device used to display an electrical quantity as a numeric value. Meters can be used to show measurements such as voltage, current, or resistance.

T6D05. What type of circuit controls the amount of voltage from a power supply?

A. Regulator
B. Oscillator
C. Filter
D. Phase inverter

A: A regulator circuit controls the amount of voltage from a power supply.

T6D06. What component changes 120 V AC power to a lower AC voltage for other uses?

A. Variable capacitor
B. Transformer
C. Transistor
D. Diode

B: A transformer is commonly used to change 120V AC house current to a lower AC voltage for other uses.

T6D07. Which of the following is commonly used as a visual indicator?

A. LED
B. FET
C. Zener diode
D. All these choices are correct

A: LED is commonly used as a visual indicator.

T6D08. Which of the following is combined with an inductor to make a resonant circuit?

A. Resistor
B. Zener diode
C. Potentiometer
D. Capacitor

D: A capacitor is used along with an inductor to make a resonant circuit.

T6D09. What is the name of a device that combines several semiconductors and other components into one package?

A. Transducer
B. Multi-pole relay
C. Integrated circuit
D. Transformer

C: An integrated circuit combines several semiconductors and other components into one package. All of these semiconductors and other components are either imprinted or etched on a thin slice of a semiconducting material, as for instance silicon.

T6D10. What is the function of component 2 in the figure below?

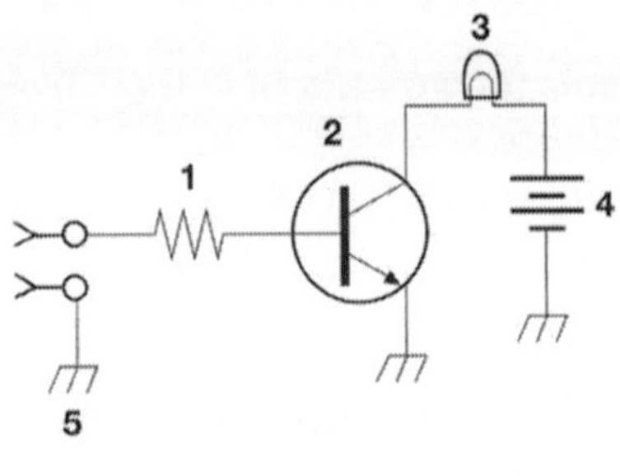

A. Give off light when current flows through it
B. Supply electrical energy
C. Control the flow of current
D. Convert electrical energy into radio waves

C: In the figure, the function of component 2 is to control the flow of current.

T6D11. Which of the following is a resonant or tuned circuit?

A. An inductor and a capacitor in series or parallel
B. A linear voltage regulator
C. A resistor circuit used for reducing standing wave ratio
D. A circuit designed to provide high-fidelity audio

A: A simple resonant or tuned circuit is a circuit containing an inductor and a capacitor, connected either in series or in parallel, which functions to filter out certain frequencies.

T7 – Practical Circuits

T7A – Station Equipment: Receivers, Transceivers, Transmitter Amplifiers, RF Preamplifiers, Transverters; Basic Radio Circuit Concepts and Terminology: Sensitivity, Selectivity, Mixers, Oscillators, Push-To-Talk (PTT), VFO, Modulation

T7A01. Which term describes the ability of a receiver to detect the presence of a signal?

A. RF gain
B. Sensitivity
C. Selectivity
D. Total Harmonic Distortion

B: The ability of a receiver to detect the presence of a signal is measured in terms of its sensitivity.

T7A02. What is a transceiver?

A. A device that combines a receiver and transmitter
B. A device for matching feed line impedance to 50 ohms
C. A device for automatically sending and decoding Morse code
D. A device for converting receiver and transmitter frequencies to another band

A: A transceiver is a device that combines the functions of a transmitter and a receiver.

T7A03. Which of the following is used to convert a signal from one frequency to another?

A. Phase splitter
B. Mixer
C. Inverter
D. Amplifier

B: A mixer is a device used to convert radio signals from one frequency to another.

T7A04. Which term describes the ability of a receiver to discriminate between multiple signals?

A. Discrimination ratio
B. Sensitivity
C. Selectivity
D. Harmonic distortion

C: A receiver's ability to discriminate among multiple radio signals is referred to as its selectivity.

T7A05. What is the name of a circuit that generates a signal at a specific frequency?

A. Reactance modulator
B. Phase modulator
C. Low-pass filter
D. Oscillator

D: An oscillator is a circuit that produces an oscillating signal at a desired frequency.

T7A06. What device converts the RF input and output of a transceiver to another band?

A. High-pass filter
B. Low-pass filter
C. Transverter
D. Phase converter

C: A transverter takes the output of a low-powered 28 MHz SSB exciter and produces a 222 MHz output signal. Transverters are a single unit that includes both an upconverter and a downconverter. The transverter enables the transceiver to communicate over a broad range of frequencies.

T7A07. What is the function of a transceiver's PTT input?

A. Input for a key used to send CW
B. Switches transceiver from receive to transmit when grounded
C. Provides a transmit tuning tone when grounded
D. Input for a preamplifier tuning tone

B: The term PTT stands for push-to-talk, a setup in which the transceiver is set to receive when the button is not pushed, and transmit when the button is pushed (when the switch is grounded).

T7A08. Which of the following describes combining speech with an RF carrier signal?

A. Impedance matching
B. Oscillation
C. Modulation
D. Low-pass filtering

C: The process of combining speech with an RF carrier signal is referred to as modulation.

T7A09. What is the function of the switch which selects either SSB or CW-FM on some VHF power amplifiers?

A. Change the mode of the transmitted signal
B. Set the amplifier for proper operation in the selected mode
C. Change the frequency range of the amplifier to operate in the proper segment of the band
D. Reduce the received signal noise

B: Single Side Band/Continuous Wave - FM switch on a VHF amplifier sets the amplifier to the selected mode. The switch provides an easy toggle between settings.

T7A10. What can be added to the output of a transceiver to increase the transmitted output power?

A. A potentiometer
B. An RF power amplifier
C. An impedance multiplier
D. All these choices are correct

B: An RF power amplifier increases the low-power output from a handheld transceiver.

T7A11. What is the function of the Variable Frequency Oscillator (VFO) circuit in a transceiver?

A. Set the receive and transmit frequency
B. Provide automatic frequency control
C. Inject a variable frequency to allow CW reception
D. Generate and demodulate single sideband signals

A: The Variable Frequency Oscillator (VFO) circuit in a transceiver sets the receive and transmit frequency.

T7B – Symptoms, Causes, and Cures of Common Transmitter and Receiver Problems: Overload and Overdrive, Distortion, Interference and Consumer Electronics, RF Feedback

T7B01. What can you do if you are told your FM handheld or mobile transceiver is over-deviating?

A. Talk louder into the microphone
B. Let the transceiver cool off
C. Change to a higher power level
D. Talk farther away from the microphone

D: If you are told your FM handheld or mobile transceiver is over deviating, you can talk farther away from the microphone.

T7B02. What would cause a broadcast AM or FM radio to receive an amateur radio transmission unintentionally?

A. The receiver is unable to reject strong signals outside the AM or FM band
B. The microphone gain of the transmitter is turned up too high
C. The audio amplifier of the transmitter is overloaded
D. The deviation of an FM transmitter is set too low

A: If a broadcast AM/FM radio is unintentionally receiving amateur radio transmissions, the most likely explanation is that the receiver is unable to reject strong signals outside of the AM/FM bands.

T7B03. Which of the following can cause radio frequency interference?

A. Fundamental overload
B. Harmonics
C. Spurious emissions
D. All these choices are correct

D: Radio frequency interference may be caused by fundamental overload, harmonics, or spurious emissions. A spurious emission is any radio frequency that was not created or transmitted on purpose.

T7B04. Which of the following might be the cause of low RF power output from a solid-state transceiver?

A. Poor amplifier noise figure
B. Poor amplifier linearity
C. Low SWR
D. High SWR

D: High SWR might be the cause of low RF power output from a solid-state transceiver.

T7B05. Which of the following might reduce interference by an amateur station to a non-amateur over-the-air radio receiver?

A. Block the amateur signal with a filter at the antenna input of the affected receiver
B. Block the interfering signal with a filter on the amateur transmitter
C. Switch the transmitter from FM to SSB
D. Switch the transmitter to a narrow-band mode

A: Filtering out an unwanted amateur radio signal at the receiver of the impacted device is the best way to reduce or eliminate overload on a TV or radio.

T7B06. Which of the following actions should you take if a neighbor tells you that your station's transmissions are interfering with their radio or TV reception?

A. Make sure that your station is functioning properly and that it does not cause interference to your own radio or television when it is tuned to the same channel
B. Immediately turn off your transmitter and contact the nearest FCC office for assistance
C. Install a harmonic doubler on the output of your transmitter and tune it until the interference is eliminated
D. All these choices are correct

A: If someone tells you that your station's transmissions are interfering with their radio or TV reception, your first step should be to make sure that your station is functioning properly and that it does not cause interference to your own television.

T7B07. Which of the following can reduce interference to a 2-meter band transceiver from a nearby commercial FM station?

A. Installing an RF preamplifier
B. Using double-shielded coaxial cable
C. Installing bypass capacitors on the microphone cable
D. Installing a band-reject filter

D: The purpose of a band reject filter is specifically for blocking specific signals, especially if they are strong, to prevent signal overload.

T7B08. What should you do if something in a neighbor's home is causing harmful interference to your amateur station?

A. Work with your neighbor to identify the offending device
B. Politely inform your neighbor that FCC rules prohibit the use of devices that cause interference
C. Make sure your station meets the standards of good amateur practice
D. All these choices are correct

D: If you believe something in your neighbor's house is causing harmful interference to your amateur station, there are a few things you can or should do. First, make sure that your station is set up properly and that a faulty setup is not causing the interference problems. If that is not successful, talk to your neighbor about the interference problems you are experiencing, and politely let him know about the FCC rules that govern harmful interference. If your neighbor is amenable, work with him to locate the source of the interference and find a solution. Always remain courteous.

T7B09. What should be the first step to resolve non-fiber optic cable TV interference caused by your amateur radio transmission?

A. Add a low-pass filter to the TV antenna input
B. Add a high-pass filter to the TV antenna input
C. Add a preamplifier to the TV antenna input
D. Be sure all TV feed line coaxial connectors are installed properly

D: To remedy any non-fiber optic cable TV interference caused by your amateur radio transmission, ensure that all TV feed line coaxial connectors are installed properly.

T7B10. What might be a problem if you receive a report that your audio signal through an FM repeater is distorted or unintelligible?

A. Your transmitter is slightly off frequency
B. You are speaking too loudly or too close to the microphone
C. You are in a bad location
D. All these choices are correct

D: If you receive a report that your audio signal through the repeater is distorted or unintelligible, this may be because your transmitter is slightly off frequency, your batteries are running low, or you're in a bad location.

T7B11. Which of the following can eliminate distorted voice transmissions?

A. Adding extra feedline to the antenna to lower SWR
B. Turning the radio on and off to reset the computer-controlled circuitry
C. Adding a clip-on ferrite "choke" to the microphone cable to prevent the transmitted signal from feeding back into the transmitter
D. Turning the squelch control fully clockwise to prevent the transmitted signal from triggering the squelch circuit

C: Adding a clip-on ferrite choke to the microphone cable can eliminate distorted voice transmissions by preventing transmitted RF from feeding back into the transmitter.

T7C – Antenna and Transmission Line Measurements and Troubleshooting: Measuring SWR, Effects of High SWR, Causes of Feed Line Failures; Basic Coaxial Cable Characteristics; Use of Dummy Loads When Testing

T7C01. What is the primary purpose of a dummy load?

A. To prevent transmitting signals over the air when making tests
B. To prevent over-modulation of a transmitter
C. To improve the efficiency of an antenna
D. To improve the signal-to-noise ratio of a receiver

A: The primary purpose of a dummy load is to prevent the radiation of signals when making tests. The dummy load, also known as a dummy antenna, is a station accessory that enables the user to test and finetune equipment without actually broadcasting a signal.

T7C02. Which of the following is used to determine if an antenna is resonant at the desired operating frequency?

A. A VTVM
B. An antenna analyzer
C. A Q meter
D. A frequency counter

B: An antenna analyzer can be used to determine if an antenna is resonant at the desired operating frequency. Antenna analyzers assess the efficiency of antenna systems.

T7C03. What does a typical RF dummy load consist of?

A. A low-voltage power supply and an AC relay
B. A 50-ohm non-inductive resistor mounted on a heat sink
C. A low-voltage power supply and a DC relay
D. A 50-ohm inductive reactance mounted in a shielded enclosure

B: A typical RF dummy load consists of a 50-ohm non-inductive resistor mounted on a heat sink. It is designed to absorb transmitter power without radiating a signal.

T7C04. What reading on an SWR meter indicates a perfect impedance match between the antenna and the feed line?

A. 50:50
B. Zero
C. 1:1
D. Full Scale

C: An SWR meter reading of 1:1 indicates a perfect impedance match between the antenna and the feed line. This means that all of the transmitted power is being delivered to the load with no reflected power.

T7C05. Why do most solid-state transmitters reduce output power as SWR increases beyond a certain level?

A. To protect the RF output amplifier transistors
B. To comply with FCC rules on spectral purity
C. Because power supplies cannot supply enough current at high SWR
D. To lower the SWR on the transmission line

A: Solid-state radios will automatically reduce the power output in order to prevent damage, specifically to output amplifier transistors, from an increase in SWR.

T7C06. What does an SWR reading of 4:1 indicate?

A. Loss of -4 dB
B. Good impedance match
C. Gain of +4 dB
D. Impedance mismatch

D: An SWR reading of 4:1 indicates an impedance mismatch.

T7C07. What happens to power lost in a feed line?

A. It increases the SWR
B. It is radiated as harmonics
C. It is converted into heat
D. It distorts the signal

C: The power lost in a feed line is converted into heat. If the cable has cracks or dents, it will be more likely to lose power in this manner. A ham radio operator should always use the best feed line he or she can afford.

T7C08. Which instrument can be used to determine SWR?

A. Voltmeter
B. Ohmmeter
C. Iambic pentameter
D. Directional wattmeter

D: Besides an SWR meter, one could also use a directional wattmeter to determine if a feed line and antenna are properly matched. An SWR (standing wave ratio) meter can evaluate the effectiveness of impedance matching, and can also identify the degree of mismatch between a transmission line and its load. A directional wattmeter is capable of differentiating between the forward and reflected waves.

T7C09. Which of the following causes failure of coaxial cables?

A. Moisture contamination
B. Solder flux contamination
C. Rapid fluctuation in transmitter output power
D. Operation at 100% duty cycle for an extended period

A: The most common cause of failure in coaxial cables is moisture contamination. Coaxial cable, also known as coax, is composed of a central wire surrounded by hollow tube. The center wire is called the center conductor, and the outer conductor is known as the braid, or shield.

T7C10. Why should the outer jacket of coaxial cable be resistant to ultraviolet light?

A. Ultraviolet light can increase the resistance of the conductors
B. Ultraviolet light can increase losses in the cable's jacket
C. Ultraviolet and RF signals can mix, causing interference
D. Ultraviolet light can damage the jacket and allow water to enter the cable

D: The outer jacket of a coaxial cable should be resistant to ultraviolet light because this light can damage the jacket and allow water to enter the cable.

T7C11. What is an advantage of foam-dielectric versus solid-dielectric coaxial cable?

A. It is more resistant to moisture contamination
B. It has higher voltage breakdown
C. It has less loss per foot
D. It has a better impedance match to 50 ohms

C: Foam-dielectric coaxial cable has an advantage over solid-dielectric coaxial cable because it has less loss per foot.

T7D – Using basic test instruments: voltmeter, ammeter, and ohmmeter; Soldering

T7D01. Which instrument would you use to measure electric potential?

A. An ammeter
B. A voltmeter
C. A potentiometer
D. An ohmmeter

B: A voltmeter is used to measure electric potential or electromotive force. It accomplishes this by identifying the electric potential difference between two conductors.

T7D02. How is a voltmeter connected to a component to measure applied voltage?

A. In series
B. In parallel
C. In quadrature
D. In phase

B: The correct way to connect a voltmeter to a circuit is in parallel with the circuit. An analog voltmeter, on the other hand, is a moving coil galvanometer that works as a voltmeter after a resistor is installed in series with it.

T7D03. When configured to measure current, how is a multimeter connected to a component?

A. In series
B. In parallel
C. In quadrature
D. In phase

A: An ammeter is usually connected in series with the circuit. In most cases, an ammeter is combined with a voltmeter and ohmmeter in a single instrument.

T7D04. Which instrument is used to measure electric current?

A. An ohmmeter
B. An electrometer
C. A voltmeter
D. An ammeter

D: An ammeter is used to measure electric current. Typically, the current will need to be at least a few amperes to be susceptible to measurement by the ammeter.

T7D05. How does an ohmmeter measure the resistance of a circuit or component?

A. By applying a small current and measuring the resulting voltage
B. By placing a variable resistor in parallel with the circuit
C. By placing a variable resistor in series with the circuit
D. By applying a variable voltage and measuring the resulting current change

A: An ohmmeter measures resistance by applying a small current and measuring the resulting voltage.

T7D06. Which of the following can damage a multimeter?

A. Attempting to measure resistance using the voltage setting
B. Failing to connect one of the probes to ground
C. Attempting to measure voltage when using the resistance setting
D. Not allowing it to warm up properly

C: Attempting to measure voltage when using the resistance setting might damage a multimeter. Multimeters are capable of measuring the following values: current, resistance, and the current potential differences of alternating and direct current.

T7D07. Which of the following measurements are made using a multimeter?

A. Signal strength and noise
B. Impedance and reactance
C. Voltage and resistance
D. All these choices are correct

C: Voltage and resistance measurements are commonly made using a multimeter. The multimeter is sometimes referred to as a volt-ohm meter.

T7D08. Which of the following types of solder should not be used for radio and electronic applications?

A. Acid-core solder
B. Lead-tin solder
C. Rosin-core solder
D. Tin-copper solder

A: Rosin-core solder is best for radio and electronic use. Acid-core should not be used.

T7D09. What is the characteristic appearance of a cold tin-lead solder joint?

A. Dark black spots
B. A bright or shiny surface
C. A rough or lumpy surface
D. A greenish tinge

C: Cold tin-lead solder joints typically have a rough or lumpy surface.

T7D10. What reading indicates that an ohmmeter is connected across a large, discharged capacitor?

A. Increasing resistance with time
B. Decreasing resistance with time
C. Steady full-scale reading
D. Alternating between open and short circuit

A: When an ohmmeter is connected across a large, discharged capacitor it will show increasing resistance over time.

T7D11. Which of the following precautions should be taken when measuring in-circuit resistance with an ohmmeter?

A. Ensure that the applied voltages are correct
B. Ensure that the circuit is not powered
C. Ensure that the circuit is grounded
D. Ensure that the circuit is operating at the correct frequency

B: When measuring in-circuit resistance with an ohmmeter, one should ensure that the circuit is not powered.

T8 – SIGNALS AND EMISSIONS

T8A – BASIC CHARACTERISTICS OF FM AND SSB; BANDWIDTH OF VARIOUS MODULATION MODES: CW, SSB, FM, FAST-SCAN TV; CHOICE OF EMISSION TYPE: SELECTION OF USB VS LSB, USE OF SSB FOR WEAK SIGNAL WORK, USE OF FM FOR VHF PACKET AND REPEATERS

T8A01. Which of the following is a form of amplitude modulation?

A. Spread spectrum
B. Packet radio
C. Single sideband
D. Phase shift keying (PSK)

C: Single sideband is a form of amplitude modulation. Indeed, single sideband is the most common mode of voice transmission on the high-frequency bands. Unlike an a.m. transmission, in which two identical versions of the message are broadcast, an SSB transmission only broadcasts one. For this reason, single sideband communications are more efficient and are better at conserving space on the radio spectrum.

T8A02. What type of modulation is commonly used for VHF packet radio transmissions?

A. FM or PM
B. SSB
C. AM
D. PSK

A: The type of modulation most commonly used for VHF packet radio transmission is either FM or PM.

T8A03. Which type of voice mode is often used for long-distance (weak signal) contacts on the VHF and UHF bands?

A. FM
B. DRM
C. SSB
D. PM

C: The type of voice modulation often used for long-distance or weak signal contacts on the VHF and UHF bands is SSB.

T8A04. Which type of modulation is commonly used for VHF and UHF voice repeaters?

A. AM
B. SSB
C. PSK
D. FM or PM

D: The type of modulation most commonly used for VHF and UHF voice repeaters is either FM or PM.

T8A05. Which of the following signal types has the narrowest bandwidth?

A. FM voice
B. SSB voice
C. CW
D. Slow-scan TV

C: CW has a narrower bandwidth than FM voice, SSB voice, or slow-scan TV emission.

T8A06. Which sideband is normally used for 10-meter HF, VHF, and UHF single-sideband communications?

A. Upper sideband
B. Lower sideband
C. Suppressed sideband
D. Inverted sideband

A: The upper sideband is normally used for 10 meter HF, VHF, and UHF single-sideband communications.

T8A07. What is one characteristic of single sideband (SSB) compared to FM?

A. SSB signals are easier to tune in correctly
B. SSB signals are less susceptible to interference
C. SSB signals have narrower bandwidth
D. SSB signals are less susceptible to high SWR

C: The primary advantage of single sideband over FM is that SSB signals have narrower bandwidth.

T8A08. What is the approximate bandwidth of a typical single sideband (SSB) voice signal?

A. 1 kHz
B. 3 kHz
C. 6 kHz
D. 15 kHz

B: The approximate bandwidth of a single sideband voice signal is 3 kHz.

T8A09. What is the approximate bandwidth of an FM voice signal on VHF repeaters?

A. Less than 500 Hz
B. About 150 kHz
C. Between 10 and 15 kHz
D. Between 50 and 125 kHz

C: The approximate bandwidth of a VHF repeater FM voice signal is between 10 and 15 kHz.

T8A10. What is the approximate bandwidth of AM fast-scan TV transmissions?

A. More than 10 MHz
B. About 6 MHz
C. About 3 MHz
D. About 1 MHz

B: The typical bandwidth of AM fast-scan TV transmissions on the 70 cm band is about 6 MHz.

T8A11. What is the approximate bandwidth required to transmit a CW signal?

A. 2.4 kHz
B. 150 Hz
C. 1000 Hz
D. 15 kHz

B: The approximate bandwidth required to transmit a CW signal is 150 Hz.

T8A12. Which of the following is a disadvantage of FM compared with single sideband?

A. Voice quality is poorer
B. Only one signal can be received at a time
C. FM signals are harder to tune
D. FM signals are more susceptible to high SWR

B: A disadvantage of FM when compared to single sideband is that only one signal can be received at a time.

T8B – Amateur satellite operation: Doppler shift, basic orbits, operating protocols, modulation mode selection, transmitter power considerations, telemetry, satellite tracking programs, beacons, uplink and downlink mode definitions, spin fading, definition of "LEO", setting uplink power

T8B01. What telemetry information is typically transmitted by satellite beacons?

A. The signal strength of received signals
B. Time of day accurate to plus or minus 1/10 second
C. Health and status of the satellite
D. All these choices are correct

C: Health and status are the most common telemetry datapoints that are transmitted by satellite beacons.

T8B02. What is the impact of using excessive effective radiated power on a satellite uplink?

A. Possibility of commanding the satellite to an improper mode
B. Blocking access by other users
C. Overloading the satellite batteries
D. Possibility of rebooting the satellite control computer

B: The result can be that the signal-to-noise ratio received by the repeater can be overpowered by a single signal and thus won't transmit other valid, but weaker signals.

T8B03. Which of the following are provided by satellite tracking programs?

A. Maps showing the real-time position of the satellite track over Earth
B. The time, azimuth, and elevation of the start, maximum altitude, and end of a pass
C. The apparent frequency of the satellite transmission, including effects of Doppler shift
D. All these choices are correct

D: Satellite tracking programs provide a wealth of information about the path and position of orbiting satellites, as well as their operation.

T8B04. What mode of transmission is commonly used by amateur radio satellites?

A. SSB
B. FM
C. CW/data
D. All these choices are correct

D: The three most common transmission modes are SSB, FM, and CW/data.

T8B05. What is a satellite beacon?

A. The primary transmit antenna on the satellite
B. An indicator light that shows where to point your antenna
C. A reflective surface on the satellite
D. A transmission from a satellite that contains status information

D: A satellite beacon is a transmission from a space station that contains information about a satellite. These transmissions are used for maintenance and guidance.

T8B06. Which of the following are inputs to a satellite tracking program?

A. The satellite transmitted power
B. The Keplerian elements
C. The last observed time of zero Doppler shift
D. All these choices are correct

B: The six Keplerian elements precisely define the orbit of a satellite. The six elements are: (1) eccentricity, (2) semi-major axis, (3) inclination, (4) longitude of the ascending node, (5) argument of periapsis, and (6) mean anomaly at epoch.

T8B07. What is Doppler shift in reference to satellite communications?

A. A change in the satellite orbit
B. A mode where the satellite receives signals on one band and transmits on another
C. An observed change in signal frequency caused by relative motion between the satellite and Earth station
D. A special digital communications mode for some satellites

C: With regard to satellite communications, Doppler shift is an observed change in signal frequency caused by relative motion between the satellite and the earth station. When the satellite is approaching the earth station, the wavelength will be shorter; as the satellite moves away from the earth station, the wave length will gradually expand.

T8B08. What does it mean if a satellite is operating in U/V mode?

A. The satellite uplink is in the 15-meter band and the downlink is in the 10 meter band
B. The satellite uplink is in the 70-centimeter band and the downlink is in the 2-meter band
C. The satellite operates using ultraviolet frequencies
D. The satellite frequencies are usually variable

B: When it is said that a satellite is operating in "U/V mode," this means that the satellite uplink is in the 70 cm band and the downlink is in the 2-meter band. In ham radio, modes are particular types of modulation, and modulations are the systems for adding information to a radio signal to be broadcast over the air.

T8B09. What causes spin fading of satellite signals?

A. Circular polarized noise interference radiated from the sun
B. Rotation of the satellite and its antennas
C. Doppler shift of the received signal
D. Interfering signals within the satellite uplink band

B: Spin fading with respect to satellite signals is caused by the rotation of the satellite and its antennas.

T8B10. What does the term LEO mean in reference to communication satellites?

A. Low Energy Orbit, which conserves battery power
B. Low Elevation Orbit, which appears close to the horizon from the earth station
C. Low Equilibrium Orbit, which has a slightly unstable period
D. Low Earth Orbit, which has a period of around 100 minutes

D: The initials LEO indicate that the satellite is in a Low Earth Orbit. This means that the path of the satellite is less than 1000 miles above the surface of the Earth.

T8B11. Who is permitted to receive telemetry from an amateur radio satellite?

A. Anyone
B. Only the satellite control operator
C. Only the control operator or a licensed radio amateur who has received the encryption key from the control operator
D. Only a licensed radio amateur who has received the encryption key from AMSAT

A: Anyone is permitted to receive telemetry from an amateur radio satellite.

T8B12. What is a way to determine whether your satellite uplink power into a linear transponder satellite is neither too low nor too high?

A. Check your signal strength report in the telemetry data
B. Listen for distortion on your downlink signal
C. Your signal strength on the downlink should be about the same as the beacon
D. Compare your signal to others on the downlink using an internet SDR receiver

C: Your signal strength on the downlink should be about the same as the beacon.

T8C – Operating Activities: Radio Direction Finding, Contests, Linking over the Internet, Exchanging Grid Locators

T8C01. Which of the following methods is used to locate sources of noise interference or jamming?

A. Echolocation
B. Doppler radar
C. Radio direction finding
D. Phase locking

C: Radio direction finding is used to locate sources of noise interference or jamming.

T8C02. Which of these items would be useful for a hidden transmitter hunt?

A. Calibrated SWR meter
B. A directional antenna
C. A directional wattmeter
D. All these choices are correct

B: A directional antenna would be useful for a hidden transmitter hunt. Directional antennas send and receive signals in some directions more than others. Therefore, these antennas are able to ascertain from which direction a signal is being broadcast.

T8C03. What operating activity involves contacting as many stations as possible during a specified period?

A. Simulated emergency exercises
B. Net operations
C. Hidden transmitter hunts
D. Contesting

D: Contesting involves contacting as many stations as possible during a specified period of time.

T8C04. Which of the following is good practice when contacting another station in a contest?

A. Signing only the last two letters of your call if there are many other stations calling
B. Contacting the station twice to be sure that you are in his log
C. Sending only the minimum information needed for proper identification and the contest exchange
D. Adding "Please copy" before your exchange

C: Sending only the minimum information needed for proper identification and the contest exchange is good procedure when contacting another station in a radio contest.

T8C05. What is a grid locator?

A. A letter-number designator assigned to a geographic location
B. A letter-number designator assigned to an azimuth and elevation
C. An instrument for locating faults in power amplifiers
D. An instrument for radio direction finding

A: A grid locator is a letter-number designator assigned to a geographic location. The latitude and the longitude of the location are compressed into a brief string of characters, in alternating pairs of letters and numbers.

T8C06. How is over the air access to Internet Radio Linking Project (IRLP) nodes accomplished?

A. By obtaining a password that is sent via voice to the node
B. By using Dual-Tone Multi-Frequency (DTMF) signals
C. By entering the proper internet password
D. By using Continuous Tone-Coded Squelch System (CTCSS) tone codes

B: Internet Radio Linking Project (IRLP) nodes consist of a radio attached to an internet-connected computer running specialized software. It allows amateur radio users to communicate with other users anywhere in the world near another IRLP node. Users access the node using Dual-Tone Multi-Frequency (DTMF) signals.

T8C07. What is Voice Over Internet Protocol (VoIP)?

A. A set of rules specifying how to identify your station when linked over the internet to another station
B. A technique employed to "spot" DX stations via the internet
C. A technique for measuring the modulation quality of a transmitter using remote sites monitored via the internet
D. A method of delivering voice communications over the internet using digital techniques

D: Voice-over-Internet Protocol (VoIP) is a method of delivering voice communications over the Internet. It is an integral part of the Internet Radio Linking Project (IRLP).

T8C08. What is the Internet Radio Linking Project (IRLP)?

A. A technique to connect amateur radio systems, such as repeaters, via the internet
B. A system for providing access to websites via amateur radio
C. A system for informing amateurs in real time of the frequency of active DX stations
D. A technique for measuring signal strength of an amateur transmitter via the internet

A: The IRLP is a project that makes use of the Internet to connect amateur radio stations to one another from all over the world.

T8C09. Which of the following protocols enables an amateur station to transmit through a repeater without using a radio to initiate the transmission?

A. IRLP
B. D-STAR
C. DMR
D. EchoLink

D: EchoLink enables an amateur station to transmit through a repeater without using a radio to initiate the transmission.

T8C10. What is required before using the EchoLink system?

A. Complete the required EchoLink training
B. Purchase a license to use the EchoLink software
C. Register your call sign and provide proof of license
D. At least a General Class license

C: You must provide your call sign and proof of license since this type of use is a type of remote control of a station.

T8C11. What is an amateur radio station that connects other amateur stations to the internet?

A. A gateway
B. A repeater
C. A digipeater
D. A beacon

A: A gateway is an amateur radio station that is used to connect other amateur stations to the Internet.

T8D – Non-voice and digital communications: image signals and definition of NTSC, CW, packet radio, PSK, APRS, error detection and correction, amateur radio networking, DMR, WSJT modes, Broadband-Hamnet

T8D01. Which of the following is a digital communications mode?

A. Packet radio
B. IEEE 802.11
C. FT8
D. All these choices are correct

D: Packet, IEEE 802.11, and FT8 are all examples of digital communications methods.

T8D02. What is FT8?

A. A wideband FM voice mode
B. A digital mode capable of low signal-to-noise operation
C. An eight-channel multiplex mode for FM repeaters
D. A digital slow-scan TV mode with forward error correction and automatic color compensation

B: FT8 is a digital mode capable of low signal-to-noise operation.

T8D03. What kind of data can be transmitted by APRS?

A. GPS position data
B. Text messages
C. Weather data
D. All these choices are correct

D: GPS position data, text messages, and weather data can all be transmitted by APRS.

T8D04. What is meant by the term "NTSC?"

A. A digital transmission standard for encrypting data
B. A special mode for satellite uplink
C. An analog fast-scan color TV signal
D. A frame compression scheme for TV signals

C: The term NTSC indicates an analog fast scan color TV signal.

T8D05. Which of the following is an application of APRS?

A. Providing real-time tactical digital communications in conjunction with a map showing the locations of stations
B. Automatically showing the number of packets transmitted via PACTOR during a specific time interval
C. Providing voice over internet connection between repeaters
D. Providing information on the number of stations signed into a repeater

A: The Automatic Packet Reporting System (APRS) is a system designed to provide real-time tactical digital communications along with a map indicating the sources of the signals carrying the communication.

T8D06. What does the abbreviation "PSK" mean?

A. Pulse Shift Keying
B. Phase Shift Keying
C. Packet Sampled Keying
D. Power Sampled Keying

B: The abbreviation PSK means phase shift keying. Phase shift keying is a strategy for digital modes in the high frequency spectrum. In this system, the components of code are indicated with shifts in the timing relationship between a continuously transmitted tone and a reference tone. This enables the user to transmit a signal in very limited space.

T8D07. Which of the following describes DMR?

A. A technique for time-multiplexing two digital voice signals on a single 12.5 kHz repeater channel
B. An automatic position tracking mode for FM mobiles communicating through repeaters
C. An automatic computer logging technique for hands-off logging when communicating while operating a vehicle
D. A digital technique for transmitting on two repeater inputs simultaneously for automatic error correction

A: DMR is specifically a way to time-multiplex two signals on a single channel.

T8D08. Which of the following is included in packet radio transmissions?

A. A checksum that permits error detection
B. A header that contains the call sign of the station to which the information is being sent
C. Automatic repeat request in case of error
D. All these choices are correct

D: Packet transmissions may include a checksum which permits error detection, a header which contains the call sign of the station to which the information is being sent, and an automatic repeat request in case of error.

T8D09. What is CW?

A. A type of electromagnetic propagation
B. A digital mode used primarily on 2-meter FM
C. Error correction for digital transmission using code words
D. Another name for a Morse code transmission

D: CW is another name for a Morse code transmission.

T8D10. Which of the following operating activities is supported by digital mode software in the WSJT-X software suite?

A. Earth-Moon-Earth
B. Weak signal propagation beacons
C. Meteor scatter
D. All these choices are correct

D: Earth-Moon-Earth, weak signal propagation beacons, and meteor scatter are all well suited to the short transmissions of WSJT.

T8D11. What is the role of ARQ in a transmission system?

A. A special transmission format limited to video signals
B. A system used to encrypt command signals to an amateur radio satellite
C. An error correction method in which the receiving station detects errors and sends a request for retransmission
D. A method of compressing data using autonomous reiterative Q codes prior to final encoding

C: An Automatic Repeat Query (ARQ) transmission system is a system designed to catch errors in transmission. From the receiving station, it detects errors in the transmission and automatically sends a request to retransmit the information.

T8D12. Which of the following best describes an amateur radio mesh network?

A. An amateur-radio data network using commercial Wi-Fi equipment with modified firmware
B. A wide-bandwidth digital voice mode employing DMR protocols
C. An amateur-radio satellite communications network using modified commercial satellite TV hardware
D. An internet linking protocol allowing communication through repeaters around the world

A: An amateur radio mesh network is an amateur-radio based data network using commercial Wi-Fi equipment with modified firmware.

T9 – Antennas and Feed Lines

T9A – Antennas: Vertical and Horizontal Polarization, Concept of Antenna Gain, Definition and Types of Beam Antennas, Antenna Loading, Common Portable and Mobile Antennas, Relationships Between Resonant Length and Frequency, Dipole Pattern

T9A01. What is a beam antenna?

A. An antenna built from square aluminum beams
B. An omnidirectional antenna invented by Clarence Beam
C. An antenna that concentrates signals in one direction
D. An antenna that focuses the signal into two intense rays

C: A beam antenna concentrates signals in one direction. Beam antennas, also known as beamforming antennas, are sometimes composed of a simple system made of two wires. The most popular beam antenna is the Yagi, which consists of two conducting elements running parallel to each other and 1/10 of a wavelength apart.

T9A02. Which of the following describes a type of antenna loading?

A. Electrically lengthening by inserting inductors in radiating elements
B. Inserting a resistor in the radiating portion of the antenna to make it resonant
C. Installing a spring in the base of a mobile vertical antenna to make it more flexible
D. Strengthening the radiating elements of a beam antenna to better resist wind damage

A: Antenna loading is the term for placing an inductor in series with the antenna so that it reduces the resonant frequency of the antenna.

T9A03. How is the polarization of an antenna described?

A. By the shape of the driven element
B. By the orientation of the electric field
C. By the orientation of the magnetic field
D. By the direction of radiation

B: The polarization of an antenna is described by the orientation of the electric field.

T9A04. What is a disadvantage of a handheld radio transceiver's short flexible antenna compared to a full-sized quarter-wave antenna?

A. It has low efficiency
B. It transmits only circularly polarized signals
C. It is more susceptible to receiver desensitization
D. It only works on analog signals, not digital ones

A: One disadvantage of the antenna supplied with most handheld radio transceivers is it does not transmit or receive as effectively as a full-sized antenna.

T9A05. Which of the following increases the resonant frequency of a dipole antenna?

A. Lengthening it
B. Inserting coils in series with radiating wires
C. Shortening it
D. Adding capacitive loading to the ends of the radiating wires

C: To make a dipole antenna resonant on a higher frequency, shorten it.

T9A06. Which of the following types of antennas offers the greatest gain?

A. 5/8 wave vertical
B. Isotropic
C. J pole
D. Yagi

D: When compared to 5/8 wave vertical, isotropic, and J pole antennas, Yagi antennas offer the greatest gain.

T9A07. What is a potential drawback of using a handheld VHF transceiver inside a vehicle that lacks an externally mounted antenna?

A. Signal strength is reduced due to the shielding effect of the vehicle
B. The bandwidth of the antenna will decrease, increasing SWR
C. The SWR might decrease, decreasing the signal strength
D. The handheld will overheat due to reflected power in the vehicle

A: One good reason not to use a "rubber duck" antenna inside your car is that signals can be significantly weaker than when it is outside the vehicle.

T9A08. Why is a 19-inch-long vertical antenna often used on 2 meters?

A. It has high gain
B. It is a resonant half-wave
C. It is a resonant quarter-wave
D. It has low RF radiation exposure

C: A 19-inch-long vertical antenna is often used on 2 meters because it is a resonant quarter-wave.

T9A09. What is an advantage of a 5/8-wavelength whip antenna for VHF or UHF mobile service compared to a 1/4-wave antenna?

A. It has more gain
B. It radiates at a higher angle
C. It has lower SWR
D. It has lower impedance

A: A 5/8-wavelength whip antenna has an advantage over a 1/4-wave antenna because it has more gain.

T9A10. In which direction does a half-wave dipole antenna radiate the strongest signal?

A. Equally in all directions
B. Off the ends of the antenna
C. In the direction of the feed line
D. Broadside to the antenna

D: The radiation is strongest from a half-wave dipole antenna in free space broadside to the antenna.

T9A11. What is antenna gain?

A. The additional power that is added to the transmitter power
B. The additional power that is required in the antenna when transmitting on a higher frequency
C. The increase in signal strength in a specified direction compared to a reference antenna
D. The increase in impedance on receive or transmit compared to a reference antenna

C: The gain of an antenna is the increase in signal strength in a specified direction when compared to a reference antenna.

T9B – Feed lines: types, attenuation vs frequency, selecting; SWR concepts; Antenna tuners (couplers); RF Connectors: selecting, weather protection

T9B01. Which of the following connectors should be carefully taped for weather protection when used outdoors?

A. PL259
B. BNC
C. Type N
D. All these choices are correct

D: All these choices are correct because PL259, BNC, and Type N connectors should all be carefully taped for weather protection when used outdoors.

T9B02. What is the most common impedance of coaxial cables used in amateur radio?

A. 8 ohms
B. 50 ohms
C. 600 ohms
D. 12 ohms

B: The impedance of the most commonly used coaxial cable in typical amateur radio installations is 50 ohms. Impedance is the measure of the total opposition to current flow in an alternating current circuit, composed of reactance and ohmic resistance.

T9B03. Why is coaxial cable the most common feed line for amateur radio antenna systems?

A. It is easy to use and requires few special installation considerations
B. It has less loss than any other type of feed line
C. It can handle more power than any other type of feed line
D. It is less expensive than any other type of feed line

A: Coaxial cable is used more often than any other feed lines for amateur radio antenna systems because it is easy to use and requires few special installation considerations.

T9B04. What is the major function of an antenna tuner (antenna coupler)?

A. It matches the antenna system impedance to the transceiver's output impedance
B. It helps a receiver automatically tune in weak stations
C. It allows an antenna to be used on both transmit and receive
D. It automatically selects the proper antenna for the frequency band being used

A: An antenna tuner matches the antenna system impedance to the transceiver's output impedance.

T9B05. What happens as the frequency of a signal in coaxial cable is increased?

A. The characteristic impedance decreases
B. The loss decreases
C. The characteristic impedance increases
D. The loss increases

D: As the frequency of a signal passing through coaxial cable is increased, the loss generally increases as well.

T9B06. Which of the following connector types is most suitable as an RF connector for frequencies above 400 MHz?

A. PL-259
B. Type N
C. RS-213
D. DB-25

B: A Type N connector is most suitable for frequencies above 400 MHz. Type N connectors are threaded RF connectors used to join coaxial cables. These cables are able to carry microwave frequency signals.

T9B07. Which of the following is true of PL-259 type coax connectors?

A. They are preferred for microwave operation
B. They are watertight
C. They are commonly used at HF and VHF frequencies
D. They are a bayonet-type connector

C: PL–259 type coax connectors are commonly used at HF and VHF frequencies.

T9B08. Which of the following is a source of loss in coaxial feed line?

A. Water intrusion into coaxial connectors
B. High SWR
C. Multiple connectors in the line
D. All these choices are correct

D: Water intrusion into coaxial connectors, high SWR, and multiple connectors in the line are all sources of loss in a coaxial feed line.

T9B09. What can cause erratic changes in SWR?

A. Local thunderstorm
B. Loose connection in the antenna or feed line
C. Over-modulation
D. Overload from a strong local station

B: A loose connection in an antenna or a feed line might cause erratic changes in SWR readings.

T9B10. What is the electrical difference between RG-58 and RG-213 coaxial cable?

A. There is no significant difference between the two types
B. RG-58 cable has two shields
C. RG-213 cable has less loss at a given frequency
D. RG-58 cable can handle higher power levels

C: An RG-213 cable has less loss at a given frequency than an RG-58 cable.

T9B11. Which of the following types of feed line has the lowest loss?

A. 50-ohm flexible coax
B. Multi-conductor unbalanced cable
C. Air-insulated hardline
D. 75-ohm flexible coax

C: Air-insulated hardline is the type of feed line that has the lowest loss.

T9B12. What is standing wave ratio (SWR)?

A. A measure of how well a load is matched to a transmission line
B. The ratio of amplifier power output to input
C. The transmitter efficiency ratio
D. An indication of the quality of your station's ground connection

A: In general terms, standing wave ratio (SWR) is a measure of how well a load is matched to a transmission line. This is a measure of the impedance match between the antenna and the feedline. It is the ratio of the maximum voltage to the minimum voltage along the feedline. If a transmitter is being used, standing wave ratio is the impedance match between the feedline from the transmitter and the antenna system. If the antenna is a purely resistive load, the standing wave ratio is the ratio of antenna impedance to feedline impedance.

T0 –Safety

T0A – Power circuits and hazards: hazardous voltages, fuses and circuit breakers, grounding, electrical code compliance; Lightning protection; Battery safety

T0A01. Which of the following is a safety hazard of a 12-volt storage battery that lacks internal protection circuitry?

A. Touching both terminals with your hands can cause electrical shock
B. Shorting the terminals can cause burns, fire, or an explosion
C. RF emissions from a nearby transmitter can cause the electrolyte to emit poison gas
D. All these choices are correct

B: In order for electrical shock from a 12-volt battery to be hazardous, the circuit would typically need to be connected on or near one's chest. The primary hazard associated with a 12-volt battery is shorting the terminals with low resistance materials such as metal wires or rods, potentially resulting in burns, fires, or explosions.

T0A02. What health hazard is posed by electrical current flowing through the body?

A. It may cause injury by heating body tissue
B. It may disrupt the electrical functions of cells
C. It may cause involuntary muscle contractions
D. All these choices are correct

D: Electric shock may result in any of the following: cell damage, electrical function disruption in cells, tissue heating, muscle contraction, or burns.

T0A03. In the United States, what circuit does black wire insulation indicate in a three-wire 120 V AC cable?

A. Neutral
B. Hot
C. Equipment ground
D. Negative

B: In a three-wire electrical AC plug, the black wire is hot.

T0A04. What is the purpose of a fuse in an electrical circuit?

A. To prevent power supply ripple from damaging a component
B. To remove power in case of an overload
C. To limit current and prevent shocks
D. All these choices are correct

B: The purpose of a fuse in an electrical circuit is to interrupt power in case of overload.

T0A05. Why should a 5-ampere fuse never be replaced with a 20-ampere fuse?

A. The larger fuse would be likely to blow because it is rated for higher current
B. The power supply ripple would greatly increase
C. Excessive current could cause a fire
D. Voltage drop in the higher current fuse could result in excessively low voltage to the device

C: It is unwise to install a 20-ampere fuse in the place of a 5-ampere fuse because the excessive current could cause a fire.

T0A06. What is a good way to guard against electrical shock at your station?

A. Use three-wire cords and plugs for all AC powered equipment
B. Connect all AC powered station equipment to a common safety ground
C. Ensure all capacitors used for high-voltage DC are fully discharged before working inside equipment
D. All these choices are correct

D: There are several good ways to guard against electrical shock at your station. Use three-wire cords and plugs for all AC-powered equipment. Connect all AC-powered station equipment to a common safety ground. Also, ensure that capacitors used for high-voltage DC are fully discharged before working inside equipment.

T0A07. Where should a lightning arrester be installed in a coaxial feed line?

A. At the output connector of a transceiver
B. At the antenna feed point
C. At the AC power service panel
D. On a grounded panel near where feed lines enter the building

D: When installing a lightning arrester in a coaxial cable feed line, it should be near where the feed lines enter the building and grounded to a common plate which is in turn connected to an external ground.

T0A08. Where should a fuse or circuit breaker be installed in a 120V AC power circuit?

A. In series with the hot conductor only
B. In series with the hot and neutral conductors
C. In parallel with the hot conductor only
D. In parallel with the hot and neutral conductors

A: Home-built equipment that is powered with 120V AC power should always include a fuse or circuit breaker in series with the hot power line to reduce the risk of electrocution hazard.

T0A09. What should be done to all external ground rods or earth connections?

A. Waterproof them with silicone caulk or electrical tape
B. Keep them as far apart as possible
C. Bond them together with heavy wire or conductive strap
D. Tune them for resonance on the lowest frequency of operation

C: The best practice for ensuring safety regarding ground rods and earth connections is to bond them together. This can be done with heavy gauge wire or a large conductive strap.

T0A10. What hazard exists when rapidly charging or discharging an unprotected battery?

A. Overheating or out-gassing
B. Excess output ripple
C. Electric shock
D. Overvoltage

A: If a battery is charged or discharged too quickly, the battery could overheat and give off flammable gas, or explode.

T0A11. What hazard exists in a power supply immediately after turning it off?

A. Circulating currents in the dc filter
B. Leakage flux in the power transformer
C. Voltage transients from kickback diodes
D. Charge stored in filter capacitors

D: When a power supply is turned off and disconnected, a person still might receive an electric shock from the stored charge in large capacitors.

T0A12. Which of the following precautions should be taken when measuring high voltages with a voltmeter?

A. Ensure that the voltmeter has very low impedance
B. Ensure that the voltmeter and its leads are rated for use at the voltages being measured
C. Ensure that the circuit is grounded through the voltmeter
D. Ensure that the voltmeter is set to the correct frequency

B: When dealing with high voltages, safety should always be your foremost concern. If you need to measure the voltage on a high voltage circuit, always make sure that the voltmeter you are using and the attached leads are rated for use at the voltages you will be measuring.

T0B – Antenna Safety: Tower Safety and Grounding, Installing Antennas, Antenna Supports

T0B01. Which of the following is good practice when installing ground wires on a tower for lightning protection?

A. Put a drip loop in the ground connection to prevent water damage to the ground system
B. Make sure all ground wire bends are right angles
C. Ensure that connections are short and direct
D. All these choices are correct

C: When installing ground wires on a tower for lightning protection it is always good practice to ensure that connections are short and direct.

T0B02. What is required when climbing an antenna tower?

A. Have sufficient training on safe tower climbing techniques
B. Use appropriate tie-off to the tower at all times
C. Always wear an approved climbing harness
D. All these choices are correct

D: When climbing an antenna tower it is essential that you have sufficient training on safe tower climbing techniques, use appropriate tie-off to the tower at all times, and wear an approved climbing harness.

T0B03. Under what circumstances is it safe to climb a tower without a helper or observer?

A. When no electrical work is being performed
B. When no mechanical work is being performed
C. When the work being done is not more than 20 feet above the ground
D. Never

D: It is never safe to climb a tower without a helper or observer.

T0B04. Which of the following is an important safety precaution to observe when putting up an antenna tower?

A. Wear a ground strap connected to your wrist at all times
B. Insulate the base of the tower to avoid lightning strikes
C. Look for and stay clear of any overhead electrical wires
D. All these choices are correct

C: When putting up an antenna tower, it is important to look for and stay clear of any overhead electric wires.

T0B05. What is the purpose of a safety wire through a turnbuckle used to tension guy lines?

A. Secure the guy line if the turnbuckle breaks
B. Prevent loosening of the turnbuckle from vibration
C. Provide a ground path for lightning strikes
D. Provide an ability to measure for proper tensioning

B: The safety wire prevents the turnbuckle from turning. This will mediate any potential loosening of the turnbuckle due to vibration.

T0B06. What is the minimum safe distance from a power line to allow when installing an antenna?

A. Add the height of the antenna to the height of the power line and multiply by a factor of 1.5
B. The height of the power line above ground
C. 1/2 wavelength at the operating frequency
D. Enough so that if the antenna falls, no part of it can come within 10 feet of the power wires

D: The minimum safe distance from a power line when installing an antenna is such that, if the antenna falls unexpectedly, no part of it can come closer than 10 feet to the power wires.

T0B07. Which of the following is an important safety rule to remember when using a crank-up tower?

A. This type of tower must never be painted
B. This type of tower must never be grounded
C. This type of tower must not be climbed unless it is retracted, or mechanical safety locking devices have been installed
D. All these choices are correct

C: An important safety rule to remember when using a crank-up tower is that this type of tower must never be climbed unless it is in the fully retracted position. Crank-up towers are kept stable by a concrete foundation rather than by guy wires.

T0B08. Which is a proper grounding method for a tower?

A. A single four-foot ground rod, driven into the ground no more than 12 inches from the base
B. A ferrite-core RF choke connected between the tower and ground
C. A connection between the tower base and a cold-water pipe
D. Separate eight-foot ground rods for each tower leg, bonded to the tower and each other

D: Separate eight-foot long ground rods for each tower leg, bonded to the tower and each other, are considered to be a proper grounding method for a tower.

T0B09. Why should you avoid attaching an antenna to a utility pole?

A. The antenna will not work properly because of induced voltages
B. The antenna may unbalance the power transformer, causing power fluctuations
C. The antenna could contact high-voltage power lines
D. All these choices are correct

C: You should avoid attaching an antenna to a utility pole because the antenna could contact high-voltage power wires.

T0B10. Which of the following is true when installing grounding conductors used for lightning protection?

A. Use only non-insulated wire
B. Wires must be carefully routed with precise right-angle bends
C. Sharp bends must be avoided
D. Common grounds must be avoided

C: Sharp bends must be avoided in the grounding conductors used for lightning protection.

T0B11. Which of the following establishes grounding requirements for an amateur radio tower or antenna?

A. FCC Part 97 rules
B. Local electrical codes
C. FAA tower lighting regulations
D. UL recommended practices

B: Local electrical codes establish grounding requirements for an amateur radio tower or antenna.

T0C – RF HAZARDS: RADIATION EXPOSURE, PROXIMITY TO ANTENNAS, RECOGNIZED SAFE POWER LEVELS, RADIATION TYPES, DUTY CYCLE

T0C01. What type of radiation are radio signals?

A. Gamma radiation
B. Ionizing radiation
C. Alpha radiation
D. Non-ionizing radiation

D: Radio signals are nonionizing radiation. That is, they are electromagnetic radiation without enough energy to knock electrons off of atoms or molecules, which would create an ion.

T0C02. Which of the following bands has the lowest maximum permissible exposure for RF safety?

A. 3.5 MHz
B. 50 MHz
C. 440 MHz
D. 1296 MHz

B: 50 MHz has a lower maximum permissible exposure limit than 3.5 MHz, 440 MHz, or 1296 MHz.

T0C03. How does the allowable power density for RF safety change if duty cycle changes from 100 percent to 50 percent?

A. It increases by a factor of 3
B. It decreases by 50 percent
C. It increases by a factor of 2
D. There is no adjustment allowed for lower duty cycle

C: When duty cycle changes from 100 percent to 50 percent, the allowable power density for RF safety increases by a factor of 2.

T0C04. What factors affect the RF exposure of people near an amateur station antenna?

A. Frequency and power level of the RF field
B. Distance from the antenna to a person
C. Radiation pattern of the antenna
D. All these choices are correct

D: Several factors affect the RF exposure of people near an amateur station antenna. These factors include the frequency and power level of the RF field, the distance from the antenna to a person, and the radiation pattern of the antenna.

T0C05. Why do exposure limits vary with frequency?

A. Lower frequency RF fields have more energy than higher frequency fields
B. Lower frequency RF fields do not penetrate the human body
C. Higher frequency RF fields are transient in nature
D. The human body absorbs more RF energy at some frequencies than at others

D: Exposure limits vary with frequency because the human body absorbs more RF energy at some frequencies than at others.

T0C06. Which of the following is an acceptable method to determine whether your station complies with FCC RF exposure regulations?

A. By calculation based on FCC OET Bulletin 65
B. By calculation based on computer modeling
C. By measurement of field strength using calibrated equipment
D. All these choices are correct

D: It is acceptable to determine that your station complies with FCC RF exposure regulations by calculation based on FCC OET Bulletin 65, by calculation based on computer modeling, or by measurement of field strength using calibrated equipment.

T0C07. What hazard is created by touching an antenna during a transmission?

A. Electrocution
B. RF burn to skin
C. Exposure to ionizing radiation
D. All these choices are correct

B: If a person accidentally touched your antenna while you were transmitting, they might receive a painful RF burn.

T0C08. Which of the following actions can reduce exposure to RF radiation?

A. Relocate antennas
B. Relocate the transmitter
C. Increase the duty cycle
D. All these choices are correct

A: Amateur operators might relocate antennas to prevent exposure to RF radiation in excess of FCC-supplied limits.

T0C09. How can you make sure your station stays in compliance with RF safety regulations?

A. By informing the FCC of any changes made in your station
B. By re-evaluating the station whenever an item in the transmitter or antenna system is changed
C. By making sure your antennas have low SWR
D. By using only Underwriter Laboratories approved transmitting equipment

B: A station may ensure compliance by re-evaluating the station whenever an item of equipment is changed.

T0C10. Why is duty cycle one of the factors used to determine safe RF radiation exposure levels?

A. It affects the average exposure to radiation
B. It affects the peak exposure to radiation
C. It takes into account the antenna feed line loss
D. It takes into account the thermal effects of the final amplifier

A: Duty cycle is one of the factors used to determine safe RF radiation exposure levels because it affects the average exposure of people to radiation. If the duty cycle is lower, then there is less RF radiation exposure with no change in peak envelope power output.

T0C11. What is the definition of duty cycle during the averaging time for RF exposure?

A. The difference between the lowest and highest power output of a transmitter
B. The difference between the PEP and the average power output of a transmitter
C. The percentage of time that a transmitter is transmitting
D. The percentage of time that a transmitter is not transmitting

C: In the context of determining RF exposure, the duty cycle is the percentage of the time that the transmitter is actually transmitting.

T0C12. How does RF radiation differ from ionizing radiation (radioactivity)?

A. RF radiation does not have sufficient energy to cause chemical changes in cells and damage DNA
B. RF radiation can only be detected with an RF dosimeter
C. RF radiation is limited in range to a few feet
D. RF radiation is perfectly safe

A: Unlike most ionizing radiation, RF radiation does not carry sufficient energy to cause genetic damage to living creatures.

T0C13. Who is responsible for ensuring that no person is exposed to RF energy above the FCC exposure limits?

A. The FCC
B. The station licensee
C. Anyone who is near an antenna
D. The local zoning board

B: The station licensee is responsible for ensuring that no person is exposed to RF energy above the FCC exposure limits.

Ham Radio Technician Practice Tests

Want to take this practice test in an online interactive format?
Check out the online resources page, which includes interactive practice questions and much more: **mometrix.com/resources719/hamradiotech**

Test #1 Practice Questions

1. Which of the following is part of the Basis and Purpose of the Amateur Radio Service?

A. Providing personal radio communications for as many citizens as possible
B. Providing communications for international contesting
C. Advancing skills in the technical and communication phases of the radio art
D. All these choices are correct

2. Which of the following frequency ranges are available for phone operation by Technician licensees?

A. 28.050 MHz to 28.150 MHz
B. 28.100 MHz to 28.300 MHz
C. 28.300 MHz to 28.500 MHz
D. 28.500 MHz to 28.600 MHz

3. For which classes of amateur radio licenses does the FCC currently issue new licenses?

A. Novice, Technician, General, Amateur Extra
B. Technician, Technician Plus, General, Amateur Extra
C. Novice, Technician Plus, General, Advanced
D. Technician, General, Amateur Extra

4. With which countries are FCC-licensed amateur radio stations prohibited from exchanging communications?

A. Any country whose administration has notified the International Telecommunication Union (ITU) that it objects to such communications
B. Any country whose administration has notified the American Radio Relay League (ARRL) that it objects to such communications
C. Any country banned from such communications by the International Amateur Radio Union (IARU)
D. Any country banned from making such communications by the American Radio Relay League (ARRL)

5. When may an amateur station transmit without a control operator?

A. When using automatic control, such as in the case of a repeater
B. When the station licensee is away and another licensed amateur is using the station
C. When the transmitting station is an auxiliary station
D. Never

6. When must the station licensee make the station and the station records available for inspection?

A. At any time ten days after notification by the FCC of such an inspection
B. At any time upon request by an FCC representative
C. At any time after a written notification by the FCC of such inspection
D. Only when presented with a valid warrant by an FCC official or government agent

7. What is a common repeater frequency offset in the 2-meter band?

A. Plus or minus 5 MHz
B. Plus or minus 600 kHz
C. Plus or minus 500 kHz
D. Plus or minus 1 MHz

8. What is the purpose of the reverse function on a VHF/UHF transceiver?

A. To reduce power output
B. To increase power output
C. To listen on a repeater's input frequency
D. To listen on a repeater's output frequency

9. When do the FCC Part 97 Amateur Radio Service rules NOT apply to the operation of an amateur station?

A. When operating under RACES rules
B. When operating under FEMA rules
C. When operating under ARES rules
D. FCC rules always apply

10. Why do VHF signal strengths sometimes vary greatly when the antenna is moved only a few feet?

A. The signal path encounters different concentrations of water vapor
B. VHF ionospheric propagation is very sensitive to path length
C. Multipath propagation cancels or reinforces signals
D. The Doppler effect causes slight frequency shifts which result in changes in signal strength

11. What is the relationship between the electric and magnetic fields of an electromagnetic wave?

A. They travel at different speeds
B. They are in parallel
C. They revolve in opposite directions
D. They are at right angles

12. Why are simplex UHF signals rarely heard beyond their radio horizon?

A. They are too weak to go very far
B. FCC regulations prohibit them from going more than 50 miles
C. UHF signals are usually not propagated by the ionosphere
D. UHF signals are absorbed by the ionospheric D region

13. Which of the following is an appropriate power supply rating for a typical 50-watt output mobile FM transceiver?

A. 24.0 volts at 4 amperes
B. 13.8 volts at 4 amperes
C. 24.0 volts at 12 amperes
D. 13.8 volts at 12 amperes

14. What is the effect of excessive microphone gain on SSB transmissions?

A. Frequency instability
B. Distorted transmitted audio
C. Increased SWR
D. Sideband inversion

15. Electrical current is measured in which of the following units?

A. Volts
B. Watts
C. Ohms
D. Amperes

16. How many milliamperes is 1.5 amperes?

A. 0.0000015 milliamperes
B. 0.0015 milliamperes
C. 1500 milliamperes
D. 1,500,000 milliamperes

17. What describes the ability to store energy in an electric field?

A. Inductance
B. Resistance
C. Frequency
D. Capacitance

18. What formula is used to calculate current in a circuit?

A. $I = E \times R$
B. $I = E / R$
C. $I = E2 \times R$
D. $I = E2 / R$

19. What electrical component opposes the flow of current in a DC circuit?

A. Inductor
B. Resistor
C. Inverter
D. Transformer

20. Which is true about forward voltage drop in a diode?

A. It is lower in some diode types than in others
B. It is proportional to peak inverse voltage
C. It indicates that the diode is defective
D. It has no impact on the voltage delivered to the load

21. What is an electrical diagram using standard component symbols called?

A. Connection chart
B. Instrumentation system
C. Schematic
D. Flow chart

22. Which of the following devices or circuits changes an alternating current into a varying direct current signal?

A. Transformer
B. Rectifier
C. Amplifier
D. Reflector

23. Which term describes the ability of a receiver to detect the presence of a signal?

A. RF gain
B. Sensitivity
C. Selectivity
D. Total Harmonic Distortion

24. What can you do if you are told your FM handheld or mobile transceiver is over-deviating?

A. Talk louder into the microphone
B. Let the transceiver cool off
C. Change to a higher power level
D. Talk farther away from the microphone

25. What is the primary purpose of a dummy load?

A. To prevent transmitting signals over the air when making tests
B. To prevent over-modulation of a transmitter
C. To improve the efficiency of an antenna
D. To improve the signal-to-noise ratio of a receiver

26. Which instrument would you use to measure electric potential?

A. An ammeter
B. A voltmeter
C. A potentiometer
D. An ohmmeter

27. Which of the following is a form of amplitude modulation?

A. Spread spectrum
B. Packet radio
C. Single sideband
D. Phase shift keying (PSK)

28. What telemetry information is typically transmitted by satellite beacons?

A. The signal strength of received signals
B. Time of day accurate to plus or minus 1/10 second
C. Health and status of the satellite
D. All these choices are correct

29. Which of the following methods is used to locate sources of noise interference or jamming?

A. Echolocation
B. Doppler radar
C. Radio direction finding
D. Phase locking

30. Which of the following is a digital communications mode?

A. Packet radio
B. IEEE 802.11
C. FT8
D. All these choices are correct

31. What is a beam antenna?

A. An antenna built from square aluminum beams
B. An omnidirectional antenna invented by Clarence Beam
C. An antenna that concentrates signals in one direction
D. An antenna that focuses the signal into two intense rays

32. Which of the following connectors should be carefully taped for weather protection when used outdoors?

A. PL259
B. BNC
C. Type N
D. All these choices are correct

33. Which of the following is a safety hazard of a 12-volt storage battery that lacks internal protection circuitry?

A. Touching both terminals with your hands can cause electrical shock
B. Shorting the terminals can cause burns, fire, or an explosion
C. RF emissions from a nearby transmitter can cause the electrolyte to emit poison gas
D. All these choices are correct

34. Which of the following is good practice when installing ground wires on a tower for lightning protection?

A. Put a drip loop in the ground connection to prevent water damage to the ground system
B. Make sure all ground wire bends are right angles
C. Ensure that connections are short and direct
D. All these choices are correct

35. What type of radiation are radio signals?

A. Gamma radiation
B. Ionizing radiation
C. Alpha radiation
D. Non-ionizing radiation

Test #1 Answer Key and Explanations

1. C: As stated in the FCC rules, advancing skills in the technical and communication phases of the radio art is a purpose of the Amateur Radio Service

2. C: Frequencies in the 28.300 MHz to 28.500 MHz range are available for phone operation by Technician licensees. [97.301(e)]

3. D: The classes of amateur operator license grants are: Technician, General, and Amateur Extra. The person named in the operator license grant is authorized to be the control operator of an amateur station with the privileges authorized to the operator class specified on the license grant. [97.9(a), 97.17(a)]

4. A: FCC-licensed amateur stations are prohibited from exchanging communications with any country whose administration has notified the ITU that it objects to such communications. [97.111(a)(1)]

5. D: When transmitting, each amateur station must have a control operator. [97.7(a)]

6. B: The station licensee must make the station and the station records available for inspection upon request by an FCC representative. [97.103(c)]

7. B: The most common repeater frequency offset in the 2-meter band is plus or minus 600 kHz.

8. C: A VHF/UHF transceiver's "reverse" function is used to listen on a repeater's input frequency.

9. D: FCC rules always apply to the operation of an amateur station. [97.103(a)]

10. C: If a signal is experiencing multipath propagation, it can easily cancel itself out or reinforce itself over a distance of a few feet.

11. D: The electric and magnetic fields of electromagnetic waves are at right angles (perpendicular) to each other.

12. C: Simplex (that is, not by means of a repeater) UHF signals are rarely heard from stations outside the local coverage area because UHF signals are usually not reflected by the ionosphere.

13. D: For a typical 50 watt output mobile FM transceiver, 13.8 volts at 12 amperes would be an appropriate power supply rating.

14. B: If a transmitter is operated with the microphone gain set too high, the output signal might become distorted.

15. D: Electrical current is measured in amperes, usually referred to as amps. Current is the amount of electrons flowing through a circuit.

16. C: 1.5 amperes is equivalent to 1500 mA. The prefix milli- means thousandth, so a milliampere is a thousandth of an ampere. Therefore, 1.5 amperes can be converted to milliamperes by multiplying by a thousand: 1.5 x 1000 = 1500.

17. D: The ability to store energy in an electric field is called capacitance. Capacitance can also be defined as the ratio of the electric charge that is shifted from one conductor to another to the resulting potential difference between them.

18. B: The formula for calculating current in a circuit is current equals voltage divided by resistance.

19. B: The electrical component used to oppose the flow of current in a DC circuit is a resistor. For ham radio technicians, the most commonly required resistors are quarter- and half-watt fixed value resistors and 100, 500, 1k, 5k, 10k, and 100k ohm variable resistors.

20. A: Forward voltage drop is lower in some diode types than in others.

21. C: An electrical diagram with standard wiring component symbols is called a schematic.

22. B: A rectifier changes an alternating current into a varying direct current signal. Specifically, it is a switch that blocks the current in one direction but permits it in the other.

23. B: The ability of a receiver to detect the presence of a signal is measured in terms of its sensitivity.

24. D: If you are told your FM handheld or mobile transceiver is over deviating, you can talk farther away from the microphone.

25. A: The primary purpose of a dummy load is to prevent the radiation of signals when making tests. The dummy load, also known as a dummy antenna, is a station accessory that enables the user to test and finetune equipment without actually broadcasting a signal.

26. B: A voltmeter is used to measure electric potential or electromotive force. It accomplishes this by identifying the electric potential difference between two conductors.

27. C: Single sideband is a form of amplitude modulation. Indeed, single sideband is the most common mode of voice transmission on the high-frequency bands. Unlike an a.m. transmission, in which two identical versions of the message are broadcast, an SSB transmission only broadcasts one. For this reason, single sideband communications are more efficient and are better at conserving space on the radio spectrum.

28. C: Health and status are the most common telemetry datapoints that are transmitted by satellite beacons.

29. C: Radio direction finding is used to locate sources of noise interference or jamming.

30. D: Packet, IEEE 802.11, and FT8 are all examples of digital communications methods.

31. C: A beam antenna concentrates signals in one direction. Beam antennas, also known as beamforming antennas, are sometimes composed of a simple system made of two wires. The most popular beam antenna is the Yagi, which consists of two conducting elements running parallel to each other and 1/10 of a wavelength apart.

32. D: All these choices are correct because PL259, BNC, and Type N connectors should all be carefully taped for weather protection when used outdoors.

33. B: In order for electrical shock from a 12-volt battery to be hazardous, the circuit would typically need to be connected on or near one's chest. The primary hazard associated with a 12-volt battery is shorting the terminals with low resistance materials such as metal wires or rods, potentially resulting in burns, fires, or explosions.

34. C: When installing ground wires on a tower for lightning protection it is always good practice to ensure that connections are short and direct.

35. D: Radio signals are nonionizing radiation. That is, they are electromagnetic radiation without enough energy to knock electrons off of atoms or molecules, which would create an ion.

Test #2 Practice Questions

1. Which agency regulates and enforces the rules for the Amateur Radio Service in the United States?

A. ARRL
B. Homeland Security
C. The FCC
D. All these choices are correct

2. Which of the following U.S. amateur radio operators are allowed to contact the International Space Station (ISS) on VHF bands?

A. Only amateurs with a General class or higher license
B. Any amateur with a Technician class or higher license
C. Only amateurs with a General class or higher license, and NASA approval
D. Any amateurs with a Technician class or higher license, and NASA approval

3. Who may select a desired call sign under the vanity call sign rules?

A. Only a licensed amateur with a General or Amateur Extra Class license
B. Only a licensed amateur with an Amateur Extra Class license
C. Only a licensed amateur who has been licensed continuously for more than 10 years
D. Any licensed amateur

4. Under which of the following circumstances are one-way transmissions by an amateur station prohibited?

A. Announcements of upcoming ham radio operating events
B. Broadcasting
C. International Morse Code Practice
D. Telecommand or transmissions of telemetry

5. Who may be the control operator of a station communicating through an amateur satellite or space station?

A. Only an Amateur Extra Class operator
B. A General class or higher licensee with a satellite operator certification
C. Only an Amateur Extra Class operator who is also an AMSAT member
D. Any amateur allowed to transmit on the satellite uplink frequency

6. How often must you identify with your FCC-assigned call sign when using tactical call signs such as "Race Headquarters"?

A. Never, the tactical call is sufficient
B. Once every hour
C. At least every 10 minutes during and at the end of a communication
D. At the end of every transmission

7. What is the national calling frequency for FM simplex operations in the 2-meter band?

A. 146.520 MHz
B. 145.000 MHz
C. 432.100 MHz
D. 446.000 MHz

8. What term describes the use of a sub-audible tone transmitted along with normal voice audio to open the squelch of a receiver?

A. Carrier squelch
B. Tone burst
C. DTMF
D. CTCSS

9. Which of the following are typical duties of a Net Control Station?

A. Choose the regular net meeting time and frequency
B. Ensure that all stations checking into the net are properly licensed for operation on the net frequency
C. Call the net to order and direct communications between stations checking in
D. All these choices are correct

10. How does vegetation affect UHF and microwave signals?

A. Causes knife-edge diffraction, distorting voice peaks
B. Absorbs signals, leading to poor reception of weak signals
C. Amplifies signals, improving reception of weak signals
D. Has no effect

11. What property of a radio wave defines its polarization?

A. The orientation of the electric field
B. The orientation of the magnetic field
C. The ratio of the energy in the magnetic field to the energy in the electric field
D. The ratio of the velocity to the wavelength

12. What is a characteristic of HF communication compared with communications on VHF and higher frequencies?

A. HF antennas are generally smaller
B. HF accommodates wider bandwidth signals
C. Long-distance ionospheric propagation is far more common on HF
D. There is less atmospheric interference (static) on HF

13. Which of the following should be considered when selecting an accessory SWR meter?

A. The frequency and power level at which the measurements will be made
B. The distance that the meter will be located from the antenna
C. The maximum SWR anticipated on the transmission line
D. The ability of the meter to compensate for a poor transmission line match to the antenna

14. Which of the following can be used to enter a transceiver's operating frequency?

A. The keypad or VFO knob
B. The CTCSS or DTMF encoder
C. The Automatic Frequency Control
D. All these choices are correct

15. Electrical power is measured in which of the following units?

A. Volts
B. Watts
C. Watt-hours
D. Amperes

16. Which is equal to 1,500,000 hertz?

A. 1500 kHz
B. 1500 MHz
C. 15 GHz
D. 150 kHz

17. What is the unit of capacitance?

A. Farad
B. Ohm
C. Volt
D. Henry

18. What formula is used to calculate voltage in a circuit?

A. $E = I \times R$
B. $E = I / R$
C. $E = I2 \times R$
D. $E = I2 / R$

19. What type of component is often used as an adjustable volume control?

A. Fixed resistor
B. Power resistor
C. Potentiometer
D. Transformer

20. What electronic component allows current to flow in only one direction?

A. Resistor
B. Fuse
C. Diode
D. Driven element

21. What is component 1 in the figure below?

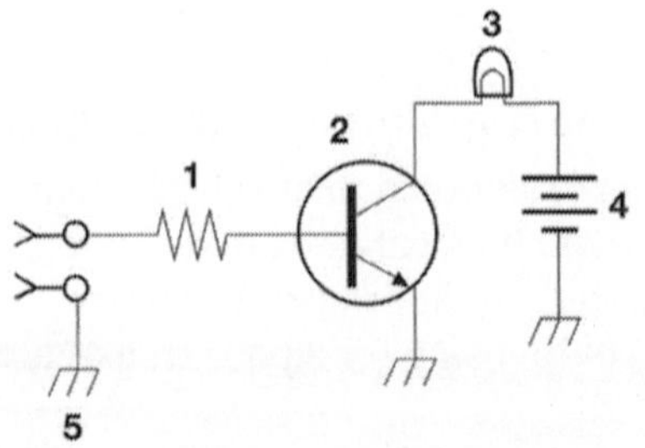

A. Resistor
B. Transistor
C. Battery
D. Connector

22. What is a relay?

A. An electrically-controlled switch
B. A current-controlled amplifier
C. An inverting amplifier
D. A pass transistor

23. What is a transceiver?

A. A device that combines a receiver and transmitter
B. A device for matching feed line impedance to 50 ohms
C. A device for automatically sending and decoding Morse code
D. A device for converting receiver and transmitter frequencies to another band

24. What would cause a broadcast AM or FM radio to receive an amateur radio transmission unintentionally?

A. The receiver is unable to reject strong signals outside the AM or FM band
B. The microphone gain of the transmitter is turned up too high
C. The audio amplifier of the transmitter is overloaded
D. The deviation of an FM transmitter is set too low

25. Which of the following is used to determine if an antenna is resonant at the desired operating frequency?

A. A VTVM
B. An antenna analyzer
C. A Q meter
D. A frequency counter

26. How is a voltmeter connected to a component to measure applied voltage?

A. In series
B. In parallel
C. In quadrature
D. In phase

27. What type of modulation is commonly used for VHF packet radio transmissions?

A. FM or PM
B. SSB
C. AM
D. PSK

28. What is the impact of using excessive effective radiated power on a satellite uplink?

A. Possibility of commanding the satellite to an improper mode
B. Blocking access by other users
C. Overloading the satellite batteries
D. Possibility of rebooting the satellite control computer

29. Which of these items would be useful for a hidden transmitter hunt?

A. Calibrated SWR meter
B. A directional antenna
C. A directional wattmeter
D. All these choices are correct

30. What is FT8?

A. A wideband FM voice mode
B. A digital mode capable of low signal-to-noise operation
C. An eight-channel multiplex mode for FM repeaters
D. A digital slow-scan TV mode with forward error correction and automatic color compensation

31. Which of the following describes a type of antenna loading?

A. Electrically lengthening by inserting inductors in radiating elements
B. Inserting a resistor in the radiating portion of the antenna to make it resonant
C. Installing a spring in the base of a mobile vertical antenna to make it more flexible
D. Strengthening the radiating elements of a beam antenna to better resist wind damage

32. What is the most common impedance of coaxial cables used in amateur radio?

A. 8 ohms
B. 50 ohms
C. 600 ohms
D. 12 ohms

33. What health hazard is posed by electrical current flowing through the body?

A. It may cause injury by heating body tissue
B. It may disrupt the electrical functions of cells
C. It may cause involuntary muscle contractions
D. All these choices are correct

34. What is required when climbing an antenna tower?

A. Have sufficient training on safe tower climbing techniques
B. Use appropriate tie-off to the tower at all times
C. Always wear an approved climbing harness
D. All these choices are correct

35. Which of the following bands has the lowest maximum permissible exposure for RF safety?

A. 3.5 MHz
B. 50 MHz
C. 440 MHz
D. 1296 MHz

Test #2 Answer Key and Explanations

1. C: The Federal Communications Commission (FCC) is the agency that regulates and enforces the rules for the Amateur Radio Service in the United States.

2. B: For a station having a control operator who has been granted a Technician, General, Advanced, or Amateur Extra Class operator license or who holds a CEPT radio-amateur license or IARP of any class. The following frequency bands and segments are authorized to space stations:

(1) The 17 m, 15 m, 12 m, and 10 m bands, 6 mm, 4 mm, 2 mm and 1 mm bands; and

(2) The 7.0-7.1 MHz, 14.00-14.25 MHz, 144-146 MHz, 435-438 MHz, 2400-2450 MHz, 3.40-3.41 GHz, 5.83-5.85 GHz, 10.45-10.50 GHz, and 24.00-24.05 GHz segments.

[97.301, 97.207(c)]

3. D: The person named in an operator/primary station license grant or in a club station license grant is eligible to make application for modification of the license grant, or the renewal thereof, to show a call sign selected by the vanity call sign system. [97.19]

4. B: While an amateur station is broadcasting, one-way transmissions are prohibited. [97.113(b), 97.111(b)]

5. D: Any amateur station may be a space station. A holder of any class operator license may be the control operator of a space station, subject to the privileges of the class of operator license held by the control operator. [97.301, 97.207(c)]

6. C: When using tactical identifiers, a station must transmit its FCC-assigned call sign every 10 minutes. [97.119(a)]

7. A: 146.520 and 446.000 are both simplex frequencies, but only 146.520 is in the 2m band.

8. D: CTCSS is the use of a sub-audible tone transmitted with normal voice audio to open the squelch of the receiver.

9. C: A typical duty of a Net Control Station is to call the net to order and direct communications between stations checking in. The Net Control Station helps maintain order and manages the flow of traffic on the net.

10. B: Vegetation can absorb UHF and microwave signals, significantly weakening them in areas with dense vegetation.

11. A: The orientation of a radio wave's electric field determines its polarization.

12. C: The main benefit to HF radio waves is that they typically bounce off the ionosphere and therefore can have a much greater range. Higher frequencies penetrate the ionosphere and therefore aren't propagated.

13. A: The frequency and power level at which the measurements will be made should be considered when selecting an accessory SWR meter.

14. A: The keypad or the VFO knob can be used to enter the operating frequency on a modern transceiver. A transceiver is a single unit that contains both a radio transmitter and receiver.

15. B: Electrical power is measured in watts. Electrical power is the rate at which electricity can be converted into other types of energy. It is calculated by multiplying the current and the voltage drop. A watt is equal to one joule per second.

16. A: Another way to specify a radio signal frequency of 1,500,000 Hz is 1500 kHz. In the metric system, the prefix kilo- means thousand, so a kilohertz is equal to 1000 hertz. Therefore, 1,500,000 Hz can be converted to kHz by dividing by a thousand: 1,500,000/1000 = 1500 kHz.

17. A: The basic unit of capacitance is the farad. One farad is equal to the capacitance of a capacitor that has an equal and opposite charge of 1 coulomb on each of its plates, and 1 V of potential difference between those plates.

18. A: The formula for calculating voltage in a circuit is voltage equals current multiplied by resistance.

19. C: A potentiometer is often used as an adjustable volume control. A potentiometer is an instrument that measures an unknown voltage by comparing it to a standard voltage.

20. C: A diode allows current to flow in only one direction. A diode is an electronic device that includes two electrodes, an anode and a cathode. These devices can be used to convert an alternating current into a direct current.

21. A: In the figure, component 1 is a resistor.

22. A: A relay may best be described as a switch controlled by an electromagnet. When the device senses a miniscule voltage or current change, it activates a switch or another component in the electric circuit.

23. A: A transceiver is a device that combines the functions of a transmitter and a receiver.

24. A: If a broadcast AM/FM radio is unintentionally receiving amateur radio transmissions, the most likely explanation is that the receiver is unable to reject strong signals outside of the AM/FM bands.

25. B: An antenna analyzer can be used to determine if an antenna is resonant at the desired operating frequency. Antenna analyzers assess the efficiency of antenna systems.

26. B: The correct way to connect a voltmeter to a circuit is in parallel with the circuit. An analog voltmeter, on the other hand, is a moving coil galvanometer that works as a voltmeter after a resistor is installed in series with it.

27. A: The type of modulation most commonly used for VHF packet radio transmission is either FM or PM.

28. B: The result can be that the signal-to-noise ratio received by the repeater can be overpowered by a single signal and thus won't transmit other valid, but weaker signals.

29. B: A directional antenna would be useful for a hidden transmitter hunt. Directional antennas send and receive signals in some directions more than others. Therefore, these antennas are able to ascertain from which direction a signal is being broadcast.

30. B: FT8 is a digital mode capable of low signal-to-noise operation.

31. A: Antenna loading is the term for placing an inductor in series with the antenna so that it reduces the resonant frequency of the antenna.

32. B: The impedance of the most commonly used coaxial cable in typical amateur radio installations is 50 ohms. Impedance is the measure of the total opposition to current flow in an alternating current circuit, composed of reactance and ohmic resistance.

33. D: Electric shock may result in any of the following: cell damage, electrical function disruption in cells, tissue heating, muscle contraction, or burns.

34. D: When climbing an antenna tower it is essential that you have sufficient training on safe tower climbing techniques, use appropriate tie-off to the tower at all times, and wear an approved climbing harness.

35. B: 50 MHz has a lower maximum permissible exposure limit than 3.5 MHz, 440 MHz, or 1296 MHz.

Test #3 Practice Questions

1. What do the FCC rules state regarding the use of a phonetic alphabet for station identification in the Amateur Radio Service?

A. It is required when transmitting emergency messages
B. It is encouraged when using phone emissions
C. It is required when in contact with foreign stations
D. All these choices are correct

2. Which frequency is in the 6-meter amateur band?

A. 49.00 MHz
B. 52.525 MHz
C. 28.50 MHz
D. 222.15 MHz

3. What types of international communications are FCC-licensed amateur radio stations permitted to make?

A. Communications incidental to the purposes of the Amateur Radio Service and remarks of a personal character
B. Communications incidental to conducting business or remarks of a personal nature
C. Only communications incidental to contest exchanges; all other communications are prohibited
D. Any communications that would be permitted by an international broadcast station

4. When is it permissible to transmit messages encoded to obscure their meaning?

A. Only when using a remote station during a contest
B. Only when transmitting certain approved digital codes
C. Only when transmitting control commands to space stations or model craft
D. Never

5. Who must designate the station control operator?

A. The station licensee
B. The FCC
C. The frequency coordinator
D. Any licensed operator

6. When are you required to transmit your assigned call sign?

A. At the beginning of each contact, and every 10 minutes thereafter
B. At least once during each transmission
C. At least every 15 minutes during and at the end of a communication
D. At least every 10 minutes during and at the end of a communication

7. What is a common repeater frequency offset in the 70-centimeter band?

A. Plus or minus 5 MHz
B. Plus or minus 600 kHz
C. Plus or minus 500 kHz
D. Plus or minus 1 MHz

8. Which of the following describes a linked repeater network?

A. A network of repeaters in which signals received by one repeater are transmitted by all the repeaters in the network
B. A single repeater with more than one receiver
C. Multiple repeaters with the same control operator
D. A system of repeaters linked by APRS

9. What technique is used to ensure that voice messages containing unusual words are received correctly?

A. Send the words by voice and Morse code
B. Use the Q-code "QSR" to ask the receiving station to repeat the words back
C. Spell the words using a standard phonetic alphabet
D. All these choices are correct

10. What antenna polarization is normally used for long-distance CW and SSB contacts on the VHF and UHF bands?

A. Right-hand circular
B. Left-hand circular
C. Horizontal
D. Vertical

11. What are the two components of a radio wave?

A. Impedance and reactance
B. Voltage and current
C. Electric and magnetic fields
D. Ionizing and non-ionizing radiation

12. What is one characteristic of VHF signals received via auroral backscatter?

A. They are often received from 10,000 miles or more
B. They are distorted, with a characteristic raspy sound
C. They occur only during winter nighttime hours
D. They are generally strongest when your antenna is aimed west

13. Why are short, heavy-gauge wires used for a transceiver's DC power connection?

A. To minimize voltage drop when transmitting
B. To provide a close match to the power supply output impedance
C. To avoid RF interference
D. To minimize radiative losses in the power cable

14. How is squelch adjusted so that a weak FM signal can be heard?

A. Set the squelch threshold so that receiver output audio is on all the time
B. Turn up the audio level until it overcomes the squelch threshold
C. Turn on the anti-squelch function
D. Enable squelch enhancement

15. What is the term for the flow of electrons in an electric circuit?

A. Voltage
B. Amperes per second
C. Volts per second
D. Current

16. Which is equal to one kilovolt?

A. One one-thousandth of a volt
B. One hundred volts
C. One thousand volts
D. One million volts

17. What describes the ability to store energy in a magnetic field?

A. Admittance
B. Capacitance
C. Resistance
D. Inductance

18. What formula is used to calculate resistance in a circuit?

A. R = E × I
B. R = E / I
C. R = E + I
D. R = E - I

19. What electrical parameter is controlled by a potentiometer?

A. Inductance
B. Resistance
C. Capacitance
D. Field strength

20. Which of these components can be used as an electronic switch?

A. Varistor
B. Potentiometer
C. Transistor
D. Thermistor

21. What is component 2 in the figure below?

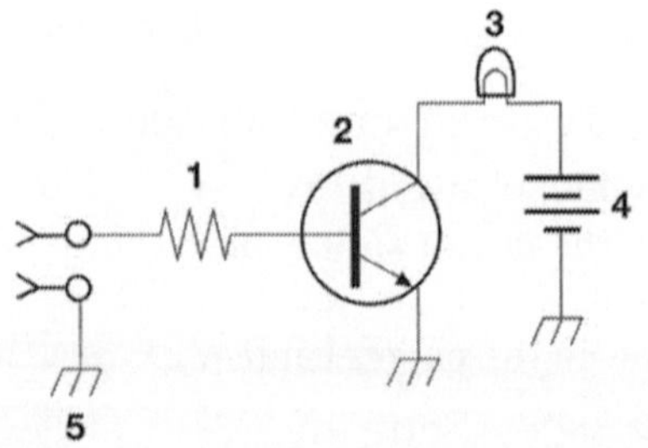

A. Resistor
B. Transistor
C. Indicator lamp
D. Connector

22. Which of the following is a reason to use shielded wire?

A. To decrease the resistance of DC power connections
B. To increase the current carrying capability of the wire
C. To prevent coupling of unwanted signals to or from the wire
D. To reduce receiver overload

23. Which of the following is used to convert a signal from one frequency to another?

A. Phase splitter
B. Mixer
C. Inverter
D. Amplifier

24. Which of the following can cause radio frequency interference?

A. Fundamental overload
B. Harmonics
C. Spurious emissions
D. All these choices are correct

25. What does a typical RF dummy load consist of?

A. A low-voltage power supply and an AC relay
B. A 50-ohm non-inductive resistor mounted on a heat sink
C. A low-voltage power supply and a DC relay
D. A 50-ohm inductive reactance mounted in a shielded enclosure

26. When configured to measure current, how is a multimeter connected to a component?

A. In series
B. In parallel
C. In quadrature
D. In phase

27. Which type of voice mode is often used for long-distance (weak signal) contacts on the VHF and UHF bands?

A. FM
B. DRM
C. SSB
D. PM

28. Which of the following are provided by satellite tracking programs?

A. Maps showing the real-time position of the satellite track over Earth
B. The time, azimuth, and elevation of the start, maximum altitude, and end of a pass
C. The apparent frequency of the satellite transmission, including effects of Doppler shift
D. All these choices are correct

29. What operating activity involves contacting as many stations as possible during a specified period?

A. Simulated emergency exercises
B. Net operations
C. Hidden transmitter hunts
D. Contesting

30. What kind of data can be transmitted by APRS?

A. GPS position data
B. Text messages
C. Weather data
D. All these choices are correct

31. How is the polarization of an antenna described?

A. By the shape of the driven element
B. By the orientation of the electric field
C. By the orientation of the magnetic field
D. By the direction of radiation

32. Why is coaxial cable the most common feed line for amateur radio antenna systems?

A. It is easy to use and requires few special installation considerations
B. It has less loss than any other type of feed line
C. It can handle more power than any other type of feed line
D. It is less expensive than any other type of feed line

33. In the United States, what circuit does black wire insulation indicate in a three-wire 120 V AC cable?

A. Neutral
B. Hot
C. Equipment ground
D. Negative

34. Under what circumstances is it safe to climb a tower without a helper or observer?

A. When no electrical work is being performed
B. When no mechanical work is being performed
C. When the work being done is not more than 20 feet above the ground
D. Never

35. How does the allowable power density for RF safety change if duty cycle changes from 100 percent to 50 percent?

A. It increases by a factor of 3
B. It decreases by 50 percent
C. It increases by a factor of 2
D. There is no adjustment allowed for lower duty cycle

Test #3 Answer Key and Explanations

1. B: By a phone emission in the English language. Use of a phonetic alphabet as an aid for correct station identification is encouraged.

2. B: 52.525 MHz is within the 6-meter band. [97.301(a)]

3. A: FCC-licensed amateur stations are permitted to make international communications incidental to the purposes of the amateur service and remarks of a personal character. [97.117]

4. C: An amateur station is allowed to hide the meaning of a transmitted message with codes or ciphers only when transmitting control commands to space stations or radio control craft. [97.211(b), 97.215(b), 97.113(a)(4)]

5. A: The station licensee must designate the station control operator. [97.103(b)]

6. D: An amateur station is required to transmit its assigned call sign at least every 10 minutes during and at the end of a communication. [97.119(a)]

7. A: A common repeater frequency offset in the 70 cm band is plus or minus 5 MHz.

8. A: A linked repeater network is a network of repeaters that are all repeating the signal received by one repeater of the network.

9. C: To ensure that any proper names and unusual words are copied correctly by the receiving station, it is good practice to spell them out using a standard phonetic alphabet.

10. C: A horizontal antenna polarization is normally used for long-distance weak-signal CW and SSB contacts using the VHF and UHF bands.

11. C: The two components of a radio wave are electric and magnetic fields. This is because a radio wave is an electromagnetic wave.

12. B: A characteristic of VHF signals received via auroral backscatter is that the signals exhibit rapid fluctuations of strength and often sound distorted.

13. A: Heavier gauge wire and short lengths will reduce the resistance as much as possible, thus maintaining sufficient voltage for peak performance.

14. A: Setting the squelch threshold so that receiver output audio is on all the time will help a weak FM signal be heard.

15. D: The flow of electrons in an electric circuit is the current. Current is measured in amperes, also known as amps.

16. C: 1000 V is equal to 1 kV. The metric prefix kilo- means thousand, so a thousand volts is the same as one kilovolt. Therefore, V can be converted to kV by dividing by a thousand: 1000/1000 = 1.

17. D: The ability to store energy in a magnetic field is called inductance. Inductance can also be defined as the characteristic of an electric circuit that enables electromagnetic force to be created in it through a varying magnetic flux.

18. B: The formula for calculating resistance in a circuit is resistance (R) equals voltage (E) divided by current (I). Resistance is the opposition to the passage of current, the result of which is the conversion of electrical energy into heat or another type of energy.

19. B: Resistance is controlled by a potentiometer. A potentiometer will typically have a resistance element connected to the circuit with three terminals. Two of these are attached to the two input voltage conductors of the circuit, and the third is connected to the circuit output. The third terminal is typically able to move across the resistance element, which enables the magnitude of the input voltage to be adjusted.

20. C: A transistor can be used as an electronic switch. It may also be used as a detector.

21. B: In the figure, component 2 is a transistor.

22. C: Shielding a wire is necessary to prevent coupling of unwanted signals to or from the wire.

23. B: A mixer is a device used to convert radio signals from one frequency to another.

24. D: Radio frequency interference may be caused by fundamental overload, harmonics, or spurious emissions. A spurious emission is any radio frequency that was not created or transmitted on purpose.

25. B: A typical RF dummy load consists of a 50-ohm non-inductive resistor mounted on a heat sink. It is designed to absorb transmitter power without radiating a signal.

26. A: An ammeter is usually connected in series with the circuit. In most cases, an ammeter is combined with a voltmeter and ohmmeter in a single instrument.

27. C: The type of voice modulation often used for long-distance or weak signal contacts on the VHF and UHF bands is SSB.

28. D: Satellite tracking programs provide a wealth of information about the path and position of orbiting satellites, as well as their operation.

29. D: Contesting involves contacting as many stations as possible during a specified period of time.

30. D: GPS position data, text messages, and weather data can all be transmitted by APRS.

31. B: The polarization of an antenna is described by the orientation of the electric field.

32. A: Coaxial cable is used more often than any other feed lines for amateur radio antenna systems because it is easy to use and requires few special installation considerations.

33. B: In a three-wire electrical AC plug, the black wire is hot.

34. D: It is never safe to climb a tower without a helper or observer.

35. C: When duty cycle changes from 100 percent to 50 percent, the allowable power density for RF safety increases by a factor of 2.

Seven Additional Ham Radio Technician Practice Tests

To take these additional practice tests, visit the online resources page:
mometrix.com/resources719/hamradiotech

General Class Question Pool

G1 – Commission's Rules

G1A – General Class Control Operator Frequency Privileges; Primary and Secondary Allocations

On which HF and/or MF amateur bands are there portions where General class licensees cannot transmit?

A. 60 meters, 30 meters, 17 meters, and 12 meters
B. 160 meters, 60 meters, 15 meters, and 12 meters
C. 80 meters, 40 meters, 20 meters, and 15 meters
D. 80 meters, 20 meters, 15 meters, and 10 meters

G1A01 Answer: C. There are portions of the 80-, 40-, 20-, and 15-meter bands on which General Class license holders cannot transmit. However, they are granted all amateur frequency privileges on the 160-, 60-, 30-, 17-, 12-, and 10-meter bands. [97.301(d)]

On which of the following bands is phone operation prohibited?

A. 160 meters
B. 30 meters
C. 17 meters
D. 12 meters

G1A02 Answer: B. Phone operation is prohibited on the 30-meter band. In ham radio, phone operation is the generic term for voice communication. There are a number of different ways to communicate by voice using ham radio technology. However, this type of communication is considered to be too cumbersome for the 30-meter band. [97.305]

On which of the following bands is image transmission prohibited?

A. 160 meters
B. 30 meters
C. 20 meters
D. 12 meters

G1A03 Answer: B. Image transmission is prohibited on the 30-meter band. This is because the transmission of images requires an amount of traffic that would obstruct the band for other users. [97.305]

Which of the following amateur bands is restricted to communication only on specific channels, rather than frequency ranges?

A. 11 meters
B. 12 meters
C. 30 meters
D. 60 meters

G1A04 Answer: D. The 60-meter amateur band is restricted to communication on only specific channels, rather than frequency ranges. This is in contrast to the other amateur bands, on which frequency ranges rather than channels are restricted. [97.303(h)]

On which of the following frequencies are General class licensees prohibited from operating as control operator?

A. 7.125 MHz to 7.175 MHz
B. 28.000 MHz to 28.025 MHz
C. 21.275 MHz to 21.300 MHz
D. All these choices are correct

G1A05 Answer: A. General class licensees prohibited from operating as control operator on the 7.125 MHz to 7.175 MHz frequencies. [97.301(d)]

Which of the following applies when the FCC rules designate the amateur service as a secondary user on a band?

A. Amateur stations must record the call sign of the primary service station before operating on a frequency assigned to that station
B. Amateur stations may use the band only during emergencies
C. Amateur stations must not cause harmful interference to primary users and must accept interference from primary users
D. Amateur stations may only operate during specific hours of the day, while primary users are permitted 24-hour use of the band

G1A06 Answer: C. When the FCC rules designate the Amateur Service as a secondary user on a band, amateur stations are allowed to use the band only if they do not cause harmful interference to primary users. The Amateur Service is reserved for people who are interested in improving their ham radio skills simply for personal reasons (that is, not for pecuniary gain). The Amateur Service can be used for self-training, communication, and technical inquiries. [97.303]

On which amateur frequencies in the 10-meter band may stations with a General class control operator transmit CW emissions?

A. 28.000 MHz to 28.025 MHz only
B. 28.000 MHz to 28.300 MHz only
C. 28.025 MHz to 28.300 MHz only
D. The entire band

G1A07 Answer: D. Stations with a General class control operator may transmit CW emissions on the entire band 10-meter band. [97.305(a)]

Which HF bands have segments exclusively allocated to Amateur Extra licensees?

A. All HF bands
B. 80 meters, 40 meters, 20 meters, and 15 meters
C. All HF bands except 160 meters and 10 meters
D. 60 meters, 30 meters, 17 meters, and 12 meters

G1A08 Answer: B. Amateur Extra licensees have segments exclusively allocated on the 80-, 40-, 20-, and 15-meter HF bands. [97.301(b)]

Which of the following frequencies is within the General class portion of the 15-meter band?

A. 14250 kHz
B. 18155 kHz
C. 21300 kHz
D. 24900 kHz

G1A09 Answer: C. The 21300 kHz frequency is within the General Class portion of the 15-meter band. [97.301(d)]

What portion of the 10-meter band is available for repeater use?

A. The entire band
B. The portion between 28.1 MHz and 28.2 MHz
C. The portion between 28.3 MHz and 28.5 MHz
D. The portion above 29.5 MHz

G1A10 Answer: D. The portion above 29.5 MHz of the 10-meter band is available for repeater use. [97.205(b)]

When General class licensees are not permitted to use the entire voice portion of a band, which portion of the voice segment is available to them?

A. The lower frequency portion
B. The upper frequency portion
C. The lower frequency portion on frequencies below 7.3 MHz, and the upper portion on frequencies above 14.150 MHz
D. The upper frequency portion on frequencies below 7.3 MHz, and the lower portion on frequencies above 14.150 MHz

G1A11 Answer: B. When General Class licensees are not permitted to use the entire voice portion of a particular band, the upper frequency portion of the voice segment is generally available to them. [97.301]

G1B – Antenna Structure Limitations; Good Engineering and Good Amateur Practice; Beacon Operation; Prohibited Transmissions; Retransmitting Radio Signals

What is the maximum height above ground for an antenna structure not near a public use airport without requiring notification to the FAA and registration with the FCC?

A. 50 feet
B. 100 feet
C. 200 feet
D. 250 feet

G1B01 Answer: C. The maximum height above ground for an antenna structure not near a public use airport without requiring notification to the FAA and registration with the FCC, is 200 feet. For most ham radio operators, this will not be a problem. [97.15(a)]

With which of the following conditions must beacon stations comply?

A. No more than one beacon station may transmit in the same band from the same station location
B. The frequency must be coordinated with the National Beacon Organization
C. The frequency must be posted on the internet or published in a national periodical
D. All these choices are correct

G1B02 Answer: A. There must be no more than one beacon signal in the same band from a single location. The use of multiple beacon signals may confuse those whom the signals were intended to inform. [97.203(b)]

Which of the following is a purpose of a beacon station as identified in the FCC rules?

A. Observation of propagation and reception
B. Automatic identification of repeaters
C. Transmission of bulletins of general interest to amateur radio licensees
D. All these choices are correct

G1B03 Answer: A. The FCC Rules state that one purpose of a beacon station is the observation of propagation and reception. Beacon stations communicate only for experimental purposes, most often to observe propagation and reception. Ham radio operators often use these stations as reference points or to calibrate their equipment. [97.3(a)(9)]

Which of the following transmissions is permitted for all amateur stations?

A. Unidentified transmissions of less than 10 seconds duration for test purposes only
B. Automatic retransmission of other amateur signals by any amateur station
C. Occasional retransmission of weather and propagation forecast information from US government stations
D. Encrypted messages, if not intended to facilitate a criminal act

G1B04 Answer: C. Occasional retransmission of weather and propagation forecast information from US government stations is permitted. [97.113(c)]

Which of the following one-way transmissions are permitted?

A. Unidentified test transmissions of less than 10 seconds in duration
B. Transmissions to assist with learning the International Morse code
C. Regular transmissions offering equipment for sale, if intended for amateur radio use
D. All these choices are correct

G1B05 Answer: B. One-way transmissions necessary to assist learning the International Morse code are permitted. [97.111((5)(b)]

Under what conditions are state and local governments permitted to regulate amateur radio antenna structures?

A. Under no circumstances, FCC rules take priority
B. At any time and to any extent necessary to accomplish a legitimate purpose of the state or local entity, provided that proper filings are made with the FCC
C. Only when such structures exceed 50 feet in height and are clearly visible 1,000 feet from the structure
D. Amateur Service communications must be reasonably accommodated, and regulations must constitute the minimum practical to accommodate a legitimate purpose of the state or local entity

G1B06 Answer: D. Amateur Service communications must be reasonably accommodated, and regulations must constitute the minimum practical to accommodate a legitimate purpose of the state or local entity. [97.15(b), PRB-1, 101 FCC 2d 952 (1985)]

What are the restrictions on the use of abbreviations or procedural signals in the amateur service?

A. Only "Q" signals are permitted
B. They may be used if they do not obscure the meaning of a message
C. They are not permitted
D. They are limited to those expressly listed in Part 97 of the FCC rules

G1B07 Answer: B. In the Amateur Service, abbreviations or procedural signals may be used if they do not obscure the meaning of a message. Procedural signals, also known as prosigns, are shorthand messages that indicate the immediate intentions of the operator. A procedural signal may consist of a single letter or two letters transmitted as a single character. [97.113(a)(4)]

When is it permissible to communicate with amateur stations in countries outside the areas administered by the Federal Communications Commission?

A. Only when the foreign country has a formal third-party agreement filed with the FCC
B. When the contact is with amateurs in any country except those whose administrations have notified the ITU that they object to such communications
C. Only when the contact is with amateurs licensed by a country which is a member of the United Nations, or by a territory possessed by such a country
D. Only when the contact is with amateurs licensed by a country which is a member of the International Amateur Radio Union, or by a territory possessed by such a country

G1B08 Answer: B. It is permissible to communicate with amateur stations in countries outside the areas administered by the Federal Communications Commission when the contact is with amateurs in any country except those whose administrations have notified the ITU that they object to such communications. [97.111(a)(1)]

On what HF frequencies are automatically controlled beacons permitted?

A. On any frequency if power is less than 1 watt
B. On any frequency if transmissions are in Morse code
C. 21.08 MHz to 21.09 MHz
D. 28.20 MHz to 28.30 MHz

G1B09 Answer: D. Automatically controlled beacons are permitted on 28.20 MHz to 28.30 MHz HF frequencies. [97.203(d)]

What is the power limit for beacon stations?

A. 10 watts PEP output
B. 20 watts PEP output
C. 100 watts PEP output
D. 200 watts PEP output

G1B10 Answer: C. The power limit for beacon stations is 100 watts PEP output. [97.203(c)]

Who or what determines "good engineering and good amateur practice," as applied to the operation of an amateur station in all respects not covered by the Part 97 rules?

A. The FCC
B. The control operator
C. The IEEE
D. The ITU

G1B11 Answer: A. The FCC determines "good engineering and good amateur practice" as applied to the operation of an amateur station in all respects not covered by the Part 97 rules. The FCC is generally willing to respond to novice operators who are unsure whether their operations are in keeping with these standards. [97.101(a)]

G1C – Transmitter Power Regulations; Data Emission Standards; 60-Meter Operation Requirements

What is the maximum transmitter power an amateur station may use on 10.140 MHz?

A. 200 watts PEP output
B. 1000 watts PEP output
C. 1500 watts PEP output
D. 2000 watts PEP output

G1C01 Answer: A. The maximum transmitter power an amateur station may use on 10.140 MHz is 200 watts PEP output. [97.313(c)(1)]

What is the maximum transmitter power an amateur station may use on the 12-meter band?

A. 50 watts PEP output
B. 200 watts PEP output
C. 1500 watts PEP output
D. An effective radiated power equivalent to 100 watts from a half-wave dipole

G1C02 Answer: C. The maximum transmitter power an amateur station may use on the 12-meter band is 1500 watts PEP output. [97.313]

What is the maximum bandwidth permitted by FCC rules for amateur radio stations transmitting on USB frequencies in the 60-meter band?

A. 2.8 kHz
B. 5.6 kHz
C. 1.8 kHz
D. 3 kHz

G1C03 Answer: A. The maximum bandwidth permitted by FCC rules for Amateur Radio stations when transmitting on USB frequencies in the 60-meter band is 2.8 kHz. [97.303(h)(1)]

Which of the following is required by the FCC rules when operating in the 60-meter band?

A. If you are using an antenna other than a dipole, you must keep a record of the gain of your antenna
B. You must keep a record of the date, time, frequency, power level, and stations worked
C. You must keep a record of all third-party traffic
D. You must keep a record of the manufacturer of your equipment and the antenna used

G1C04 Answer: A. When operating in the 60-meter band, the FCC rules require that you keep a record of the gain of your antenna, if you are using other than a dipole antenna. [97.303(i)]

What is the limit for transmitter power on the 28 MHz band for a General Class control operator?

A. 100 watts PEP output
B. 1000 watts PEP output
C. 1500 watts PEP output
D. 2000 watts PEP output

G1C05 Answer: C. On the 28 MHz band, the limitation on transmitter power is 1500 watts PEP output. [97.313]

What is the limit for transmitter power on the 1.8 MHz band?

A. 200 watts PEP output
B. 1000 watts PEP output
C. 1200 watts PEP output
D. 1500 watts PEP output

G1C06 Answer: D. On the 1.8 MHz band, the limitation on transmitter power is 1500 watts PEP output. [97.313]

What must be done before using a new digital protocol on the air?

A. Type-certify equipment to FCC standards
B. Obtain an experimental license from the FCC
C. Publicly document the technical characteristics of the protocol
D. Submit a rule-making proposal to the FCC describing the codes and methods of the technique

G1C07 Answer: C. Before using a new digital protocol on the air, one must publicly document the technical characteristics of the protocol. [97.309(a)(4)]

What is the maximum power limit on the 60-meter band?

A. 1500 watts PEP
B. 10 watts RMS
C. ERP of 100 watts PEP with respect to a dipole
D. ERP of 100 watts PEP with respect to an isotropic antenna

G1C09 Answer: C. ERP of 100 watts PEP with respect to a dipole is the maximum power limit on the 60-meter band. [97.313(i)]

What measurement is specified by FCC rules that regulate maximum power?

A. RMS output from the transmitter
B. RMS input to the antenna
C. PEP input to the antenna
D. PEP output from the transmitter

G1C11 Answer: D. PEP output from the transmitter is specified by FCC rules to regulate maximum power and it varies according to the band used. [97.313]

G1D – Volunteer Examiners and Volunteer Examiner Coordinators; Temporary Identification; Element Credit; Remote Operation

Who may receive partial credit for the elements represented by an expired amateur radio license?

A. Any person who can demonstrate that they once held an FCC-issued General, Advanced, or Amateur Extra class license that was not revoked by the FCC
B. Anyone who held an FCC-issued amateur radio license that expired not less than 5 and not more than 15 years ago
C. Any person who previously held an amateur license issued by another country, but only if that country has a current reciprocal licensing agreement with the FCC
D. Only persons who once held an FCC issued Novice, Technician, or Technician Plus license

G1D01 Answer: A. As long as you can demonstrate that you have previously held a General, Advanced, or Amateur Extra class license issued by the FCC and that it was not revoked, you may receive partial credit for all the elements represented. [97.501, 97.505(a)]

What license examinations may you administer as an accredited Volunteer Examiner holding a General class operator license?

A. General and Technician
B. None, only Amateur Extra class licensees may be accredited
C. Technician only
D. Amateur Extra, General, and Technician

G1D02 Answer: C. When you are an accredited Volunteer Examiner holding a General Class operator license, you may only administer the Technician license exam. Volunteer Examiners are only allowed to proctor exams at a level below their own level. Any licensed amateur may become a Volunteer Examiner by completing the qualification process administered by the VEC. [97.509(b)(3)(i)]

On which of the following band segments may you operate if you are a Technician class operator and have an unexpired Certificate of Successful Completion of Examination (CSCE) for General class privileges?

A. Only the Technician band segments until your upgrade is posted in the FCC database
B. Only on the Technician band segments until you have a receipt for the FCC application fee payment
C. On any General or Technician class band segment
D. On any General or Technician class band segment except 30 meters and 60 meters

G1D03 Answer: C. You may operate on any General or Technician Class band segment if you are a Technician Class operator and have a CSCE for General Class privileges. [97.9(b)]

Who must observe the administration of a Technician class license examination?

A. At least three Volunteer Examiners of General class or higher
B. At least two Volunteer Examiners of General class or higher
C. At least two Volunteer Examiners of Technician class or higher
D. At least three Volunteer Examiners of Technician class

G1D04 Answer: A. In order for a Technician class license examination to be administered, at least three Volunteer examiners of General class or higher must be present. [97.509(3)(i)(c)]

When operating a US station by remote control from outside the country, what license is required of the control operator?

A. A US operator/primary station license
B. Only an appropriate US operator/primary license and a special remote station permit from the FCC
C. Only a license from the foreign country, as long as the call sign includes identification of portable operation in the US
D. A license from the foreign country and a special remote station permit from the FCC

G1D05 Answer: A. A US operator/primary station license is required when operating a US station by remote control from outside the country. [97.7]

Until an upgrade to General class is shown in the FCC database, when must a Technician licensee identify with "AG" after their call sign?

A. Whenever they operate using General class frequency privileges
B. Whenever they operate on any amateur frequency
C. Whenever they operate using Technician frequency privileges
D. A special identifier is not required if their General class license application has been filed with the FCC

G1D06 Answer: A. Adding the special identifier "AG" after their call sign indicates that their actual status will not be reflected in the FCC database. [97.119(f)(2)]

Volunteer Examiners are accredited by what organization?

A. The Federal Communications Commission
B. The Universal Licensing System
C. A Volunteer Examiner Coordinator
D. The Wireless Telecommunications Bureau

G1D07 Answer: C. Volunteer Examiners are accredited by the Volunteer Examiner Coordinator. VECs are recognized by the American Radio Relay League. [97.509(b)(1)]

Which of the following criteria must be met for a non-US citizen to be an accredited Volunteer Examiner?

A. The person must be a resident of the US for a minimum of 5 years
B. The person must hold an FCC granted amateur radio license of General class or above
C. The person's home citizenship must be in ITU region 2
D. None of these choices is correct; a non-US citizen cannot be a Volunteer Examiner

G1D08 Answer: B. For a non-US citizen to be an accredited Volunteer Examiner, the person must hold an FCC granted Amateur Radio license of General Class or above. [97.509(b)(3)]

How long is a Certificate of Successful Completion of Examination (CSCE) valid for exam element credit?

A. 30 days
B. 180 days
C. 365 days
D. For as long as your current license is valid

G1D09 Answer: C. A Certificate of Successful Completion of Examination (CSCE) is valid for exam element credit for 365 days. [97.9(b)]

What is the minimum age that one must be to qualify as an accredited Volunteer Examiner?

A. 16 years
B. 18 years
C. 21 years
D. There is no age limit

G1D10 Answer: B. One must be at least 18 years old to qualify as an accredited Volunteer Examiner. Each licensing exam requires the presence of three Volunteer Examiners, each of which needs to sign the paperwork for the exam to be valid. [97.509(b)(2)]

What action is required to obtain a new General class license after a previously held license has expired and the two-year grace period has passed?

A. They must have a letter from the FCC showing they once held an amateur or commercial license
B. There are no requirements other than being able to show a copy of the expired license
C. Contact the FCC to have the license reinstated
D. The applicant must show proof of the appropriate expired license grant and pass the current Element 2 exam

G1D11 Answer: D. A person with an expired FCC issued amateur radio license of General Class or higher must show proof of the appropriate expired license grant and pass the current Element 2 exam before they can receive a new license. [97.505]

When operating a station in South America by remote control over the internet from the US, what regulations apply?

A. Those of both the remote station's country and the FCC
B. Those of the remote station's country and the FCC's third-party regulations
C. Only those of the remote station's country
D. Only those of the FCC

G1D12 Answer: C. When operating a station in South America by remote control over the internet from the US, only the regulations of the remote station's country apply. [97.507]

G1E – Control Categories; Repeater Regulations; Third-Party Rules; ITU Regions; Automatically Controlled Digital Station

Which of the following would disqualify a third party from participating in sending a message via an amateur station?

A. The third party's amateur license has been revoked and not reinstated
B. The third party is not a US citizen
C. The third party is speaking in a language other than English
D. All these choices are correct

G1E01 Answer: A. A third party would be disqualified from participating in stating a message via an amateur station if their amateur license had ever been revoked. Typically, third-party participation is the only way an unlicensed person can join in on amateur communications. The responsibility for ensuring that all communications follow the rules is held by the control operator. [97.115(b)(2)]

When may a 10-meter repeater retransmit the 2-meter signal from a station that has a Technician class control operator?

A. Under no circumstances
B. Only if the station on 10-meters is operating under a Special Temporary Authorization allowing such retransmission
C. Only during an FCC-declared general state of communications emergency
D. Only if the 10-meter repeater control operator holds at least a General class license

G1E02 Answer: D. A 10-meter repeater may retransmit the 2-meter signal from a station having a Technician Class control operator only if the 10-meter repeater control operator holds at least a General Class license. [97.205(b)]

What is required to conduct communications with a digital station operating under automatic control outside the automatic control band segments?

A. The station initiating the contact must be under local or remote control
B. The interrogating transmission must be made by another automatically controlled station
C. No third-party traffic may be transmitted
D. The control operator of the interrogating station must hold an Amateur Extra class license

G1E03 Answer: A. To communicate with a digital station operating under automatic control outside the automatic control band segments, the station initiating contact must be under local or remote control. [97.221]

Which of the following conditions require a licensed amateur radio operator to take specific steps to avoid harmful interference to other users or facilities?

A. When operating within one mile of an FCC Monitoring Station
B. When using a band where the Amateur Service is secondary
C. When a station is transmitting spread spectrum emissions
D. All these choices are correct

G1E04 Answer: D. An Amateur Radio station licensee is required to take specific steps to avoid harmful interference to other users or facilities when the following conditions apply: when operating within one mile of an FCC Monitoring Station; when using a band where the Amateur Service is secondary; and when a station is transmitting spread spectrum emissions. All of these conditions place the responsibility for avoiding interference on the shoulders of the amateur operator. [97.13(b), 97.303, 97.311(b)]

What are the restrictions on messages sent to a third party in a country with which there is a Third-Party Agreement?

A. They must relate to emergencies or disaster relief
B. They must be for other licensed amateurs
C. They must relate to amateur radio, or remarks of a personal character, or messages relating to emergencies or disaster relief
D. The message must be limited to no longer than 1 minute in duration and the name of the third party must be recorded in the station log

G1E05 Answer: C. Messages sent to a third party in a country with which there is a Third-Party Agreement must relate to amateur radio, or remarks of a personal character, or messages relating to emergencies or disaster relief. [97.115(a)(2), 97.117]

The frequency allocations of which ITU region apply to radio amateurs operating in North and South America?

A. Region 4
B. Region 3
C. Region 2
D. Region 1

G1E06 Answer: C. The frequency allocations of which ITU Region 2 apply to radio amateurs operating in North and South America. [97.301, ITU Radio Regulations]

In what part of the 2.4 GHz band may an amateur station communicate with non-licensed Wi-Fi stations?

A. Anywhere in the band
B. Channels 1 through 4
C. Channels 42 through 45
D. No part

G1E07 Answer: D. In no part of the 2.4 GHz band may an amateur station communicate with non-licensed Wi-Fi stations. [97.111]

What is the maximum PEP output allowed for spread spectrum transmissions?

A. 100 milliwatts
B. 10 watts
C. 100 watts
D. 1500 watts

G1E08 Answer: B. 10 watts is the maximum PEP output allowed for spread spectrum transmissions. [97.313(j)]

Why should an amateur operator normally avoid transmitting on 14.100, 18.110, 21.150, 24.930 and 28.200 MHz?

A. A system of propagation beacon stations operates on those frequencies
B. A system of automatic digital stations operates on those frequencies
C. These frequencies are set aside for emergency operations
D. These frequencies are set aside for bulletins from the FCC

G1E10 Answer: A. An amateur operator should normally avoid transmitting on 14.100, 18.110, 21.150, 24.930 and 28.200 MHz because a system of propagation beacon stations operates on those frequencies. [97.101]

On what bands may automatically controlled stations transmitting RTTY or data emissions communicate with other automatically controlled digital stations?

A. On any band segment where digital operation is permitted
B. Anywhere in the non-phone segments of the 10-meter or shorter wavelength bands
C. Only in the non-phone Extra Class segments of the bands
D. Anywhere in the 6-meter or shorter wavelength bands, and in limited segments of some of the HF bands

G1E11 Answer: D. An automatically controlled station transmitting RTTY or data emissions communicate with other automatically controlled digital stations anywhere in the 6-meter or shorter wavelength bands, and in limited segments of the HF bands. [97.221, 97.305]

When may third-party messages be transmitted via remote control?

A. Under any circumstances in which third party messages are permitted by FCC rules
B. Under no circumstances except for emergencies
C. Only when the message is intended for licensed radio amateurs
D. Only when the message is intended for third parties in areas where licensing is controlled by the FCC

G1E12 Answer: A. Third-party messages may be transmitted via remote control under any circumstances in which third party messages are permitted by FCC rules. [97.115]

G2 – Operating Procedures

G2A – Phone Operating Procedures: USB/LSB Conventions, Breaking into a Contact, Transmitter Setup for Voice Operation; Answering DX Stations

Which mode is most commonly used for voice communications on frequencies of 14 MHz or higher?

A. Upper sideband
B. Lower sideband
C. Suppressed sideband
D. Double sideband

G2A01 Answer: A. The upper sideband is the most commonly used for voice communications on frequencies of 14 MHz or higher.

Which mode is most commonly used for voice communications on the 160-, 75-, and 40-meter bands?

A. Upper sideband
B. Lower sideband
C. Suppressed sideband
D. Double sideband

G2A02 Answer: B. The lower sideband is most commonly used for voice communications on the 160-, 75-, and 40-meter bands. It is also the preferred operating mode on the 80-meter amateur bands. For voice communication on the HF bands, ham operators are most likely to use single sideband. Signals are designated as upper or lower sideband depending on whether they are above or below the carrier frequency displayed on the radio. According to tradition, voice operation on HF bands above 9 MHz is on the upper sideband, and voice operation below 9 MHz occurs on the lower sideband. The four basic steps for tuning in an SSB signal are as follows: set your rig to receive LSB or USB signals; select the widest SSB filter; adjust the tuning dial until the SSB frequency can be heard; and adjust the tuning until the voice sounds normal.

Which mode is most commonly used for SSB voice communications in the VHF and UHF bands?

A. Upper sideband
B. Lower sideband
C. Suppressed sideband
D. Double sideband

G2A03 Answer: A. The upper sideband is most commonly used for SSB voice communications in the VHF and UHF bands.

Which mode is most commonly used for voice communications on the 17- and 12-meter bands?

A. Upper sideband
B. Lower sideband
C. Suppressed sideband
D. Double sideband

G2A04 Answer: A. The upper sideband is the mode most commonly used for voice communications on the 17- and 12-meter bands. Indeed, the upper sideband is the preferred operating mode on the 20-, 17-, 15-, 12-, and 10-meter HF amateur bands. In addition, the upper sideband is preferred on all the VHF and UHF bands.

Which mode of voice communication is most commonly used on the HF amateur bands?

A. Frequency modulation
B. Double sideband
C. Single sideband
D. Single phase modulation

G2A05 Answer: C. The single-sideband mode of voice communication is most commonly used on the high frequency amateur bands. This is more because of convention than for any technical reasons.

Which of the following is an advantage of using single sideband, as compared to other analog voice modes on the HF amateur bands?

A. Very high-fidelity voice modulation
B. Less subject to interference from atmospheric static crashes
C. Ease of tuning on receive and immunity to impulse noise
D. Less bandwidth used and greater power efficiency

G2A06 Answer: D. When using single sideband as compared to other analog voice modes on the HF amateur bands, less bandwidth used and higher power efficiency is an advantage.

Which of the following statements is true of single sideband (SSB)?

A. Only one sideband and the carrier are transmitted; the other sideband is suppressed
B. Only one sideband is transmitted; the other sideband and carrier are suppressed
C. SSB is the only voice mode authorized on the 20-, 15-, and 10-meter amateur bands
D. SSB is the only voice mode authorized on the 160-, 75-, and 40-meter amateur bands

G2A07 Answer: B. In single sideband (SSB), only one sideband is transmitted; the other sideband and carrier are suppressed. This means that SSB transmission consumes considerably less power.

What is the recommended way to break into a phone contact?

A. Say "QRZ" several times, followed by your call sign
B. Say your call sign once
C. Say "Breaker Breaker"
D. Say "CQ" followed by the call sign of either station

G2A08 Answer: B. Saying your call sign once is the recommended way to break in to a phone contact.

Why do most amateur stations use lower sideband on the 160-, 75-, and 40-meter bands?

A. Lower sideband is more efficient than upper sideband at these frequencies
B. Lower sideband is the only sideband legal on these frequency bands
C. Because it is fully compatible with an AM detector
D. It is commonly accepted amateur practice

G2A09 Answer: D. Most amateur stations use lower sideband on the 160-, 75-, and 40-meter bands simply because this is commonly accepted amateur practice. The separation between the bands used by the upper sideband and those used by the lower sideband is largely arbitrary and based on tradition.

Which of the following statements is true of VOX operation versus PTT operation?

A. The received signal is more natural sounding
B. It allows "hands free" operation
C. It occupies less bandwidth
D. It provides more power output

G2A10 Answer: B. SSB VOX allows "hands free" operation.

Generally, who should respond to a station in the contiguous 48 states calling "CQ DX"?

A. Any caller is welcome to respond
B. Only stations in Germany
C. Any stations outside the lower 48 states
D. Only contest stations

G2A11 Answer: C. Any stations outside the lower 48 states should respond to a station in the contiguous 48 states who calls "CQ DX."

What control is typically adjusted for proper ALC setting on a single sideband transceiver?

A. RF clipping level
B. Transmit audio or microphone gain
C. Antenna inductance or capacitance
D. Attenuator level

G2A12 Answer: B. Transmit audio or microphone gain is typically adjusted for proper ALC setting on a single sideband transceiver.

G2B – Operating Effectively; Band Plans; Drills and Emergencies; RACES Operation

Which of the following is true concerning access to frequencies?

A. Nets have priority
B. QSOs in progress have priority
C. Except during emergencies, no amateur station has priority access to any frequency
D. Contest operations should yield to non-contest use of frequencies

G2B01 Answer: C. No one has priority access to frequencies, common courtesy should always be a guide. [97.101(b), (c)]

What is the first thing you should do if you are communicating with another amateur station and hear a station in distress break in?

A. Inform your local emergency coordinator
B. Acknowledge the station in distress and determine what assistance may be needed
C. Immediately decrease power to avoid interfering with the station in distress
D. Immediately cease all transmissions

G2B02 Answer: B. If you are communicating with another amateur station and hear a station in distress break in, the first thing you should do is acknowledge the station in distress and determine what assistance may be needed. You should note the time and frequency of the call as soon as possible. Specifically, it is important to note the address, or, if an address cannot be obtained, the latitude and longitude of the emergency. You should also try to learn the nature of the problem and the sort of assistance required. After obtaining this information, you should ask the station in distress to remain on frequency as you contact the appropriate emergency services.

What is good amateur practice if propagation changes during a contact creating interference from other stations using the frequency?

A. Advise the interfering stations that you are on the frequency and that you have priority
B. Decrease power and continue to transmit
C. Attempt to resolve the interference problem with the other stations in a mutually acceptable manner
D. Switch to the opposite sideband

G2B03 Answer: C. Attempting to resolve the interference problem with the other stations in a mutually acceptable manner is good amateur practice if propagation changes during a contact create interference from other stations using the frequency.

When selecting a CW transmitting frequency, what minimum separation from other stations should be used to minimize interference to stations on adjacent frequencies?

A. 5 Hz to 50 Hz
B. 150 Hz to 500 Hz
C. 1 kHz to 3 kHz
D. 3 kHz to 6 kHz

G2B04 Answer: B. When selecting a CW transmitting frequency, you should allow a minimum frequency separation of 150 Hz to 500 Hz in order to minimize interference to stations on adjacent frequencies. CW transmissions, otherwise known as Morse code, are a series of on and off keys.

When selecting an SSB transmitting frequency, what minimum separation should be used to minimize interference to stations on adjacent frequencies?

A. 5 Hz to 50 Hz
B. 150 Hz to 500 Hz
C. 2 kHz to 3 kHz
D. Approximately 6 kHz

G2B05 Answer: C. When selecting an SSB transmitting frequency, 2–3 kHz of separation should be used to minimize interference to stations on adjacent frequencies.

How can you avoid harmful interference on an apparently clear frequency before calling CQ on CW or phone?

A. Send "QRL?" on CW, followed by your call sign; or, if using phone, ask if the frequency is in use, followed by your call sign
B. Listen for 2 minutes before calling CQ
C. Send the letter "V" in Morse code several times and listen for a response, or say "test" several times and listen for a response
D. Send "QSY" on CW or if using phone, announce "the frequency is in use," then give your call sign and listen for a response

G2B06 Answer: A. A way to avoid harmful interference on an apparently clear frequency before calling CQ on CW or phone is to send "QRL?" on CW, followed by your call sign; or if using phone, ask if the frequency is in use, followed by your call sign. The Q-signal QRL, when issued as a question, means "Is the frequency busy?" When this same Q-signal is issued as a response, it means, "The frequency is busy. Please do not interfere."

Which of the following complies with commonly accepted amateur practice when choosing a frequency on which to initiate a call?

A. Listen on the frequency for at least two minutes to be sure it is clear
B. Identify your station by transmitting your call sign at least 3 times
C. Follow the voluntary band plan
D. All these choices are correct

G2B07 Answer: C. Following the voluntary band plan complies with commonly accepted amateur practice when choosing a frequency on which to initiate a call.

What is the voluntary band plan restriction for US stations transmitting within the 48 contiguous states in the 50.1 MHz to 50.125 MHz band segment?

A. Only contacts with stations not within the 48 contiguous states
B. Only contacts with other stations within the 48 contiguous states
C. Only digital contacts
D. Only SSTV contacts

G2B08 Answer: A. The voluntary band plan restriction for US stations transmitting within the 48 contiguous states in the 50.1 MHz to 50.125 MHz band segment limits contacts to only those with stations not within the 48 contiguous states.

Who may be the control operator of an amateur station transmitting in RACES to assist relief operations during a disaster?

A. Only a person holding an FCC-issued amateur operator license
B. Only a RACES net control operator
C. A person holding an FCC-issued amateur operator license or an appropriate government official
D. Any control operator when normal communication systems are operational

G2B09 Answer: A. Only a person holding an FCC-issued amateur operator license may be the control operator of an amateur station transmitting in RACES to assist relief operations during a disaster. RACES (the Radio Amateur Civil Emergency Service) is administered by the Federal Emergency Management Agency (FEMA). In order to be a part of RACES, an operator must also have membership in the relevant local group charged with disaster relief. Ham radio operators may obtain membership in RACES by contacting their state's Auxiliary Communications Service. [97.407(a)]

Which of the following is good amateur practice for net management?

A. Always use multiple sets of phonetics during check-in
B. Have a backup frequency in case of interference or poor conditions
C. Transmit the full net roster at the beginning of every session
D. All these choices are correct

G2B10 Answer: B. Having a backup frequency in case of interference or poor conditions is good amateur practice for net management.

How often may RACES training drills and tests be routinely conducted without special authorization?

A. No more than 1 hour per month
B. No more than 2 hours per month
C. No more than 1 hour per week
D. No more than 2 hours per week

G2B11 Answer: C. Without special authorization, RACES training drills and tests may be routinely conducted no more than 1 hour per week. [97.407(d)(4)]

G2C – CW Operating Procedures and Procedural Signals; Q Signals; Full Break-In

Which of the following describes full break-in CW operation (QSK)?

A. Breaking stations send the Morse code prosign "BK"
B. Automatic keyers, instead of hand keys, are used to send Morse code
C. An operator must activate a manual send/receive switch before and after every transmission
D. Transmitting stations can receive between code characters and elements

G2C01 Answer: D. In full break-in CW operation (QSK), transmitting stations can receive between code characters and elements. This mode of operation is only possible when the radio rig has the ability to switch very quickly between transmit and receive. When using full break-in CW operation, the operator has the ability to hear the activity on the band between code characters and elements. However, the VOX operation must be turned off in order for this mode to work properly.

What should you do if a CW station sends "QRS?"

A. Send slower
B. Change frequency
C. Increase your power
D. Repeat everything twice

G2C02 Answer: A. If a CW station sends "QRS," you should send slower. The Q-signal QRS, when issued as a question, means "Shall I send more slowly?" When it is issued as a response, it means "Please send more slowly." It is often accompanied by the requested rate in words per minute.

What does it mean when a CW operator sends "KN" at the end of a transmission?

A. No US stations should call
B. Operating full break-in
C. Listening only for a specific station or stations
D. Closing station now

G2C03 Answer: C. When a CW operator sends "KN" at the end of a transmission, it means that the operator is listening only for a specific station or stations.

What does the Q signal "QRL?" mean?

A. "Will you keep the frequency clear?"
B. "Are you operating full break-in?" or "Can you operate full break-in?"
C. "Are you listening only for a specific station?"
D. "Are you busy?" or "Is this frequency in use?"

G2C04 Answer: D. When a CW operator sends "QRL?," he or she is either asking if a frequency is being used or if the receiver is busy.

What is the best speed to use when answering a CQ in Morse code?

A. The fastest speed at which you are comfortable copying, but no slower than the CQ
B. The fastest speed at which you are comfortable copying, but no faster than the CQ
C. At the standard calling speed of 10 wpm
D. At the standard calling speed of 5 wpm

G2C05 Answer: B. The best speed to use when answering a CQ in Morse code is the fastest speed at which you are comfortable copying, but no faster than the CQ.

What does the term "zero beat" mean in CW operation?

A. Matching the speed of the transmitting station
B. Operating split to avoid interference on frequency
C. Sending without error
D. Matching the transmit frequency to the frequency of a received signal

G2C06 Answer: D. In CW operation, the term "zero beat" means matching your transmit frequency to the frequency of a received signal.

When sending CW, what does a "C" mean when added to the RST report?

A. Chirpy or unstable signal
B. Report was read from an S meter rather than estimated
C. 100 percent copy
D. Key clicks

G2C07 Answer: A. When sending CW, a "C" added to the RST report means chirpy or unstable signal. RST stands for readability, strength, and tone. When single-sideband phones are being used, only R and S reports are necessary. In an RST report, readability is measured on a scale from 1 to 5, with 1 being unreadable and 5 being perfectly readable. Strength, meanwhile, is measured on a scale from 1 to 9, with a 1 indicating a barely perceptible signal and a 9 indicating a very strong signal. Tone is measured on a scale from 1 to 9, with 1 indicating sixty cycle a.c. or less, and a 9 indicating perfect tone with no trace of ripple or modulation of any kind.

What prosign is sent to indicate the end of a formal message when using CW?

A. SK
B. BK
C. AR
D. KN

G2C08 Answer: C. The prosign AR is sent to indicate the end of a formal message when using CW. Prosigns, otherwise known as procedural signals, are one- or two-letter signals that indicate the intention of the operator. The prosign AR means "end of message." Some of the other common prosigns are AA (new line), AS (wait), BK (break), BT (space down two lines), CL (going off the air), CT (start of transmission), DO (shift to wabun code), K (go or over; that is, an invitation for another station to speak), KN (invitation to a specific station to transmit), SK (end of contact), SN (understood), and SOS (serious distress, assistance required).

What does the Q signal "QSL" mean?

A. Send slower
B. We have already confirmed the contact
C. I have received and understood
D. We have worked before

G2C09 Answer: C. The Q signal "QSL" means "I have received and understood." If this Q-signal is issued as a question, it means "Did you receive and understand my transmission?"

What does the Q signal "QRN" mean?

A. Send more slowly
B. Stop sending
C. Zero beat my signal
D. I am troubled by static

G2C10 Answer: D. The Q signal "QRN" means "noise from natural sources." When issued as a query, this Q signal means "Are you troubled by static?"

What does the Q signal "QRV" mean?

A. You are sending too fast
B. There is interference on the frequency
C. I am quitting for the day
D. I am ready to receive

G2C11 Answer: D. The Q signal "QRV" means "I am ready to receive." When this Q signal is issued as a query, it means "Are you ready to receive?"

G2D – Volunteer Monitor Program; HF Operations

What is the Volunteer Monitor Program?

A. Amateur volunteers who are formally enlisted to monitor the airwaves for rules violations
B. Amateur volunteers who conduct amateur licensing examinations
C. Amateur volunteers who conduct frequency coordination for amateur VHF repeaters
D. Amateur volunteers who use their station equipment to help civil defense organizations in times of emergency

G2D01 Answer: A. The Volunteer Monitor Program consists of amateur volunteers who are formally enlisted to monitor the airwaves for rules violations.

Which of the following are objectives of the Volunteer Monitor Program?

A. To conduct efficient and orderly amateur licensing examinations
B. To provide emergency and public safety communications
C. To coordinate repeaters for efficient and orderly spectrum usage
D. To encourage amateur radio operators to self-regulate and comply with the rules

G2D02 Answer: D. One of the objectives of the Volunteer Monitor Program is to encourage amateur radio operators to self-regulate and comply with the rules.

What procedure may be used by Volunteer Monitors to localize a station whose continuous carrier is holding a repeater on in their area?

A. Compare vertical and horizontal signal strengths on the input frequency
B. Compare beam headings on the repeater input from their home locations with that of other Volunteer Monitors
C. Compare signal strengths between the input and output of the repeater
D. All these choices are correct

G2D03 Answer: B. Comparing beam headings on the repeater input from their home locations with that of other Volunteer Monitors may help localize a station whose continuous carrier is holding a repeater on in their area.

Which of the following describes an azimuthal projection map?

A. A map that shows accurate land masses
B. A map that shows true bearings and distances from a specific location
C. A map that shows the angle at which an amateur satellite crosses the equator
D. A map that shows the number of degrees longitude that an amateur satellite appears to move westward at the equator with each orbit

G2D04 Answer: B. An azimuthal projection map is a map that shows true bearings and distances from a specific location. When the operator's station is positioned at the center of the map, the path of any transmission to or from the station will be a radial line straight to the other station.

Which of the following indicates that you are looking for an HF contact with any station?

A. Sign your call sign once, followed by the words "listening for a call" -- if no answer, change frequency and repeat
B. Say "QTC" followed by "this is" and your call sign -- if no answer, change frequency and repeat
C. Repeat "CQ" a few times, followed by "this is," then your call sign a few times, then pause to listen, repeat as necessary
D. Transmit an unmodulated carried for approximately 10 seconds, followed by "this is" and your call sign, and pause to listen -- repeat as necessary

G2D05 Answer: C. To indicate that you are looking for an HF contact with any station, repeat "CQ" a few times, followed by "this is," then your call sign a few times, then pause to listen, and repeat as necessary.

How is a directional antenna pointed when making a "long-path" contact with another station?

A. Toward the rising sun
B. Along the gray line
C. 180 degrees from the station's short-path heading
D. Toward the north

G2D06 Answer: C. When making a long-path contact with another station, a directional antenna should be pointed 180 degrees from its short-path heading.

Which of the following are examples of the NATO Phonetic Alphabet?

A. Able, Baker, Charlie, Dog
B. Adam, Boy, Charles, David
C. America, Boston, Canada, Denmark
D. Alpha, Bravo, Charlie, Delta

G2D07 Answer: D. Alpha, Bravo, Charlie, and Delta of the NATO Phonetic Alphabet are equivalent to A, B, C, and D, respectively.

Why do many amateurs keep a station log?

A. The FCC requires a log of all international contacts
B. The FCC requires a log of all international third-party traffic
C. The log provides evidence of operation needed to renew a license without retest
D. To help with a reply if the FCC requests information about your station

G2D08 Answer: D. Many amateurs keep a log even though the FCC doesn't require it to help with a reply if the FCC requests information about their station.

Which of the following is required when participating in a contest on HF frequencies?

A. Submit a log to the contest sponsor
B. Send a QSL card to the stations worked, or QSL via Logbook of The World
C. Identify your station according to normal FCC regulations
D. All these choices are correct

G2D09 Answer: C. When participating in a contest on HF frequencies, you must identify your station per normal FCC regulations.

What is QRP operation?

A. Remote piloted model control
B. Low-power transmit operation
C. Transmission using Quick Response Protocol
D. Traffic relay procedure net operation

G2D10 Answer: B. QRP operation is low power transmit operation. This method of operation is preferred by many because it requires incredible precision and skill. QRP means no more than 5 watts of transmitter output power for Morse code, and no more than 10 watts of peak power on voice transmission. For the most part, QRP occurs in Morse code and on HF.

Why are signal reports typically exchanged at the beginning of an HF contact?

A. To allow each station to operate according to conditions
B. To be sure the contact will count for award programs
C. To follow standard radiogram structure
D. To allow each station to calibrate their frequency display

G2D11 Answer: A. Signal reports are typically exchanged at the beginning of an HF contact to allow each station to operate according to conditions.

G2E – Digital Mode Operating Procedures

Which mode is normally used when sending RTTY signals via AFSK with an SSB transmitter?

A. USB
B. DSB
C. CW
D. LSB

G2E01 Answer: D. The LSB mode is normally used when sending an RTTY signal via AFSK with an SSB transmitter.

What is VARA?

A. A low signal-to-noise digital mode used for EME (moonbounce)
B. A digital protocol used with Winlink
C. A radio direction finding system used on VHF and UHF
D. A DX spotting system using a network of software defined radios

G2E02 Answer: B. VARA is a digital protocol used with Winlink.

What symptoms may result from other signals interfering with a PACTOR or VARA transmission?

A. Frequent retries or timeouts
B. Long pauses in message transmission
C. Failure to establish a connection between stations
D. All these choices are correct

G2E03 Answer: D. These are all possible symptoms of other signals interfering with a PACTOR or VARA transmission.

Which of the following is good practice when choosing a transmitting frequency to answer a station calling CQ using FT8?

A. Always call on the station's frequency
B. Call on any frequency in the waterfall except the station's frequency
C. Find a clear frequency during the same time slot as the calling station
D. Find a clear frequency during the alternate time slot to the calling station

G2E04 Answer: D. Finding a clear frequency during the alternate time slot to the calling station is good practice when choosing a transmitting frequency to answer a station calling CQ using FT8.

What is the standard sideband for JT65, JT9, FT4, or FT8 digital signal when using AFSK?

A. LSB
B. USB
C. DSB
D. SSB

G2E05 Answer: B. USB is the standard sideband for JT65, JT9, FT4, or FT8 digital signal when using AFSK.

What is the most common frequency shift for RTTY emissions in the amateur HF bands?

A. 85 Hz
B. 170 Hz
C. 425 Hz
D. 850 Hz

G2E06 Answer: B. 170 Hz is the most common frequency shift for RTTY emissions in the amateur HF bands.

Which of the following is required when using FT8?

A. A special hardware modem
B. Computer time accurate to within approximately 1 second
C. Receiver attenuator set to -12 dB
D. A vertically polarized antenna

G2E07 Answer: B. Computer time accurate to within approximately 1 second is required when using FT8.

In what segment of the 20-meter band are most digital mode operations commonly found?

A. At the bottom of the slow-scan TV segment, near 14.230 MHz
B. At the top of the SSB phone segment, near 14.325 MHz
C. In the middle of the CW segment, near 14.100 MHz
D. Between 14.070 MHz and 14.100 MHz

G2E08 Answer: D. Most digital mode operations are commonly found between 14.070 MHz and 14.100 MHz on the 20-meter band.

How do you join a contact between two stations using the PACTOR protocol?

A. Send broadcast packets containing your call sign while in MONITOR mode
B. Transmit a steady carrier until the PACTOR protocol times out and disconnects
C. Joining an existing contact is not possible, PACTOR connections are limited to two stations
D. Send a NAK code

G2E09 Answer: C. It is not possible to join a contact between two stations using a PACTOR protocol.

Which of the following is a way to establish contact with a digital messaging system gateway station?

A. Send an email to the system control operator
B. Send QRL in Morse code
C. Respond when the station broadcasts its SSID
D. Transmit a connect message on the station's published frequency

G2E10 Answer: D. To establish contact with a digital messaging system gateway station, just transmit a connect message on the station's published frequency.

What is the primary purpose of an Amateur Radio Emergency Data Network (AREDN) mesh network?

A. To provide FM repeater coverage in remote areas
B. To provide real time propagation data by monitoring amateur radio transmissions worldwide
C. To provide high-speed data services during an emergency or community event
D. To provide DX spotting reports to aid contesters and DXers

G2E11 Answer: C. The primary purpose of an AREDN mesh network is to provide high-speed data services during an emergency or community event.

Which of the following describes Winlink?

A. An amateur radio wireless network to send and receive email on the internet
B. A form of Packet Radio
C. A wireless network capable of both VHF and HF band operation
D. All these choices are correct

G2E12 Answer: D. Winlink is an amateur radio wireless network capable of both VHF and HF band operation that is used to send and receive email on the internet and a form of Packet Radio.

What is another name for a Winlink Remote Message Server?

A. Terminal Node Controller
B. Gateway
C. RJ-45
D. Printer/Server

G2E13 Answer: B. Gateway is another name for a Winlink Remote Message Server.

What could be wrong if you cannot decode an RTTY or other FSK signal even though it is apparently tuned in properly?

A. The mark and space frequencies may be reversed
B. You may have selected the wrong baud rate
C. You may be listening on the wrong sideband
D. All these choices are correct

G2E14 Answer: D. All of these are possibly wrong of you cannot decode an RTTY or other FSK signal that is tuned properly.

Which of the following is a common location for FT8?

A. Anywhere in the voice portion of the band
B. Anywhere in the CW portion of the band
C. Approximately 14.074 MHz to 14.077 MHz
D. Approximately 14.110 MHz to 14.113 MHz

G2E15 Answer: C. A common location for FT8 is approximately 14.074 MHz to 14.077 MHz.

G3 – Radio Wave Propagation

G3A – Sunspots and Solar Radiation; Geomagnetic Field and Stability Indices

How does a higher sunspot number affect HF propagation?

A. Higher sunspot numbers generally indicate a greater probability of good propagation at higher frequencies
B. Lower sunspot numbers generally indicate greater probability of sporadic E propagation
C. A zero sunspot number indicates that radio propagation is not possible on any band
D. A zero sunspot number indicates undisturbed conditions

G3A01 Answer: A. The sunspot number is a measure of solar activity based on counting sunspots and sunspot groups. This is a number used to indicate the general amount of sunspot activity, with higher numbers generally indicating a greater probability of good propagation at higher frequencies. It is sometimes referred to as relative sunspot number, Zurich number, or Wolf number. It is calculated with the equation $R = k(10g + f)$, in which f is the number of distinct spots, g is the number of spot groups, and k is a factor based on the location and equipment of the observer.

What effect does a sudden ionospheric disturbance have on the daytime ionospheric propagation?

A. It enhances propagation on all HF frequencies
B. It disrupts signals on lower frequencies more than those on higher frequencies
C. It disrupts communications via satellite more than direct communications
D. None, because only areas on the night side of the Earth are affected

G3A02 Answer: B. A sudden ionospheric disturbance disrupts signals on lower frequencies more than those on higher frequencies. A sudden ionospheric disturbance is a complicated set of rapid fluctuations in the ionosphere, typically occurring after a period of solar flares. This phenomenon, also known as the Dellinger effect or the Mogel-Dellinger effect, is observable as a rapid increase in the radio-wave absorption, particularly in the lower HF and upper MF ranges. Sudden ionospheric disturbance can be very disruptive to telecommunications systems, including ham radio. The effects are most dire in the regions around the equator, and may last from a few minutes to several hours.

Approximately how long does it take the increased ultraviolet and X-ray radiation from a solar flare to affect radio propagation on Earth?

A. 28 days
B. 1 to 2 hours
C. 8 minutes
D. 20 to 40 hours

G3A03 Answer: C. It takes the increased ultraviolet and X-ray radiation from solar flares approximately eight minutes to affect radio-wave propagation on the Earth. A solar flare is a rapid increase in the brightness of a particular area of the sun, representing a release of up to one-sixth of the sun's normal energy output. The solar flare is typically followed by a coronal mass ejection.

Which of the following are the least reliable bands for long-distance communications during periods of low solar activity?

A. 80 meters and 160 meters
B. 60 meters and 40 meters
C. 30 meters and 20 meters
D. 15 meters, 12 meters, and 10 meters

G3A04 Answer: D. During periods of low solar activity the 15-meters, 12-meters, and 10-meters bands are least reliable for long distance communication.

What is the solar flux index?

A. A measure of the highest frequency that is useful for ionospheric propagation between two points on Earth
B. A count of sunspots that is adjusted for solar emissions
C. Another name for the American sunspot number
D. A measure of solar radiation with a wavelength of 10.7 centimeters

G3A05 Answer: D. The solar flux index is a measure of solar radiation at 10.7 cm. The measure of 10.7 cm is important because it is the wavelength of radio signals at 2800 MHz. Although the solar flux index is proportional to the amount of sunspot activity at any given time, the ionization levels in the ionosphere can now be more accurately measured by assessing the X-ray flux from the Sun.

What is a geomagnetic storm?

A. A sudden drop in the solar flux index
B. A thunderstorm that affects radio propagation
C. Ripples in the geomagnetic force
D. A temporary disturbance in Earth's geomagnetic field

G3A06 Answer: D. A geomagnetic storm is a temporary disturbance in the Earth's geomagnetic field. These storms may be caused by magnetic field clouds and solar wind shock waves. A geomagnetic storm may cause rapid fluctuations and unpredictable propagation paths for radio signals. Radio operators in the HF bands may utilize solar and geomagnetic alerts that will enable them to avoid major problems caused by geomagnetic storms.

At what point in the solar cycle does the 20-meter band usually support worldwide propagation during daylight hours?

A. At the summer solstice
B. Only at the maximum point
C. Only at the minimum point
D. At any point

G3A07 Answer: D. The 20-meter band usually supports worldwide propagation during daylight hours at any point in the solar cycle.

How can a geomagnetic storm affect HF propagation?

A. Improve high-latitude HF propagation
B. Degrade ground wave propagation
C. Improve ground wave propagation
D. Degrade high-latitude HF propagation

G3A08 Answer: D. A geomagnetic storm can degrade high-latitude HF propagation.

How can high geomagnetic activity benefit radio communications?

A. Creates auroras that can reflect VHF signals
B. Increases signal strength for HF signals passing through the polar regions
C. Improve HF long path propagation
D. Reduce long delayed echoes

G3A09 Answer: A. High geomagnetic activity can cause auroras that can reflect VHF signals.

What causes HF propagation conditions to vary periodically in a 26- to 28-day cycle?

A. Long term oscillations in the upper atmosphere
B. Cyclic variation in Earth's radiation belts
C. Rotation of the Sun's surface layers around its axis
D. The position of the Moon in its orbit

G3A10 Answer: C. The rotation of the Sun's surface layers around its axis causes HF propagation conditions to vary periodically in a 26- to 28-day cycle.

How long does it take a coronal mass ejection to affect radio propagation on Earth?

A. 28 days
B. 14 days
C. 4 to 8 minutes
D. 15 hours to several days

G3A11 Answer: D. It can take 15 hours to several days for charged particles from coronal mass ejections to affect radio-wave propagation on the Earth. A coronal mass ejection is an enormous burst of solar wind and magnetic fields. It is most common for coronal mass ejections to occur in areas where there are flaring sunspots.

What does the K-index measure?

A. The relative position of sunspots on the surface of the Sun
B. The short-term stability of Earth's geomagnetic field
C. The short-term stability of the Sun's magnetic field
D. The solar radio flux at Boulder, Colorado

G3A12 Answer: B. The K-index indicates the short-term stability of the Earth's geomagnetic field. The level of disturbance in the Earth's geomagnetic field is described by an integer between 0 and 9. In this scale, values at either end indicate calm, while a value of 5 indicates a geomagnetic storm.

What does the A-index measure?

A. The relative position of sunspots on the surface of the Sun
B. The amount of polarization of the Sun's electric field
C. The long-term stability of Earth's geomagnetic field
D. The solar radio flux at Boulder, Colorado

G3A13 Answer: C. The A-index indicates the long-term stability of the Earth's geomagnetic field. It provides a daily average level of geomagnetic activity.

How is long distance radio communication usually affected by the charged particles that reach Earth from solar coronal holes?

A. HF communication is improved
B. HF communication is disturbed
C. VHF/UHF ducting is improved
D. VHF/UHF ducting is disturbed

G3A14 Answer: B. HF radio communication is usually disturbed by the charged particles that reach the Earth from solar coronal holes. A coronal hole is a place on the Sun where the corona is darker and colder. The solar wind is able to travel faster along the open magnetic field lines that pass through coronal holes, which makes them likely to disturb HF radio communication.

G3B – Maximum Usable Frequency; Lowest Usable Frequency; Short Path and Long Path Propagation; Determining Propagation Conditions; Ionospheric Refraction

What is a characteristic of skywave signals arriving at your location by both short-path and long-path propagation?

A. Periodic fading approximately every 10 seconds
B. Signal strength increased by 3 dB
C. The signal might be cancelled causing severe attenuation
D. A slightly delayed echo might be heard

G3B01 Answer: D. Skywave signals arriving at your location by both short-path and long-path propagation often produce a slightly delayed echo.

What factors affect the MUF?

A. Path distance and location
B. Time of day and season
C. Solar radiation and ionospheric disturbances
D. All these choices are correct

G3B02 Answer: D. Path distance and location, time of day and season, as well as solar radiation and ionospheric disturbances can affect the MUF.

Which frequency will have the least attenuation for long-distance skip propagation?

A. Just below the MUF
B. Just above the LUF
C. Just below the critical frequency
D. Just above the critical frequency

G3B03 Answer: A. Selecting a frequency just below the MUF will give the lowest attenuation for long-distance skip propagation.

Which of the following is a way to determine current propagation on a desired band from your station?

A. Use a network of automated receiving stations on the internet to see where your transmissions are being received
B. Check the A-index
C. Send a series of dots and listen for echoes
D. All these choices are correct

G3B04 Answer: A. Using a network of automated receiving stations on the internet to see where your transmissions are being received is a way to determine current propagation on a desired band from your station.

How does the ionosphere affect radio waves with frequencies below the MUF and above the LUF?

A. They are refracted back to Earth
B. They pass through the ionosphere
C. They are amplified by interaction with the ionosphere
D. They are refracted and trapped in the ionosphere to circle Earth

G3B05 Answer: A. Radio waves with frequencies below the Maximum Usable Frequency (MUF) and above the Lowest Usable Frequency (LUF) are refracted back to the Earth when they are sent into the ionosphere. The maximum usable frequency is the highest frequency at which a signal may still be transmitted between two points with skip reflection (that is, the reflection of waves from the ionosphere). When the frequency of a signal increases, the refractive index of the ionosphere decreases, which is why there is an upper limit to usable frequency. If a signal has a higher frequency than that, it will pass through the ionosphere into space rather than being reflected by it. Lowest usable frequency, on the other hand, is the HF band frequency that has a received field intensity high enough to create the necessary signal-to-noise ratio.

What usually happens to radio waves with frequencies below the LUF?

A. They are refracted back to Earth
B. They pass through the ionosphere
C. They are attenuated before reaching the destination
D. They are refracted and trapped in the ionosphere to circle Earth

G3B06 Answer: C. Radio waves with frequencies below the Lowest Usable Frequency (LUF) are attenuated before reaching the destination.

What does LUF stand for?

A. The Lowest Usable Frequency for communications between two specific points
B. Lowest Usable Frequency for communications to any point outside a 100-mile radius
C. The Lowest Usable Frequency during a 24-hour period
D. Lowest Usable Frequency during the past 60 minutes

G3B07 Answer: A. LUF stands for the Lowest Usable Frequency for communications between two specific points.

What does MUF stand for?

A. The Minimum Usable Frequency for communications between two points
B. The Maximum Usable Frequency for communications between two points
C. The Minimum Usable Frequency during a 24-hour period
D. The Maximum Usable Frequency during a 24-hour period

G3B08 Answer: B. MUF stands for the Maximum Usable Frequency for communications between two points. The maximum usable frequency is the highest radio signal frequency that will reach a given destination using skip, or skywave, propagation. The maximum usable frequency will not be the same for all destinations with respect to the same transmitter.

What is the approximate maximum distance along the Earth's surface normally covered in one hop using the F2 region?

A. 180 miles
B. 1,200 miles
C. 2,500 miles
D. 12,000 miles

G3B09 Answer: C. The approximate maximum distance along the Earth's surface that is normally covered in one hop using the F2 region is 2,500 miles. The F2 region is part of the ionosphere's F layer, also known as the Appleton layer. The F layer lies in between the E region and the protonosphere. It is useful for the propagation of high frequency radio waves. The greatest concentration of free electrons and ions in the atmosphere is found in the F region. The F1 region lies below the F2 region during the day, but at night these regions are one and the same. The F2 region is found between 220 and 800 km above the surface of the Earth.

What is the approximate maximum distance along the Earth's surface normally covered in one hop using the E region?

A. 180 miles
B. 1,200 miles
C. 2,500 miles
D. 12,000 miles

G3B10 Answer: B. The approximate maximum distance along the Earth's surface that is normally covered in one hop using the E region is 1,200 miles. The E region, also known as the Kennelly-Heaviside layer, is the section of the ionosphere that lies approximately 90 to 150 kilometers above the Earth's surface. This layer can reflect medium frequency radio waves, particularly at night when the ionosphere is dragged further away from the Earth by solar wind. The distance which the E layer can transmit signals is also influenced by the season and the level of sunspot activity.

What happens to HF propagation when the LUF exceeds the MUF?

A. Propagation via ordinary skywave communications is not possible over that path
B. HF communications over the path are enhanced
C. Double-hop propagation along the path is more common
D. Propagation over the path on all HF frequencies is enhanced

G3B11 Answer: A. When the Lowest Usable Frequency exceeds the Maximum Usable Frequency, propagation via ordinary skywave communications is not possible over that path.

Which of the following is typical of the lower HF frequencies during the summer?

A. Poor propagation at any time of day
B. World-wide propagation during daylight hours
C. Heavy distortion on signals due to photon absorption
D. High levels of atmospheric noise or static

G3B12 Answer: D. During the summer, high levels of atmospheric noise or static is typical of the lower HF frequencies.

G3C – Ionospheric Regions; Critical Angle and Frequency; HF Scatter; Near Vertical Incidence Skywave (NVIS)

Which ionospheric region is closest to the surface of Earth?

A. The D region
B. The E region
C. The F1 region
D. The F2 region

G3C01 Answer: A. The D region of the ionosphere is closest to the surface of the Earth. The D region extends from roughly 60 to 90 km above the surface of the Earth. Because of extensive electron collisions, high frequency radio waves are absorbed rather than reflected. That is, HF radio waves actually decrease in intensity as they pass through the D region.

What is meant by the term "critical frequency" at a given incidence angle?

A. The highest frequency which is refracted back to Earth
B. The lowest frequency which is refracted back to Earth
C. The frequency at which the signal-to-noise ratio approaches unity
D. The frequency at which the signal-to-noise ratio is 6 dB

G3C02 Answer: A. The critical frequency at a given incidence angle is the highest frequency which is refracted back to Earth.

Why is skip propagation via the F2 region longer than that via the other ionospheric regions?

A. Because it is the densest
B. Because of the Doppler effect
C. Because it is the highest
D. Because of temperature inversions

G3C03 Answer: C. Skip propagation via the F2 region is longer than that via the other ionospheric regions because it is the highest ionospheric region. It lies approximately 220 to 800 km above the surface of the Earth. It is the primary reflecting layer for HF communications both at night and during the day.

What does the term "critical angle" mean, as applied to radio wave propagation?

A. The long path azimuth of a distant station
B. The short path azimuth of a distant station
C. The lowest takeoff angle that will return a radio wave to Earth under specific ionospheric conditions
D. The highest takeoff angle that will return a radio wave to Earth under specific ionospheric conditions

G3C04 Answer: D. In radio wave propagation, the term "critical angle" means the highest takeoff angle that will return a radio wave to the Earth under specific ionospheric conditions. The critical angle is the highest possible angle for successful radio wave transmission. At angles higher than this, the radio wave will be reflected back upon itself, and will therefore not reach its destination.

Why is long-distance communication on the 40-, 60-, 80-, and 160-meter bands more difficult during the day?

A. The F region absorbs signals at these frequencies during daylight hours
B. The F region is unstable during daylight hours
C. The D region absorbs signals at these frequencies during daylight hours
D. The E region is unstable during daylight hours

G3C05 Answer: C. Long distance communications on the 40-, 60-, 80-, and 160-meter bands is more difficult during the day because the D region absorbs signals at these frequencies during daylight hours.

What is a characteristic of HF scatter?

A. Phone signals have high intelligibility
B. Signals have a fluttering sound
C. There are very large, sudden swings in signal strength
D. Scatter propagation occurs only at night

G3C06 Answer: B. One characteristic of HF scatter signals is a wavering sound.

What makes HF scatter signals often sound distorted?

A. The ionospheric region involved is unstable
B. Ground waves are absorbing much of the signal
C. The E region is not present
D. Energy is scattered into the skip zone through several different paths

G3C07 Answer: D. HF scatter signals often sound distorted because energy is scattered into the skip zone through several different paths.

Why are HF scatter signals in the skip zone usually weak?

A. Only a small part of the signal energy is scattered into the skip zone
B. Signals are scattered from the magnetosphere, which is not a good reflector
C. Propagation is via ground waves, which absorb most of the signal energy
D. Propagation is via ducts in the F region, which absorb most of the energy

G3C08 Answer: A. HF scatter signals in the skip zone are usually weak because only a small part of the signal energy is scattered into the skip zone. A skip zone is an area in which radio transmissions cannot be received, even though reception is possible at locations both closer to and farther away from the skip zone. In radio transmission, the skip zone is the area in between the respective ranges of the ground waves and sky waves. In other words, the skip zone is beyond the reach of ground waves but too close for sky waves. The sky waves that would otherwise reach the skip zone penetrate the ionosphere and proceed into space. There is no way to eliminate a skip zone. The precise size of the zone is determined by the height and structure of the ionosphere, and therefore is variable.

What type of propagation allows signals to be heard in the transmitting station's skip zone?

A. Faraday rotation
B. Scatter
C. Chordal hop
D. Short-path

G3C09 Answer: B. Scatter radio wave propagation allows a signal to be detected at a distance too far for ground wave propagation but too near for normal sky-wave propagation.

What is near vertical incidence skywave (NVIS) propagation?

A. Propagation near the MUF
B. Short distance MF or HF propagation at high elevation angles
C. Long path HF propagation at sunrise and sunset
D. Double hop propagation near the LUF

G3C10 Answer: B. Near vertical incidence skywave (NVIS) propagation is short distance MF or HF propagation at high elevation angles.

Which ionospheric region is the most absorbent of signals below 10 MHz during daylight hours?

A. The F2 region
B. The F1 region
C. The E region
D. The D region

G3C11 Answer: D. The D region of the ionosphere is the most absorbent of signals below 10 MHz during daylight hours.

G4 – Amateur Radio Practices

G4A – Station Configuration and Operation

What is the purpose of the notch filter found on many HF transceivers?

A. To restrict the transmitter voice bandwidth
B. To reduce interference from carriers in the receiver passband
C. To eliminate receiver interference from impulse noise sources
D. To remove interfering splatter generated by signals on adjacent frequencies

G4A01 Answer: B. The purpose of the notch filter found on many HF transceivers is to reduce interference from carriers in the receiver passband. A notch filter is a form of band-stop filter in which the stopband is particularly narrow (that is, it has a high Q factor). A band-stop filter, also known as a band-rejection filter, minimizes the frequencies within a specific range. This sort of filter is effective for eliminating a single interfering tone.

What is the benefit of using the opposite or "reverse" sideband when receiving CW?

A. Interference from impulse noise will be eliminated
B. More stations can be accommodated within a given signal passband
C. It may be possible to reduce or eliminate interference from other signals
D. Accidental out-of-band operation can be prevented

G4A02 Answer: C. One advantage of selecting the opposite or "reverse" sideband when receiving CW is that it may be possible to reduce or eliminate interference from other signals.

How does a noise blanker work?

A. By temporarily increasing received bandwidth
B. By redirecting noise pulses into a filter capacitor
C. By reducing receiver gain during a noise pulse
D. By clipping noise peaks

G4A03 Answer: C. A noise blanker works by reducing receiver gain during a noise pulse.

What is the effect on plate current of the correct setting of a vacuum-tube RF power amplifier's TUNE control?

A. A pronounced peak
B. A pronounced dip
C. No change will be observed
D. A slow, rhythmic oscillation

G4A04 Answer: B. A plate current of the correct setting of a vacuum-tube RF power amplifier's TUNE control will produce a pronounced dip. An RF power amplifier is used to change a low-power radio-frequency signal into a stronger signal. RF power amplifiers typically have excellent heat dissipation, output compression, gain, and return loss on the input and output.

Why is automatic level control (ALC) used with an RF power amplifier?

A. To balance the transmitter audio frequency response
B. To reduce harmonic radiation
C. To prevent excessive drive
D. To increase overall efficiency

G4A05 Answer: C. The purpose of using automatic level control with a RF power amplifier is to prevent excessive drive.

What is the purpose of an antenna tuner?

A. Reduce the SWR in the feed line to the antenna
B. Reduce the power dissipation in the feedline to the antenna
C. Increase power transfer from the transmitter to the feed line
D. All these choices are correct

G4A06 Answer: C. The purpose of an antenna tuner is to increase power transfer from the transmitter to the feed line.

What happens as a receiver's noise reduction control level is increased?

A. Received signals may become distorted
B. Received frequency may become unstable
C. CW signals may become severely attenuated
D. Received frequency may shift several kHz

G4A07 Answer: A. Received signals may become distorted when a receiver's noise reduction control level is increased.

What is the correct adjustment for the LOAD or COUPLING control of a vacuum tube RF power amplifier?

A. Minimum SWR on the antenna
B. Minimum plate current without exceeding maximum allowable grid current
C. Highest plate voltage while minimizing grid current
D. Desired power output without exceeding maximum allowable plate current

G4A08 Answer: D. The correct adjustment for the load or coupling control of a vacuum tube RF power amplifier is desired power output without exceeding maximum allowable plate current.

What is the purpose of delaying RF output after activating a transmitter's keying line to an external amplifier?

A. To prevent key clicks on CW
B. To prevent transient overmodulation
C. To allow time for the amplifier to switch the antenna between the transceiver and the amplifier output
D. To allow time for the amplifier power supply to reach operating level

G4A09 Answer: C. The purpose of delaying RF output after activating a transmitter's keying line to an external amplifier is to allow time for the amplifier to switch the antenna between the transceiver and the amplifier output.

What is the function of an electronic keyer?

A. Automatic transmit/receive switching
B. Automatic generation of dots and dashes for CW operation
C. To allow time for switching the antenna from the receiver to the transmitter
D. Computer interface for PSK and RTTY operation

G4A10 Answer: B. The purpose of an electronic keyer is the automatic generation of dots and dashes for CW operation.

Why should the ALC system be inactive when transmitting AFSK data signals?

A. ALC will invert the modulation of the AFSK mode
B. The ALC action distorts the signal
C. When using digital modes, too much ALC activity can cause the transmitter to overheat
D. All these choices are correct

G4A11 Answer: B. The ALC system should be inactive when transmitting AFSK data signals because the ALC action distorts the signal.

Which of the following is a common use of the dual-VFO feature on a transceiver?

A. To allow transmitting on two frequencies at once
B. To permit full duplex operation — that is, transmitting and receiving at the same time
C. To transmit on one frequency and listen on another
D. To improve frequency accuracy by allowing variable frequency output (VFO) operation

G4A12 Answer: C. One common use for the dual VFO feature on a transceiver is to ease the process of monitoring the transmit and receive frequencies when they are not the same. The variable frequency oscillator (VFO) is the circuit in a transmitter or receiver that is used for controlling the operating frequency.

What is the purpose of using a receive attenuator?

A. To prevent receiver overload from strong incoming signals
B. To reduce the transmitter power when driving a linear amplifier
C. To reduce power consumption when operating from batteries
D. To reduce excessive audio level on strong signals

G4A13 Answer: A. A receive attenuator diminishes the power of the radio signal without altering its waveform significantly. One way to think of an attenuator is as the opposite of an amplifier.

G4B – Tests and Test Equipment

What item of test equipment contains horizontal and vertical channel amplifiers?

A. An ohmmeter
B. A signal generator
C. An ammeter
D. An oscilloscope

G4B01 Answer: D. An oscilloscope contains horizontal and vertical channel amplifiers. An oscilloscope enables the user to observe a continuous variation of signal voltages. In most cases, this variation is displayed as a graph in which electrical potential difference is on the y-axis and time is on the x-axis.

Which of the following is an advantage of an oscilloscope versus a digital voltmeter?

A. An oscilloscope uses less power
B. Complex impedances can be easily measured
C. Greater precision
D. Complex waveforms can be measured

G4B02 Answer: D. One advantage of an oscilloscope versus a digital voltmeter is that complex waveforms can be measured. A digital voltmeter is an effective tool for measuring electrical potential difference between two distinct points in an electric circuit; it employs an analog-to-digital converter to create a numerical reading of voltage.

Which of the following is the best instrument to use for checking the keying waveform of a CW transmitter?

A. An oscilloscope
B. A field strength meter
C. A sidetone monitor
D. A wavemeter

G4B03 Answer: A. An oscilloscope is the best instrument to use for checking the keying waveform of a CW transmitter. An oscilloscope assesses the change of an electrical signal over time, and creates a graphical representation of the alterations in voltage and time. The resulting shape is called a waveform.

What signal source is connected to the vertical input of an oscilloscope when checking the RF envelope pattern of a transmitted signal?

A. The local oscillator of the transmitter
B. An external RF oscillator
C. The transmitter balanced mixer output
D. The attenuated RF output of the transmitter

G4B04 Answer: D. When checking the RF envelope pattern of a transmitted signal, the attenuated RF output of the transmitter is connected to the vertical input of an oscilloscope.

Why do voltmeters have high input impedance?

A. It improves the frequency response
B. It allows for higher voltages to be safely measured
C. It improves the resolution of the readings
D. It decreases the loading on circuits being measured

G4B05 Answer: D. Voltmeters have high input impedance because it decreases the loading on circuits being measured.

What is an advantage of a digital multimeter as compared to an analog multimeter?

A. Better for measuring computer circuits
B. Less prone to overload
C. Higher precision
D. Faster response

G4B06 Answer: C. One advantage of a digital multimeter over an analog multimeter is that a digital multimeter has higher precision.

What signals are used to conduct a two-tone test?

A. Two audio signals of the same frequency shifted 90 degrees
B. Two non-harmonically related audio signals
C. Two swept frequency tones
D. Two audio frequency range square wave signals of equal amplitude

G4B07 Answer: B. A two-tone test is conducted with two non-harmonically related audio signals.

What transmitter performance parameter does a two-tone test analyze?

A. Linearity
B. Percentage of suppression of the carrier and undesired sideband for SSB
C. Percentage of frequency modulation
D. Percentage of carrier phase shift

G4B08 Answer: A. Linearity is the transmitter performance parameter that a two-tone test analyzes.

When is an analog multimeter preferred to a digital multimeter?

A. When testing logic circuits
B. When high precision is desired
C. When measuring the frequency of an oscillator
D. When adjusting circuits for maximum or minimum values

G4B09 Answer: D. When adjusting circuits for maximum or minimum values, an analog multimeter is preferred to a digital multimeter.

Which of the following can be determined with a directional wattmeter?

A. Standing wave ratio
B. Antenna front-to-back ratio
C. RF interference
D. Radio wave propagation

G4B10 Answer: A. Standing wave ratio can be determined with a directional wattmeter. The standing wave ratio is the relationship of the amplitude of a partial standing wave at an antinode to the amplitude at the next node. Standing wave ratio, or SWR, is often used as an indicator of the efficiency of a radio frequency transmission. The best possible SWR is 1:1, which would mean that the entirety of the power is reaching its destination, and no part of the signal is reflected.

Which of the following must be connected to an antenna analyzer when it is being used for SWR measurements?

A. Receiver
B. Transmitter
C. Antenna and feed line
D. All these choices are correct

G4B11 Answer: C. An antenna and feed line must be connected to an antenna analyzer when it is being used for SWR measurements. Antenna analyzers are used for measuring the efficiency of antenna systems in radio electronics applications.

What effect can strong signals from nearby transmitters have on an antenna analyzer?

A. Desensitization which can cause intermodulation products which interfere with impedance readings
B. Received power that interferes with SWR readings
C. Generation of harmonics which interfere with frequency readings
D. All these choices are correct

G4B12 Answer: B. Received power that interferes with SWR readings can result from strong signals from nearby transmitters have on an antenna analyzer.

Which of the following can be measured with an antenna analyzer?

A. Front-to-back ratio of an antenna
B. Power output from a transmitter
C. Impedance of coaxial cable
D. Gain of a directional antenna

G4B13 Answer: C. An antenna analyzer can measure the impedance of coaxial cable.

G4C – Interference to Consumer Electronics; Grounding and Bonding

Which of the following might be useful in reducing RF interference to audio frequency circuits?

A. Bypass inductor
B. Bypass capacitor
C. Forward-biased diode
D. Reverse-biased diode

G4C01 Answer: B. A bypass capacitor might be useful in reducing RF interference to audio frequency circuits. A bypass capacitor, otherwise known as a decoupling capacitor, is a device for separating the various parts of an electrical circuit. The result of using a bypass capacitor is that noise created in one part of the system can be removed from the other parts.

Which of the following could be a cause of interference covering a wide range of frequencies?

A. Not using a balun or line isolator to feed balanced antennas
B. Lack of rectification of the transmitter's signal in power conductors
C. Arcing at a poor electrical connection
D. Using a balun to feed an unbalanced antenna

G4C02 Answer: C. One cause of interference over a wide range of frequencies could be arcing at a poor electrical connection. Arcing is the flow of current through media that normally do not conduct, as for instance air.

What sound is heard from an audio device experiencing RF interference from a single sideband phone transmitter?

A. A steady hum whenever the transmitter is on the air
B. On-and-off humming or clicking
C. Distorted speech
D. Clearly audible speech

G4C03 Answer: C. An audio device experiencing interference from a single sideband phone transmitter will produce distorted speech.

What sound is heard from an audio device experiencing RF interference from a CW transmitter?

A. On-and-off humming or clicking
B. A CW signal at a nearly pure audio frequency
C. A chirpy CW signal
D. Severely distorted audio

G4C04 Answer: A. An audio device may present on-and-off humming or clicking if there is interference from a CW transmitter.

What is a possible cause of high voltages that produce RF burns?

A. Flat braid rather than round wire has been used for the ground wire
B. Insulated wire has been used for the ground wire
C. The ground rod is resonant
D. The ground wire has high impedance on that frequency

G4C05 Answer: D. If the ground wire has high impedance on a particular HF band, you may receive an RF burn when touching your equipment while transmitting on that frequency.

What is a possible effect of a resonant ground connection?

A. Overheating of ground straps
B. Corrosion of the ground rod
C. High RF voltages on the enclosures of station equipment
D. A ground loop

G4C06 Answer: C. A resonant ground connection may cause high RF voltages on the enclosures of station equipment. A ground connection is any connection made to the ground for the purposes of safety. A ham radio operator may establish indoor or outdoor ground connections.

Why should soldered joints not be used in lightning protection ground connections?

A. A soldered joint will likely be destroyed by the heat of a lightning strike
B. Solder flux will prevent a low conductivity connection
C. Solder has too high a dielectric constant to provide adequate lightning protection
D. All these choices are correct

G4C07 Answer: A. Soldered joints should not be used in lightning protection ground connections because they will likely be destroyed by the heat of a lightning strike.

Which of the following would reduce RF interference caused by common-mode current on an audio cable?

A. Place a ferrite choke on the cable
B. Connect the center conductor to the shield of all cables to short circuit the RFI signal
C. Ground the center conductor of the audio cable causing the interference
D. Add an additional insulating jacket to the cable

G4C08 Answer: A. Placing a ferrite choke on the cable would reduce RF interference caused by common-mode current on an audio cable. Ferrite chokes are passive electric components capable of diminishing high frequency noise in electronic circuits. The choke itself is a ceramic cylinder, which operates by concentrating the magnetic field, which has the effect of increasing the inductance and thereby increasing the reactance. The increased reactance impedes the unwanted noise.

How can the effects of ground loops be minimized?

A. Connect all ground conductors in series
B. Connect the AC neutral conductor to the ground wire
C. Avoid using lock washers and star washers when making ground connections
D. Bond equipment enclosures together

G4C09 Answer: D. The effect of ground loops can be minimized by connecting all ground conductors to a single point. A ground loop is an unexpected and unwanted current flowing between two points that are incorrectly believed to have the same electric potential. The most common consequences of a ground loop are noise and interference, but there can also be a risk of electric shock. Some other strategies for reducing the risk of ground loop are to position the most powerful devices closest to the power source, to use differential signals, and to check isolated power supplies for component, parasitic, or internal PCB power plane capacitance.

What could be a symptom caused by a ground loop in your station's audio connections?

A. You receive reports of "hum" on your station's transmitted signal
B. The SWR reading for one or more antennas is suddenly very high
C. An item of station equipment starts to draw excessive amounts of current
D. You receive reports of harmonic interference from your station

G4C10 Answer: A. If you receive reports of "hum" on your station's transmitted signal, this may be a symptom of a ground loop. Ground loops are often responsible for noise and interference, and in some cases may even present a risk of electric shock.

What technique helps to minimize RF "hot spots" in an amateur station?

A. Building all equipment in a metal enclosure
B. Using surge suppressor power outlets
C. Bonding all equipment enclosures together
D. Placing low-pass filters on all feed lines

G4C11 Answer: C. Bonding all equipment enclosures together helps to minimize RF "hot spots" in an amateur station.

Why must all metal enclosures of station equipment be grounded?

A. It prevents a blown fuse in the event of an internal short circuit
B. It prevents signal overload
C. It ensures that the neutral wire is grounded
D. It ensures that hazardous voltages cannot appear on the chassis

G4C12 Answer: D. Grounding all metal enclosures of station equipment ensures that hazardous voltages cannot appear on the chassis.

G4D – Speech Processors; S Meters; Sideband Operation Near Band Edges

What is the purpose of a speech processor in a transceiver?

A. Increase the apparent loudness of transmitted voice signals
B. Increase transmitter bass response for more natural-sounding SSB signals
C. Prevent distortion of voice signals
D. Decrease high-frequency voice output to prevent out-of-band operation

G4D01 Answer: A. The purpose of a speech processor in a transceiver is to increase the apparent loudness of transmitted voice signals. A speech processor is able to clean up voice communications so that they are easier to understand.

How does a speech processor affect a single sideband phone signal?

A. It increases peak power
B. It increases average power
C. It reduces harmonic distortion
D. It reduces intermodulation distortion

G4D02 Answer: B. A speech processor increases the average power of a single sideband phone signal. This is one of the ways in which it improves the general clarity and intelligibility of the voice signal.

What is the effect of an incorrectly adjusted speech processor?

A. Distorted speech
B. Excess intermodulation products
C. Excessive background noise
D. All these choices are correct

G4D03 Answer: D. Distorted speech, excess intermodulation products, and excessive background pickup can all result from an incorrectly adjusted speech processor.

What does an S meter measure?

A. Carrier suppression
B. Impedance
C. Received signal strength
D. Transmitter power output

G4D04 Answer: C. An S meter measures received signal strength. An S meter, otherwise known as a signal strength meter, indicates signal strength on an arbitrary scale ranging from S1 to S9. Ham radio operators will often use the expression "S unit" to describe the amount of change in signal strength required to move the S meter from one level to an adjacent level on the S meter.

How does a signal that reads 20 dB over S9 compare to one that reads S9 on a receiver, assuming a properly calibrated S meter?

A. It is 10 times less powerful
B. It is 20 times less powerful
C. It is 20 times more powerful
D. It is 100 times more powerful

G4D05 Answer: D. Assuming a properly calibrated S meter, an S meter reading of 20 dB over S-9 is 100 times stronger than an S-9 signal.

How much change in signal strength is typically represented by one S unit?

A. 6 dB
B. 12 dB
C. 15 dB
D. 18 dB

G4D06 Answer: A. One S unit typically represents a 6 dB change in signal strength.

How much must the power output of a transmitter be raised to change the S meter reading on a distant receiver from S8 to S9?

A. Approximately 1.5 times
B. Approximately 2 times
C. Approximately 4 times
D. Approximately 8 times

G4D07 Answer: C. The power output of a transmitter must be raised approximately four times to change the S-meter reading on a distant receiver from S8 to S9.

What frequency range is occupied by a 3 kHz LSB signal when the displayed carrier frequency is set to 7.178 MHz?

A. 7.178 MHz to 7.181 MHz
B. 7.178 MHz to 7.184 MHz
C. 7.175 MHz to 7.178 MHz
D. 7.1765 MHz to 7.1795 MHz

G4D08 Answer: C. A 3 kHz LSB signal occupies a frequency range of 7.175 to 7.178 MHz when the displayed carrier frequency is set to 7.178MHz.

What frequency range is occupied by a 3 kHz USB signal with the displayed carrier frequency set to 14.347 MHz?

A. 14.347 MHz to 14.647 MHz
B. 14.347 MHz to 14.350 MHz
C. 14.344 MHz to 14.347 MHz
D. 14.3455 MHz to 14.3485 MHz

G4D09 Answer: B. A 3 kHz USB signal with the displayed carrier frequency set to 14.347 MHz occupies a frequency range from 14.347 to 14.350 MHz.

How close to the lower edge of a band's phone segment should your displayed carrier frequency be when using 3 kHz wide LSB?

A. At least 3 kHz above the edge of the segment
B. At least 3 kHz below the edge of the segment
C. At least 1 kHz below the edge of the segment
D. At least 1 kHz above the edge of the segment

G4D10 Answer: A. Your displayed carrier frequency, when using 3 kHz wide LSB, should be at least 3 kHz above the lower edge of a band's phone segment.

How close to the upper edge of a band's phone segment should your displayed carrier frequency be when using 3 kHz wide USB?

A. At least 3 kHz above the edge of the band
B. At least 3 kHz below the edge of the band
C. At least 1 kHz above the edge of the segment
D. At least 1 kHz below the edge of the segment

G4D11 Answer: B. Your displayed carrier frequency, when using 3 kHz wide USB, should be at least 3 kHz below the upper edge of a band's phone segment.

G4E – Mobile and Portable HF Stations; Alternative Energy Source Operation

What is the purpose of a capacitance hat on a mobile antenna?

A. To increase the power handling capacity of a whip antenna
B. To reduce radiation resistance
C. To electrically lengthen a physically short antenna
D. To lower the radiation angle

G4E01 Answer: C. When referring to a mobile antenna, a "capacitance hat" is a device to electrically lengthen a physically short antenna. Capacitance hats may be composed of a metal disk, a wire basket, or a pyramid of wires. The capacitance hat regulates the flow of current through the antenna, so that more of the signal will propagate at the top. This has the effect of increasing the functional length of the antenna.

What is the purpose of a corona ball on an HF mobile antenna?

A. To narrow the operating bandwidth of the antenna
B. To increase the "Q" of the antenna
C. To reduce the chance of damage if the antenna should strike an object
D. To reduce RF voltage discharge from the tip of the antenna while transmitting

G4E02 Answer: D. The purpose of a corona ball on an HF mobile antenna is to reduce RF voltage discharge from the tip of the antenna while transmitting.

Which of the following direct, fused power connections would be the best for a 100-watt HF mobile installation?

A. To the battery using heavy-gauge wire
B. To the alternator or generator using heavy-gauge wire
C. To the battery using insulated heavy duty balanced transmission line
D. To the alternator or generator using insulated heavy duty balanced transmission line

G4E03 Answer: A. A direct, fused power connection to the battery using heavy gauge wire would be better than a direct, fused connection to the alternator or generator using heavy gauge wire. It would also be better than direct, fused power connections to the battery or to the alternator or generator using resistor wire.

Why should DC power for a 100-watt HF transceiver not be supplied by a vehicle's auxiliary power socket?

A. The socket is not wired with an RF-shielded power cable
B. The socket's wiring may be inadequate for the current drawn by the transceiver
C. The DC polarity of the socket is reversed from the polarity of modern HF transceivers
D. Drawing more than 50 watts from this socket could cause the engine to overheat

G4E04 Answer: B. It is best not to draw the DC power for a 100-watt HF transceiver from a vehicle's auxiliary power socket because the socket's wiring may be inadequate for the current being drawn by the transceiver.

Which of the following most limits an HF mobile installation?

A. "Picket fencing"
B. The wire gauge of the DC power line to the transceiver
C. Efficiency of the electrically short antenna
D. FCC rules limiting mobile output power on the 75-meter band

G4E05 Answer: C. The efficiency of the electrically short antenna is a significant limiting factor for an HF mobile station.

What is one disadvantage of using a shortened mobile antenna as opposed to a full-size antenna?

A. Short antennas are more likely to cause distortion of transmitted signals
B. Q of the antenna will be very low
C. Operating bandwidth may be very limited
D. Harmonic radiation may increase

G4E06 Answer: C. One disadvantage of using a shortened mobile antenna as opposed to a full size antenna is that operating bandwidth may be very limited.

Which of the following may cause receive interference to an HF transceiver installed in a vehicle?

A. The battery charging system
B. The fuel delivery system
C. The control computers
D. All these choices are correct

G4E07 Answer: D. The battery charging system, the fuel delivery system, and the control computers may cause receive interference in an HF transceiver installed in a vehicle.

In what configuration are the individual cells in a solar panel connected together?

A. Series-parallel
B. Shunt
C. Bypass
D. Full-wave bridge

G4E08 Answer: A. The individual cells in a solar panel connected together in a series-parallel configuration.

What is the approximate open-circuit voltage from a fully illuminated silicon photovoltaic cell?

A. 0.02 VDC
B. 0.5 VDC
C. 0.2 VDC
D. 1.38 VDC

G4E09 Answer: B. The approximate open-circuit voltage from a modern, well-illuminated photovoltaic cell is 0.5 VDC.

Why should a series diode be connected between a solar panel and a storage battery that is being charged by the panel?

A. To prevent overload by regulating the charging voltage
B. To prevent discharge of the battery through the panel during times of low or no illumination
C. To limit the current flowing from the panel to a safe value
D. To prevent damage to the battery due to excessive voltage at high illumination levels

G4E10 Answer: B. A series diode is connected between a solar panel and a storage battery that is being charged by the panel to prevent discharge of the battery through the panel during times of low or no illumination. Diodes are two-terminal electronic components that offer little resistance in one direction and total resistance in the other.

What precaution should be taken when connecting a solar panel to a lithium iron phosphate battery?

A. Ground the solar panel outer metal framework
B. Ensure the battery is placed terminals-up
C. A series resistor must be in place
D. The solar panel must have a charge controller

G4E11 Answer: D. When connecting a solar panel to a lithium iron phosphate battery, the solar panel must have a charge controller.

G5 – Electrical Principles

G5A – Reactance; Inductance; Capacitance; Impedance; Impedance Transformation; Resonance

What happens when inductive and capacitive reactance are equal in a series LC circuit?

A. Resonance causes impedance to be very high
B. Impedance is equal to the geometric mean of the inductance and capacitance
C. Resonance causes impedance to be very low
D. Impedance is equal to the arithmetic mean of the inductance and capacitance

G5A01 Answer: C. Resonance causes impedance to be very low when inductive and capacitive reactance are equal in a series LC circuit.

What is reactance?

A. Opposition to the flow of direct current caused by resistance
B. Opposition to the flow of alternating current caused by capacitance or inductance
C. Reinforcement of the flow of direct current caused by resistance
D. Reinforcement of the flow of alternating current caused by capacitance or inductance

G5A02 Answer: B. Reactance is opposition to the flow of alternating current caused by capacitance or inductance. The amount of reactance in a circuit element depends on the inductance or capacitance of the element. If there is an established electric field, it will work against the voltage change on the element. At the same time, a magnetic field will have a natural resistance to a change in current. A perfect resistor will have a reactance of zero, while perfect inductors and capacitors will be entirely composed of reactance. This is because an ideal inductor will have zero resistance, and an ideal capacitor will have infinite resistance.

Which of the following is opposition to the flow of alternating current in an inductor?

A. Conductance
B. Reluctance
C. Admittance
D. Reactance

G5A03 Answer: D. Reactance is opposition to the flow of alternating current in an inductor. Another way of expressing this is that reactance is the opposition to the change in current caused by inductance.

Which of the following is opposition to the flow of alternating current in a capacitor?

A. Conductance
B. Reluctance
C. Reactance
D. Admittance

G5A04 Answer: C. Reactance is opposition to the flow of alternating current in a capacitor. Another way of expressing this is that reactance is the opposition to the change in voltage caused by capacitance.

How does an inductor react to AC?

A. As the frequency of the applied AC increases, the reactance decreases
B. As the amplitude of the applied AC increases, the reactance increases
C. As the amplitude of the applied AC increases, the reactance decreases
D. As the frequency of the applied AC increases, the reactance increases

G5A05 Answer: D. As the frequency of the applied AC increases, the reactance of an inductor increases. An inductor is a passive electrical component with two terminals. Its function is to resist alterations in an electric current. The most common structure of an inductor is a coil of wire. The passage of current through the wire creates a magnetic field; when the current changes, a voltage is produced by the inductor. The inductance of the component is the ratio of the voltage to the rate of change of current.

How does a capacitor react to AC?

A. As the frequency of the applied AC increases, the reactance decreases
B. As the frequency of the applied AC increases, the reactance increases
C. As the amplitude of the applied AC increases, the reactance increases
D. As the amplitude of the applied AC increases, the reactance decreases

G5A06 Answer: A. As the frequency of the applied AC increases, the reactance of a capacitor decreases. A capacitor is a passive electrical component with two terminals. Its function is to store energy in an electrical field. The basic structure of a capacitor is a pair of conductors separated by a dielectric, or insulator. However, there are capacitors that are much more complex. The capacitor operates by creating a potential difference between the conductors, which produces an electric field across the dielectric. That is, one of the plates of the dielectric has a positive charge, and the other has a negative charge. This electrostatic field becomes a repository of energy.

What is the term for the inverse of impedance?

A. Conductance
B. Susceptance
C. Reluctance
D. Admittance

G5A07 Answer: D. Admittance is the inverse of impedance.

What is impedance?

A. The ratio of current to voltage
B. The product of current and voltage
C. The ratio of voltage to current
D. The product of current and reactance

G5A08 Answer: C. Impedance is the opposition to the flow of current in an AC circuit. Another way of describing impedance is as the ratio of the voltage to the current in an alternating current circuit. Whereas resistance has only magnitude, impedance has both magnitude and phase. The concept of impedance is necessary for alternating current because they have the electrostatic storage of charge induced by voltages between conductors, or capacitance, and the induction of voltages in conductors that is self induced by the magnetic fields of the currents, known as inductance.

What unit is used to measure reactance?

A. Farad
B. Ohm
C. Ampere
D. Siemens

G5A09 Answer: B. The ohm is used to measure reactance. Specifically, the ohm is equal to the resistance created between two points of a conductor when a continuous potential difference of one volt is applied and produces a current of one ampere. The multimeter is the standard instrument for measuring resistance in ohms.

Which of the following devices can be used for impedance matching at radio frequencies?

A. A transformer
B. A Pi-network
C. A length of transmission line
D. All these choices are correct

G5A10 Answer: D. A transformer, a Pi-network, and a length of transmission line can all be used for impedance matching at radio frequencies.

What letter is used to represent reactance?

A. Z
B. X
C. B
D. Y

G5A11 Answer: B. The letter X is used to represent reactance.

What occurs in an LC circuit at resonance?

A. Current and voltage are equal
B. Resistance is cancelled
C. The circuit radiates all its energy in the form of radio waves
D. Inductive reactance and capacitive reactance cancel

G5A12 Answer: D. When an LC circuit is at resonance, inductive reactance and capacitive reactance cancel.

G5B – The Decibel; Current and Voltage Dividers; Electrical Power Calculations; Sine Wave Root-Mean-Square (RMS) Values; PEP Calculations

What dB change represents a factor of two increase or decrease in power?

A. Approximately 2 dB
B. Approximately 3 dB
C. Approximately 6 dB
D. Approximately 9 dB

G5B01 Answer: B. A two-times increase or decrease in power results in a change of approximately 3 dB. The amount of decibel change produced by a change in power is a proportional relationship.

How does the total current relate to the individual currents in a circuit of parallel resistors?

A. It equals the average of the branch currents
B. It decreases as more parallel branches are added to the circuit
C. It equals the sum of the currents through each branch
D. It is the sum of the reciprocal of each individual voltage drop

G5B02 Answer: C. The total current equals the sum of the individual currents in each branch of a parallel circuit.

How many watts of electrical power are consumed if 400 VDC is supplied to an 800-ohm load?

A. 0.5 watts
B. 200 watts
C. 400 watts
D. 3200 watts

G5B03 Answer: B. If 400 VDC is supplied to an 800-ohm load, 200 watts of electrical power are consumed. The amount of power used is calculated by dividing the voltage by the resistance and then multiplying by 100.

How many watts of electrical power are consumed by a 12 VDC light bulb that draws 0.2 amperes?

A. 2.4 watts
B. 24 watts
C. 6 watts
D. 60 watts

G5B04 Answer: A. A 12-VDC light bulb that draws 0.2 amperes uses 2.4 watts of electrical power. The amount of electrical power used is calculated by dividing the voltage by the amperage.

How many watts are consumed when a current of 7.0 milliamperes flows through a 1,250-ohm resistance?

A. Approximately 61 milliwatts
B. Approximately 61 watts
C. Approximately 11 milliwatts
D. Approximately 11 watts

G5B05 Answer: A. When a current of 7.0 milliamperes flows through 1.25 kilohms, approximately 61 milliwatts are consumed.

What is the PEP produced by 200 volts peak-to-peak across a 50-ohm dummy load?

A. 1.4 watts
B. 100 watts
C. 353.5 watts
D. 400 watts

G5B06 Answer: B. The PEP produced by 200 volts peak-to-peak across a 50-ohm dummy load is 100 watts. Peak envelope power is calculated by dividing the square of the voltage by the resistance.

What value of an AC signal produces the same power dissipation in a resistor as a DC voltage of the same value?

A. The peak-to-peak value
B. The peak value
C. The RMS value
D. The reciprocal of the RMS value

G5B07 Answer: C. The RMS value of an AC signal results in the same power dissipation as a DC voltage of the same value. RMS (root mean square) value is necessary for determining the amount of power being dissipated by an electrical resistance. The RMS value is only required for this purpose when the current is varying over time.

What is the peak-to-peak voltage of a sine wave with an RMS voltage of 120 volts?

A. 84.8 volts
B. 169.7 volts
C. 240.0 volts
D. 339.4 volts

G5B08 Answer: D. The peak-to-peak voltage of a sine wave with an RMS voltage of 120.0 volts is 2sqrt(2)*Vrms=339.4 volts.

What is the RMS voltage of a sine wave with a value of 17 volts peak?

A. 8.5 volts
B. 12 volts
C. 24 volts
D. 34 volts

G5B09 Answer: B. The RMS voltage of a sine wave with a value of 17 volts peak is 12 volts. RMS voltage is calculated by dividing the peak voltage by 1.414.

What percentage of power loss is equivalent to a loss of 1 dB?

A. 10.9 percent
B. 12.2 percent
C. 20.6 percent
D. 25.9 percent

G5B10 Answer: C. A line loss of 1 dB is equivalent to a power loss of 20.5%.

What is the ratio of PEP to average power for an unmodulated carrier?

A. 0.707
B. 1.00
C. 1.414
D. 2.00

G5B11 Answer: B. The ratio of peak envelope power to average power for an unmodulated carrier is 1.00. Peak envelope power is the highest envelope power a transmitter can deliver to the antenna transmission line during an undistorted RF cycle.

What is the RMS voltage across a 50-ohm dummy load dissipating 1,200 watts?

A. 173 volts
B. 245 volts
C. 346 volts
D. 692 volts

G5B12 Answer: B. The RMS voltage across a 50-ohm dummy load dissipating 1,200 watts would be 245 volts. The RMS voltage is calculated by finding the square root of the product of the load and the dissipated power.

What is the output PEP of an unmodulated carrier if the average power is 1,060 watts?

A. 530 watts
B. 1060 watts
C. 1500 watts
D. 2120 watts

G5B13 Answer: B. The output PEP of an unmodulated carrier if an average reading wattmeter connected to the transmitter output indicates 1,060 watts is 1,060 watts.

What is the output PEP of 500 volts peak-to-peak across a 50-ohm load?

A. 8.75 watts
B. 625 watts
C. 2500 watts
D. 5000 watts

G5B14 Answer: B. The output PEP of 500 volts peak-to-peak across a 50-ohm load would be 625 watts. First, peak-to-peak voltage is converted to RMS voltage by multiplying peak voltage (or, peak-to-peak divided by 2) it by 0.707. Then, the output PEP is found by squaring the RMS voltage and dividing it by the resistance.

G5C – Resistors, Capacitors, and Inductors in Series and Parallel; Transformers

What causes a voltage to appear across the secondary winding of a transformer when an AC voltage source is connected across its primary winding?

A. Capacitive coupling
B. Displacement current coupling
C. Mutual inductance
D. Mutual capacitance

G5C01 Answer: C. Mutual inductance causes a voltage to appear across the secondary winding of a transformer when an AC voltage source is connected across its primary winding. Mutual inductance exists when the current change in one inductor initiates a voltage in some other inductor.

What is the output voltage if an input signal is applied to the secondary winding of a 4:1 voltage step-down transformer instead of the primary winding?

A. The input voltage is multiplied by 4
B. The input voltage is divided by 4
C. Additional resistance must be added in series with the primary to prevent overload
D. Additional resistance must be added in parallel with the secondary to prevent overload

G5C02 Answer: A. If an input signal is applied to the secondary winding of a 4:1 voltage step-down transformer instead of the primary winding, then the output voltage is equal to the input voltage multiplied by 4.

What is the total resistance of a 10-, a 20-, and a 50-ohm resistor connected in parallel?

A. 5.9 ohms
B. 0.17 ohms
C. 17 ohms
D. 80 ohms

G5C03 Answer: A. The total resistance of a 10-, a 20-, and a 50-ohm resistor connected in parallel is 5.9 ohms. Total resistance of resistors in parallel is the reciprocal of the sum of their reciprocals:
$1/(1/10+1/20+1/50)=1/(10/100+5/100+2/100)=100/17\approx5.9$

What is the approximate total resistance of a 100- and a 200-ohm resistor in parallel?

A. 300 ohms
B. 150 ohms
C. 75 ohms
D. 67 ohms

G5C04 Answer: D. The total resistance of a 100- and a 200-ohm resistor connected in parallel is approximately 67 ohms. Total resistance of resistors in parallel is the reciprocal of the sum of their reciprocals:
$1/(1/100+1/200)=1/(2/200+1/200)=200/3\approx67$

Why is the primary winding wire of a voltage step-up transformer usually a larger size than that of the secondary winding?

A. To improve the coupling between the primary and secondary
B. To accommodate the higher current of the primary
C. To prevent parasitic oscillations due to resistive losses in the primary
D. To ensure that the volume of the primary winding is equal to the volume of the secondary winding

G5C05 Answer: B. The primary winding wire of a voltage step-up transformer is usually a larger size than that of the secondary winding to accommodate the higher current of the primary.

What is the voltage output of a transformer with a 500-turn primary and a 1500-turn secondary when 120 VAC is applied to the primary?

A. 360 volts
B. 120 volts
C. 40 volts
D. 25.5 volts

G5C06 Answer: A. The voltage output for a transformer with a 500-turn primary and a 1500-turn secondary when 120 VAC is applied to the primary is 360 volts.

What transformer turns ratio matches an antenna's 600-ohm feed point impedance to a 50-ohm coaxial cable?

A. 3.5 to 1
B. 12 to 1
C. 24 to 1
D. 144 to 1

G5C07 Answer: A. The turns ratio of a transformer used to match an antenna's 600-ohm feed point impedance to a 50-ohm coaxial cable is 3.5 to 1.

What is the equivalent capacitance of two 5.0-nanofarad capacitors and one 750-picofarad capacitor connected in parallel?

A. 576.9 nanofarads
B. 1,733 picofarads
C. 3,583 picofarads
D. 10.750 nanofarads

G5C08 Answer: D. The equivalent capacitance of two 5.0-nanofarad capacitors and one 750-picofarad capacitor connected in parallel would be 10,750 picofarads. The equivalent capacitance of capacitors in parallel is found by adding the individual capacitances.

What is the capacitance of three 100-microfarad capacitors connected in series?

A. 0.33 microfarads
B. 3.0 microfarads
C. 33.3 microfarads
D. 300 microfarads

G5C09 Answer: C. The capacitance of three 100-microfarad capacitors connected in series would be 33.3 microfarads. When all of the capacitors in a series have the same capacitance, the total capacitance can be calculated by dividing the capacitance of a single capacitor by the number of capacitors.

What is the inductance of three 10-millihenry inductors connected in parallel?

A. 0.30 henries
B. 3.3 henries
C. 3.3 millihenries
D. 30 millihenries

G5C10 Answer: C. The inductance of three 10-millihenry inductors connected in parallel would be 3.3 millihenries. One divided by the total inductance is equal to the sum of one divided by each of the individual inductances.

What is the inductance of a circuit with a 20-millihenry inductor connected in series with a 50-millihenry inductor?

A. 7 millihenries
B. 14.3 millihenries
C. 70 millihenries
D. 1,000 millihenries

G5C11 Answer: C. The inductance of a 20-millihenry inductor in series with a 50-millihenry inductor would be 70 millihenries. The total inductance of inductors connected in series is equal to the sum of the individual inductances.

What is the capacitance of a 20-microfarad capacitor connected in series with a 50-microfarad capacitor?

A. 0.07 microfarads
B. 14.3 microfarads
C. 70 microfarads
D. 1,000 microfarads

G5C12 Answer: B. The capacitance of a 20-microfarad capacitor in series with a 50-microfarad capacitor would be 14.3 microfarads. One divided by the total capacitance is equal to the sums of one divided by each of the individual capacitances.

Which of the following components should be added to a capacitor to increase the capacitance?

A. An inductor in series
B. An inductor in parallel
C. A capacitor in parallel
D. A capacitor in series

G5C13 Answer: C. Adding a capacitor in parallel with another capacitor would increase capacitance.

Which of the following components should be added to an inductor to increase the inductance?

A. A capacitor in series
B. A capacitor in parallel
C. An inductor in parallel
D. An inductor in series

G5C14 Answer: D. Adding an inductor in series to another inductor would increase the inductance.

G6 – Circuit Components

G6A – Resistors; Capacitors; Inductors; Rectifiers; Solid-State Diodes and Transistors; Vacuum Tubes; Batteries

What is the minimum allowable discharge voltage for maximum life of a standard 12-volt lead-acid battery?

A. 6 volts
B. 8.5 volts
C. 10.5 volts
D. 12 volts

G6A01 Answer: C. The minimum allowable discharge voltage for maximum life of a standard 12-volt lead acid battery is 10.5 volts.

What is an advantage of batteries with low internal resistance?

A. Long life
B. High discharge current
C. High voltage
D. Rapid recharge

G6A02 Answer: B. One advantage of batteries with low internal resistance is a high discharge current. Batteries convert chemical energy into electrical energy.

What is the approximate forward threshold voltage of a germanium diode?

A. 0.1 volt
B. 0.3 volts
C. 0.7 volts
D. 1.0 volts

G6A03 Answer: B. The approximate forward threshold voltage of a germanium diode is 0.3 volts. The forward threshold voltage is the amount of voltage the diode can handle.

Which of the following is characteristic of an electrolytic capacitor?

A. Tight tolerance
B. Much less leakage than any other type
C. High capacitance for a given volume
D. Inexpensive RF capacitor

G6A04 Answer: C. One characteristic of an electrolytic capacitor is a high capacitance for a given volume.

What is the approximate forward threshold voltage of a silicon junction diode?

A. 0.1 volt
B. 0.3 volts
C. 0.7 volts
D. 1.0 volts

G6A05 Answer: C. The approximate forward threshold voltage of a conventional silicon diode is 0.7 volts. The forward threshold voltage is the maximum amount of current that can be handled by a component without damage.

Why should wire-wound resistors not be used in RF circuits?

A. The resistor's tolerance value would not be adequate
B. The resistor's inductance could make circuit performance unpredictable
C. The resistor could overheat
D. The resistor's internal capacitance would detune the circuit

G6A06 Answer: B. One reason not to use wire-wound resistors in an RF circuit is that the resistor's inductance could make circuit performance unpredictable.

What are the operating points for a bipolar transistor used as a switch?

A. Saturation and cutoff
B. The active region (between cutoff and saturation)
C. Peak and valley current points
D. Enhancement and depletion modes

G6A07 Answer: A. The operating points for a bipolar transistor used as a switch are its saturation and cutoff regions.

Which of the following is characteristic of low voltage ceramic capacitors?

A. Tight tolerance
B. High stability
C. High capacitance for given volume
D. Comparatively low cost

G6A08 Answer: D. Low voltage ceramic capacitors have a comparatively low cost.

Which of the following describes MOSFET construction?

A. The gate is formed by a back-biased junction
B. The gate is separated from the channel by a thin insulating layer
C. The source is separated from the drain by a thin insulating layer
D. The source is formed by depositing metal on silicon

G6A09 Answer: B. In a MOSFET, the gate is separated from the channel by a thin insulating layer. A MOSFET, or metal-oxide-semiconductor field effect transistor, is used to switch or amplify electronic signals. A MOSFET has four terminals: source, gate, drain, and body.

Which element of a vacuum tube regulates the flow of electrons between cathode and plate?

A. Control grid
B. Suppressor grid
C. Screen grid
D. Trigger electrode

G6A10 Answer: A. The control grid of a vacuum tube is used to regulate the flow of electrons between cathode and plate.

What happens when an inductor is operated above its self-resonant frequency?

A. Its reactance increases
B. Harmonics are generated
C. It becomes capacitive
D. Catastrophic failure is likely

G6A11 Answer: C. When an inductor is operated above its self-resonant frequency it becomes capacitive.

What is the primary purpose of a screen grid in a vacuum tube?

A. To reduce grid-to-plate capacitance
B. To increase efficiency
C. To increase the control grid resistance
D. To decrease plate resistance

G6A12 Answer: A. The primary purpose of a screen grid in a vacuum tube is to reduce grid-to-plate capacitance. It is typical for the screen grid to be connected to a positive DC voltage that is set slightly lower than the plate voltage. The screen grid will also be bypassed to the cathode with a capacitor.

G6B – Analog and Digital Integrated Circuits (ICs); Microwave ICs (MMICs); Display Devices; RF Connectors; Ferrite Cores

What determines the performance of a ferrite core at different frequencies?

A. Its conductivity
B. Its thickness
C. The composition, or "mix," of materials used
D. The ratio of outer diameter to inner diameter

G6B01 Answer: C. The composition, or "mix," of materials used determines the performance of a ferrite core at different frequencies.

What is meant by the term MMIC?

A. Multi-Mode Integrated Circuit
B. Monolithic Microwave Integrated Circuit
C. Metal Monolayer Integrated Circuit
D. Mode Modulated Integrated Circuit

G6B02 Answer: B. The term MMIC means Monolithic Microwave Integrated Circuit. This is a type of integrated circuit that is capable of operating at microwave frequencies. The most common uses for these devices are high-frequency switching, low-noise amplification, power amplification, and microwave mixing.

Which of the following is an advantage of CMOS integrated circuits compared to TTL integrated circuits?

A. Low power consumption
B. High power handling capability
C. Better suited for RF amplification
D. Better suited for power supply regulation

G6B03 Answer: A. Low power consumption is one advantage of CMOS integrated circuits as compared to TTL integrated circuits. CMOS (complementary metal-oxide-semiconductor) circuits are commonly used in microcontrollers and microprocessors. These circuits also have a high noise immunity. They only use a little bit of power because at least one of the two transistors is always off. In a TTL (transistor-transistor logic) circuit, on the other hand, a great deal of power is wasted through the heat emission.

What is a typical upper frequency limit for low SWR operation of 50-ohm BNC connectors?

A. 50 MHz
B. 500 MHz
C. 4 GHz
D. 40 GHz

G6B04 Answer: C. A typical upper frequency limit for low SWR operation of 50-ohm BNC connectors is 4 GHz.

What is an advantage of using a ferrite core toroidal inductor?

A. Large values of inductance may be obtained
B. The magnetic properties of the core may be optimized for a specific range of frequencies
C. Most of the magnetic field is contained in the core
D. All these choices are correct

G6B05 Answer: D. There are several advantages of using a ferrite core toroidal inductor. To begin with, large values of inductance may be obtained. Also, the magnetic properties of the core may be optimized for a specific range of frequencies. Finally, most of the magnetic field is contained in the core. A toroidal inductor is a passive electronic component.

What kind of device is an integrated circuit operational amplifier?

A. Digital
B. MMIC
C. Programmable Logic
D. Analog

G6B06 Answer: D. An integrated circuit operational amplifier is analog.

Which of the following describes a type N connector?

A. A moisture-resistant RF connector useful to 10 GHz
B. A small bayonet connector used for data circuits
C. A low noise figure VHF connector
D. A nickel plated version of the PL-259

G6B07 Answer: A. A type-N connector is a moisture-resistant RF connector useful up to 10 GHz.

How is an LED biased when emitting light?

A. In the tunnel-effect region
B. At the Zener voltage
C. Reverse biased
D. Forward biased

G6B08 Answer: D. An LED is forward biased when emitting light.

How does a ferrite bead or core reduce common-mode RF current on the shield of a coaxial cable?

A. By creating an impedance in the current's path
B. It converts common-mode current to differential mode current
C. By creating an out-of-phase current to cancel the common-mode current
D. Ferrites expel magnetic fields

G6B10 Answer: A. A ferrite bead or core reduces common-mode RF current on the shield of a coaxial cable by creating an impedance in the current's path.

What is an SMA connector?

A. A type-S to type-M adaptor
B. A small threaded connector suitable for signals up to several GHz
C. A connector designed for serial multiple access signals
D. A type of push-on connector intended for high-voltage applications

G6B11 Answer: B. An SMA connector is a small threaded connector suitable for signals up to several GHz.

Which of these connector types is commonly used for low frequency or dc signal connections to a transceiver?

A. PL-259
B. BNC
C. RCA Phono
D. Type N

G6B12 Answer: C. RCA Phono connectors are commonly used for low frequency or dc signal connections to a transceiver.

G7 – Practical Circuits

G7A – Power Supplies; Schematic Symbols

What is the function of a power supply bleeder resistor?

A. It acts as a fuse for excess voltage
B. It discharges the filter capacitors when power is removed
C. It removes shock hazards from the induction coils
D. It eliminates ground loop current

G7A01 Answer: B. The power-supply bleeder resistor discharges the filter capacitors when power is removed.

Which of the following components are used in a power supply filter network?

A. Diodes
B. Transformers and transducers
C. Capacitors and inductors
D. All these choices are correct

G7A02 Answer: C. Capacitors and inductors are used in a power-supply filter network.

Which type of rectifier circuit uses two diodes and a center-tapped transformer?

A. Full-wave
B. Full-wave bridge
C. Half-wave
D. Synchronous

G7A03 Answer: A. A full-wave rectifier circuit uses two diodes and a center-tapped transformer.

What is characteristic of a half-wave rectifier in a power supply?

A. Only one diode is required
B. The ripple frequency is twice that of a full-wave rectifier
C. More current can be drawn from the half-wave rectifier
D. The output voltage is two times the peak input voltage

G7A04 Answer: A. In a half-wave rectifier in a power supply, only one diode is required.

What portion of the AC cycle is converted to DC by a half-wave rectifier?

A. 90 degrees
B. 180 degrees
C. 270 degrees
D. 360 degrees

G7A05 Answer: B. 180 degrees of the AC cycle is converted to DC by a half-wave rectifier. This device earns its name by rectifying half of the sine wave.

What portion of the AC cycle is converted to DC by a full-wave rectifier?

A. 90 degrees
B. 180 degrees
C. 270 degrees
D. 360 degrees

G7A06 Answer: D. 360 degrees of the AC cycle is converted to DC by a full-wave rectifier. In other words, a full-wave rectifier operates on the entirety of the sine wave.

What is the output waveform of an unfiltered full-wave rectifier connected to a resistive load?

A. A series of DC pulses at twice the frequency of the AC input
B. A series of DC pulses at the same frequency as the AC input
C. A sine wave at half the frequency of the AC input
D. A steady DC voltage

G7A07 Answer: A. The output waveform of an unfiltered full-wave rectifier connected to a resistive load is a series of DC pulses at twice the frequency of the AC input.

Which of the following is characteristic of a switchmode power supply as compared to a linear power supply?

A. Faster switching time makes higher output voltage possible
B. Fewer circuit components are required
C. High-frequency operation allows the use of smaller components
D. Inherently more stable

G7A08 Answer: C. One characteristic of a switchmode power supply as compared to a linear power supply is that high frequency operation allows the use of smaller components.

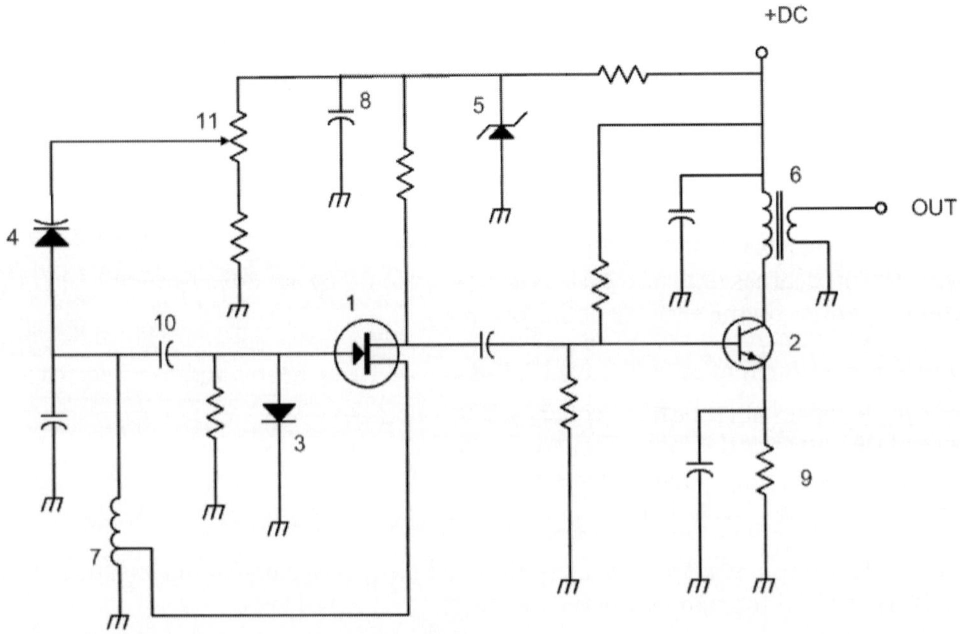

Figure G7-1

Which symbol in figure G7-1 represents a field effect transistor?

A. Symbol 2
B. Symbol 5
C. Symbol 1
D. Symbol 4

G7A09 Answer: C. In figure G7-1, symbol 1 represents a field effect transistor.

Which symbol in figure G7-1 represents a Zener diode?

A. Symbol 4
B. Symbol 1
C. Symbol 11
D. Symbol 5

G7A10 Answer: D. In figure G7-1, symbol 5 represents a Zener diode. A Zener diode is a semiconductor made of silicon, primarily used to regulate voltage. The positive characteristic of this diode is that it can maintain a fairly consistent voltage through a broad range of currents.

Which symbol in figure G7-1 represents an NPN junction transistor?

A. Symbol 1
B. Symbol 2
C. Symbol 7
D. Symbol 11

G7A11 Answer: B. In figure G7-1, symbol 2 represents an NPN junction transistor.

Which symbol in figure G7-1 represents a solid core transformer?

A. Symbol 4
B. Symbol 7
C. Symbol 6
D. Symbol 1

G7A12 Answer: C. In figure G7-1, symbol 6 represents a multiple-winding transformer.

Which symbol in figure G7-1 represents a tapped inductor?

A. Symbol 7
B. Symbol 11
C. Symbol 6
D. Symbol 1

G7A13 Answer: A. In figure G7-1, symbol 7 represents a tapped inductor.

G7B – Digital Circuits; Amplifiers and Oscillators

What is the purpose of neutralizing an amplifier?

A. To limit the modulation index
B. To eliminate self-oscillations
C. To cut off the final amplifier during standby periods
D. To keep the carrier on frequency

G7B01 Answer: B. The amplifier is neutralized to eliminate self-oscillations.

Which of these classes of amplifiers has the highest efficiency?

A. Class A
B. Class B
C. Class AB
D. Class C

G7B02 Answer: D. Class C amplifiers have the highest efficiency. A Class C amplifier is biased such that the active device conducts for less than 180 degrees of the input waveform.

Which of the following describes the function of a two-input AND gate?

A. Output is high when either or both inputs are low
B. Output is high only when both inputs are high
C. Output is low when either or both inputs are high
D. Output is low only when both inputs are high

G7B03 Answer: B. In a two input AND gate, output is high only when both inputs are high.

In a Class A amplifier, what percentage of the time does the amplifying device conduct?

A. 100%
B. More than 50% but less than 100%
C. 50%
D. Less than 50%

G7B04 Answer: A. In a Class A amplifier, the amplifying device conducts 100% of the time.

How many states does a 3-bit binary counter have?

A. 3
B. 6
C. 8
D. 16

G7B05 Answer: C. A 3-bit binary counter has 8 states.

What is a shift register?

A. A clocked array of circuits that passes data in steps along the array
B. An array of operational amplifiers used for tri-state arithmetic operations
C. A digital mixer
D. An analog mixer

G7B06 Answer: A. A shift register is a clocked array of circuits that passes data in steps along the array. Shift registers are used to perform timing functions, serial/parallel conversion, and multiplication and division.

Which of the following are basic components of a sine wave oscillator?

A. An amplifier and a divider
B. A frequency multiplier and a mixer
C. A circulator and a filter operating in a feed-forward loop
D. A filter and an amplifier operating in a feedback loop

G7B07 Answer: D. The basic components of virtually all sine wave oscillators are a filter and an amplifier operating in a feedback loop. A sine-wave oscillator produces an output voltage that is a sine-wave function of time.

How is the efficiency of an RF power amplifier determined?

A. Divide the DC input power by the DC output power
B. Divide the RF output power by the DC input power
C. Multiply the RF input power by the reciprocal of the RF output power
D. Add the RF input power to the DC output power

G7B08 Answer: B. The efficiency of an RF power amplifier is determined by dividing the RF output power by the DC input power.

What determines the frequency of an LC oscillator?

A. The number of stages in the counter
B. The number of stages in the divider
C. The inductance and capacitance in the tank circuit
D. The time delay of the lag circuit

G7B09 Answer: C. The frequency of an LC oscillator is determined by the inductance and capacitance in the tank circuit.

Which of the following describes a linear amplifier?

A. Any RF power amplifier used in conjunction with an amateur transceiver
B. An amplifier in which the output preserves the input waveform
C. A Class C high efficiency amplifier
D. An amplifier used as a frequency multiplier

G7B10 Answer: B. A linear amplifier is an amplifier in which the output preserves the input waveform. The Class A amplifier is a good example of a linear amplifier.

For which of the following modes is a Class C power stage appropriate for amplifying a modulated signal?

A. SSB
B. FM
C. AM
D. All these choices are correct

G7B11 Answer: B. FM modes is a Class C power stage appropriate for amplifying a modulated signal.

G7C – Transceiver Design; Filters; Oscillators; Digital Signal Processing (DSP)

What circuit is used to select one of the sidebands from a balanced modulator?

A. Carrier oscillator
B. Filter
C. IF amplifier
D. RF amplifier

G7C01 Answer: B. A filter is used to select one of the sidebands from a balanced modulator . Filters are circuits that allow some signals to pass through but greatly reduce the strength of other signals.

What output is produced by a balanced modulator?

A. Frequency modulated RF
B. Audio with equalized frequency response
C. Audio extracted from the modulation signal
D. Double-sideband modulated RF

G7C02 Answer: D. A balanced modulator produces a double-sideband modulated RF output.

What is one reason to use an impedance matching transformer at a transmitter output?

A. To minimize transmitter power output
B. To present the desired impedance to the transmitter and feed line
C. To reduce power supply ripple
D. To minimize radiation resistance

G7C03 Answer: B. One reason to use an impedance matching transformer at a transmitter output is to present the desired impedance to the transmitter and feed line.

How is a product detector used?

A. Used in test gear to detect spurious mixing products
B. Used in transmitter to perform frequency multiplication
C. Used in an FM receiver to filter out unwanted sidebands
D. Used in a single sideband receiver to extract the modulated signal

G7C04 Answer: D. A product detector is used in a single sideband receiver to extract the modulated signal. A product detector is a piece of equipment that gives a receiver the ability to process both CW and SSB signals.

Which of the following is characteristic of a direct digital synthesizer (DDS)?

A. Extremely narrow tuning range
B. Relatively high-power output
C. Pure sine wave output
D. Variable output frequency with the stability of a crystal oscillator

G7C05 Answer: D. A characteristic of a transceiver controlled by a direct digital synthesizer (DDS) is variable output frequency with the stability of a crystal oscillator. A direct digital synthesizer can make arbitrary waveforms based on the inputs from a clock.

Which of the following is an advantage of a digital signal processing (DSP) filter compared to an analog filter?

A. A wide range of filter bandwidths and shapes can be created
B. Fewer digital components are required
C. Mixing products are greatly reduced
D. The DSP filter is much more effective at VHF frequencies

G7C06 Answer: A. One advantage of a receiver DSP filter as compared to an analog filter is that a wide range of filter bandwidths and shapes can be created.

What term specifies a filter's attenuation inside its passband?

A. Insertion loss
B. Return loss
C. Q
D. Ultimate rejection

G7C07 Answer: A. Insertion loss specifies a filter's attenuation inside its passband.

Which parameter affects receiver sensitivity?

A. Input amplifier gain
B. Demodulator stage bandwidth
C. Input amplifier noise figure
D. All these choices are correct

G7C08 Answer: D. Receiver sensitivity is affected by both the gain and noise figure of the input amplifier as well as demodulator stage bandwidth.

What is the phase difference between the I and Q RF signals that software-defined radio (SDR) equipment uses for modulation and demodulation?

A. Zero
B. 90 degrees
C. 180 degrees
D. 45 degrees

G7C09 Answer: B. The phase difference between the I and Q RF signals that software-defined radio (SDR) equipment uses for modulation and demodulation is 90 degrees.

What is an advantage of using I-Q modulation with software-defined radios (SDRs)?

A. The need for high resolution analog-to-digital converters is eliminated
B. All types of modulation can be created with appropriate processing
C. Minimum detectible signal level is reduced
D. Automatic conversion of the signal from digital to analog

G7C10 Answer: B. When using I-Q modulation with software-defined radios (SDRs), all types of modulation can be created with appropriate processing.

Which of these functions is performed by software in a software-defined radio (SDR)?

A. Filtering
B. Detection
C. Modulation
D. All these choices are correct

G7C11 Answer: D. An SDR has many functions in the software including filtering, detection, modulation, amplification, and mixing.

What is the frequency above which a low-pass filter's output power is less than half the input power?

A. Notch frequency
B. Neper frequency
C. Cutoff frequency
D. Rolloff frequency

G7C12 Answer: C. A low-pass filter's output power is less than half the input power when it is above the cutoff frequency.

What term specifies a filter's maximum ability to reject signals outside its passband?

A. Notch depth
B. Rolloff
C. Insertion loss
D. Ultimate rejection

G7C13 Answer: D. Ultimate rejection specifies a filter's maximum ability to reject signals outside its passband.

The bandwidth of a band-pass filter is measured between what two frequencies?

A. Upper and lower half-power
B. Cutoff and rolloff
C. Pole and zero
D. Image and harmonic

G7C14 Answer: A. The bandwidth of a band-pass filter is measured between upper and lower half-power frequencies.

G8 – Signals and Emissions

G8A – Carriers and Modulation: AM, FM, and Single Sideband; Modulation Envelope; Digital Modulation; Overmodulation; Link Budgets and Link Margins

How is direct binary FSK modulation generated?

A. By keying an FM transmitter with a sub-audible tone
B. By changing an oscillator's frequency directly with a digital control signal
C. By using a transceiver's computer data interface protocol to change frequencies
D. By reconfiguring the CW keying input to act as a tone generator

G8A01 Answer: B. A direct binary FSK modulation is generated by changing an oscillator's frequency directly with a digital control signal.

What is the name of the process that changes the phase angle of an RF signal to convey information?

A. Phase convolution
B. Phase modulation
C. Phase transformation
D. Phase inversion

G8A02 Answer: B. Phase modulation is the process that changes the phase angle of an RF wave to convey information.

What is the name of the process that changes the instantaneous frequency of an RF wave to convey information?

A. Frequency convolution
B. Frequency transformation
C. Frequency conversion
D. Frequency modulation

G8A03 Answer: D. Frequency modulation is the process which changes the frequency of an RF wave to convey information. Most repeaters use frequency modulated phone signals to communicate via voice. When this is done, the RF carrier frequency is altered by the voice data.

What emission is produced by a reactance modulator connected to a transmitter RF amplifier stage?

A. Multiplex modulation
B. Phase modulation
C. Amplitude modulation
D. Pulse modulation

G8A04 Answer: B. Phase modulation is the emission produced by a reactance modulator connected to an RF power amplifier.

What type of modulation varies the instantaneous power level of the RF signal?

A. Power modulation
B. Phase modulation
C. Frequency modulation
D. Amplitude modulation

G8A05 Answer: D. Amplitude modulation varies the instantaneous power level of the RF signal.

Which of the following is characteristic of QPSK31?

A. It is sideband sensitive
B. Its encoding provides error correction
C. Its bandwidth is approximately the same as BPSK31
D. All these choices are correct

G8A06 Answer: D. QPSK31 is sideband sensitive, its encoding provides error correction, and its bandwidth is approximately the same as BPSK31.

Which of the following phone emissions uses the narrowest bandwidth?

A. Single sideband
B. Vestigial sideband
C. Phase modulation
D. Frequency modulation

G8A07 Answer: A. Single sideband phone emissions uses the narrowest frequency bandwidth. Unlike an AM transmission, which requires two matching copies of the voice information to be sent out, an SSB transmission only requires one. Therefore it takes up considerably less of the radio spectrum.

Which of the following is an effect of overmodulation?

A. Insufficient audio
B. Insufficient bandwidth
C. Frequency drift
D. Excessive bandwidth

G8A08 Answer: D. Excessive bandwidth is an effect of over-modulation.

What type of modulation is used by FT8?

A. 8-tone frequency shift keying
B. Vestigial sideband
C. Amplitude compressed AM
D. 8-bit direct sequence spread spectrum

G8A09 Answer: A. An 8-tone frequency shift keying modulation is used by FT8.

What is meant by the term "flat-topping," when referring to an amplitude-modulated phone signal?

A. Signal distortion caused by insufficient collector current
B. The transmitter's automatic level control (ALC) is properly adjusted
C. Signal distortion caused by excessive drive or speech levels
D. The transmitter's carrier is properly suppressed

G8A10 Answer: C. In an amplitude-modulated phone signal, flat-topping is signal distortion caused by excessive drive or speech levels.

What is the modulation envelope of an AM signal?

A. The waveform created by connecting the peak values of the modulated signal
B. The carrier frequency that contains the signal
C. Spurious signals that envelop nearby frequencies
D. The bandwidth of the modulated signal

G8A11 Answer: A. The modulation envelope of an AM signal is the waveform created by connecting the peak values of the modulated signal.

What is QPSK modulation?

A. Modulation using quasi-parallel to serial conversion to reduce bandwidth
B. Modulation using quadra-pole sideband keying to generate spread spectrum signals
C. Modulation using Fast Fourier Transforms to generate frequencies at the first, second, third, and fourth harmonics of the carrier frequency to improve noise immunity
D. Modulation in which digital data is transmitted using 0-, 90-, 180- and 270-degrees phase shift to represent pairs of bits

G8A12 Answer: D. QSPK modulation transmits digital data using 0-, 90-, 180- and 270-degrees phase shift to represent pairs of bits.

What is a link budget?

A. The financial costs associated with operating a radio link
B. The sum of antenna gains minus system losses
C. The sum of transmit power and antenna gains minus system losses as seen at the receiver
D. The difference between transmit power and receiver sensitivity

G8A13 Answer: C. A link budget is the sum of transmit power and antenna gains minus system losses as seen at the receiver.

What is link margin?

A. The opposite of fade margin
B. The difference between received power level and minimum required signal level at the input to the receiver
C. Transmit power minus receiver sensitivity
D. Receiver sensitivity plus 3 dB

G8A14 Answer: B. A link margin is the difference between received power level and minimum required signal level at the input to the receiver.

G8B – Frequency Changing; Bandwidths of Various Modes; Deviation; Intermodulation

Which mixer input is varied or tuned to convert signals of different frequencies to an intermediate frequency (IF)?

A. Image frequency
B. Local oscillator
C. RF input
D. Beat frequency oscillator

G8B01 Answer: B. The local oscillator is varied or tuned to convert signals of different frequencies to an intermediate frequency (IF).

What is the term for interference from a signal at twice the IF frequency from the desired signal?

A. Quadrature response
B. Image response
C. Mixer interference
D. Intermediate interference

G8B02 Answer: B. Interference from a signal at twice the IF frequency from the desired signal is called image response interference.

What is another term for the mixing of two RF signals?

A. Heterodyning
B. Synthesizing
C. Frequency inversion
D. Phase inversion

G8B03 Answer: A. Heterodyning is another term for the mixing of two RF signals. In this process, an electronic circuit is used to combine an input radio frequency with a generated frequency: the result is one frequency that is a sum of the frequencies and one frequency that is the difference between the frequencies.

What is the stage in a VHF FM transmitter that generates a harmonic of a lower frequency signal to reach the desired operating frequency?

A. Mixer
B. Reactance modulator
C. Balanced converter
D. Multiplier

G8B04 Answer: D. The multiplier stage in a VHF FM transmitter generates a harmonic of a lower frequency signal to reach the desired operating frequency.

Which intermodulation products are closest to the original signal frequencies?

A. Second harmonics
B. Even-order
C. Odd-order
D. Intercept point

G8B05 Answer: C. Odd-order intermodulation products are closest to the original signal frequencies.

What is the total bandwidth of an FM phone transmission having 5 kHz deviation and 3 kHz modulating frequency?

A. 3 kHz
B. 5 kHz
C. 8 kHz
D. 16 kHz

G8B06 Answer: D. The total bandwidth of an FM-phone transmission having a 5 kHz deviation and a 3 kHz modulating frequency is 16 kHz.

What is the frequency deviation for a 12.21 MHz reactance modulated oscillator in a 5 kHz deviation, 146.52 MHz FM phone transmitter?

A. 101.75 Hz
B. 416.7 Hz
C. 5 kHz
D. 60 kHz

G8B07 Answer: B. The frequency deviation for a 12.21-MHz reactance-modulated oscillator in a 5-kHz deviation, 146.52-MHz FM-phone transmitter is 416.7 Hz.

Why is it important to know the duty cycle of the mode you are using when transmitting?

A. To aid in tuning your transmitter
B. Some modes have high duty cycles that could exceed the transmitter's average power rating
C. To allow time for the other station to break in during a transmission
D. To prevent overmodulation

G8B08 Answer: B. It is important to know the duty cycle of the data mode you are using when transmitting because some modes have high duty cycles which could exceed the transmitter's average power rating. The duty cycle of a transmitter is the amount of time it spends operating at full output power during each transmission. When a transmitter has a higher duty cycle, this means that it creates more RF radiation exposure for an equivalent PEP output.

Why is it good to match receiver bandwidth to the bandwidth of the operating mode?

A. It is required by FCC rules
B. It minimizes power consumption in the receiver
C. It improves impedance matching of the antenna
D. It results in the best signal-to-noise ratio

G8B09 Answer: D. Matching receiver bandwidth to the bandwidth of the operating mode results in the best signal to noise ratio. The receiver is the piece of equipment that converts radio waves into signals that can be heard or seen by the operator.

What is the relationship between transmitted symbol rate and bandwidth?

A. Symbol rate and bandwidth are not related
B. Higher symbol rates require wider bandwidth
C. Lower symbol rates require wider bandwidth
D. Bandwidth is half the symbol rate

G8B10 Answer: B. The relationship between transmitted symbol rate and bandwidth is the higher symbol rates require wider bandwidth.

What combination of a mixer's Local Oscillator (LO) and RF input frequencies is found in the output?

A. The ratio
B. The average
C. The sum and difference
D. The arithmetic product

G8B11 Answer: C. The sum and difference of a mixer's Local Oscillator (LO) and RF input frequencies is found in the output.

What process combines two signals in a non-linear circuit to produce unwanted spurious outputs?

A. Intermodulation
B. Heterodyning
C. Detection
D. Rolloff

G8B12 Answer: A. Intermodulation combines two signals in a non-linear circuit to produce unwanted spurious outputs.

Which of the following is an odd-order intermodulation product of frequencies F1 and F2?

A. 5F1-3F2
B. 3F1-F2
C. 2F1-F2
D. All these choices are correct

G8B13 Answer: C. 2F1-F2 is an odd-order intermodulation product of frequencies F1 and F2.

G8C – Digital Emission Modes

Which digital mode is used as a low-power beacon for assessing HF propagation?

A. WSPR
B. MFSK16
C. PSK31
D. SSB-SC

G8C02 Answer: A. WSPR mode is used as a low-power beacon for assessing HF propagation.

What part of a packet radio frame contains the routing and handling information?

A. Directory
B. Preamble
C. Header
D. Trailer

G8C03 Answer: C. The header of a data packet contains the routing and handling information. The trailer of a data packet may also contain the routing and handling information, which is also known as the control information. The main content of the message is called the user data, or payload.

Which of the following describes Baudot code?

A. A 7-bit code with start, stop, and parity bits
B. A code using error detection and correction
C. A 5-bit code with additional start and stop bits
D. A code using SELCAL and LISTEN

G8C04 Answer: C. Baudot code is a five-bit code with additional start and stop bits. It is used in RTTY (radioteletype) communications. In Baudot code, characters of plain text are sent as five-bit codes composed of patterns of marks and spaces. The modulation created by this succession of frequencies is called frequency shift keying.

In an ARQ mode, what is meant by a NAK response to a transmitted packet?

A. Request retransmission of the packet
B. Packet was received without error
C. Receiving station connected and ready for transmissions
D. Entire file received correctly

G8C05 Answer: A. In an ARQ mode, an NAK response to a transmitted packet means that the receiver is requesting the packet be retransmitted.

What action results from a failure to exchange information due to excessive transmission attempts when using an ARQ mode?

A. The checksum overflows
B. The connection is dropped
C. Packets will be routed incorrectly
D. Encoding reverts to the default character set

G8C06 Answer: B. When using an ARQ mode and there is a failure to exchange information due to excessive transmission attempts, the connection is dropped.

Which of the following narrow-band digital modes can receive signals with very low signal-to-noise ratios?

A. MSK144
B. FT8
C. AMTOR
D. MFSK32

G8C07 Answer: B. FT8 can receive signals with very low signal-to-noise ratios.

Which of the following statements is true about PSK31?

A. Upper case letters are sent with more power
B. Upper case letters use longer Varicode bit sequences and thus slow down transmission
C. Error correction is used to ensure accurate message reception
D. Higher power is needed as compared to RTTY for similar error rates

G8C08 Answer: B. In PSK31 the upper case letters use longer Varicode signals and thus slow down transmission.

Which is true of mesh network microwave nodes?

A. Having more nodes increases signal strengths
B. If one node fails, a packet may still reach its target station via an alternate node
C. Links between two nodes in a network may have different frequencies and bandwidths
D. More nodes reduce overall microwave out of band interference

G8C09 Answer: B. For mesh network microwave nodes, if one node fails, a packet may still reach its target station via an alternate node.

How does forward error correction (FEC) allow the receiver to correct data errors?

A. By controlling transmitter output power for optimum signal strength
B. By using the Varicode character set
C. By transmitting redundant information with the data
D. By using a parity bit with each character

G8C10 Answer: C. FEC allows the receiver to correct data errors by transmitting redundant information with the data.

How are the two separate frequencies of a Frequency Shift Keyed (FSK) signal identified?

A. Dot and dash
B. On and off
C. High and low
D. Mark and space

G8C11 Answer: D. The two separate frequencies of a FSK signal are identified by a mark and space.

Which type of code is used for sending characters in a PSK31 signal?

A. Varicode
B. Viterbi
C. Volumetric
D. Binary

G8C12 Answer: A. In a PSK31 signal Varicode is used to send characters.

What is indicated on a waterfall display by one or more vertical lines on either side of a data mode or RTTY signal?

A. Long path propagation
B. Backscatter propagation
C. Insufficient modulation
D. Overmodulation

G8C13 Answer: D. One or more vertical lines on either side of a data mode or RTTY signal on a waterfall display indicates overmodulation.

Which of the following describes a waterfall display?

A. Frequency is horizontal, signal strength is vertical, time is intensity
B. Frequency is vertical, signal strength is intensity, time is horizontal
C. Frequency is horizontal, signal strength is intensity, time is vertical
D. Frequency is vertical, signal strength is horizontal, time is intensity

G8C14 Answer: C. In a waterfall display the frequency is horizontal, the signal strength is intensity and the time is vertical.

What does an FT8 signal report of +3 mean?

A. The signal is 3 times the noise level of an equivalent SSB signal
B. The signal is S3 (weak signals)
C. The signal-to-noise ratio is equivalent to +3dB in a 2.5 kHz bandwidth
D. The signal is 3 dB over S9

G8C15 Answer: C. An FT8 signal report of +3 means that the signal-to-noise ratio is equivalent to +3dB in a 2.5 kHz bandwidth.

Which of the following provide digital voice modes?

A. WSPR, MFSK16, and EasyPAL
B. FT8, FT4, and FST4
C. Winlink, PACTOR II, and PACTOR III
D. DMR, D-STAR, and SystemFusion

G8C16 Answer: D. DMR, D-STAR, and SystemFusion all provide digital voice modes.

G9 – Antennas and Feed Lines

G9A – Feed Lines: Characteristic Impedance and Attenuation; standing wave ratio (SWR) Calculation, Measurement, and Effects; Antenna Feed Point Matching

Which of the following factors determine the characteristic impedance of a parallel conductor feed line?

A. The distance between the centers of the conductors and the radius of the conductors
B. The distance between the centers of the conductors and the length of the line
C. The radius of the conductors and the frequency of the signal
D. The frequency of the signal and the length of the line

G9A01 Answer: A. The distance between the centers of the conductors and the radius of the conductors determines the characteristic impedance of a parallel conductor feed line.

What is the relationship between high standing wave ratio (SWR) and transmission line loss?

A. There is no relationship between transmission line loss and SWR
B. High SWR increases loss in a lossy transmission line
C. High SWR makes it difficult to measure transmission line loss
D. High SWR reduces the relative effect of transmission line loss

G9A02 Answer: B. High SWR increases loss in a lossy transmission line, so it is critical to minimize SWR.

What is the nominal characteristic impedance of "window line" transmission line?

A. 50 ohms
B. 75 ohms
C. 100 ohms
D. 450 ohms

G9A03 Answer: D. The nominal characteristic impedance of "window line" transmission line is 450 ohms.

What causes reflected power at an antenna's feed point?

A. Operating an antenna at its resonant frequency
B. Using more transmitter power than the antenna can handle
C. A difference between feed line impedance and antenna feed point impedance
D. Feeding the antenna with unbalanced feed line

G9A04 Answer: C. At the point where a feed line connects to an antenna, a difference between feed line impedance and antenna feed point impedance results in reflected power.

How does the attenuation of coaxial cable change with increasing frequency?

A. Attenuation is independent of frequency
B. Attenuation increases
C. Attenuation decreases
D. Attenuation follows Marconi's Law of Attenuation

G9A05 Answer: B. The attenuation of coaxial cable increases as the frequency of the signal it is carrying increases. A coaxial cable is a type of feedline in which one conductor is entirely inside another.

In what units is RF feed line loss usually expressed?

A. Ohms per 1,000 feet
B. Decibels per 1,000 feet
C. Ohms per 100 feet
D. Decibels per 100 feet

G9A06 Answer: D. RF feed line losses are usually expressed in dB per 100 ft.

What must be done to prevent standing waves on a feed line connected to an antenna?

A. The antenna feed point must be at DC ground potential
B. The feed line must be an odd number of electrical quarter wavelengths long
C. The feed line must be an even number of physical half wavelengths long
D. The antenna feed point impedance must be matched to the characteristic impedance of the feed line

G9A07 Answer: D. To prevent standing waves on an antenna feed line, the antenna feed point impedance must be matched to the characteristic impedance of the feed line.

If the SWR on an antenna feed line is 5:1, and a matching network at the transmitter end of the feed line is adjusted to present a 1:1 SWR to the transmitter, what is the resulting SWR on the feed line?

A. 1:1
B. 5:1
C. Between 1:1 and 5:1 depending on the characteristic impedance of the line
D. Between 1:1 and 5:1 depending on the reflected power at the transmitter

G9A08 Answer: B. If the SWR on an antenna line is 5:1, and a matching network at the transmitter end of the feed line is adjusted to present a 1:1 SWR, the resulting SWR on the feed line is 5:1. The standing wave ratio, also known as the voltage standing wave ratio, is an indication of the impedance match between the feedline and the antenna.

What standing wave ratio results from connecting a 50-ohm feed line to a 200-ohm resistive load?

A. 4:1
B. 1:4
C. 2:1
D. 1:2

G9A09 Answer: A. The connection of a 50-ohm feed line to a 200-ohm resistive load will result in a standing wave ratio of 4:1.

What standing wave ratio results from connecting a 50-ohm feed line to a 10-ohm resistive load?

A. 2:1
B. 1:2
C. 1:5
D. 5:1

G9A10 Answer: D. The connection of a 50-ohm feed line to a 10-ohm resistive load will result in a standing wave ratio of 5:1.

What is the effect of transmission line loss on SWR measured at the input to the line?

A. Higher loss reduces SWR measured at the input to the line
B. Higher loss increases SWR measured at the input to the line
C. Higher loss increases the accuracy of SWR measured at the input to the line
D. Transmission line loss does not affect the SWR measurement

G9A11 Answer: A. The effect is the higher the transmission line loss, the more the SWR will read artificially low.

G9B – Basic Dipole and Monopole Antennas

What is a characteristic of a random-wire HF antenna connected directly to the transmitter?

A. It must be longer than 1 wavelength
B. Station equipment may carry significant RF current
C. It produces only vertically polarized radiation
D. It is more effective on the lower HF bands than on the higher bands

G9B01 Answer: B. A characteristic of a random-wire HF antenna connected directly to the transmitter is that station equipment may carry significant RF current.

Which of the following is a common way to adjust the feed point impedance of an elevated quarter-wave ground-plane vertical antenna to be approximately 50 ohms?

A. Slope the radials upward
B. Slope the radials downward
C. Lengthen the radials beyond one wavelength
D. Coil the radials

G9B02 Answer: B. A common way to adjust the feed point impedance of a quarter-wave ground plane vertical antenna is to slope the radials downward.

Which of the following best describes the radiation pattern of a quarter-wave ground-plane vertical antenna?

A. Bi-directional in azimuth
B. Isotropic
C. Hemispherical
D. Omnidirectional in azimuth

G9B03 Answer: D. A quarter-wave ground-plane vertical antenna produces a radiation pattern that is omnidirectional in azimuth.

What is the radiation pattern of a dipole antenna in free space in a plane containing the conductor?

A. It is a figure-eight at right angles to the antenna
B. It is a figure-eight off both ends of the antenna
C. It is a circle (equal radiation in all directions)
D. It has a pair of lobes on one side of the antenna and a single lobe on the other side

G9B04 Answer: A. The low angle azimuthal radiation pattern of an ideal half-wavelength dipole antenna installed 1/2 wavelength high and parallel to the Earth is a figure-eight at right angles to the antenna.

How does antenna height affect the azimuthal radiation pattern of a horizontal dipole HF antenna at elevation angles higher than about 45 degrees?

A. If the antenna is too high, the pattern becomes unpredictable
B. Antenna height has no effect on the pattern
C. If the antenna is less than 1/2 wavelength high, the azimuthal pattern is almost omnidirectional
D. If the antenna is less than 1/2 wavelength high, radiation off the ends of the wire is eliminated

G9B05 Answer: C. If a horizontal dipole HF antenna is less than 1/2 wavelength high and at elevation angles higher than 45 degrees, then the azimuthal pattern is almost omnidirectional.

Where should the radial wires of a ground-mounted vertical antenna system be placed?

A. As high as possible above the ground
B. Parallel to the antenna element
C. On the surface or buried a few inches below the ground
D. At the center of the antenna

G9B06 Answer: C. The radial wires of a ground-mounted vertical antenna system should be placed on the surface or buried a few inches below the ground.

How does the feed point impedance of a horizontal 1/2 wave dipole antenna change as the antenna height is reduced to 1/10 wavelength above ground?

A. It steadily increases
B. It steadily decreases
C. It peaks at about 1/8 wavelength above ground
D. It is unaffected by the height above ground

G9B07 Answer: B. The feed point impedance of a 1/2 wave dipole antenna steadily decreases as the antenna is reduced to 1/10 wavelength above ground.

How does the feed point impedance of a 1/2 wave dipole change as the feed point is moved from the center toward the ends?

A. It steadily increases
B. It steadily decreases
C. It peaks at about 1/8 wavelength from the end
D. It is unaffected by the location of the feed point

G9B08 Answer: A. The feed-point impedance of a 1/2 wave dipole steadily increases as the feed-point location is moved from the center toward the ends.

Which of the following is an advantage of using a horizontally polarized as compared to a vertically polarized HF antenna?

A. Lower ground losses
B. Lower feed point impedance
C. Shorter radials
D. Lower radiation resistance

G9B09 Answer: A. Horizontally polarized HF antennas have lower ground losses than vertically polarized HF antennas.

What is the approximate length for a 1/2 wave dipole antenna cut for 14.250 MHz?

A. 8 feet
B. 16 feet
C. 24 feet
D. 33 feet

G9B10 Answer: D. The approximate length for a 1/2 wave dipole antenna cut for 14.250 MHz is 33 feet.

What is the approximate length for a 1/2 wave dipole antenna cut for 3.550 MHz?

A. 42 feet
B. 84 feet
C. 132 feet
D. 263 feet

G9B11 Answer: C. The approximate length for a 1/2 wave dipole antenna cut for 3.550 MHz is 132 feet.

What is the approximate length for a 1/4 wave monopole antenna cut for 28.5 MHz?

A. 8 feet
B. 11 feet
C. 16 feet
D. 21 feet

G9B12 Answer: A. The approximate length for a 1/4 wave monopole antenna cut for 28.5 MHz is 8 feet.

G9C – Directional Antennas

Which of the following would increase the bandwidth of a Yagi antenna?

A. Larger-diameter elements
B. Closer element spacing
C. Loading coils in series with the element
D. Tapered-diameter elements

G9C01 Answer: A. Larger diameter elements would increase the bandwidth of a Yagi antenna. The Yagi antenna is the most popular form of amateur directional antenna. It has one driven element and additional elements.

What is the approximate length of the driven element of a Yagi antenna?

A. 1/4 wavelength
B. 1/2 wavelength
C. 3/4 wavelength
D. 1 wavelength

G9C02 Answer: B. The approximate length of the driven element of a Yagi antenna is 1/2 wavelength.

How do the lengths of a three-element Yagi reflector and director compare to that of the driven element?

A. The reflector is longer, and the director is shorter
B. The reflector is shorter, and the director is longer
C. They are all the same length
D. Relative length depends on the frequency of operation

G9C03 Answer: A. In a three-element Yagi, the reflector is longer and the director is shorter than those of the driven element.

How does antenna gain in dBi compare to gain stated in dBd for the same antenna?

A. Gain in dBi is 2.15 dB lower
B. Gain in dBi is 2.15 dB higher
C. Gain in dBd is 1.25 dBd lower
D. Gain in dBd is 1.25 dBd higher

G9C04 Answer: B. The antenna gain in dBi is 2.15 dB higher than the same antenna gain stated in dBd.

What is the primary effect of increasing boom length and adding directors to a Yagi antenna?

A. Gain increases
B. Beamwidth increases
C. Front-to-back ratio decreases
D. Resonant frequency is lower

G9C05 Answer: A. The primary effect of increasing the boom length and adding directors is increasing the gain of a Yagi antenna.

What does "front-to-back ratio" mean in reference to a Yagi antenna?

A. The number of directors versus the number of reflectors
B. The relative position of the driven element with respect to the reflectors and directors
C. The power radiated in the major lobe compared to that in the opposite direction
D. The ratio of forward gain to dipole gain

G9C07 Answer: C. In reference to a Yagi antenna, "front-to-back ratio" means the power radiated in the major lobe compared to that in the opposite direction.

What is meant by the "main lobe" of a directive antenna?

A. The magnitude of the maximum vertical angle of radiation
B. The point of maximum current in a radiating antenna element
C. The maximum voltage standing wave point on a radiating element
D. The direction of maximum radiated field strength from the antenna

G9C08 Answer: D. The "main lobe" of a directive antenna is the direction of maximum radiated field strength from the antenna.

In free space, how does the gain of two three-element, horizontally polarized Yagi antennas spaced vertically 1/2 wavelength apart typically compare to the gain of a single three-element Yagi?

A. Approximately 1.5 dB higher
B. Approximately 3 dB higher
C. Approximately 6 dB higher
D. Approximately 9 dB higher

G9C09 Answer: B. The gain of a pair of three-element, horizontally polarized Yagi antennas spaced vertically 1/2 wavelength apart is approximately 3 dB higher than the gain of a single three-element Yagi.

Which of the following can be adjusted to optimize forward gain, front-to-back ratio, or SWR bandwidth of a Yagi antenna?

A. The physical length of the boom
B. The number of elements on the boom
C. The spacing of each element along the boom
D. All these choices are correct

G9C10 Answer: D. The forward gain, front-to-back ratio, or SWR bandwidth of a Yagi antenna could be optimized by adjusting the physical length of the boom, the number of elements on the boom, and the spacing of each element along the boom.

What is a beta or hairpin match?

A. A shorted transmission line stub placed at the feed point of a Yagi antenna to provide impedance matching
B. A 1/4 wavelength section of 75-ohm coax in series with the feed point of a Yagi to provide impedance matching
C. A series capacitor selected to cancel the inductive reactance of a folded dipole antenna
D. A section of 300-ohm twin-lead transmission line used to match a folded dipole antenna

G9C11 Answer: A. A beta or hairpin match is a shorted transmission line stub placed at the feed point of a Yagi antenna to provide impedance matching.

Which of the following is a characteristic of using a gamma match with a Yagi antenna?

A. It does not require the driven element to be insulated from the boom
B. It does not require any inductors or capacitors
C. It is useful for matching multiband antennas
D. All these choices are correct

G9C12 Answer: A. One characteristic of using a gamma match with a Yagi antenna is that it does not require that the elements be insulated from the boom.

G9D – Specialized Antenna Types and Applications

Which of the following antenna types will be most effective as a near vertical incidence skywave (NVIS) antenna for short-skip communications on 40 meters during the day?

A. A horizontal dipole placed between 1/10 and 1/4 wavelength above the ground
B. A vertical antenna placed between 1/4 and 1/2 wavelength above the ground
C. A horizontal dipole placed at approximately 1/2 wavelength above the ground
D. A vertical dipole placed at approximately 1/2 wavelength above the ground

G9D01 Answer: A. A horizontal dipole antenna placed between 1/10 and 1/4 wavelength above the ground will be effective as a Near Vertical Incidence Skywave (NVIS) antenna for short-skip communications on 40 meters during the day.

What is the feed point impedance of an end-fed half-wave antenna?

A. Very low
B. Approximately 50 ohms
C. Approximately 300 ohms
D. Very high

G9D02 Answer: D. The feed-point impedance of an end-fed half-wave antenna is very high.

In which direction is the maximum radiation from a VHF/UHF "halo" antenna?

A. Broadside to the plane of the halo
B. Opposite the feed point
C. Omnidirectional in the plane of the halo
D. On the same side as the feed point

G9D03 Answer: C. The maximum radiation from a VHF/UHF "halo" antenna is omnidirectional in the plane of the halo

What is the primary function of antenna traps?

A. To enable multiband operation
B. To notch spurious frequencies
C. To provide balanced feed point impedance
D. To prevent out-of-band operation

G9D04 Answer: A. The primary purpose of antenna traps are to enable multiband operation.

What is an advantage of vertically stacking horizontally polarized Yagi antennas?

A. It allows quick selection of vertical or horizontal polarization
B. It allows simultaneous vertical and horizontal polarization
C. It narrows the main lobe in azimuth
D. It narrows the main lobe in elevation

G9D05 Answer: D. One advantage of vertically stacking horizontally polarized Yagi antennas is that it narrows the main lobe in elevation.

Which of the following is an advantage of a log-periodic antenna?

A. Wide bandwidth
B. Higher gain per element than a Yagi antenna
C. Harmonic suppression
D. Polarization diversity

G9D06 Answer: A. Wide bandwidth is one advantage of a log periodic antenna. A log periodic antenna resembles a large TV antenna, with several angled elements. These antennas have several elements so that they can function over all of the bands within a particular range. For instance, a ham radio operator may use a log periodic antenna so that a single antenna can be used to cover the 20-, 17-, 15-, 12-, and 10-meter bands.

Which of the following describes a log-periodic antenna?

A. Element length and spacing vary logarithmically along the boom
B. Impedance varies periodically as a function of frequency
C. Gain varies logarithmically as a function of frequency
D. SWR varies periodically as a function of boom length

G9D07 Answer: A. In a log periodic antenna, the length and spacing of the elements increases logarithmically from one end of the boom to the other.

How does a "screwdriver" mobile antenna adjust its feed point impedance?

A. By varying its body capacitance
B. By varying the base loading inductance
C. By extending and retracting the whip
D. By deploying a capacitance hat

G9D08 Answer: B. A "screwdriver" mobile antenna adjust its feed-point impedance by varying the base loading inductance.

What is the primary use of a Beverage antenna?

A. Directional receiving for MF and low HF bands
B. Directional transmitting for low HF bands
C. Portable direction finding at higher HF frequencies
D. Portable direction finding at lower HF frequencies

G9D09 Answer: A. One application for a Beverage antenna is directional receiving for MF and low HF bands.

In which direction or directions does an electrically small loop (less than 1/10 wavelength in circumference) have nulls in its radiation pattern?

A. In the plane of the loop
B. Broadside to the loop
C. Broadside and in the plane of the loop
D. Electrically small loops are omnidirectional

G9D10 Answer: B. Broadside to the loop, an electrically small loop (less than 1/10 wavelength in circumference) has nulls in its radiation pattern.

Which of the following is a disadvantage of multiband antennas?

A. They present low impedance on all design frequencies
B. They must be used with an antenna tuner
C. They must be fed with open wire line
D. They have poor harmonic rejection

G9D11 Answer: D. One disadvantage of multiband antennas is that they have poor harmonic rejection.

What is the common name of a dipole with a single central support?

A. Inverted V
B. Inverted L
C. Sloper
D. Lazy H

G9D12 Answer: A. A dipole with a single central support is also called an inverted V.

G0 – Electrical and RF Safety

G0A – RF Safety Principles, Rules, and Guidelines; Routine Station Evaluation

What is one way that RF energy can affect human body tissue?

A. It heats body tissue
B. It causes radiation poisoning
C. It causes the blood count to reach a dangerously low level
D. It cools body tissue

G0A01 Answer: A. RF energy can heat human body tissue.

Which of the following is used to determine RF exposure from a transmitted signal?

A. Its duty cycle
B. Its frequency
C. Its power density
D. All these choices are correct

G0A02 Answer: D. The duty cycle, frequency, and power density are all part of determining RF exposure from a transmitted signal.

How can you determine that your station complies with FCC RF exposure regulations?

A. By calculation based on FCC OET Bulletin 65
B. By calculation based on computer modeling
C. By measurement of field strength using calibrated equipment
D. All these choices are correct

G0A03 Answer: D. You can determine that your station complies with FCC RF exposure regulations by calculation based on FCC OET Bulletin 65; by calculation based on computer modeling; or by measurement of field strength using calibrated equipment. [97.13(c)(1)]

What does "time averaging" mean when evaluating RF radiation exposure?

A. The average amount of power developed by the transmitter over a specific 24-hour period
B. The average time it takes RF radiation to have any long-term effect on the body
C. The total time of the exposure
D. The total RF exposure averaged over a certain period

G0A04 Answer: D. When evaluating RF radiation exposure, "time averaging" means the total RF exposure averaged over a certain period.

What must you do if an evaluation of your station shows that the RF energy radiated by your station exceeds permissible limits for possible human absorption?

A. Take action to prevent human exposure to the excessive RF fields
B. File an Environmental Impact Statement (EIS-97) with the FCC
C. Secure written permission from your neighbors to operate above the controlled MPE limits
D. All these choices are correct

G0A05 Answer: A. If an evaluation shows that the RF energy radiated from your station exceeds permissible limits for possible human absorption, you must take action to prevent human exposure to the excessive RF fields. [97.13(c)(2), 1.1307(b)]

What must you do if your station fails to meet the FCC RF exposure exemption criteria?

A. Perform an RF Exposure Evaluation in accordance with FCC OET Bulletin 65
B. Contact the FCC for permission to transmit
C. Perform an RF exposure evaluation in accordance with World Meteorological Organization guidelines
D. Use an FCC-approved band-pass filter

G0A06 Answer: A. If your station fails to meet the FCC RF exposure exemption criteria, you must perform an RF Exposure Evaluation in accordance with FCC OET Bulletin 65. [97.13(c)(2), 1.1307(1)(b)(3)(i)]

What is the effect of modulation duty cycle on RF exposure?

A. A lower duty cycle permits greater power levels to be transmitted
B. A higher duty cycle permits greater power levels to be transmitted
C. Low duty cycle transmitters are exempt from RF exposure evaluation requirements
D. High duty cycle transmitters are exempt from RF exposure requirements

G0A07 Answer: A. Regarding RF exposure, a lower duty cycle permits greater power levels to be transmitted.

Which of the following steps must an amateur operator take to ensure compliance with RF safety regulations?

A. Post a copy of FCC Part 97.13 in the station
B. Notify neighbors within a 100-foot radius of the antenna of the existence of the station and power levels
C. Perform a routine RF exposure evaluation and prevent access to any identified high exposure areas
D. All these choices are correct

G0A08 Answer: C. To ensure compliance with RF safety regulations, an amateur operator should perform a routine RF exposure evaluation and prevent access to any identified high exposure areas. [97.13(c)(2)]

What type of instrument can be used to accurately measure an RF field strength?

A. A receiver with digital signal processing (DSP) noise reduction
B. A calibrated field strength meter with a calibrated antenna
C. An SWR meter with a peak-reading function
D. An oscilloscope with a high-stability crystal marker generator

G0A09 Answer: B. A calibrated field-strength meter with a calibrated antenna can be used to accurately measure RF field strength.

What should be done if evaluation shows that a neighbor might experience more than the allowable limit of RF exposure from the main lobe of a directional antenna?

A. Change to a non-polarized antenna with higher gain
B. Use an antenna with a higher front-to-back ratio
C. Take precautions to ensure that the antenna cannot be pointed in their direction when they are present
D. All these choices are correct

G0A10 Answer: C. If evaluation shows that a neighbor might experience more than the allowable limit of RF exposure from the main lobe of a directional antenna, the operator should take precautions to ensure that the antenna cannot be pointed in their direction when they are present.

What precaution should be taken if you install an indoor transmitting antenna?

A. Locate the antenna close to your operating position to minimize feed-line radiation
B. Position the antenna along the edge of a wall to reduce parasitic radiation
C. Make sure that MPE limits are not exceeded in occupied areas
D. Make sure the antenna is properly shielded

G0A11 Answer: C. If you install an indoor transmitting antenna, you should make sure that MPE limits are not exceeded in occupied areas.

What stations are subject to the FCC rules on RF exposure?

A. All commercial stations; amateur radio stations are exempt
B. Only stations with antennas lower than one wavelength above the ground
C. Only stations transmitting more than 500 watts PEP
D. All stations with a time-averaged transmission of more than one milliwatt

G0A12 Answer: D. All stations with a time-averaged transmission of more than one milliwatt are subject to the FCC rules on RF exposure. [1.1307(1)(b)(3)(i)(A)]

G0B – Station Safety: Electrical Shock, Grounding, Fusing, Interlocks, and Wiring; Antenna and Tower Safety

Which wire or wires in a four-conductor 240 VAC circuit should be attached to fuses or circuit breakers?

A. Only the hot wires
B. Only the neutral wire
C. Only the ground wire
D. All wires

G0B01 Answer: A. In a four-conductor 240 VAC circuit, only the hot wires should be attached to fuses or circuit breakers.

According to the National Electrical Code, what is the minimum wire size that may be used safely for wiring with a 20-ampere circuit breaker?

A. AWG number 20
B. AWG number 16
C. AWG number 12
D. AWG number 8

G0B02 Answer: C. The minimum wire size that may be safely used for a circuit that draws up to 20 amperes of continuous current is AWG number 12.

Which size of fuse or circuit breaker would be appropriate to use with a circuit that uses AWG number 14 wiring?

A. 30 amperes
B. 25 amperes
C. 20 amperes
D. 15 amperes

G0B03 Answer: D. A fuse or circuit breaker of 15 amperes would be appropriate to use with a circuit that uses AWG number 14 wiring.

Where should the station's lightning protection ground system be located?

A. As close to the station equipment as possible
B. Outside the building
C. Next to the closest power pole
D. Parallel to the water supply line

G0B04 Answer: B. A station's lightning protection ground system should be located outside the building.

Which of the following conditions will cause a ground fault circuit interrupter (GFCI) to disconnect AC power?

A. Current flowing from one or more of the hot wires to the neutral wire
B. Current flowing from one or more of the hot wires directly to ground
C. Overvoltage on the hot wires
D. All these choices are correct

G0B05 Answer: B. Current flowing from one or more of the hot wires directly to ground will cause a ground fault circuit interrupter (GFCI) to disconnect AC power.

Which of the following is covered by the National Electrical Code?

A. Acceptable bandwidth limits
B. Acceptable modulation limits
C. Electrical safety of the station
D. RF exposure limits of the human body

G0B06 Answer: C. The National Electrical Code only pertains to electrical safety and building guidelines.

Which of these choices should be observed when climbing a tower using a safety harness?

A. Always hold on to the tower with one hand
B. Confirm that the harness is rated for the weight of the climber and that it is within its allowable service life
C. Ensure that all heavy tools are securely fastened to the harness
D. All these choices are correct

G0B07 Answer: B. When climbing on a tower using a safety harness, always confirm that the harness is rated for the weight of the climber and that it is within its allowable service life.

What should be done before climbing a tower that supports electrically powered devices?

A. Notify the electric company that a person will be working on the tower
B. Make sure all circuits that supply power to the tower are locked out and tagged
C. Unground the base of the tower
D. All these choices are correct

G0B08 Answer: B. Any person preparing to climb a tower that supports electrically powered devices should make sure all circuits that supply power to the tower are locked out and tagged.

Which of the following is true of an emergency generator installation?

A. The generator should be operated in a well-ventilated area
B. The generator must be insulated from ground
C. Fuel should be stored near the generator for rapid refueling in case of an emergency
D. All these choices are correct

G0B09 Answer: A. In an emergency generator installation, the generator should only be operated in a well-ventilated area. This is also true when the ham radio rig is to be powered by an automobile battery.

Which of the following is a danger from lead-tin solder?

A. Lead can contaminate food if hands are not washed carefully after handling the solder
B. High voltages can cause lead-tin solder to disintegrate suddenly
C. Tin in the solder can "cold flow," causing shorts in the circuit
D. RF energy can convert the lead into a poisonous gas

G0B10 Answer: A. One danger of lead-tin solder is that the lead can contaminate food if hands are not washed carefully after handling.

Which of the following is required for lightning protection ground rods?

A. They must be bonded to all buried water and gas lines
B. Bends in ground wires must be made as close as possible to a right angle
C. Lightning grounds must be connected to all ungrounded wiring
D. They must be bonded together with all other grounds

G0B11 Answer: D. It is required for lightning protection grounds to be bonded together with all other grounds.

What is the purpose of a power supply interlock?

A. To prevent unauthorized changes to the circuit that would void the manufacturer's warranty
B. To shut down the unit if it becomes too hot
C. To ensure that dangerous voltages are removed if the cabinet is opened
D. To shut off the power supply if too much voltage is produced

G0B12 Answer: C. The purpose of a transmitter power supply interlock is to ensure that dangerous voltages are removed if the cabinet is opened.

Where should lightning arrestors be located?

A. Where the feed lines enter the building
B. On the antenna, opposite the feed point
C. In series with each ground lead
D. At the closest power pole ground electrode

G0B13 Answer: A. Lightning arrestors should be located where the feed lines enter the building.

Ham Radio General Class Practice Tests

Want to take this practice test in an online interactive format?
Check out the online resources page, which includes interactive practice questions and much more: **mometrix.com/resources719/hamradiogen**

Test #1 Practice Questions

1. How are the two separate frequencies of a Frequency Shift Keyed (FSK) signal identified?

a. Dot and dash
b. On and off
c. High and low
d. Mark and space

2. What is the maximum height above ground for an antenna structure not near a public use airport without requiring notification to the FAA and registration with the FCC?

a. 50 feet
b. 100 feet
c. 200 feet
d. 250 feet

3. What is the maximum transmitter power an amateur station may use on 10.140 MHz?

a. 200 watts PEP output
b. 1000 watts PEP output
c. 1500 watts PEP output
d. 2000 watts PEP output

4. Who may receive partial credit for the elements represented by an expired amateur radio license?

a. Any person who can demonstrate that they once held an FCC-issued General, Advanced, or Amateur Extra class license that was not revoked by the FCC
b. Anyone who held an FCC-issued amateur radio license that expired not less than 5 and not more than 15 years ago
c. Any person who previously held an amateur license issued by another country, but only if that country has a current reciprocal licensing agreement with the FCC
d. Only persons who once held an FCC issued Novice, Technician, or Technician Plus license

5. Which of the following would disqualify a third party from participating in sending a message via an amateur station?

a. The third party's amateur license has been revoked and not reinstated
b. The third party is not a US citizen
c. The third party is speaking in a language other than English
d. All these choices are correct

6. Which mode is most commonly used for voice communications on frequencies of 14 MHz or higher?

a. Upper sideband
b. Lower sideband
c. Suppressed sideband
d. Double sideband

7. Which of the following is true concerning access to frequencies?

a. Nets have priority
b. QSOs in progress have priority
c. Except during emergencies, no amateur station has priority access to any frequency
d. Contest operations should yield to non-contest use of frequencies

8. Which of the following describes full break-in CW operation (QSK)?

a. Breaking stations send the Morse code prosign "BK"
b. Automatic keyers, instead of hand keys, are used to send Morse code
c. An operator must activate a manual send/receive switch before and after every transmission
d. Transmitting stations can receive between code characters and elements

9. What is the Volunteer Monitor Program?

a. Amateur volunteers who are formally enlisted to monitor the airwaves for rules violations
b. Amateur volunteers who conduct amateur licensing examinations
c. Amateur volunteers who conduct frequency coordination for amateur VHF repeaters
d. Amateur volunteers who use their station equipment to help civil defense organizations in times of emergency

10. Which mode is normally used when sending RTTY signals via AFSK with an SSB transmitter?

a. USB
b. DSB
c. CW
d. LSB

11. How does a higher sunspot number affect HF propagation?

a. Higher sunspot numbers generally indicate a greater probability of good propagation at higher frequencies
b. Lower sunspot numbers generally indicate greater probability of sporadic E propagation
c. A zero sunspot number indicates that radio propagation is not possible on any band
d. A zero sunspot number indicates undisturbed conditions

12. What is a characteristic of skywave signals arriving at your location by both short-path and long-path propagation?

a. Periodic fading approximately every 10 seconds
b. Signal strength increased by 3 dB
c. The signal might be cancelled causing severe attenuation
d. A slightly delayed echo might be heard

13. Which ionospheric region is closest to the surface of Earth?

a. The D region
b. The E region
c. The F1 region
d. The F2 region

14. What is the purpose of the notch filter found on many HF transceivers?

a. To restrict the transmitter voice bandwidth
b. To reduce interference from carriers in the receiver passband
c. To eliminate receiver interference from impulse noise sources
d. To remove interfering splatter generated by signals on adjacent frequencies

15. What item of test equipment contains horizontal and vertical channel amplifiers?

a. An ohmmeter
b. A signal generator
c. An ammeter
d. An oscilloscope

16. Which of the following might be useful in reducing RF interference to audio frequency circuits?

a. Bypass inductor
b. Bypass capacitor
c. Forward-biased diode
d. Reverse-biased diode

17. What is the purpose of a speech processor in a transceiver?

a. Increase the apparent loudness of transmitted voice signals
b. Increase transmitter bass response for more natural-sounding SSB signals
c. Prevent distortion of voice signals
d. Decrease high-frequency voice output to prevent out-of-band operation

18. What is the purpose of a capacitance hat on a mobile antenna?

a. To increase the power handling capacity of a whip antenna
b. To reduce radiation resistance
c. To electrically lengthen a physically short antenna
d. To lower the radiation angle

19. What happens when inductive and capacitive reactance are equal in a series LC circuit?

a. Resonance causes impedance to be very high
b. Impedance is equal to the geometric mean of the inductance and capacitance
c. Resonance causes impedance to be very low
d. Impedance is equal to the arithmetic mean of the inductance and capacitance

20. What dB change represents a factor of two increase or decrease in power?

a. Approximately 2 dB
b. Approximately 3 dB
c. Approximately 6 dB
d. Approximately 9 dB

21. What causes a voltage to appear across the secondary winding of a transformer when an AC voltage source is connected across its primary winding?

a. Capacitive coupling
b. Displacement current coupling
c. Mutual inductance
d. Mutual capacitance

22. What is the minimum allowable discharge voltage for maximum life of a standard 12-volt lead-acid battery?

a. 6 volts
b. 8.5 volts
c. 10.5 volts
d. 12 volts

23. What determines the performance of a ferrite core at different frequencies?

a. Its conductivity
b. Its thickness
c. The composition, or "mix," of materials used
d. The ratio of outer diameter to inner diameter

24. What is the function of a power supply bleeder resistor?

a. It acts as a fuse for excess voltage
b. It discharges the filter capacitors when power is removed
c. It removes shock hazards from the induction coils
d. It eliminates ground loop current

25. What is the purpose of neutralizing an amplifier?

a. To limit the modulation index
b. To eliminate self-oscillations
c. To cut off the final amplifier during standby periods
d. To keep the carrier on frequency

26. What circuit is used to select one of the sidebands from a balanced modulator?

a. Carrier oscillator
b. Filter
c. IF amplifier
d. RF amplifier

27. How is direct binary FSK modulation generated?

a. By keying an FM transmitter with a sub-audible tone
b. By changing an oscillator's frequency directly with a digital control signal
c. By using a transceiver's computer data interface protocol to change frequencies
d. By reconfiguring the CW keying input to act as a tone generator

28. Which mixer input is varied or tuned to convert signals of different frequencies to an intermediate frequency (IF)?

a. Image frequency
b. Local oscillator
c. RF input
d. Beat frequency oscillator

29. On what band do amateurs share channels with the unlicensed Wi-Fi service?

a. 432 MHz
b. 902 MHz
c. 2.4 GHz
d. 10.7 GHz

30. Which of the following factors determine the characteristic impedance of a parallel conductor feed line?

a. The distance between the centers of the conductors and the radius of the conductors
b. The distance between the centers of the conductors and the length of the line
c. The radius of the conductors and the frequency of the signal
d. The frequency of the signal and the length of the line

31. What is a characteristic of a random-wire HF antenna connected directly to the transmitter?

a. It must be longer than 1 wavelength
b. Station equipment may carry significant RF current
c. It produces only vertically polarized radiation
d. It is more effective on the lower HF bands than on the higher bands

32. Which of the following would increase the bandwidth of a Yagi antenna?

a. Larger-diameter elements
b. Closer element spacing
c. Loading coils in series with the element
d. Tapered-diameter elements

33. Which of the following antenna types will be most effective as a near vertical incidence skywave (NVIS) antenna for short-skip communications on 40 meters during the day?

a. A horizontal dipole placed between 1/10 and 1/4 wavelength above the ground
b. A vertical antenna placed between 1/4 and 1/2 wavelength above the ground
c. A horizontal dipole placed at approximately 1/2 wavelength above the ground
d. A vertical dipole placed at approximately 1/2 wavelength above the ground

34. What is one way that RF energy can affect human body tissue?

a. It heats body tissue
b. It causes radiation poisoning
c. It causes the blood count to reach a dangerously low level
d. It cools body tissue

35. Which wire or wires in a four-conductor 240 VAC circuit should be attached to fuses or circuit breakers?

a. Only the hot wires
b. Only the neutral wire
c. Only the ground wire
d. All wires

Test #1 Answer Key and Explanations

1. D: The two separate frequencies of a FSK signal are identified by a mark and space.

2. C: The maximum height above ground for an antenna structure not near a public use airport without requiring notification to the FAA and registration with the FCC, is 200 feet. For most ham radio operators, this will not be a problem. [97.15(a)]

3. A: The maximum transmitter power an amateur station may use on 10.140 MHz is 200 watts PEP output. [97.313(c)(1)]

4. A: As long as you can demonstrate that you have previously held a General, Advanced, or Amateur Extra class license issued by the FCC and that it was not revoked, you may receive partial credit for all the elements represented. [97.501, 97.505(a)]

5. A: A third party would be disqualified from participating in stating a message via an amateur station if their amateur license had ever been revoked. Typically, third-party participation is the only way an unlicensed person can join in on amateur communications. The responsibility for ensuring that all communications follow the rules is held by the control operator. [97.115(b)(2)]

6. A: The upper sideband is the most commonly used for voice communications on frequencies of 14 MHz or higher.

7. C: No one has priority access to frequencies, common courtesy should always be a guide. [97.101(b), (c)]

8. D: In full break-in CW operation (QSK), transmitting stations can receive between code characters and elements. This mode of operation is only possible when the radio rig has the ability to switch very quickly between transmit and receive. When using full break-in CW operation, the operator has the ability to hear the activity on the band between code characters and elements. However, the VOX operation must be turned off in order for this mode to work properly.

9. A: The Volunteer Monitor Program consists of amateur volunteers who are formally enlisted to monitor the airwaves for rules violations.

10. D: The LSB mode is normally used when sending an RTTY signal via AFSK with an SSB transmitter.

11. A: The sunspot number is a measure of solar activity based on counting sunspots and sunspot groups. This is a number used to indicate the general amount of sunspot activity, with higher numbers generally indicating a greater probability of good propagation at higher frequencies. It is sometimes referred to as relative sunspot number, Zurich number, or Wolf number. It is calculated with the equation $R = k(10g + f)$, in which f is the number of distinct spots, g is the number of spot groups, and k is a factor based on the location and equipment of the observer.

12. D: Skywave signals arriving at your location by both short-path and long-path propagation often produce a slightly delayed echo.

13. A: The D region of the ionosphere is closest to the surface of the Earth. The D region extends from roughly 60 to 90 km above the surface of the Earth. Because of extensive electron collisions, high frequency radio waves are absorbed rather than reflected. That is, HF radio waves actually decrease in intensity as they pass through the D region.

14. B: The purpose of the notch filter found on many HF transceivers is to reduce interference from carriers in the receiver passband. A notch filter is a form of band-stop filter in which the stopband is particularly narrow (that is, it has a high Q factor). A band-stop filter, also known as a band-rejection filter, minimizes the frequencies within a specific range. This sort of filter is effective for eliminating a single interfering tone.

15. D: An oscilloscope contains horizontal and vertical channel amplifiers. An oscilloscope enables the user to observe a continuous variation of signal voltages. In most cases, this variation is displayed as a graph in which electrical potential difference is on the y-axis and time is on the x-axis.

16. B: A bypass capacitor might be useful in reducing RF interference to audio frequency circuits. A bypass capacitor, otherwise known as a decoupling capacitor, is a device for separating the various parts of an electrical circuit. The result of using a bypass capacitor is that noise created in one part of the system can be removed from the other parts.

17. A: The purpose of a speech processor in a transceiver is to increase the apparent loudness of transmitted voice signals. A speech processor is able to clean up voice communications so that they are easier to understand.

18. C: When referring to a mobile antenna, a "capacitance hat" is a device to electrically lengthen a physically short antenna. Capacitance hats may be composed of a metal disk, a wire basket, or a pyramid of wires. The capacitance hat regulates the flow of current through the antenna, so that more of the signal will propagate at the top. This has the effect of increasing the functional length of the antenna.

19. C: Resonance causes impedance to be very low when inductive and capacitive reactance are equal in a series LC circuit.

20. B: A two-times increase or decrease in power results in a change of approximately 3 dB. The amount of decibel change produced by a change in power is a proportional relationship.

21. C: Mutual inductance causes a voltage to appear across the secondary winding of a transformer when an AC voltage source is connected across its primary winding. Mutual inductance exists when the current change in one inductor initiates a voltage in some other inductor.

22. C: The minimum allowable discharge voltage for maximum life of a standard 12-volt lead acid battery is 10.5 volts.

23. C: The composition, or "mix," of materials used determines the performance of a ferrite core at different frequencies.

24. B: The power-supply bleeder resistor discharges the filter capacitors when power is removed.

25. B: The amplifier is neutralized to eliminate self-oscillations.

26. B: A filter is used to select one of the sidebands from a balanced modulator . Filters are circuits that allow some signals to pass through but greatly reduce the strength of other signals.

27. B: A direct binary FSK modulation is generated by changing an oscillator's frequency directly with a digital control signal.

28. B: The local oscillator is varied or tuned to convert signals of different frequencies to an intermediate frequency (IF).

29. C: Amateurs share channels with the unlicensed Wi-Fi service on the 2.4 GHz band.

30. A: The distance between the centers of the conductors and the radius of the conductors determines the characteristic impedance of a parallel conductor feed line.

31. B: A characteristic of a random-wire HF antenna connected directly to the transmitter is that station equipment may carry significant RF current.

32. A: Larger diameter elements would increase the bandwidth of a Yagi antenna. The Yagi antenna is the most popular form of amateur directional antenna. It has one driven element and additional elements.

33. A: A horizontal dipole antenna placed between 1/10 and 1/4 wavelength above the ground will be effective as a Near Vertical Incidence Skywave (NVIS) antenna for short-skip communications on 40 meters during the day.

34. A: RF energy can heat human body tissue.

35. A: In a four-conductor 240 VAC circuit, only the hot wires should be attached to fuses or circuit breakers.

Test #2 Practice Questions

1. On which of the following bands is phone operation prohibited?

a. 160 meters
b. 30 meters
c. 17 meters
d. 12 meters

2. With which of the following conditions must beacon stations comply?

a. No more than one beacon station may transmit in the same band from the same station location
b. The frequency must be coordinated with the National Beacon Organization
c. The frequency must be posted on the internet or published in a national periodical
d. All these choices are correct

3. What is the maximum transmitter power an amateur station may use on the 12-meter band?

a. 50 watts PEP output
b. 200 watts PEP output
c. 1500 watts PEP output
d. An effective radiated power equivalent to 100 watts from a half-wave dipole

4. What license examinations may you administer as an accredited Volunteer Examiner holding a General class operator license?

a. General and Technician
b. None, only Amateur Extra class licensees may be accredited
c. Technician only
d. Amateur Extra, General, and Technician

5. When may a 10-meter repeater retransmit the 2-meter signal from a station that has a Technician class control operator?

a. Under no circumstances
b. Only if the station on 10-meters is operating under a Special Temporary Authorization allowing such retransmission
c. Only during an FCC-declared general state of communications emergency
d. Only if the 10-meter repeater control operator holds at least a General class license

6. Which mode is most commonly used for voice communications on the 160-, 75-, and 40-meter bands?

a. Upper sideband
b. Lower sideband
c. Suppressed sideband
d. Double sideband

7. What is the first thing you should do if you are communicating with another amateur station and hear a station in distress break in?

a. Inform your local emergency coordinator
b. Acknowledge the station in distress and determine what assistance may be needed
c. Immediately decrease power to avoid interfering with the station in distress
d. Immediately cease all transmissions

8. What should you do if a CW station sends "QRS?"

a. Send slower
b. Change frequency
c. Increase your power
d. Repeat everything twice

9. Which of the following are objectives of the Volunteer Monitor Program?

a. To conduct efficient and orderly amateur licensing examinations
b. To provide emergency and public safety communications
c. To coordinate repeaters for efficient and orderly spectrum usage
d. To encourage amateur radio operators to self-regulate and comply with the rules

10. What is VARA?

a. A low signal-to-noise digital mode used for EME (moonbounce)
b. A digital protocol used with Winlink
c. A radio direction finding system used on VHF and UHF
d. A DX spotting system using a network of software defined radios

11. What effect does a sudden ionospheric disturbance have on the daytime ionospheric propagation?

a. It enhances propagation on all HF frequencies
b. It disrupts signals on lower frequencies more than those on higher frequencies
c. It disrupts communications via satellite more than direct communications
d. None, because only areas on the night side of the Earth are affected

12. What factors affect the MUF?

a. Path distance and location
b. Time of day and season
c. Solar radiation and ionospheric disturbances
d. All these choices are correct

13. What is meant by the term "critical frequency" at a given incidence angle?

a. The highest frequency which is refracted back to Earth
b. The lowest frequency which is refracted back to Earth
c. The frequency at which the signal-to-noise ratio approaches unity
d. The frequency at which the signal-to-noise ratio is 6 dB

14. What is the benefit of using the opposite or "reverse" sideband when receiving CW?

a. Interference from impulse noise will be eliminated
b. More stations can be accommodated within a given signal passband
c. It may be possible to reduce or eliminate interference from other signals
d. Accidental out-of-band operation can be prevented

15. Which of the following is an advantage of an oscilloscope versus a digital voltmeter?

a. An oscilloscope uses less power
b. Complex impedances can be easily measured
c. Greater precision
d. Complex waveforms can be measured

16. Which of the following could be a cause of interference covering a wide range of frequencies?

a. Not using a balun or line isolator to feed balanced antennas
b. Lack of rectification of the transmitter's signal in power conductors
c. Arcing at a poor electrical connection
d. Using a balun to feed an unbalanced antenna

17. How does a speech processor affect a single sideband phone signal?

a. It increases peak power
b. It increases average power
c. It reduces harmonic distortion
d. It reduces intermodulation distortion

18. What is the purpose of a corona ball on an HF mobile antenna?

a. To narrow the operating bandwidth of the antenna
b. To increase the "Q" of the antenna
c. To reduce the chance of damage if the antenna should strike an object
d. To reduce RF voltage discharge from the tip of the antenna while transmitting

19. What is reactance?

a. Opposition to the flow of direct current caused by resistance
b. Opposition to the flow of alternating current caused by capacitance or inductance
c. Reinforcement of the flow of direct current caused by resistance
d. Reinforcement of the flow of alternating current caused by capacitance or inductance

20. How does the total current relate to the individual currents in a circuit of parallel resistors?

a. It equals the average of the branch currents
b. It decreases as more parallel branches are added to the circuit
c. It equals the sum of the currents through each branch
d. It is the sum of the reciprocal of each individual voltage drop

21. What is the output voltage if an input signal is applied to the secondary winding of a 4:1 voltage step-down transformer instead of the primary winding?

a. The input voltage is multiplied by 4
b. The input voltage is divided by 4
c. Additional resistance must be added in series with the primary to prevent overload
d. Additional resistance must be added in parallel with the secondary to prevent overload

22. What is an advantage of batteries with low internal resistance?

a. Long life
b. High discharge current
c. High voltage
d. Rapid recharge

23. What is meant by the term MMIC?

a. Multi-Mode Integrated Circuit
b. Monolithic Microwave Integrated Circuit
c. Metal Monolayer Integrated Circuit
d. Mode Modulated Integrated Circuit

24. Which of the following components are used in a power supply filter network?

a. Diodes
b. Transformers and transducers
c. Capacitors and inductors
d. All these choices are correct

25. Which of these classes of amplifiers has the highest efficiency?

a. Class A
b. Class B
c. Class AB
d. Class C

26. What output is produced by a balanced modulator?

a. Frequency modulated RF
b. Audio with equalized frequency response
c. Audio extracted from the modulation signal
d. Double-sideband modulated RF

27. What is the name of the process that changes the phase angle of an RF signal to convey information?

a. Phase convolution
b. Phase modulation
c. Phase transformation
d. Phase inversion

28. What is the term for interference from a signal at twice the IF frequency from the desired signal?

a. Quadrature response
b. Image response
c. Mixer interference
d. Intermediate interference

29. Which digital mode is used as a low-power beacon for assessing HF propagation?

a. WSPR
b. MFSK16
c. PSK31
d. SSB-SC

30. What is the relationship between high standing wave ratio (SWR) and transmission line loss?

a. There is no relationship between transmission line loss and SWR
b. High SWR increases loss in a lossy transmission line
c. High SWR makes it difficult to measure transmission line loss
d. High SWR reduces the relative effect of transmission line loss

31. Which of the following is a common way to adjust the feed point impedance of an elevated quarter-wave ground-plane vertical antenna to be approximately 50 ohms?

a. Slope the radials upward
b. Slope the radials downward
c. Lengthen the radials beyond one wavelength
d. Coil the radials

32. What is the approximate length of the driven element of a Yagi antenna?

a. 1/4 wavelength
b. 1/2 wavelength
c. 3/4 wavelength
d. 1 wavelength

33. What is the feed point impedance of an end-fed half-wave antenna?

a. Very low
b. Approximately 50 ohms
c. Approximately 300 ohms
d. Very high

34. Which of the following is used to determine RF exposure from a transmitted signal?

a. Its duty cycle
b. Its frequency
c. Its power density
d. All these choices are correct

35. According to the National Electrical Code, what is the minimum wire size that may be used safely for wiring with a 20-ampere circuit breaker?

a. AWG number 20
b. AWG number 16
c. AWG number 12
d. AWG number 8

Test #2 Answer Key and Explanations

1. B: Phone operation is prohibited on the 30-meter band. In ham radio, phone operation is the generic term for voice communication. There are a number of different ways to communicate by voice using ham radio technology. However, this type of communication is considered to be too cumbersome for the 30-meter band. [97.305]

2. A: There must be no more than one beacon signal in the same band from a single location. The use of multiple beacon signals may confuse those whom the signals were intended to inform. [97.203(b)]

3. C: The maximum transmitter power an amateur station may use on the 12-meter band is 1500 watts PEP output. [97.313]

4. C: When you are an accredited Volunteer Examiner holding a General Class operator license, you may only administer the Technician license exam. Volunteer Examiners are only allowed to proctor exams at a level below their own level. Any licensed amateur may become a Volunteer Examiner by completing the qualification process administered by the VEC. [97.509(b)(3)(i)]

5. D: A 10-meter repeater may retransmit the 2-meter signal from a station having a Technician Class control operator only if the 10-meter repeater control operator holds at least a General Class license. [97.205(b)]

6. B: The lower sideband is most commonly used for voice communications on the 160-, 75-, and 40-meter bands. It is also the preferred operating mode on the 80-meter amateur bands. For voice communication on the HF bands, ham operators are most likely to use single sideband. Signals are designated as upper or lower sideband depending on whether they are above or below the carrier frequency displayed on the radio. According to tradition, voice operation on HF bands above 9 MHz is on the upper sideband, and voice operation below 9 MHz occurs on the lower sideband. The four basic steps for tuning in an SSB signal are as follows: set your rig to receive LSB or USB signals; select the widest SSB filter; adjust the tuning dial until the SSB frequency can be heard; and adjust the tuning until the voice sounds normal.

7. B: If you are communicating with another amateur station and hear a station in distress break in, the first thing you should do is acknowledge the station in distress and determine what assistance may be needed. You should note the time and frequency of the call as soon as possible. Specifically, it is important to note the address, or, if an address cannot be obtained, the latitude and longitude of the emergency. You should also try to learn the nature of the problem and the sort of assistance required. After obtaining this information, you should ask the station in distress to remain on frequency as you contact the appropriate emergency services.

8. A: If a CW station sends "QRS," you should send slower. The Q-signal QRS, when issued as a question, means "Shall I send more slowly?" When it is issued as a response, it means "Please send more slowly." It is often accompanied by the requested rate in words per minute.

9. D: One of the objectives of the Volunteer Monitor Program is to encourage amateur radio operators to self-regulate and comply with the rules.

10. B: VARA is a digital protocol used with Winlink.

11. B: A sudden ionospheric disturbance disrupts signals on lower frequencies more than those on higher frequencies. A sudden ionospheric disturbance is a complicated set of rapid fluctuations in the ionosphere, typically occurring after a period of solar flares. This phenomenon, also known as the Dellinger effect or the Mogel-Dellinger effect, is observable as a rapid increase in the radio-wave absorption, particularly in the lower HF and upper MF ranges. Sudden ionospheric disturbance can be very disruptive to telecommunications systems, including ham radio. The effects are most dire in the regions around the equator, and may last from a few minutes to several hours.

12. D: Path distance and location, time of day and season, as well as solar radiation and ionospheric disturbances can affect the MUF.

13. A: The critical frequency at a given incidence angle is the highest frequency which is refracted back to Earth.

14. C: One advantage of selecting the opposite or "reverse" sideband when receiving CW is that it may be possible to reduce or eliminate interference from other signals.

15. D: One advantage of an oscilloscope versus a digital voltmeter is that complex waveforms can be measured. A digital voltmeter is an effective tool for measuring electrical potential difference between two distinct points in an electric circuit; it employs an analog-to-digital converter to create a numerical reading of voltage.

16. C: One cause of interference over a wide range of frequencies could be arcing at a poor electrical connection. Arcing is the flow of current through media that normally do not conduct, as for instance air.

17. B: A speech processor increases the average power of a single sideband phone signal. This is one of the ways in which it improves the general clarity and intelligibility of the voice signal.

18. D: The purpose of a corona ball on an HF mobile antenna is to reduce RF voltage discharge from the tip of the antenna while transmitting.

19. B: Reactance is opposition to the flow of alternating current caused by capacitance or inductance. The amount of reactance in a circuit element depends on the inductance or capacitance of the element. If there is an established electric field, it will work against the voltage change on the element. At the same time, a magnetic field will have a natural resistance to a change in current. A perfect resistor will have a reactance of zero, while perfect inductors and capacitors will be entirely composed of reactance. This is because an ideal inductor will have zero resistance, and an ideal capacitor will have infinite resistance.

20. C: The total current equals the sum of the individual currents in each branch of a parallel circuit.

21. A: If an input signal is applied to the secondary winding of a 4:1 voltage step-down transformer instead of the primary winding, then the output voltage is equal to the input voltage multiplied by 4.

22. B: One advantage of batteries with low internal resistance is a high discharge current. Batteries convert chemical energy into electrical energy.

23. B: The term MMIC means Monolithic Microwave Integrated Circuit. This is a type of integrated circuit that is capable of operating at microwave frequencies. The most common uses for these devices are high-frequency switching, low-noise amplification, power amplification, and microwave mixing.

24. C: Capacitors and inductors are used in a power-supply filter network.

25. D: Class C amplifiers have the highest efficiency. A Class C amplifier is biased such that the active device conducts for less than 180 degrees of the input waveform.

26. D: A balanced modulator produces a double-sideband modulated RF output.

27. B: Phase modulation is the process that changes the phase angle of an RF wave to convey information.

28. B: Interference from a signal at twice the IF frequency from the desired signal is called image response interference.

29. A: WSPR mode is used as a low-power beacon for assessing HF propagation.

30. B: High SWR increases loss in a lossy transmission line, so it is critical to minimize SWR.

31. B: A common way to adjust the feed point impedance of a quarter-wave ground plane vertical antenna is to slope the radials downward.

32. B: The approximate length of the driven element of a Yagi antenna is 1/2 wavelength.

33. D: The feed-point impedance of an end-fed half-wave antenna is very high.

34. D: The duty cycle, frequency, and power density are all part of determining RF exposure from a transmitted signal.

35. C: The minimum wire size that may be safely used for a circuit that draws up to 20 amperes of continuous current is AWG number 12.

Test #3 Practice Questions

1. On which of the following bands is image transmission prohibited?

a. 160 meters
b. 30 meters
c. 20 meters
d. 12 meters

2. Which of the following is a purpose of a beacon station as identified in the FCC rules?

a. Observation of propagation and reception
b. Automatic identification of repeaters
c. Transmission of bulletins of general interest to amateur radio licensees
d. All these choices are correct

3. What is the maximum bandwidth permitted by FCC rules for amateur radio stations transmitting on USB frequencies in the 60-meter band?

a. 2.8 kHz
b. 5.6 kHz
c. 1.8 kHz
d. 3 kHz

4. On which of the following band segments may you operate if you are a Technician class operator and have an unexpired Certificate of Successful Completion of Examination (CSCE) for General class privileges?

a. Only the Technician band segments until your upgrade is posted in the FCC database
b. Only on the Technician band segments until you have a receipt for the FCC application fee payment
c. On any General or Technician class band segment
d. On any General or Technician class band segment except 30 meters and 60 meters

5. What is required to conduct communications with a digital station operating under automatic control outside the automatic control band segments?

a. The station initiating the contact must be under local or remote control
b. The interrogating transmission must be made by another automatically controlled station
c. No third-party traffic may be transmitted
d. The control operator of the interrogating station must hold an Amateur Extra class license

6. Which mode is most commonly used for SSB voice communications in the VHF and UHF bands?

a. Upper sideband
b. Lower sideband
c. Suppressed sideband
d. Double sideband

7. What is good amateur practice if propagation changes during a contact creating interference from other stations using the frequency?

a. Advise the interfering stations that you are on the frequency and that you have priority
b. Decrease power and continue to transmit
c. Attempt to resolve the interference problem with the other stations in a mutually acceptable manner
d. Switch to the opposite sideband

8. What does it mean when a CW operator sends "KN" at the end of a transmission?

a. No US stations should call
b. Operating full break-in
c. Listening only for a specific station or stations
d. Closing station now

9. What procedure may be used by Volunteer Monitors to localize a station whose continuous carrier is holding a repeater on in their area?

a. Compare vertical and horizontal signal strengths on the input frequency
b. Compare beam headings on the repeater input from their home locations with that of other Volunteer Monitors
c. Compare signal strengths between the input and output of the repeater
d. All these choices are correct

10. What symptoms may result from other signals interfering with a PACTOR or VARA transmission?

a. Frequent retries or timeouts
b. Long pauses in message transmission
c. Failure to establish a connection between stations
d. All these choices are correct

11. Approximately how long does it take the increased ultraviolet and X-ray radiation from a solar flare to affect radio propagation on Earth?

a. 28 days
b. 1 to 2 hours
c. 8 minutes
d. 20 to 40 hours

12. Which frequency will have the least attenuation for long-distance skip propagation?

a. Just below the MUF
b. Just above the LUF
c. Just below the critical frequency
d. Just above the critical frequency

13. Why is skip propagation via the F2 region longer than that via the other ionospheric regions?

a. Because it is the densest
b. Because of the Doppler effect
c. Because it is the highest
d. Because of temperature inversions

14. How does a noise blanker work?

a. By temporarily increasing received bandwidth
b. By redirecting noise pulses into a filter capacitor
c. By reducing receiver gain during a noise pulse
d. By clipping noise peaks

15. Which of the following is the best instrument to use for checking the keying waveform of a CW transmitter?

a. An oscilloscope
b. A field strength meter
c. A sidetone monitor
d. A wavemeter

16. What sound is heard from an audio device experiencing RF interference from a single sideband phone transmitter?

a. A steady hum whenever the transmitter is on the air
b. On-and-off humming or clicking
c. Distorted speech
d. Clearly audible speech

17. What is the effect of an incorrectly adjusted speech processor?

a. Distorted speech
b. Excess intermodulation products
c. Excessive background noise
d. All these choices are correct

18. Which of the following direct, fused power connections would be the best for a 100-watt HF mobile installation?

a. To the battery using heavy-gauge wire
b. To the alternator or generator using heavy-gauge wire
c. To the battery using insulated heavy duty balanced transmission line
d. To the alternator or generator using insulated heavy duty balanced transmission line

19. Which of the following is opposition to the flow of alternating current in an inductor?

a. Conductance
b. Reluctance
c. Admittance
d. Reactance

20. How many watts of electrical power are consumed if 400 VDC is supplied to an 800-ohm load?

a. 0.5 watts
b. 200 watts
c. 400 watts
d. 3200 watts

21. What is the total resistance of a 10-, a 20-, and a 50-ohm resistor connected in parallel?

a. 5.9 ohms
b. 0.17 ohms
c. 17 ohms
d. 80 ohms

22. What is the approximate forward threshold voltage of a germanium diode?

a. 0.1 volt
b. 0.3 volts
c. 0.7 volts
d. 1.0 volts

23. Which of the following is an advantage of CMOS integrated circuits compared to TTL integrated circuits?

a. Low power consumption
b. High power handling capability
c. Better suited for RF amplification
d. Better suited for power supply regulation

24. Which type of rectifier circuit uses two diodes and a center-tapped transformer?

a. Full-wave
b. Full-wave bridge
c. Half-wave
d. Synchronous

25. Which of the following describes the function of a two-input AND gate?

a. Output is high when either or both inputs are low
b. Output is high only when both inputs are high
c. Output is low when either or both inputs are high
d. Output is low only when both inputs are high

26. What is one reason to use an impedance matching transformer at a transmitter output?

a. To minimize transmitter power output
b. To present the desired impedance to the transmitter and feed line
c. To reduce power supply ripple
d. To minimize radiation resistance

27. What is the name of the process that changes the instantaneous frequency of an RF wave to convey information?

a. Frequency convolution
b. Frequency transformation
c. Frequency conversion
d. Frequency modulation

28. What is another term for the mixing of two RF signals?

a. Heterodyning
b. Synthesizing
c. Frequency inversion
d. Phase inversion

29. What part of a packet radio frame contains the routing and handling information?

a. Directory
b. Preamble
c. Header
d. Trailer

30. What is the nominal characteristic impedance of "window line" transmission line?

a. 50 ohms
b. 75 ohms
c. 100 ohms
d. 450 ohms

31. Which of the following best describes the radiation pattern of a quarter-wave ground-plane vertical antenna?

a. Bi-directional in azimuth
b. Isotropic
c. Hemispherical
d. Omnidirectional in azimuth

32. How do the lengths of a three-element Yagi reflector and director compare to that of the driven element?

a. The reflector is longer, and the director is shorter
b. The reflector is shorter, and the director is longer
c. They are all the same length
d. Relative length depends on the frequency of operation

33. In which direction is the maximum radiation from a VHF/UHF "halo" antenna?

a. Broadside to the plane of the halo
b. Opposite the feed point
c. Omnidirectional in the plane of the halo
d. On the same side as the feed point

34. How can you determine that your station complies with FCC RF exposure regulations?

a. By calculation based on FCC OET Bulletin 65
b. By calculation based on computer modeling
c. By measurement of field strength using calibrated equipment
d. All these choices are correct

35. Which size of fuse or circuit breaker would be appropriate to use with a circuit that uses AWG number 14 wiring?

a. 30 amperes
b. 25 amperes
c. 20 amperes
d. 15 amperes

Test #3 Answer Key and Explanations

1. B: Image transmission is prohibited on the 30-meter band. This is because the transmission of images requires an amount of traffic that would obstruct the band for other users. [97.305]

2. A: The FCC Rules state that one purpose of a beacon station is the observation of propagation and reception. Beacon stations communicate only for experimental purposes, most often to observe propagation and reception. Ham radio operators often use these stations as reference points or to calibrate their equipment. [97.3(a)(9)]

3. A: The maximum bandwidth permitted by FCC rules for Amateur Radio stations when transmitting on USB frequencies in the 60-meter band is 2.8 kHz. [97.303(h)(1)]

4. C: You may operate on any General or Technician Class band segment if you are a Technician Class operator and have a CSCE for General Class privileges. [97.9(b)]

5. A: To communicate with a digital station operating under automatic control outside the automatic control band segments, the station initiating contact must be under local or remote control. [97.221]

6. A: The upper sideband is most commonly used for SSB voice communications in the VHF and UHF bands.

7. C: Attempting to resolve the interference problem with the other stations in a mutually acceptable manner is good amateur practice if propagation changes during a contact create interference from other stations using the frequency.

8. C: When a CW operator sends "KN" at the end of a transmission, it means that the operator is listening only for a specific station or stations.

9. B: Comparing beam headings on the repeater input from their home locations with that of other Volunteer Monitors may help localize a station whose continuous carrier is holding a repeater on in their area.

10. D: These are all possible symptoms of other signals interfering with a PACTOR or VARA transmission.

11. C: It takes the increased ultraviolet and X-ray radiation from solar flares approximately eight minutes to affect radio-wave propagation on the Earth. A solar flare is a rapid increase in the brightness of a particular area of the sun, representing a release of up to one-sixth of the sun's normal energy output. The solar flare is typically followed by a coronal mass ejection.

12. A: Selecting a frequency just below the MUF will give the lowest attenuation for long-distance skip propagation.

13. C: Skip propagation via the F2 region is longer than that via the other ionospheric regions because it is the highest ionospheric region. It lies approximately 220 to 800 km above the surface of the Earth. It is the primary reflecting layer for HF communications both at night and during the day.

14. C: A noise blanker works by reducing receiver gain during a noise pulse.

15. A: An oscilloscope is the best instrument to use for checking the keying waveform of a CW transmitter. An oscilloscope assesses the change of an electrical signal over time, and creates a graphical representation of the alterations in voltage and time. The resulting shape is called a waveform.

16. C: An audio device experiencing interference from a single sideband phone transmitter will produce distorted speech.

17. D: Distorted speech, excess intermodulation products, and excessive background pickup can all result from an incorrectly adjusted speech processor.

18. A: A direct, fused power connection to the battery using heavy gauge wire would be better than a direct, fused connection to the alternator or generator using heavy gauge wire. It would also be better than direct, fused power connections to the battery or to the alternator or generator using resistor wire.

19. D: Reactance is opposition to the flow of alternating current in an inductor. Another way of expressing this is that reactance is the opposition to the change in current caused by inductance.

20. B: If 400 VDC is supplied to an 800-ohm load, 200 watts of electrical power are consumed. The amount of power used is calculated by dividing the voltage by the resistance and then multiplying by 100.

21. A: The total resistance of a 10-, a 20-, and a 50-ohm resistor connected in parallel is 5.9 ohms. Total resistance of resistors in parallel is the reciprocal of the sum of their reciprocals: $1/(1/10+1/20+1/50)=1/(10/100+5/100+2/100)=100/17\approx5.9$

22. B: The approximate forward threshold voltage of a germanium diode is 0.3 volts. The forward threshold voltage is the amount of voltage the diode can handle.

23. A: Low power consumption is one advantage of CMOS integrated circuits as compared to TTL integrated circuits. CMOS (complementary metal-oxide-semiconductor) circuits are commonly used in microcontrollers and microprocessors. These circuits also have a high noise immunity. They only use a little bit of power because at least one of the two transistors is always off. In a TTL (transistor-transistor logic) circuit, on the other hand, a great deal of power is wasted through the heat emission.

24. A: A full-wave rectifier circuit uses two diodes and a center-tapped transformer.

25. B: In a two input AND gate, output is high only when both inputs are high.

26. B: One reason to use an impedance matching transformer at a transmitter output is to present the desired impedance to the transmitter and feed line.

27. D: Frequency modulation is the process which changes the frequency of an RF wave to convey information. Most repeaters use frequency modulated phone signals to communicate via voice. When this is done, the RF carrier frequency is altered by the voice data.

28. A: Heterodyning is another term for the mixing of two RF signals. In this process, an electronic circuit is used to combine an input radio frequency with a generated frequency: the result is one frequency that is a sum of the frequencies and one frequency that is the difference between the frequencies.

29. C: The header of a data packet contains the routing and handling information. The trailer of a data packet may also contain the routing and handling information, which is also known as the control information. The main content of the message is called the user data, or payload.

30. D: The nominal characteristic impedance of "window line" transmission line is 450 ohms.

31. D: A quarter-wave ground-plane vertical antenna produces a radiation pattern that is omnidirectional in azimuth.

32. A: In a three-element Yagi, the reflector is longer and the director is shorter than those of the driven element.

33. C: The maximum radiation from a VHF/UHF "halo" antenna is omnidirectional in the plane of the halo

34. D: You can determine that your station complies with FCC RF exposure regulations by calculation based on FCC OET Bulletin 65; by calculation based on computer modeling; or by measurement of field strength using calibrated equipment. [97.13(c)(1)]

35. D: A fuse or circuit breaker of 15 amperes would be appropriate to use with a circuit that uses AWG number 14 wiring.

Seven Additional Ham Radio General Class Practice Tests

To take these additional practice tests, visit the online resources page:
mometrix.com/resources719/hamradiogen

Extra Class Question Pool

E1 – Commission Rules

E1A – Frequency Privileges; Signal Frequency Range; Automatic Message Forwarding; Stations Abroad Ships or Aircraft; Power Restriction on 630- and 2200-Meter Bands

Why is it not legal to transmit a 3 kHz bandwidth USB signal with a carrier frequency of 14.348 MHz?

A. USB is not used on 20-meter phone
B. The lower 1 kHz of the signal is outside the 20-meter band
C. 14.348 MHz is outside the 20-meter band
D. The upper 1 kHz of the signal is outside the 20-meter band

E1A01 Answer: D. It is not legal to transmit a 3 kHz bandwidth USB signal with a carrier frequency of 14.348 MHz because the upper 1 kHz of the signal is outside the 20-meter band. [97.305, 97.307(b)]

When using a transceiver that displays the carrier frequency of phone signals, which of the following displayed frequencies represents the lowest frequency at which a properly adjusted LSB emission will be totally within the band?

A. The exact lower band edge
B. 300 Hz above the lower band edge
C. 1 kHz above the lower band edge
D. 3 kHz above the lower band edge

E1A02 Answer: D. The lowest frequency at which a properly adjusted LSB emission will be totally within the band is 3 kHz above the lower band edge. [97.301, 97.305]

What is the highest legal carrier frequency on the 20-meter band for transmitting a 2.8 kHz wide USB digital signal?

A. 14.0708 MHz
B. 14.1002 MHz
C. 14.1472 MHz
D. 14.3490 MHz

E1A03 Answer: C. 14.1472 MHz is the maximum legal carrier frequency on the 20-meter band for transmitting a 2.8 kHz wide USB data signal. [97.305, 97.307(b)]

May an Extra class operator answer the CQ of a station on 3.601 MHz LSB phone?

A. Yes, the entire signal will be inside the SSB allocation for Extra class operators
B. Yes, the displayed frequency is within the 75-meter phone band segment
C. No, the sideband components will extend beyond the edge of the phone band segment
D. No, US stations are not permitted to use phone emissions below 3.610 MHz

E1A04 Answer: C. An Extra class operator may not answer the CQ of a station on a 3.601 MHz LSB phone because the sideband components will extend beyond the edge of the phone band segment. [97.301, 97.305]

Who must be in physical control of the station apparatus of an amateur station aboard any vessel or craft that is documented or registered in the United States?

A. Only a person with an FCC Marine Radio license grant
B. Only a person named in an amateur station license grant
C. Any person holding an FCC issued amateur license or who is authorized for alien reciprocal operation
D. Any person named in an amateur station license grant or a person holding an unrestricted Radiotelephone Operator Permit

E1A05 Answer: C. Any person holding an FCC issued amateur license or who is authorized for alien reciprocal operation must be in physical control of the station apparatus of an amateur station aboard any vessel or craft that is documented or registered in the United States. [97.5]

What is the required transmit frequency of a CW signal for channelized 60 meter operation?

A. At the lowest frequency of the channel
B. At the center frequency of the channel
C. At the highest frequency of the channel
D. On any frequency where the signal's sidebands are within the channel

E1A06 Answer: B. The required transmit frequency of a CW signal channelized for 60 meter operation must be set at the center frequency of the channel. [97.303(h)(1)]

What is the maximum power permitted on the 2200-meter band?

A. 50 watts PEP (peak envelope power)
B. 100 watts PEP (peak envelope power)
C. 1 watt EIRP (equivalent isotropic radiated power)
D. 5 watts EIRP (equivalent isotropic radiated power)

E1A07 Answer: C. The maximum power permitted on the 2200-meter band is 1 watt EIRP (equivalent isotropic radiated power). [97.313(k)]

If a station in a message forwarding system inadvertently forwards a message that is in violation of FCC rules, who is primarily accountable for the rules violation?

A. The control operator of the packet bulletin board station
B. The control operator of the originating station
C. The control operators of all the stations in the system
D. The control operators of all the stations in the system not authenticating the source from which they accept communications

E1A08 Answer: B. The control operator of the originating station is primarily accountable if a forwarded message violates FCC rules. [97.219]

Except in some parts of Alaska, what is the maximum power permitted on the 640-meter band?

A. 50 watts PEP (peak envelope power)
B. 100 watts PEP (peak envelope power)
C. 1 watt EIRP (equivalent isotropic radiated power)
D. 5 watts EIRP (equivalent isotropic radiated power)

E1A09 Answer: D. The maximum power permitted on the 640-meter band is 5 watts EIRP (equivalent isotropic radiated power), except in some parts of Alaska. [97.313(l)]

If an amateur station is installed aboard a ship or aircraft, what condition must be met before the station is operated?

A. Its operation must be approved by the master of the ship or the pilot in command of the aircraft
B. The amateur station operator must agree not to transmit when the main radio of the ship or aircraft is in use
C. The amateur station must have a power supply that is completely independent of the main ship or aircraft power supply
D. The amateur station must operate only in specific segments of the amateur service HF and VHF bands

E1A10 Answer: A. Amateur stations aboard ships or aircraft do not need special endorsement so long as permission is obtained from the captain or pilot of the craft and all applicable rules are followed. [97.11]

What licensing is required when operating an amateur station aboard a US-registered vessel in international waters?

A. Any amateur license with an FCC Marine or Aircraft endorsement
B. Any FCC-issued amateur license
C. Only General class or higher amateur licenses
D. An unrestricted Radiotelephone Operator Permit

E1A11 Answer: B. Any FCC-issued amateur license is suitable for operating an amateur station aboard a US-registered vessel in international waters. [97.5]

E1B – Station Restrictions and Special Operations: Restrictions on Station Location; General Operating Restrictions; Spurious Emissions; Antenna Structure Restrictions; RACES Operations

Which of the following constitutes a spurious emission?

A. An amateur station transmission made without the proper call sign identification
B. A signal transmitted to prevent its detection by any station other than the intended recipient
C. Any transmitted signal that unintentionally interferes with another licensed radio station and whose levels exceed 40 dB below the fundamental power level
D. An emission outside the signal's necessary bandwidth that can be reduced or eliminated without affecting the information transmitted

E1B01 Answer: D. A spurious emission is an emission outside the signal's necessary bandwidth that can be reduced or eliminated without affecting the information transmitted. [97.3]

Which of the following is an acceptable bandwidth for digital voice or slow-scan TV transmissions made on the HF amateur bands?

A. 3 kHz
B. 10 kHz
C. 15 kHz
D. 20 kHz

E1B02 Answer: A. 3 KHz is an acceptable bandwidth for digital voice or slow-scan TV transmissions made on the HF amateur bands. [97.307(f)(2)]

Within what distance must an amateur station protect an FCC monitoring facility from harmful interference?

A. 1 mile
B. 3 miles
C. 10 miles
D. 30 miles

E1B03 Answer: A. An amateur station located within 1 mile (1600 m) of an FCC monitoring facility must protect it from harmful interference. [97.13]

What must the control operator of a repeater operating in the 70-centimeter band do if a radiolocation system experiences interference from that repeater?

A. Reduce the repeater antenna HAAT (Height Above Average Terrain)
B. File an FAA NOTAM (Notice to Air Missions) with the repeater system's ERP, call sign, and six-character grid locator
C. Cease operation or make changes to the repeater that mitigate the interference
D. All these choices are correct

E1B04 Answer: C. A control operator of a repeater operating in the 70-centimeter band must cease operation or make changes to the repeater that mitigate the interference if a radiolocation system experiences interference from that repeater. [97.303(b)]

What is the National Radio Quiet Zone?

A. An area surrounding the FCC monitoring station in Laurel, Maryland
B. An area in New Mexico surrounding the White Sands Test Area
C. An area surrounding the National Radio Astronomy Observatory
D. An area in Florida surrounding Cape Canaveral

E1B05 Answer: C. The National Radio Quiet Zone is an area surrounding the National Radio Astronomy Observatory. [97.3]

Which of the following additional rules apply if you are erecting an amateur station antenna structure at a site at or near a public use airport?

A. You may have to notify the Federal Aviation Administration and register it with the FCC as required by Part 17 of the FCC rules
B. You may have to enter the height above ground in meters, and the latitude and longitude in degrees, minutes, and seconds on the FAA website
C. You must file an Environmental Impact Statement with the EPA before construction begins
D. You must obtain a construction permit from the airport zoning authority per Part 119 of the FAA regulations

E1B06 Answer: A. If installing an amateur station antenna at a site at or near a public use airport, you may have to notify the Federal Aviation Administration and register it with the FCC as required by Part 17 of FCC rules. [97.15]

To what type of regulations does PRB-1 apply?

A. Homeowners associations
B. FAA tower height limits
C. State and local zoning
D. Use of wireless devices in vehicles

E1B07 Answer: C. PRB-1 applies to state and local zoning. [97.15]

What limitations may the FCC place on an amateur station if its signal causes interference to domestic broadcast reception, assuming that the receivers involved are of good engineering design?

A. The amateur station must cease operation
B. The amateur station must cease operation on all frequencies below 30 MHz
C. The amateur station must cease operation on all frequencies above 30 MHz
D. The amateur station must avoid transmitting during certain hours on frequencies that cause the interference

E1B08 Answer: D. If an amateur station causes interference to domestic broadcast reception, the FCC may require that the station avoid transmitting during certain hours on frequencies that cause the interference. [97.121]

Which amateur stations may be operated under RACES rules?

A. Only those club stations licensed to Amateur Extra class operators
B. Any FCC-licensed amateur station except a Technician class
C. Any FCC-licensed amateur station certified by the responsible civil defense organization for the area served
D. Only stations meeting the FCC Part 97 technical standards for operation during an emergency

E1B09 Answer: C. Any FCC-licensed amateur station certified by the responsible civil defense organization for the area served may be operated under RACES rules. [97.407]

What frequencies are authorized to an amateur station operating under RACES rules?

A. All amateur service frequencies authorized to the control operator
B. Specific segments in the amateur service MF, HF, VHF and UHF bands
C. Specific local government channels
D. All these choices are correct

E1B10 Answer: A. An amateur station operating under RACES rules may use all amateur service frequencies authorized to the control operator. [97.407]

What does PRB-1 require of state and local regulations affecting amateur radio antenna size and structures?

A. No limitations may be placed on antenna size or placement
B. Reasonable accommodations of amateur radio must be made
C. Such structures must be permitted when use for emergency communications can be demonstrated
D. Such structures must be permitted if certified by a registered professional engineer

E1B11 Answer: B. PRB-1 requires state and local regulations to make reasonable accommodations of amateur radio. [97.15]

E1C –Automatic and Remote Control; Band-Specific Regulations; Operating in and Communicating with Foreign Countries; Spurious Emission Standards; HF Modulation Index Limit; Band-Specific Rules

What is the maximum bandwidth for a data emission on 60 meters?

A. 60 Hz
B. 170 Hz
C. 1.5 kHz
D. 2.8 kHz

E1C01 Answer: D. The maximum bandwidth for a data emission on 60 meters is 2.8 kHz. [97.303]

Which of the following apply to communications transmitted to amateur foreign stations in foreign countries?

A. Third party traffic must be limited to that intended for the exclusive use of government and non-Government Organization (NGOs) involved in emergency relief activities
B. All transmissions must be in English
C. Communications must be limited to those incidental to the purpose of the amateur service and remarks of a personal nature
D. All these choices are correct

E1C02 Answer: C. Communications transmitted to amateur foreign stations in foreign countries must be limited to those incidental to the purpose of the amateur service and remarks of a personal nature. [97.117]

How long must an operator wait after filing a notification with the Utilities Technology Council (UTC) before operating on the 2200-meter or 630-meter band?

A. Operators must not operate until approval is received
B. Operators may operate after 30 days, providing they have not been told that their station is within 1 kilometer of PLC systems using those frequencies
C. Operators may not operate until a test signal has been transmitted in coordination with the local power company
D. Operations may commence immediately, and may continue unless interference is reported by the UTC

E1C03 Answer: B. Operators may operate on the 2200-meter or 630-meter band after 30 days, providing they have not been told that their station is within 1 kilometer of PLC systems using those frequencies, after filing a notification with the Utilities Technology Council (UTC). [97.303(g)]

What is an IARP?

A. A permit that allows US amateurs to operate in certain countries of the Americas
B. The internal amateur radio practices policy of the FCC
C. An indication of increased antenna reflected power
D. A forecast of intermittent aurora radio propagation

E1C04 Answer: A. An IARP is an international amateur radio permit that allows US amateurs to operate in certain countries of the Americas.

Under what situation may a station transmit third party communications while being automatically controlled?

A. Never
B. Only when transmitting RTTY or data emissions
C. Only when transmitting SSB or CW
D. On any mode approved by the National Telecommunication and Information Administration

E1C05 Answer: B. A station may transmit third party communications while being automatically controlled only when transmitting RTTY or data emissions. [97.221(c), 97.115(c)]

Which of the following is required in order to operate in accordance with CEPT rules in foreign countries where permitted?

A. You must identify in the official language of the country in which you are operating
B. The US embassy must approve of your operation
C. You must bring a copy of FCC Public Notice DA 16-1048
D. You must append "/CEPT" to your call sign

E1C06 Answer: C. To operate in accordance with CEPT rules in foreign countries where permitted, you must bring a copy of FCC Public Notice DA 16-1048.

What notifications must be given before transmitting on the 630- or 2200-meter bands?

A. A special endorsement must be requested from the FCC
B. An environmental impact statement must be filed with the Department of the Interior
C. Operators must inform the FAA of their intent to operate, giving their call sign and distance to the nearest runway
D. Operators must inform the Utilities Technology Council (UTC) of their call sign and coordinates of the station

E1C07 Answer: D. Operators must inform the Utilities Technology Council (UTC) of their call sign and coordinates of the station before transmitting on the 630- or 2200-meter bands. [97.303(g)]

What is the maximum permissible duration of a remotely controlled station's transmissions if its control link malfunctions?

A. 30 seconds
B. 3 minutes
C. 5 minutes
D. 10 minutes

E1C08 Answer: B. The maximum permissible duration of a remotely controlled station's transmissions if its control link malfunctions is 3 minutes. [97.213]

What is the highest modulation index permitted at the highest modulation frequency for angle modulation below 29.0 MHz?

A. 0.5
B. 1.0
C. 2.0
D. 3.0

E1C09 Answer: B. The highest modulation index permitted at the highest modulation frequency for angle modulation below 29.0 MHz is 1.0. [97.307]

What is the maximum mean power level for a spurious emission below 30 MHz with respect to the fundamental emission?

A. -43 dB
B. -53 dB
C. -63 dB
D. -73 dB

E1C10 Answer: A. The maximum mean power level for a spurious emission below 30 MHz with respect to the fundamental emission is -43 dB. [97.307]

Which of the following operating arrangements allows an FCC-licensed US citizen to operate in many European countries, and amateurs from many European countries to operate in the US?

A. CEPT
B. IARP
C. ITU reciprocal license
D. All these choices are correct

E1C11 Answer: A. A CEPT allows an FCC-licensed US citizen to operate in many European countries, and amateurs from many European countries to operate in the US. [97.5]

On what portion of the 630-meter band are phone emissions permitted?

A. None
B. Only the top 3 kHz
C. Only the bottom 3 kHz
D. The entire band

E1C12 Answer: D. Phone emissions are permitted on the entire 630-meter band. [97.305(c)]

E1D – Amateur Space and Earth Stations; Telemetry and Telecommand Rules; Identification of Balloon Transmissions; One-Way Communications

What is the definition of telemetry?

A. One-way transmission of measurements at a distance from the measuring instrument
B. Two-way transmissions in excess of 1000 feet
C. Two-way transmissions of data
D. One-way transmission that initiates, modifies, or terminates the functions of a device at a distance

E1D01 Answer: A. Telemetry is one-way transmission of measurements at a distance from the measuring instrument. [97.3]

Which of the following may transmit encrypted messages?

A. Telecommand signals to terrestrial repeaters
B. Telecommand signals from a space telecommand station
C. Auxiliary relay links carrying repeater audio
D. Mesh network backbone nodes

E1D02 Answer: B. Telecommand signals from a space telecommand station may transmit encrypted messages. [97.211(b)]

What is a space telecommand station?

A. An amateur station located on the surface of the Earth for communication with other Earth stations by means of Earth satellites
B. An amateur station that transmits communications to initiate, modify, or terminate functions of a space station
C. An amateur station located in a satellite or a balloon more than 50 kilometers above the surface of the Earth
D. An amateur station that receives telemetry from a satellite or balloon more than 50 kilometers above the surface of the Earth

E1D03 Answer: B. A space telecommand station is an amateur station that transmits communications to initiate, modify, or terminate functions of a space station. [97.3(a)(45)]

Which of the following is required in the identification transmissions from a balloon-borne telemetry station?

A. Call sign
B. The output power of the balloon transmitter
C. The station's six-character Maidenhead grid locator
D. All these choices are correct

E1D04 Answer: A. A call sign is required in the identification transmissions from a balloon-borne telemetry station. [97.119(a)]

What must be posted at the location of a station being operated by telecommand on or within 50 km of the Earth's surface?

A. A photocopy of the station license
B. A label with the name, address, and telephone number of the station licensee
C. A label with the name, address, and telephone number of the control operator
D. All these choices are correct

E1D05 Answer: D. A photocopy of the station license, a label with the name, address, and telephone number of the station licensee, and a label with the name, address, and telephone number of the control operator all must be posted at the location of a station being operated by telecommand on or within 50 km of the Earth's surface. [97.213(d)]

What is the maximum permitted transmitter output power when operating a model craft by telecommand?

A. 1 watt
B. 2 watts
C. 5 watts
D. 100 watts

E1D06 Answer: A. 1 watt is the maximum permitted transmitter output power when operating a model craft by telecommand. [97.215(c)]

Which of the following HF amateur bands include allocations for space stations?

A. 40 meters, 20 meters, 15 meters, and 10 meters
B. 30 meters, 17 meters, and 10 meters
C. Only 10 meters
D. Satellite operation is permitted on all HF bands

E1D07 Answer: A. Only the 40-, 20-, 15-, and 10-meter HF amateur bands include allocations for space stations. [97.207]

Which VHF amateur bands have frequencies authorized for space stations?

A. 6 meters and 2 meters
B. 6 meters, 2 meters, and 1.25 meters
C. 2 meters and 1.25 meters
D. 2 meters

E1D08 Answer: D. The 2-meter amateur bands have frequencies authorized for space stations. [97.207]

Which UHF amateur bands have frequencies authorized for space stations?

A. 70 centimeters only
B. 70 centimeters and 13 centimeters
C. 70 centimeters and 33 centimeters
D. 33 centimeters and 13 centimeters

E1D09 Answer: B. The 70-centimeter and 13-centimeter amateur bands have frequencies authorized for space stations. [97.207]

Which amateur stations are eligible to be telecommand stations of space stations (subject to the privileges of the class of operator license held by the control operator of the station)?

A. Any amateur station approved by AMSAT
B. Any amateur station so designated by the space station licensee
C. Any amateur station so designated by the ITU
D. All these choices are correct

E1D10 Answer: B. Any amateur station so designated by the space station licensee is eligible to be a telecommand station (subject to the privileges of the class of operator license held by the control operator of the station). [97.211]

Which amateur stations are eligible to operate as Earth stations?

A. Any amateur licensee who has successfully complete the AMSAT space communications course
B. Only those of General, Advanced or Amateur Extra class operators
C. Only those of Amateur Extra class operators
D. Any amateur station, subject to the privileges of the class of operator license held by the control operator

E1D11 Answer: D. Any amateur station is eligible to operate as an Earth station, subject to the privileges of the class of operator license held by the control operator. [97.209]

Which of the following amateur stations may transmit one-way communications?

A. A space station, beacon station, or telecommand station
B. A local repeater or linked repeater station
C. A message forwarding station or automatically controlled digital station
D. All these choices are correct

E1D12 Answer: A. A space station, beacon station, or telecommand station may transmit one-way communications. [97.207(e), 97.203(g)]

E1E – Volunteer Examiner Program: Definitions; Qualifications; Preparation and Administration of Exams; Accreditation; Question Pools; Documentation Requirements

For which types of out-of-pocket expenses do the Part 97 rules state that VEs and VECs may be reimbursed?

A. Preparing, processing, administering, and coordinating an examination for an amateur radio operator license
B. Teaching an amateur operator license examination preparation course
C. No expenses are authorized for reimbursement
D. Providing amateur operator license examination preparation training materials

E1E01 Answer: A. The Part 97 rules state that VEs and VECs may be reimbursed for preparing, processing, administering and coordinating an examination for an amateur radio license. [97.527]

Who is tasked by Part 97 with maintaining the pools of questions for all US amateur license examinations?

A. The VEs
B. The FCC
C. The VECs
D. The ARRL

E1E02 Answer: C. The VECs are tasked by Part 97 with maintaining the pools of questions for all US amateur license examinations. [97.523]

What is a Volunteer Examiner Coordinator?

A. A person who has volunteered to administer amateur operator license examinations
B. An organization paid by the volunteer examiner team to publicize and schedule examinations
C. An organization that has entered into an agreement with the FCC to coordinate, prepare, and administer amateur operator license examinations
D. The person who has entered into an agreement with the FCC to be the VE session manager

E1E03 Answer: C. A Volunteer Examiner Coordinator is an organization that has entered into an agreement with the FCC to coordinate, prepare, and administer amateur operator license examinations. [97.521]

What is required to be accredited as a Volunteer Examiner?

A. Each General, Advanced and Amateur Extra class operator is automatically accredited as a VE when the license is granted
B. The amateur operator applying must pass a VE examination administered by the FCC Enforcement Bureau
C. The prospective VE must obtain accreditation from the FCC
D. A VEC must confirms that the VE applicant meets FCC requirements to serve as an examiner

E1E04 Answer: D. The Volunteer Examiner accreditation process is the procedure by which a VEC confirms that the VE applicant meets FCC requirements to serve as an examiner. [97.509, 97.525]

What must the VE team do with the application form if the examinee does not pass the exam?

A. Maintain the application form with the VEC's records
B. Return the application document to the examinee
C. Send the application form to the FCC and inform the FCC of the grade
D. Destroy the application form

E1E05 Answer: B. The VE team must return the application document to the examinee if the examinee does not pass the exam. [97.509(j)]

Who is responsible for the proper conduct and necessary supervision during an amateur operator license examination session?

A. The VEC coordinating the session
B. The designated monitoring VE
C. Each administering VE
D. Only the VE session manager

E1E06 Answer: C. Each administering VE is responsible for the proper conduct and necessary supervision during an amateur operator license examination session. [97.509]

What should a VE do if a candidate fails to comply with the examiner's instructions during an amateur operator license examination?

A. Warn the candidate that continued failure to comply will result in termination of the examination
B. Immediately terminate the candidate's examination
C. Allow the candidate to complete the examination, but invalidate the results
D. Immediately terminate everyone's examination and close the session

E1E07 Answer: B. If a candidate fails to comply with the examiner's instructions during an amateur operator license examination, the VE should immediately terminate the candidate's examination. [97.509, 97.511]

To which of the following examinees may a VE not administer an examination?

A. Employees of the VE
B. Friends of the VE
C. Relatives of the VE as listed in the FCC rules
D. All these choices are correct

E1E08 Answer: C. A VE may not administer an examination to his or her own relatives, as listed in the FCC rules. [97.509]

What may be the penalty for a VE who fraudulently administers or certifies an examination?

A. Revocation of the VE's amateur station license grant and the suspension of the VE's amateur operator license grant
B. A fine of up to $1000 per occurrence
C. A sentence of up to one year in prison
D. All these choices are correct

E1E09 Answer: A. A VE who fraudulently administers or certifies an examination may be subject to revocation of his or her amateur station license grant and suspension of his or her amateur operator license grant. [97.509]

What must the administering VEs do after the administration of a successful examination for an amateur operator license?

A. They must collect and send the documents directly to the FCC
B. They must collect and submit the documents to the coordinating VEC for grading
C. They must submit the application document to the coordinating VEC according to the coordinating VEC instructions
D. They must return the documents to the applicant for submission to the FCC according to the FCC instructions

E1E10 Answer: C. The administering VEs must submit the application document to the coordinating VEC according to the coordinating VEC's instructions after the administration of a successful examination for an amateur operator license. [97.509(m)]

What must the VE team do if an examinee scores a passing grade on all examination elements needed for an upgrade or new license?

A. Photocopy all examination documents and forward them to the FCC for processing
B. Three VEs must certify that the examinee is qualified for the license grant and that they have complied with the administering VE requirements
C. Issue the examinee the new or upgrade license
D. All these choices are correct

E1E11 Answer: B. If an examinee scores a passing grade on all examination elements needed for an upgrade or new license, three VEs must certify that the examinee is qualified for the license grant and that they have complied with the administering VE requirements. [97.509(i)]

E1F – Miscellaneous Rules: External RF Power Amplifiers; Prohibited Communications; Spread Spectrum; Auxiliary Stations; Canadian Amateurs Operating in the US; Special Temporary Authority

On what frequencies are spread spectrum transmissions permitted?

A. Only on amateur frequencies above 50 MHz
B. Only on amateur frequencies above 222 MHz
C. Only on amateur frequencies above 420 MHz
D. Only on amateur frequencies above 144 MHz

E1F01 Answer: B. Spread spectrum transmissions are permitted only on amateur frequencies above 222 MHz. [97.305]

What privileges are authorized in the US to persons holding an amateur service license granted by the government of Canada?

A. None, they must obtain a US license
B. Full privileges of the General class license on the 80-, 40-, 20-, and 10-meter bands
C. The operating terms and conditions of the Canadian amateur service license, not to exceed US Amateur Extra class license privileges
D. Full privileges, up to and including those of the Amateur Extra class license, on the 80-, 40-, 20-, 15-, and 10-meter bands

E1F02 Answer: C. Persons in the US holding an amateur service license granted by the Government of Canada are granted the operating terms and conditions of the Canadian amateur service license, not to exceed US Amateur Extra class privileges. [97.107]

Under what circumstances may a dealer sell an external RF power amplifier capable of operation below 144 MHz if it has not been granted FCC certification?

A. Gain is less than 23 dB when driven by power of 10 watts or less
B. The equipment dealer assembled it from a kit
C. It was manufactured and certificated in a country which has a reciprocal certification agreement with the FCC
D. The amplifier is constructed or modified by an amateur radio operator for use at an amateur station

E1F03 Answer: D. A dealer may sell an external RF power amplifier capable of operation below 144 MHz if the amplified has been constructed or modified by an amateur radio operator for use at an amateur station. [97.315]

Which of the following geographic descriptions approximately describes "Line A"?

A. A line roughly parallel to and south of the border between the US and Canada
B. A line roughly parallel to and west of the US Atlantic coastline
C. A line roughly parallel to and north of the border between the US and Mexico
D. A line roughly parallel to and east of the US Pacific coastline

E1F04 Answer: A. "Line A" is a line roughly parallel to and south of the US-Canadian border. [97.3]

Amateur stations may not transmit in which of the following frequency segments if they are located in the contiguous 48 states and north of Line A?

A. 440 MHz - 450 MHz
B. 53 MHz - 54 MHz
C. 222 MHz - 223 MHz
D. 420 MHz - 430 MHz

E1F05 Answer: D. Amateur stations may not transmit on frequencies between 420 MHz and 430 MHz if they are located in the contiguous 48 states and north of Line A. [97.303]

Under what circumstances might the FCC issue a Special Temporary Authority (STA) to an amateur station?

A. To provide for experimental amateur communications
B. To allow use of a special event call sign
C. To allow a VE group with less than three VEs to administer examinations in a remote, sparsely populated area
D. To allow a licensee who has passed an upgrade exam to operate with upgraded privileges while waiting for posting on the FCC database

E1F06 Answer: A. The FCC might issue a Special Temporary Authority (STA) to an amateur station to provide for experimental amateur communications. [1.931]

When may an amateur station send a message to a business?

A. When the pecuniary interest of the amateur or his or her employer is less than $25
B. When the pecuniary interest of the amateur or his or her employer is less than $50
C. At no time
D. When neither the amateur nor his or her employer has a pecuniary interest in the communications

E1F07 Answer: D. An amateur station may send a message to a business when neither the amateur nor his or her employer has a pecuniary interest in the communications. [97.113]

Which of the following types of amateur station communications are prohibited?

A. Communications transmitted for hire or material compensation, except as otherwise provided in the rules
B. Communications that have political content, except as allowed by the Fairness Doctrine
C. Communications that have religious content
D. Communications in a language other than English

E1F08 Answer: A. Amateur station communications transmitted for hire or material compensation are prohibited, except as otherwise provided in the rules. [97.113(c)]

Which of the following cannot be transmitted over an amateur radio mesh network?

A. Third party traffic
B. Email
C. Messages encoded to obscure their meaning
D. All these choices are correct

E1F09 Answer: C. Messages encoded to obscure their meaning cannot be transmitted over an amateur radio mesh network. [97.113(a)(4)]

Who may be the control operator of an auxiliary station?

A. Any licensed amateur operator
B. Only Technician, General, Advanced or Amateur Extra class operators
C. Only General, Advanced or Amateur Extra class operators
D. Only Amateur Extra class operators

E1F10 Answer: B. Only Technician, General, Advanced or Amateur Extra class operators may be control operators of auxiliary stations. [97.201]

Which of the following best describes one of the standards that must be met by an external RF power amplifier if it is to qualify for a grant of FCC certification?

A. It must produce full legal output when driven by not more than 5 watts of mean RF input power
B. It must have received an Underwriters Laboratory certification for electrical safety as well as having met IEEE standard 14.101(b)
C. It must exhibit a gain of less than 23 dB when driven by 10 watts or less
D. It must satisfy the FCC's spurious emission standards when operated at the lesser of 1500 watts or its full output power

E1F11 Answer: D. An external RF power amplifier must satisfy the FCC's spurious emission standards when operated at the lesser of 1500 watts or its full output power if it is to qualify for a grant of FCC certification. [97.317]

E2 – Operating Procedures

E2A – Amateur Radio in Space: Amateur Satellites; Orbital Mechanics; Frequencies and Modes; Satellite Hardware; Satellite Operations

What is the direction of an ascending pass for an amateur satellite?

A. From west to east
B. From east to west
C. From south to north
D. From north to south

E2A01 Answer: C. An amateur satellite goes from south to north in an ascending pass.

Which of the following is a characteristic of an inverting linear transponder?

A. Doppler shift is reduced because the uplink and downlink shifts are in opposite directions
B. Signal position in the band is reversed
C. Upper sideband on the uplink becomes lower sideband on the downlink, and vice versa
D. All these choices are correct

E2A02 Answer: D. Characteristics of an inverting linear transponder are that the doppler shift is reduced because the uplink and downlink shifts are in opposite directions, the signal position in the band is reversed, and the upper sideband on the uplink becomes lower sideband on the downlink, and vice versa.

How is an upload signal processed by an inverting linear transponder?

A. The signal is detected and remodulated on the reverse sideband
B. The signal is passed through a nonlinear filter
C. The signal is reduced to I and Q components and the Q component is filtered out
D. The signal is mixed with a local oscillator signal and the difference product is transmitted

E2A03 Answer: D. In an inverting linear transponder, an upload signal is processed by mixing the signal with a local oscillator signal and transmitting the difference product.

What is meant by the "mode" of an amateur radio satellite?

A. Whether the satellite is in a low earth or geostationary orbit
B. The satellite's uplink and downlink frequency bands
C. The satellite's orientation with respect to the Earth
D. Whether the satellite is in a polar or equatorial orbit

E2A04 Answer: B. The term mode as applied to an amateur radio satellite refers to the satellite's uplink and downlink frequency bands.

What do the letters in a satellite's mode designator specify?

A. Power limits for uplink and downlink transmissions
B. The location of the ground control station
C. The polarization of uplink and downlink signals
D. The uplink and downlink frequency ranges

E2A05 Answer: D. The letters in a satellite's mode designator specify the uplink and downlink frequency ranges.

What are Keplerian elements?

A. Parameters that define the orbit of a satellite
B. Phase reversing elements in a Yagi antenna
C. High-emission heater filaments used in magnetron tubes
D. Encrypting codes used for spread spectrum modulation

E2A06 Answer: A. Keplerian elements are parameters that define the orbit of a satellite.

Which of the following types of signals can be relayed through a linear transponder?

A. FM and CW
B. SSB and SSTV
C. PSK and packet
D. All these choices are correct

E2A07 Answer: D. FM, CW, SSB, SSTV, PSK, and Packet signals can all be relayed through a linear transponder.

Why should effective radiated power (ERP) be limited to a satellite that uses a linear transponder?

A. To prevent creating errors in the satellite telemetry
B. To avoid reducing the downlink power to all other users
C. To prevent the satellite from emitting out-of-band signals
D. To avoid interfering with terrestrial QSOs

E2A08 Answer: B. Effective radiated power should be limited to a satellite which uses a linear transponder to avoid reducing the downlink power to all other users.

What do the terms "L band" and "S band" specify?

A. The 23-centimeter and 13-centimeter bands
B. The 2-meter and 70-centimeter bands
C. FM and digital store-and-forward systems
D. Which sideband to use

E2A09 Answer: A. The terms "L band" and "S band" specify the 23-centimeter and 13-centimeter bands, respectively, with regard to satellite communications.

What type of satellite appears to stay in one position in the sky?

A. HEO
B. Geostationary
C. Geomagnetic
D. LEO

E2A10 Answer: B. A geostationary satellite appears to stay in one position in the sky.

What type of antenna can be used to minimize the effects of spin modulation and Faraday rotation?

A. A linearly polarized antenna
B. A circularly polarized antenna
C. An isotropic antenna
D. A log-periodic dipole array

E2A11 Answer: B. A circularly polarized antenna can be used to minimize the effects of spin modulation and Faraday rotation.

What is the purpose of digital store-and-forward functions on an amateur radio satellite?

A. To upload operational software for the transponder
B. To delay download of telemetry between satellites
C. To store digital messages in the satellite for later download
D. To relay messages between satellites

E2A12 Answer: C. The purpose of digital store-and-forward functions on an Amateur Radio satellite is to store digital messages in the satellite for later download.

Which of the following techniques is used by digital satellites to relay messages?

A. Digipeating
B. Store-and-forward
C. Multisatellite relaying
D. Node hopping

E2A13 Answer: B. Store-and-forward is a technique used by digital satellites to relay messages around the world.

E2B – Television Practices: Fast Scan Television Standards and Techniques; Slow Scan Television Standards and Techniques

In digital television, what does a coding rate of ¾ mean?

A. 25% of the data sent is forward error correction data
B. Data compression reduces data rate by ¾
C. ¼ of the time interval is used as a guard interval
D. Three, four-bit words are used to transmit each pixel

E2B01 Answer: A. In digital television, a coding rate of ¾ means that 25% of the data sent is forward error correction data.

How many horizontal lines make up a fast-scan (NTSC) television frame?

A. 30
B. 60
C. 525
D. 1080

E2B02 Answer: C. There are 525 horizontal lines in a fast-scan (NTSC) television frame.

How is an interlaced scanning pattern generated in a fast-scan (NTSC) television system?

A. By scanning two fields simultaneously
B. By scanning each field from bottom to top
C. By scanning lines from left to right in one field and right to left in the next
D. By scanning odd-numbered lines in one field and even-numbered lines in the next

E2B03 Answer: D. In a fast-scan (NTSC) television system, an interlaced scanning pattern is generated by scanning odd-numbered lines in one field and even-numbered lines in the next.

How is color information sent in analog SSTV?

A. Color lines are sent sequentially
B. Color information is sent on a 2.8 kHz subcarrier
C. Color is sent in a color burst at the end of each line
D. Color is amplitude modulated on the frequency modulated intensity signal

E2B04 Answer: A. Color lines are sent sequentially in analog SSTV.

Which of the following describes the use of vestigial sideband in analog fast-scan TV transmissions?

A. The vestigial sideband carries the audio information
B. The vestigial sideband contains chroma information
C. Vestigial sideband reduces bandwidth while increasing the fidelity of low frequency video components
D. Vestigial sideband provides high frequency emphasis to sharpen the picture

E2B05 Answer: C. The use of vestigial sideband in analog fast-scan TV transmissions reduces bandwidth while increasing the fidelity of low frequency video components.

What is vestigial sideband modulation?

A. Amplitude modulation in which one complete sideband and a portion of the other are transmitted
B. A type of modulation in which one sideband is inverted
C. Narrow-band FM modulation achieved by filtering one sideband from the audio before frequency modulating the carrier
D. Spread spectrum modulation achieved by applying FM modulation following single sideband amplitude modulation

E2B06 Answer: A. Vestigial sideband modulation is amplitude modulation in which one complete sideband and a portion of the other are transmitted.

Which types of modulation are used for amateur television DVB-T signals?

A. FM and FSK
B. QAM and QPSK
C. AM and OOK
D. All these choices are correct

E2B07 Answer: B. QAM and QPSK modulation types are used for amateur television DVB-T signals.

What technique allows commercial analog TV receivers to be used for fast-scan TV operations on the 70-cm band?

A. Transmitting on channels shared with cable TV
B. Using converted satellite TV dishes
C. Transmitting on the abandoned TV channel 2
D. Using USB and demodulating the signal with a computer sound card

E2B08 Answer: A. Transmitting on channels shared with cable TV allows commercial analog TV receivers to be used for fast-scan TV operations on the 70-cm band.

What kind of receiver can be used to receive and decode SSTV using the Digital Radio Mondiale (DRM)

A. CDMA
B. AREDN
C. AM
D. SSB

E2B09 Answer: D. An SSB receiver can be used to receive and decode SSTV using the Digital Radio Mondiale (DRM).

What aspect of an analog slow-scan television signal encodes the brightness of the picture?

A. Tone frequency
B. Tone amplitude
C. Sync amplitude
D. Sync frequency

E2B10 Answer: A. The tone frequency encodes the brightness of the picture in an amateur slow-scan television signal.

What is the function of the Vertical Interval Signaling (VIS) code sent as part of an SSTV transmission?

A. To lock the color burst oscillator in color SSTV images
B. To identify the SSTV mode being used
C. To provide vertical synchronization
D. To identify the call sign of the station transmitting

E2B11 Answer: B. The Vertical Interval Signaling (VIS) code is sent as part of an SSTV transmission to identify the SSTV mode being used.

What signals SSTV receiving software to begin a new picture line?

A. Specific tone frequencies
B. Elapsed time
C. Specific tone amplitudes
D. A two-tone signal

E2B12 Answer: A. Specific tone frequencies tell SSTV receiving software to begin a new picture line.

E2C – Contest and DX operating; remote operation techniques; log data format; contract confirmation; RF network systems

What indicator is required to be used by US-licensed operators when operating a station via remote control and the remote transmitter is located in the US?

A. / followed by the USPS two-letter abbreviation for the state in which the remote station is located
B. /R# where # is the district of the remote station
C. / followed by the ARRL Section of the remote station
D. No additional indicator is required

E2C01 Answer: D. No additional indicator is required when US-licensed operators operate a station via remote control where the transmitter is located in the US.

Which of the following file formats is used for exchanging amateur radio log data?

A. NEC
B. ARLD
C. ADIF
D. OCF

E2C02 Answer: C. The ADIF file format is used for exchanging amateur radio log data.

From which of the following bands is amateur radio contesting generally excluded?

A. 30 meters
B. 6 meters
C. 70 centimeters
D. 33 centimeters

E2C03 Answer: A. Amateur radio contesting is generally excluded from the 30-meter band.

Which of the following frequencies can be used for amateur radio mesh networks?

A. HF frequencies where digital communications are permitted
B. Frequencies shared with various unlicensed wireless data services
C. Cable TV channels 41 through 43
D. The 60-meter band channel centered on 5373 kHz

E2C04 Answer: B. Frequencies shared with various unlicensed wireless data services are sometimes used for amateur radio mesh networks.

What is the function of a DX QSL Manager?

A. To allocate frequencies for DXpeditions
B. To handle the receiving and sending of confirmation for a DX station
C. To run a net to allow many stations to contact a rare DX station
D. To communicate to a DXpedition about propagation, band openings, pileup conditions, etc.

E2C05 Answer: B. A DX QSL Manager handles the receiving and sending of confirmation for a DX station.

During a VHF/UHF contest, in which band segment would you expect to find the highest level of SSB or CW activity?

A. At the top of each band, usually in a segment reserved for contests
B. In the middle of each band, usually on the national calling frequency
C. In the weak signal segment of the band, with most of the activity near the calling frequency
D. In the middle of the band, usually 25 kHz above the national calling frequency

E2C06 Answer: C. During a VHF/UHF contest, you would expect to find the highest SSB or CW activity in the weak signal segment of the band, with most of the activity near the calling frequency.

What is the Cabrillo format?

A. A standard for submission of electronic contest logs
B. A method of exchanging information during a contest QSO
C. The most common set of contest rules
D. A digital protocol specifically designed for rapid contest exchanges

E2C07 Answer: A. The Cabrillo format is a standard for submission of electronic contest logs.

Which of the following contacts may be confirmed through the Logbook of The World (LoTW)?

A. Special event contacts between stations in the US
B. Contacts between a US station and a non-US station
C. Contacts for Worked All States credit
D. All these choices are correct

E2C08 Answer: D. Special event contacts between stations in the US, contacts between a US station and a non-US station, and contacts for Worked All States credit may be confirmed through the Logbook of The World (LoTW).

What type of equipment is commonly used to implement an amateur radio mesh network?

A. A 2-meter VHF transceiver with a 1200-baud modem
B. A computer running EchoLink to provide interface from the radio to the internet
C. A wireless router running custom firmware
D. A 440 MHz transceiver with a 9600-baud modem

E2C09 Answer: C. Wireless routers running custom software are commonly used to implement amateur radio mesh networks.

Why do DX stations often transmit and receive on different frequencies?

A. Because the DX station may be transmitting on a frequency that is prohibited to some responding stations
B. To separate the calling stations from the DX station
C. To improve operating efficiency by reducing interference
D. All these choices are correct

E2C10 Answer: D. A DX station may transmit and receive on different frequencies for a number of reasons, including because they may be transmitting on a frequency that is prohibited to some responding stations, to separate the calling stations from the DX station, and to improve operating efficiency by reducing interference.

How should you generally identify your station when attempting to contact a DX station during a contest or in a pileup?

A. Send your full call sign once or twice
B. Send only the last two letters of your call sign until you make contact
C. Send your full call sign and grid square
D. Send the call sign of the DX station three times, the words "this is," then your call sign three times

E2C11 Answer: A. When attempting to contact a DX station during a contest or in a pileup, you should generally identify your station by sending your full call sign once or twice.

What indicates the delay between a control operator action and the corresponding change in the transmitted signal?

A. Jitter
B. Hang Time
C. Latency
D. Anti-VOX

E2C12 Answer: C. Latency indicates the delay between control operator action and the corresponding change in the transmitted signal.

E2D – Operating Methods: VHF and UHF Digital Modes and Procedures; APRS; EME Procedures; Meteor Scatter Procedures

Which of the following digital modes is designed for meteor scatter communications?

A. WSPR
B. MSK144
C. Hellschreiber
D. APRS

E2D01 Answer: B. The MSK144 digital mode is designed for meteor scatter communications.

What information replaces signal-to-noise ratio when using the FT8 or FT4 modes in a VHF contest?

A. RST report
B. State abbreviation
C. Serial number
D. Grid square

E2D02 Answer: D. The grid square replaces the signal-to-noise ration when using the FT8 or FT4 modes in a VHF contest.

Which of the following digital modes is designed for EME communications?

A. MSK144
B. PACTOR III
C. WSPR
D. Q65

E2D03 Answer: D. The Q65 digital mode is designed for EME communications.

What technology is used for real-time tracking of balloons carrying amateur radio transmitters?

A. FT8
B. Bandwidth compressed LORAN
C. APRS
D. PACTOR III

E2D04 Answer: C. APRS technology is used to track balloons carrying amateur radio transmitters in real time.

What is a characteristic of the JT65 mode?

A. Uses only a 65 Hz bandwidth
B. Decodes signals which have a very low signal-to-noise ratio
C. Symbol rate is 65 baud
D. Permits fast-scan TV transmissions over narrow bandwidth

E2D05 Answer: B. One characteristic of the JT65 mode is the ability to decode signals which have a very low signal-to-noise ratio.

Which of the following is a method for establishing EME contacts?

A. Time-synchronous transmissions alternating between stations
B. Storing and forwarding digital messages
C. Judging optimum transmission times by monitoring beacons reflected from the moon
D. High-speed CW identification to avoid fading

E2D06 Answer: A. Establishing EME contacts can be done by timing synchronous transmissions alternately between stations.

What digital protocol is used by APRS?

A. PACTOR
B. QAM
C. AX.25
D. AMTOR

E2D07 Answer: C. The AX.25 digital protocol is used by APRS.

What type of packet frame is used to transmit APRS beacon data?

A. Acknowledgement
B. Burst
C. Unnumbered Information
D. Connect

E2D08 Answer: C. Unnumbered Information packet frames are used to transmit APRS beacon data.

What type of modulation is used by JT65?

A. Multitone AFSK
B. PSK
C. RTTY
D. QAM

E2D09 Answer: A. JT65 contacts use multitone AFSK modulation.

What does the packet path WIDE3-1 designate?

A. Three stations are allowed on frequency, one transmitting at a time
B. Three subcarriers are permitted, subcarrier one is being used
C. Three digipeater hops are requested with one remaining
D. Three internet gateway stations may receive one transmission

E2D10 Answer: C. The packet path WIDE3-1 designates that three digipeater hops are requested with one remaining.

How do APRS stations relay data?

A. By packet ACK/NAK relay
B. By C4FM repeaters
C. By DMR repeaters
D. By packet digipeaters

E2D11 Answer: D. APRS stations relay data by packet digipeaters.

E2E – Operating Methods: Digital Modes and Procedures for HF

Which of the following types of modulation is common for data emissions below 30 MHz?

A. DTMF tones modulating an FM signal
B. FSK
C. Pulse modulation
D. Spread spectrum

E2E01 Answer: B. FSK modulation is common for data emissions below 30 MHz.

Which of the following synchronizes WSJT-X digital mode transmit/receive timing?

A. Alignment of frequency shifts
B. Synchronization of computer clocks
C. Sync-field transmission
D. Sync-pulse timing

E2E02 Answer: B. The synchronization of computer clocks synchronizes WSJT-X digital mode transmit/receive timing.

To what does the "4" in FT4 refer?

A. Multiples of 4 bits of user information
B. Four-tone continuous-phase frequency shift keying
C. Four transmit/receive cycles per minute
D. All these choices are correct

E2E03 Answer: B. The "4" in FT4 refers to the four-tone continuous-phase frequency shift keying.

Which of the following is characteristic of the FST4 mode?

A. Four-tone Gaussian frequency shift keying
B. Variable transmit/receive periods
C. Seven different tone spacings
D. All these choices are correct

E2E04 Answer: D. Four-tone Gaussian frequency shift keying, variable transmit/receive periods, and seven different tone spacings are characteristics of the FST4 mode.

Which of these digital modes does not support keyboard-to-keyboard operation?

A. WSPR
B. RTTY
C. PSK31
D. MFSK16

E2E05 Answer: A. WSPR does not support keyboard-to-keyboard operation.

What is the length of an FT8 transmission cycle?

A. It varies with the amount of data
B. 8 seconds
C. 15 seconds
D. 30 seconds

E2E06 Answer: C. An FT8 transmission cycle is 15 seconds.

How does Q65 differ from JT65?

A. Keyboard-to-keyboard operation is supported
B. Quadrature modulation is used
C. Multiple receive cycles are averaged
D. All these choices are correct

E2E07 Answer: C. Multiple receive cycles are averaged for Q65, unlike JT65.

Which of the following HF digital modes can be used to transfer binary files?

A. PSK31
B. PACTOR
C. RTTY
D. AMTOR

E2E08 Answer: B. PACTOR can be used to transfer binary files.

Which of the following HF digital modes uses variable-length coding?

A. RTTY
B. PACTOR
C. MT63
D. PSK31

E2E09 Answer: D. PSK31 uses variable-length coding.

Which of these digital modes has the narrowest bandwidth?

A. MFSK16
B. 170 Hz shift, 45-baud RTTY
C. FT8
D. PACTOR IV

E2E10 Answer: C. FT8 has a narrower bandwidth than MFSK16, 170 Hz shift, 45 baud RTTY, and PACTOR IV.

What is the difference between direct FSK and audio FSK?

A. Direct FSK modulates the transmitter VFO
B. Direct FSK occupies less bandwidth
C. Direct FSK can transmit higher baud rates
D. All these choices are correct

E2E11 Answer: A. The difference between direct FSK and audio FSK is that Direct FSK modulates the transmitter VFO.

How do ALE stations establish contact?

A. ALE constantly scans a list of frequencies, activating the radio when the designated call sign is received
B. ALE radios monitor an internet site for the frequency they are being paged on
C. ALE radios send a constant tone code to establish a frequency for future use
D. ALE radios activate when they hear their signal echoed by back scatter

E2E12 Answer: A. ALE stations establish contact by constantly scanning a list of frequencies and then activating the radio when the designated call sign is received.

Which of these digital modes has the highest data throughput under clear communication conditions?

A. MFSK16
B. 170 Hz shift, 45 baud RTTY
C. FT8
D. PACTOR IV

E2E13 Answer: D. PACTOR IV is faster than MFSK16, 170 Hz shift, 45 baud RTTY, and FT8 under clear communication conditions.

E3 – Radio Wave Propagation

E3A – Electromagnetic waves; Earth-Moon-Earth communications; meteor scatter; microwave tropospheric and scatter propagation; aurora propagation; ionospheric propagation changes over the day; circular polarization

What is the approximate maximum separation measured along the surface of the Earth between two stations communicating by EME?

A. 2,000 miles, if the Moon is at perigee
B. 2,000 miles, if the Moon is at apogee
C. 5,000 miles, if the Moon is at perigee
D. 12,000 miles, if the Moon is "visible" by both stations

E3A01 Answer: D. The approximate maximum separation measured along the surface of the Earth between two stations communicating by EME is 12,000 miles, if the Moon is "visible" by both stations.

What characterizes libration fading of an EME signal?

A. A slow change in the pitch of the CW signal
B. A fluttery, irregular fading
C. A gradual loss of signal as the sun rises
D. The returning echo is several hertz lower in frequency than the transmitted signal

E3A02 Answer: B. A fluttery, irregular fading characterizes libration fading of an EME signal.

When scheduling EME contacts, which of these conditions will generally result in the least path loss?

A. When the Moon is at perigee
B. When the Moon is full
C. When the Moon is at apogee
D. When the MUF is above 30 MHz

E3A03 Answer: A. Scheduling EME contacts when the Moon is at perigee will generally result in the least path loss.

In what direction does an electromagnetic wave travel?

A. It depends on the phase angle of the magnetic field
B. It travels parallel to the electric and magnetic fields
C. It depends on the phase angle of the electric field
D. It travels at a right angle to the electric and magnetic fields

E3A04 Answer: D. An electromagnetic wave travels at a right angle to the electric and magnetic fields.

How are the component fields of an electromagnetic wave oriented?

A. They are parallel
B. They are tangential
C. They are at right angles
D. They are 90 degrees out of phase

E3A05 Answer: C. The component fields of an electromagnetic wave are at right angles.

What should be done to continue a long-distance contact when the MUF for that path decreases due to darkness?

A. Switch to a higher frequency HF band
B. Switch to a lower frequency HF band
C. Change to an antenna with a higher takeoff angle
D. Change to an antenna with greater beam width

E3A06 Answer: B. Operators should switch to a lower frequency HF band to continue long-distance contact when the MUF for that path decreases due to darkness.

Atmospheric ducts capable of propagating microwave signals often form over what geographic feature?

A. Mountain ranges
B. Stratocumulus clouds
C. Large bodies of water
D. Nimbus clouds

E3A07 Answer: C. Atmospheric ducts capable of propagating microwave signals often form over large bodies of water.

When a meteor strikes the Earth's atmosphere, a linear ionized region is formed at what region of the ionosphere?

A. The E layer
B. The F1 layer
C. The F2 layer
D. The D layer

E3A08 Answer: A. When a meteor strikes the Earth's atmosphere, a linear ionized region is formed at the E layer of the ionosphere.

Which of the following frequency ranges is most suited for meteor scatter communications?

A. 1.8 MHz - 1.9 MHz
B. 10 MHz - 14 MHz
C. 28 MHz - 148 MHz
D. 220 MHz - 450 MHz

E3A09 Answer: C. The 28 MHz – 148 MHz range is better suited for meteor scatter communications than 1.8 MHz – 1.9 MHz, 10 MHz – 14 MHz, or 220 MHz – 450 MHz.

What determines the speed of electromagnetic waves through a medium?

A. Resistance and reactance
B. Evanescence
C. Birefringence
D. The index of refraction

E3A10 Answer: D. The index of refraction determines the speed of electromagnetic waves through a medium.

What is a typical range for tropospheric propagation of microwave signals?

A. 10 miles to 50 miles
B. 100 miles to 300 miles
C. 1,200 miles
D. 2,500 miles

E3A11 Answer: B. 100 miles to 300 miles is a typical range for tropospheric propagation of microwave signals.

What is most likely to result in auroral propagation?

A. Meteor showers
B. Quiet geomagnetic conditions
C. Severe geomagnetic storms
D. Extreme low-pressure areas in polar regions

E3A12 Answer: C. Severe geomagnetic storms are most likely to result in auroral propagation.

Which of these emission modes is best for auroral propagation?

A. CW
B. SSB
C. FM
D. RTTY

E3A13 Answer: A. CW is better for auroral propagation than FM, SSB, or RTTY.

What are circularly polarized electromagnetic waves?

A. Waves with an electric field bent into a circular shape
B. Waves with rotating electric and magnetic fields
C. Waves that circle the Earth
D. Waves produced by a loop antenna

E3A14 Answer: B. Circularly polarized electromagnetic waves are waves with rotating electric and magnetic fields.

E3B – Transequatorial Propagation; Long-Path Propagation; Ordinary and Extraordinary Waves; Sporadic E Mechanisms; Ground-Wave Propagation

Where is transequatorial propagation (TEP) most likely to occur?

A. Between points separated by 2,000 miles to 3,000 miles over a path perpendicular to the geomagnetic equator
B. Between points located 1,500 miles to 2,000 miles apart on the geomagnetic equator
C. Between points located at each other's antipode
D. Through the region where the terminator crosses the geographic equator

E3B01 Answer: A. Transequatorial propagation (TEP) is most likely to occur between points separated by 2,000 miles to 3,000 miles over a path perpendicular to the geomagnetic equator.

What is the approximate maximum range for signals using transequatorial propagation?

A. 1,000 miles
B. 2,500 miles
C. 5,000 miles
D. 7,500 miles

E3B02 Answer: C. The approximate maximum range for signals using transequatorial propagation is 5,000 miles.

At what time of day is transequatorial propagation most likely to occur?

A. Morning
B. Noon
C. Afternoon or early evening
D. Late at night

E3B03 Answer: C. Transequatorial propagation is most likely to occur in the afternoon or early evening.

What are "extraordinary" and "ordinary" waves?

A. Extraordinary waves exhibit rare long-skip propagation, compared to ordinary waves, which travel shorter distances
B. Independently propagating, elliptically polarized waves created in the ionosphere
C. Long-path and short-path waves
D. Refracted rays and reflected waves

E3B04 Answer: B. "Extraordinary" and "ordinary" waves are independently propagating, elliptically polarized waves created in the ionosphere.

Which of the following paths is most likely to support long-distance propagation on 160 meters?

A. A path entirely in sunlight
B. Paths at high latitudes
C. A direct north-south path
D. A path entirely in darkness

E3B05 Answer: D. A path entirely in darkness is most likely to support long-distance propagation on 160 meters.

On which of the following amateur bands is long-path propagation most frequent?

A. 160 meters and 80 meters
B. 40 meters and 20 meters
C. 10 meters and 6 meters
D. 6 meters and 2 meters

E3B06 Answer: B. Long-path propagation is most frequent on 40-meter and 20-meter bands.

What effect does lowering a signal's transmitted elevation angle have on ionospheric HF skip propagation?

A. Faraday rotation becomes stronger
B. The MUF decreases
C. The distance covered by each hop increases
D. The critical frequency increases

E3B07 Answer: C. Lowering a signal's transmitted elevation increases the distance covered by each hop for ionospheric HF skip propagation.

How does the maximum range of ground-wave propagation change when the signal frequency is increased?

A. It stays the same
B. It increases
C. It decreases
D. It peaks at roughly 8 MHz

E3B08 Answer: C. The maximum range of ground-wave propagation decreases when the signal frequency is increased.

At what time of year is sporadic-E propagation most likely to occur?

A. Around the solstices, especially the summer solstice
B. Around the solstices, especially the winter solstice
C. Around the equinoxes, especially the spring equinox
D. Around the equinoxes, especially the fall equinox

E3B09 Answer: A. Sporadic-E propagation most likely to occur around the solstices, especially the summer solstice.

What is the effect of chordal-hop propagation?

A. The signal experiences less loss compared to multi-hop propagation, which uses Earth as a reflector
B. The MUF for chordal-hop propagation is much lower than for normal skip propagation
C. Atmospheric noise is reduced in the direction of chordal-hop propagation
D. Signals travel faster along ionospheric chords

E3B10 Answer: A. In chordal-hop propagation, the signal experiences less loss compared to multi-hop propagation, which uses Earth as a reflector.

At what time of day is sporadic-E propagation most likely to occur?

A. Between midnight and sunrise
B. Between sunset and midnight
C. Between sunset and sunrise
D. Between sunrise and sunset

E3B11 Answer: D. Sporadic-E propagation is most likely to occur between sunrise and sunset.

What is chordal-hop propagation?

A. Propagation away from the great circle bearing between stations
B. Successive ionospheric refractions without an intermediate reflection from the ground
C. Propagation across the geomagnetic equator
D. Signals reflected back toward the transmitting station

E3B12 Answer: B. Chordal-hop propagation is successive ionospheric reflections without an intermediate reflection from the ground.

What type of polarization is supported by ground-wave propagation?

A. Vertical
B. Horizontal
C. Circular
D. Elliptical

E3B13 Answer: A. Vertical polarization is supported by ground-wave propagation.

E3C – Propagation Prediction and Reporting; Radio Horizon; Effects of Space-Weather Phenomena

What is the cause of short-term radio blackouts?

A. Coronal mass ejections
B. Sunspots on the solar equator
C. North-oriented interplanetary magnetic field
D. Solar flares

E3C01 Answer: D. Solar flares cause short-term radio blackouts.

What is indicated by a rising A- or K-index?

A. Increasing disturbance of the geomagnetic field
B. Decreasing disturbance of the geomagnetic field
C. Higher levels of solar UV radiation
D. An increase in the critical frequency

E3C02 Answer: A. A rising A- or K-index indicates increasing disturbance of the geomagnetic field.

Which of the following signal paths is most likely to experience high levels of absorption when the A-index or K-index is elevated?

A. Transequatorial
B. Through the auroral oval
C. Sporadic-E
D. NVIS

E3C03 Answer: B. Paths through the auroral oval are more likely to experience high levels of absorption when the A-index or K-index is elevated than transequatorial, sporadic-E, or NVIS propagation.

What does the value of Bz (B sub Z) represent?

A. Geomagnetic field stability
B. Critical frequency for vertical transmissions
C. North-south strength of the interplanetary magnetic field
D. Duration of long-delayed echoes

E3C04 Answer: C. Bz represents the north-south strength of the interplanetary magnetic field.

What orientation of Bz (B sub z) increases the likelihood that charged particles from the Sun will cause disturbed conditions?

A. Southward
B. Northward
C. Eastward
D. Westward

E3C05 Answer: A. A southward orientation of Bz increases the likelihood that charged particles from the Sun will cause disturbed conditions.

How does the VHF/UHF radio horizon compare to the geographic horizon?

A. It is approximately 15 percent farther
B. It is approximately 20 percent nearer
C. It is approximately 50 percent farther
D. They are approximately the same

E3C06 Answer: A. The VHF/UHF radio horizon is approximately 15 percent farther than the geographic horizon.

Which of the following descriptors indicates the greatest solar flare intensity?

A. Class A
B. Class Z
C. Class M
D. Class X

E3C07 Answer: D. A class X descriptor indicates the greatest solar flare intensity.

Which of the following is the space-weather term for an extreme geomagnetic storm?

A. B9
B. X5
C. M9
D. G5

E3C08 Answer: D. G5 is the space-weather term for a geomagnetic storm.

What type of data is reported by amateur radio propagation reporting networks?

A. Solar flux
B. Electric field intensity
C. Magnetic declination
D. Digital-mode and CW signals

E3C09 Answer: D. Digital-mode and CW signals are reported by amateur radio propagation reporting networks.

What does the 304A solar parameter measure?

A. The ratio of X-ray flux to radio flux, correlated to sunspot number
B. UV emissions at 304 angstroms, correlated to the solar flux index
C. The solar wind velocity at 304 degrees from the solar equator, correlated to geomagnetic storms
D. The solar emission at 304 GHz, correlated to X-ray flare levels

E3C10 Answer: B. The 304A solar parameter measures UV emissions at 304 angstroms, correlated to solar flux index.

What does VOACAP software model?

A. AC voltage and impedance
B. VHF radio propagation
C. HF propagation
D. AC current and impedance

E3C11 Answer: C. VOACAP software models HF propagation.

Which of the following is indicated by a sudden rise in radio background noise across a large portion of the HF spectrum?

A. A temperature inversion has occurred
B. A coronal mass ejection impact or solar flare has occurred
C. Transequatorial propagation on 6 meters is likely
D. Long-path propagation on the higher HF bands is likely

E3C12 Answer: B. A sudden rise in radio background noise across a large portion of the HF spectrum indicates that a coronal mass ejection impact or solar flare has occurred.

E4 – Amateur Practices

E4A – Test Equipment: Analog and Digital Instruments; Spectrum Analyzers; Antenna Analyzers; Oscilloscopes; RF Measurements

Which of the following limits the highest frequency signal that can be accurately displayed on a digital oscilloscope?

A. Sampling rate of the analog-to-digital converter
B. Analog-to-digital converter reference frequency
C. Q of the circuit
D. All these choices are correct

E4A01 Answer: A. The sampling rate of the analog-to-digital converter limits the highest frequency signal that can be accurately displayed on a digital oscilloscope.

Which of the following parameters does a spectrum analyzer display on the vertical and horizontal axes?

A. Signal amplitude and time
B. Signal amplitude and frequency
C. SWR and frequency
D. SWR and time

E4A02 Answer: B. A spectrum analyzer displays the signal amplitude and frequency on the vertical and horizontal axes, respectively.

Which of the following test instruments is used to display spurious signals and/or intermodulation distortion products generated by an SSB transmitter?

A. A differential resolver
B. A spectrum analyzer
C. A logic analyzer
D. A network analyzer

E4A03 Answer: B. A spectrum analyzer is used to display spurious signals and/or intermodulation distortion products generated by an SSB transmitter.

How is the compensation of an oscilloscope probe performed?

A. A square wave is displayed, and the probe is adjusted until the horizontal portions of the displayed wave are as nearly flat as possible
B. A high frequency sine wave is displayed, and the probe is adjusted for maximum amplitude
C. A frequency standard is displayed, and the probe is adjusted until the deflection time is accurate
D. A DC voltage standard is displayed, and the probe is adjusted until the displayed voltage is accurate

E4A04 Answer: A. An oscilloscope probe is typically adjusted by displaying a square wave and adjusting the probe until the horizontal portions of the displayed wave are as nearly flat as possible.

What is the purpose of using a prescaler with a frequency counter?

A. It amplifies low-level signals for more accurate counting
B. It multiplies a higher frequency signal so a low-frequency counter can display the operating frequency
C. It prevents oscillation in a low-frequency counter circuit
D. It reduces the signal frequency to within the counter's operating range

E4A05 Answer: D. Using a prescaler with a frequency counter reduces the signal frequency to within the counter's operating range.

What is the effect of aliasing on a digital oscilloscope when displaying a waveform?

A. A false, jittery low-frequency version of the waveform is displayed
B. The waveform DC offset will be inaccurate
C. Calibration of the vertical scale is no longer valid
D. Excessive blanking occurs, which prevents display of the waveform

E4A06 Answer: A. Aliasing on a digital oscilloscope caused by setting the time base too slow means that false, jittery low-frequency versions of the signals are being displayed.

Which of the following is an advantage of using an antenna analyzer compared to an SWR bridge?

A. Antenna analyzers automatically tune your antenna for resonance
B. Antenna analyzers compute SWR and impedance automatically
C. Antenna analyzers display a time-varying representation of the modulation envelope
D. All these choices are correct

E4A07 Answer: B. An advantage of using an antenna analyzer compared to an SWR bridge is that antenna analyzers compute SWR and impedance automatically.

Which of the following is used to measure SWR?

A. Directional wattmeter
B. Vector network analyzer
C. Antenna analyzer
D. All these choices are correct

E4A08 Answer: D. A directional wattmeter, a vector network analyzer, and an antenna analyzer are all used to measure SWR.

Which of the following is good practice when using an oscilloscope probe?

A. Minimize the length of the probe's ground connection
B. Never use a high-impedance probe to measure a low-impedance circuit
C. Never use a DC-coupled probe to measure an AC circuit
D. All these choices are correct

E4A09 Answer: A. When using an oscilloscope probe, you should minimize the length of the probe's ground connection.

Which trigger mode is most effective when using an oscilloscope to measure a linear power supply's output ripple?

A. Single-shot
B. Edge
C. Level
D. Line

E4A10 Answer: D. Line mode is most effective when using an oscilloscope to measure a linear power supply's output ripple.

Which of the following can be measured with an antenna analyzer?

A. Velocity factor
B. Cable length
C. Resonant frequency of a tuned circuit
D. All these choices are correct

E4A11 Answer: D. Velocity factor, cable length, and resonant frequency of a tuned circuit can all be measured with an antenna analyzer.

E4B – Measurement Technique and Limitations: Instrument Accuracy and Performance Limitations; Probes; Techniques to Minimize Errors; Measurement of Q; Instrument Calibration; S Parameters; Vector Network Analyzers; RF Signals

Which of the following factors most affects the accuracy of a frequency counter?

A. Input attenuator accuracy
B. Time base accuracy
C. Decade divider accuracy
D. Temperature coefficient of the logic

E4B01 Answer: B. Time base accuracy most affects the overall accuracy of a frequency counter.

What is the significance of voltmeter sensitivity expressed in ohms per volt?

A. The full scale reading of the voltmeter multiplied by its ohms per volt rating is the input impedance of the voltmeter
B. The reading in volts multiplied by the ohms per volt rating will determine the power drawn by the device under test
C. The reading in ohms divided by the ohms per volt rating will determine the voltage applied to the circuit
D. The full scale reading in amps divided by ohms per volt rating will determine the size of shunt needed

E4B02 Answer: A. Voltmeter sensitivity is expressed in ohms per volt because the full scale reading of the voltmeter multiplied by its ohms per volt rating is the input impedance of the voltmeter.

Which S parameter is equivalent to forward gain?

A. S11
B. S12
C. S21
D. S22

E4B03 Answer: C. The S21 parameter is equivalent to forward gain.

Which S parameter represents input port return loss or reflection coefficient (equivalent to VSWR)?

A. S11
B. S12
C. S21
D. S22

E4B04 Answer: A. S11 represents input port return loss or reflection coefficient (equivalent to VSWR).

What three test loads are used to calibrate an RF vector network analyzer?

A. 50 ohms, 75 ohms, and 90 ohms
B. Short circuit, open circuit, and 50 ohms
C. Short circuit, open circuit, and resonant circuit
D. 50 ohms through 1/8 wavelength, 1/4 wavelength, and 1/2 wavelength of coaxial cable

E4B05 Answer: B. Short circuit, open circuit, and 50 ohms test loads are used to calibrate a standard RF vector network analyzer.

How much power is being absorbed by the load when a directional power meter connected between a transmitter and a terminating load reads 100 watts forward power and 25 watts reflected power?

A. 100 watts
B. 125 watts
C. 112.5 watts
D. 75 watts

E4B06 Answer: D. 75 watts of power are being absorbed by the load when a directional power meter connected between a transmitter and a terminating load reads 100 watts forward power and 25 watts reflected power.

What do the subscripts of S parameters represent?

A. The port or ports at which measurements are made
B. The relative time between measurements
C. Relative quality of the data
D. Frequency order of the measurements

E4B07 Answer: A. The subscripts of S parameters represent the port or ports at which measurements are made.

Which of the following can be used to measure the Q of a series-tuned circuit?

A. The ratio of inductive reactance to capacitive reactance
B. The frequency shift
C. The bandwidth of the circuit's frequency response
D. The resonant frequency of the circuit

E4B08 Answer: C. The bandwidth of the circuit's frequency response can be used to measure the Q of a series-tuned circuit.

Which of the following can be measured by a two-port vector network analyzer?

A. Phase noise
B. Filter frequency response
C. Pulse rise time
D. Forward power

E4B09 Answer: B. Filter frequency response can be measured by a two-port vector network analyzer.

Which of the following methods measures intermodulation distortion in an SSB transmitter?

A. Modulate the transmitter using two RF signals having non-harmonically related frequencies and observe the RF output with a spectrum analyzer
B. Modulate the transmitter using two AF signals having non-harmonically related frequencies and observe the RF output with a spectrum analyzer
C. Modulate the transmitter using two AF signals having harmonically related frequencies and observe the RF output with a peak reading wattmeter
D. Modulate the transmitter using two RF signals having harmonically related frequencies and observe the RF output with a logic analyzer

E4B10 Answer: B. To measure intermodulation distortion in an SSB transmitter, modulate the transmitter using two AF signals having non-harmonically related frequencies and observe the RF output with a spectrum analyzer.

Which of the following can be measured with a vector network analyzer?

A. Input impedance
B. Output impedance
C. Reflection coefficient
D. All these choices are correct

E4B11 Answer: D. Input impedance, output impedance, and reflection coefficient can all be measured with a vector network analyzer.

E4C – Receiver Performance: Phase Noise, Noise Floor, Image Rejection, Minimum Detectable Signal (MDS), Increasing Signal-to-Noise Ratio and Dynamic Range, Noise Figure, Reciprocal Mixing; Selectivity; SDR Non-Linearity; Use of Attenuators at Low Frequencies

What is an effect of excessive phase noise in an SDR receiver's master clock oscillator?

A. It limits the receiver's ability to receive strong signals
B. It can affect the receiver's frequency calibration
C. It decreases the receiver's third-order intercept point
D. It can combine with strong signals on nearby frequencies to generate interference

E4C01 Answer: D. Excessive phase noise in an SDR receiver's master clock oscillator can combine with strong signals on nearby frequencies to generate interference.

Which of the following receiver circuits can be effective in eliminating interference from strong out-of-band signals?

A. A front-end filter or pre-selector
B. A narrow IF filter
C. A notch filter
D. A properly adjusted product detector

E4C02 Answer: A. A front-end filter or pre-selector can be effective in eliminating interference from strong out-of-band signals.

What is the term for the suppression in an FM receiver of one signal by another stronger signal on the same frequency?

A. Desensitization
B. Cross-modulation interference
C. Capture effect
D. Frequency discrimination

E4C03 Answer: C. Capture effect is the term for the suppression in an FM receiver of one signal by another stronger signal on the same frequency.

What is the noise figure of a receiver?

A. The ratio of atmospheric noise to phase noise
B. The ratio of the noise bandwidth in hertz to the theoretical bandwidth of a resistive network
C. The ratio in dB of the noise generated in the receiver to atmospheric noise
D. The ratio in dB of the noise generated by the receiver to the theoretical minimum noise

E4C04 Answer: D. The noise figure of a receiver is defined as the ratio in dB of the noise generated by the receiver to the theoretical minimum noise.

What does a receiver noise floor of -174 dBm represent?

A. The receiver noise is 6 dB above the theoretical minimum
B. The theoretical noise in a 1 Hz bandwidth at the input of a perfect receiver at room temperature
C. The noise figure of a 1 Hz bandwidth receiver
D. The receiver noise is 3 dB above the theoretical minimum

E4C05 Answer: B. A receiver noise floor of -174 dBm represents the theoretical noise in a 1 Hz bandwidth at the input of a perfect receiver at room temperature.

How much does increasing a receiver's bandwidth from 50 Hz to 1000 Hz increase the receiver's noise floor?

A. 3 dB
B. 5 dB
C. 10 dB
D. 13 dB

E4C06 Answer: D. Increasing a receiver's bandwidth from 50 Hz to 1000 Hz increases the receiver's noise floor by 13 dB.

What does the MDS of a receiver represent?

A. The meter display sensitivity
B. The minimum discernible signal
C. The modulation distortion specification
D. The maximum detectable spectrum

E4C07 Answer: B. The MDS of a receiver represents the minimum discernible signal.

An SDR receiver is overloaded when input signals exceed what level?

A. One-half the maximum sample rate
B. One-half the maximum sampling buffer size
C. The maximum count value of the analog-to-digital converter
D. The reference voltage of the analog-to-digital converter

E4C08 Answer: D. An SDR receiver is overloaded when input signals exceed the reference voltage of the analog-to-digital converter.

Which of the following choices is a good reason for selecting a high IF for a superheterodyne HF or VHF communications receiver?

A. Fewer components in the receiver
B. Reduced drift
C. Easier for front-end circuitry to eliminate image responses
D. Improved receiver noise figure

E4C09 Answer: C. It is good to select a high IF for a superheterodyne HF or VHF communications receiver because it makes it easier for front-end circuitry to eliminate image responses.

What is an advantage of having a variety of receiver bandwidths from which to select?

A. The noise figure of the RF amplifier can be adjusted to match the modulation type, thus increasing receiver sensitivity
B. Receiver power consumption can be reduced when wider bandwidth is not required
C. Receive bandwidth can be set to match the modulation bandwidth, maximizing signal-to-noise ratio and minimizing interference
D. Multiple frequencies can be received simultaneously if desired

E4C10 Answer: C. One advantage of having a variety of receiver IF bandwidths from which to select is that the receive bandwidth can be set to match the modulation bandwidth, maximizing signal-to-noise ratio and minimizing interference.

Why does input attenuation reduce receiver overload on the lower frequency HF bands with little or no impact of signal-to-noise ratio?

A. The attenuator has a low-pass filter to increase the strength of lower frequency signals
B. The attenuator has a noise filter to suppress interference
C. Signals are attenuated separately from the noise
D. Atmospheric noise is generally greater than internally generated noise even after attenuation

E4C11 Answer: D. Input attenuation reduces receiver overload on the lower frequency HF bands with little or no impact of the signal-to-noise ratio because atmospheric noise is generally greater than internally generated noise even after attenuation.

How does a narrow-band roofing filter affect receiver performance?

A. It improves sensitivity by reducing front-end noise
B. It improves intelligibility by using low Q circuitry to reduce ringing
C. It improves blocking dynamic range by attenuating strong signals near the receive frequency
D. All these choices are correct

E4C12 Answer: C. A narrow-band roofing filter affects receiver performance improving dynamic range by attenuating strong signals near the receive frequency.

What is reciprocal mixing?

A. Two out-of-band signals mixing to generate an in-band spurious signal
B. In-phase signals cancelling in a mixer resulting in loss of receiver sensitivity
C. Two digital signals combining from alternate time slots
D. Local oscillator phase noise mixing with adjacent strong signals to create interference to desired signals

E4C13 Answer: D. Reciprocal mixing is when local oscillator phase noise is mixed with adjacent strong signals to create interference to desired signals.

What is the purpose of the receiver IF shift control?

A. To permit listening on a different frequency from the transmitting frequency
B. To change frequency rapidly
C. To reduce interference from stations transmitting on adjacent frequencies
D. To tune in stations slightly off frequency without changing the transmit frequency

E4C14 Answer: C. The purpose of the receiver IF shift control is to reduce interference from stations transmitting on adjacent frequencies.

E4D – Receiver Performance Characteristics: Blocking Range; Intermodulation and Cross-Modulation Interference; Third-Order Intercept; Desensitization; Preselector; Sensitivity; Link Margin

What is meant by the blocking dynamic range of a receiver?

A. The difference in dB between the noise floor and the level of an incoming signal that will cause 1 dB of gain compression
B. The minimum difference in dB between the levels of two FM signals that will cause one signal to block the other
C. The difference in dB between the noise floor and the third-order intercept point
D. The minimum difference in dB between two signals which produce third-order intermodulation products greater than the noise floor

E4D01 Answer: A. The blocking dynamic range of a receiver is the difference in dB between the noise floor and the level of an incoming signal which will cause 1 dB of gain compression.

Which of the following describes problems caused by poor dynamic range in a receiver?

A. Spurious signals caused by cross-modulation and desensitization from strong adjacent signals
B. Oscillator instability requiring frequent retuning and loss of ability to recover the opposite sideband
C. Poor weak signal reception caused by insufficient local oscillator injection
D. Oscillator instability and severe audio distortion of all but the strongest received signals

E4D02 Answer: A. Spurious signals caused by cross-modulation and desensitization from strong adjacent signals are both problems caused by poor dynamic range in a receiver.

What creates intermodulation interference between two repeaters in close proximity?

A. The output signals cause feedback in the final amplifier of one or both transmitters
B. The output signals mix in the final amplifier of one or both transmitters
C. The input frequencies are harmonically related
D. The output frequencies are harmonically related

E4D03 Answer: B. Intermodulation interference between two repeaters in close proximity is created when the output signals mix in the final amplifier of one or both transmitters.

Which of the following is used to reduce or eliminate intermodulation interference in a repeater caused by a nearby transmitter?

A. A band-pass filter in the feed line between the transmitter and receiver
B. A properly terminated circulator at the output of the repeater's transmitter
C. Utilizing a Class C final amplifier
D. Utilizing a Class D final amplifier

E4D04 Answer: B. A properly terminated circulator at the output of the repeater's transmitter is used the reduce or eliminate intermodulation interference in a repeater caused by a nearby transmitter.

What transmitter frequencies would cause an intermodulation-product signal in a receiver tuned to 146.70 MHz when a nearby station transmits on 146.52 MHz?

A. 146.34 MHz and 146.61 MHz
B. 146.88 MHz and 146.34 MHz
C. 146.10 MHz and 147.30 MHz
D. 146.30 MHz and 146.90 MHz

E4D05 Answer: A. 146.34 MHz and 146.61 MHz frequencies would cause an intermodulation-product signal in a receiver tuned to 146.70 MHz when a nearby station transmits on 146.52 MHz.

What is the term for the reduction in receiver sensitivity caused by a strong signal near the received frequency?

A. Reciprocal mixing
B. Quieting
C. Desensitization
D. Cross modulation interference

E4D06 Answer: C. Desensitization is the term for the reduction in receiver sensitivity caused by a strong signal near the received frequency.

Which of the following reduces the likelihood of receiver desensitization?

A. Insert attenuation before the first RF stage
B. Raise the receiver's IF frequency
C. Increase the receiver's front end gain
D. Switch from fast AGC to slow AGC

E4D07 Answer: A. Inserting the attenuation before the first RF stage reduces the likelihood of receiver desensitization.

What causes intermodulation in an electronic circuit?

A. Negative feedback
B. Lack of neutralization
C. Nonlinear circuits or devices
D. Positive feedback

E4D08 Answer: C. Nonlinear circuits or devices cause intermodulation in an electronic circuit.

What is the purpose of the preselector in a communications receiver?

A. To store frequences that are often used
B. To provide broadband attenuation before the first RF stage to prevent intermodulation
C. To increase rejection of signals outside the band being received
D. To allow selection of the optimum RF amplifier device

E4D09 Answer: C. The purpose of the preselector in a communications receiver is to increase rejection of signals outside the band being received.

What does a third-order intercept level of 40 dBm mean with respect to receiver performance?

A. Signals less than 40 dBm will not generate audible third-order intermodulation products
B. The receiver can tolerate signals up to 40 dB above the noise floor without producing third-order intermodulation products
C. A pair of 40 dBm input signals will theoretically generate a third-order intermodulation product that has the same output amplitude as either of the input signals
D. A pair of 1 mW input signals will produce a third-order intermodulation product that is 40 dB stronger than the input signal

E4D10 Answer: C. A third-order intercept level of 40 dBm means that a pair of 40 dBm input signals will theoretically generate a third-order intermodulation product that has the same output amplitude as either of the input signals.

Why are odd-order intermodulation products, created within a receiver, of particular interest compared to other products?

A. Odd-order products of two signals in the band being received are also likely to be within the band
B. Odd-order products are more likely to overload the IF filters
C. Odd-order products are an indication of poor image rejection
D. Odd-order intermodulation produces three products for every input signal within the band of interest

E4D11 Answer: A. Third-order intermodulation products created within a receiver of particular interest are often compared to other products because the third-order product of two signals which are in the band being received is also likely to be within the band.

What is the link margin in a system with a transmit power level of 10 W (+40 dBm), a system antenna gain of 10 dBi, a cable loss of 3 dB, a path loss of 136 dB, a receiver minimum discernable signal of -103 dBm, and a required signal-to-noise ratio of 6 dB?

A. -8 dB
B. -14 dB
C. +8 dB
D. +14 dB

E4D12 Answer: C. The link margin in a system with a transmit power level of 10 W (+40 dBm), a system antenna gain of 10 dBi, a cable loss of 3 dB, a path loss of 136 dB, a receiver minimum discernable signal of -103 dBm, and a required signal-to-noise ratio of 6 dB is +8 dB.

What is the received signal level with a transmit power of 10 W (+40 dBm), a transmit antenna gain of 6 dBi, a receive antenna gain of 3 dBi, and a path loss of 100 dB?

A. -51 dBm
B. -54 dBm
C. -57 dBm
D. -60 dBm

E4D13 Answer: A. The received signal level with a transmit power of 10 W (+40 dBm), a transmit antenna gain of 6 dBi, a receive antenna gain of 3 dBi, and a path loss of 100 dB is -51 dBm.

What power level does a receiver minimum discernable signal of -100 dBm represent?

A. 100 microwatts
B. 0.1 microwatts
C. 0.001 microwatts
D. 0.1 picowatts

E4D14 Answer: D. A receiver minimum discernable signal of -100 dBm represents 0.1 picowatts.

E4E – Noise and Interference: External RF Interference; Electrical and Computer Noise; Line Noise; DSP Filtering and Noise Reduction; Common-Mode Current; Surge Protectors; Single Point Ground Panel

What problem can occur when using an automatic notch filter (ANF) to remove interfering carriers while receiving CW signals?

A. Removal of the CW signal as well as the interfering carrier
B. Any nearby signal passing through the DSP system will overwhelm the desired signal
C. Excessive ringing
D. All these choices are correct

E4E01 Answer: A. Using an automatic notch filter (ANF) to remove interfering carriers while receiving CW signals can remove the CW signal as well as the interfering carrier.

Which of the following types of noise can often be reduced by a digital noise reduction?

A. Broadband white noise
B. Ignition noise
C. Power line noise
D. All these choices are correct

E4E02 Answer: D. Broadband white noise, ignition noise, and power line noise can often be reduced by a digital noise reduction.

Which of the following types of noise are removed by a noise blanker?

A. Broadband white noise
B. Impulse noise
C. Hum and buzz
D. All these choices are correct

E4E03 Answer: B. Impulse noise is removed by a noise blanker.

How can conducted noise from an automobile battery charging system be suppressed?

A. By installing filter capacitors in series with the alternator leads
B. By installing a noise suppression resistor and a blocking capacitor at the battery
C. By installing a high-pass filter in series with the radio's power lead and a low-pass filter in parallel with the antenna feed line
D. By installing ferrite chokes on the charging system leads

E4E04 Answer: D. Conducted noise from an automobile battery charging system can be suppressed by installing ferrite chokes on the charging system leads.

What is used to suppress radio frequency interference from a line-driven AC motor?

A. A high-pass filter in series with the motor's power leads
B. A brute-force AC-line filter in series with the motor leads
C. A bypass capacitor in series with the motor's field winding
D. A bypass choke in parallel with the motor's field winding

E4E05 Answer: B. A brute-force AC-line filter in series with the motor leads is used to suppress radio frequency interference from a line-drive AC motor.

What is one type of electrical interference that might be caused by computer network equipment?

A. A loud AC hum in the audio output of your station's receiver
B. A clicking noise at intervals of a few seconds
C. The appearance of unstable modulated or unmodulated signals at specific frequencies
D. A whining-type noise that continually pulses off and on

E4E06 Answer: C. The appearance of unstable modulated or unmodulated signals at specific frequencies could be caused by computer network equipment.

Which of the following can cause shielded cables to radiate or receive interference?

A. Low inductance ground connections at both ends of the shield
B. Common-mode currents on the shield and conductors
C. Use of braided shielding material
D. Tying all ground connections to a common point resulting in differential-mode currents in the shield

E4E07 Answer: B. Common-mode currents on the shield and conductors can cause shielded cables to radiate or receive interference.

What current flows equally on all conductors of an unshielded multiconductor cable?

A. Differential-mode current
B. Common-mode current
C. Reactive current only
D. Magnetically-coupled current only

E4E08 Answer: B. Common-mode current flows equally on all conductors of an unshielded multi-conductor cable.

What undesirable effect can occur when using a noise blanker?

A. Received audio in the speech range might have an echo effect
B. The audio frequency bandwidth of the received signal might be compressed
C. Strong signals may be distorted and appear to cause spurious emissions
D. FM signals can no longer be demodulated

E4E09 Answer: C. When using a noise blanker, strong signals may be distorted and appear to cause spurious emissions.

Which of the following can create intermittent loud roaring or buzzing AC line interference?

A. Arcing contacts in a thermostatically controlled device
B. A defective doorbell or doorbell transformer inside a nearby residence
C. A malfunctioning illuminated advertising display
D. All these choices are correct

E4E10 Answer: D. Loud roaring or buzzing AC line interference that comes and goes at intervals could be caused by a number of things, including arcing contacts in a thermostatically controlled device, a defective doorbell or doorbell transformer inside a nearby residence, or a malfunctioning illuminated advertising display.

What could be the cause of local AM broadcast band signals combining to generate spurious signals on the MF or HF bands?

A. One or more of the broadcast stations is transmitting an over-modulated signal
B. Nearby corroded metal connections are mixing and re-radiating the broadcast signals
C. You are receiving skywave signals from a distant station
D. Your station receiver IF amplifier stage is overloaded

E4E11 Answer: B. A cause of local AM broadcast band signals combining to generate spurious signals of the MF or HF bands could be that nearby corroded metal connections are mixing and re-radiating the broadcast signals.

What causes interference received as a series of carriers at regular intervals across a wide frequency range?

A. Switch-mode power supplies
B. Radar transmitters
C. Wireless security camera transmitters
D. Electric fences

E4E12 Answer: A. Switch-mode power supplies cause interference received as a series of carriers at regular intervals across a wide frequency range.

Where should a station AC surge protector be installed?

A. At the AC service panel
B. At an AC outlet
C. On the single point ground panel
D. On a ground rod outside the station

E4E13 Answer: C. A station's AC surge protector should be installed on the single point ground panel.

What is the purpose of a single point ground panel?

A. Remove AC power in case of a short-circuit
B. Prevent common-mode transients in multi-wire systems
C. Eliminate air gaps between protected and non-protected circuits
D. Ensure all lightning protectors activate at the same time

E4E14 Answer: D. The purpose of a single point ground panel is to ensure that all lightning protectors activate at the same time.

E5 – Electrical Principles

E5A – Resonance and Q: Characteristics of Resonant Circuits: Series and Parallel Resonance; Definitions and Effects of Q; Half-Power Bandwidth

What can cause the voltage across reactances in a series RLC circuit to be higher than the voltage applied to the entire circuit?

A. Resonance
B. Capacitance
C. Low quality factor (Q)
D. Resistance

E5A01 Answer: A. Resonance can cause the voltage across reactances in a series RLC circuit to be higher than the voltage applied to the entire circuit.

What is the resonant frequency of an RLC circuit if R is 22 ohms, L is 50 microhenries, and C is 40 picofarads?

A. 44.72 MHz
B. 22.36 MHz
C. 3.56 MHz
D. 1.78 MHz

E5A02 Answer: C. The resonant frequency of an RLC circuit where R is 22 ohms, L is 50 microhenries, and C is 40 picofarads is 3.56 MHz.

What is the magnitude of the impedance of a series RLC circuit at resonance?

A. High, as compared to the circuit resistance
B. Approximately equal to capacitive reactance
C. Approximately equal to inductive reactance
D. Approximately equal to circuit resistance

E5A03 Answer: D. The magnitude of the impedance of a series RLC circuit at resonance is approximately equal to circuit resistance.

What is the magnitude of the impedance of a parallel RLC circuit at resonance?

A. Approximately equal to circuit resistance
B. Approximately equal to inductive reactance
C. Low compared to the circuit resistance
D. High compared to the circuit resistance

E5A04 Answer: A. The magnitude of the impedance of a parallel RLC circuit at resonance is approximately equal to circuit resistance.

What is the result of increasing the Q of an impedance-matching circuit?

A. Matching bandwidth is decreased
B. Matching bandwidth is increased
C. Losses increase
D. Harmonics increase

E5A05 Answer: A. Increasing the Q of an impedance-matching circuit will decrease the matching bandwidth.

What is the magnitude of the circulating current within the components of a parallel LC circuit at resonance?

A. It is at a minimum
B. It is at a maximum
C. It equals 1 divided by the quantity 2 times pi, multiplied by the square root of inductance L multiplied by capacitance C
D. It equals 2 multiplied by pi, multiplied by the square root of inductance L multiplied by capacitance C

E5A06 Answer: B. The magnitude of the circulating current within the components of a parallel LC circuit at resonance is at a maximum.

What is the magnitude of the current at the input of a parallel RLC circuit at resonance?

A. Minimum
B. Maximum
C. R/L
D. L/R

E5A07 Answer: A. The magnitude of the current at the input of a parallel RLC circuit at resonance is at a minimum.

What is the phase relationship between the current through and the voltage across a series resonant circuit at resonance?

A. The voltage leads the current by 90 degrees
B. The current leads the voltage by 90 degrees
C. The voltage and current are in phase
D. The voltage and current are 180 degrees out of phase

E5A08 Answer: C. In a series resonant circuit at resonance, the voltage and current are in phase.

How is the Q of an RLC parallel resonant circuit calculated?

A. Reactance of either the inductance or capacitance divided by the resistance
B. Reactance of either the inductance or capacitance multiplied by the resistance
C. Resistance divided by the reactance of either the inductance or capacitance
D. Reactance of the inductance multiplied by the reactance of the capacitance

E5A09 Answer: C. The Q of an RLC parallel resonant circuit is calculated by dividing the resistance by the reactance of either the inductance or capacitance.

What is the resonant frequency of an RLC circuit if R is 33 ohms, L is 50 microhenries, and C is 10 picofarads?

A. 7.12 MHz
B. 23.5 kHz
C. 7.12 kHz
D. 23.5 MHz

E5A10 Answer: A. The resonant frequency of an RLC circuit where R is 33 ohms, L is 50 microhenries, and C is 10 picofarads is 7.12 MHz.

What is the half-power bandwidth of a resonant circuit that has a resonant frequency of 7.1 MHz and a Q of 150?

A. 157.8 Hz
B. 315.6 Hz
C. 47.3 kHz
D. 23.67 kHz

E5A11 Answer: C. The half-power bandwidth of a resonant circuit that has a resonant frequency of 7.1 MHz and a Q of 150 is 47.3 kHz.

What is the half-power bandwidth of a resonant circuit that has a resonant frequency of 3.7 MHz and a Q of 118?

A. 436.6 kHz
B. 218.3 kHz
C. 31.4 kHz
D. 15.7 kHz

E5A12 Answer: C. The half-power bandwidth of a resonant circuit that has a resonant frequency of 3.7 MHz and a Q of 118 is 31.4 kHz.

What is an effect of increasing Q in a series resonant circuit?

A. Fewer components are needed for the same performance
B. Parasitic effects are minimized
C. Internal voltages increase
D. Phase shift can become uncontrolled

E5A13 Answer: C. Increasing Q in a series resonant circuit can cause internal voltages to increase.

E5B – Time Constants and Phase Relationships: RL and RC Time Constants; Phase Angle in Reactive Circuits and Components; Admittance and Susceptance

What is the term for the time required for the capacitor in an RC circuit to be charged to 63.2% of the applied voltage or to discharge to 36.8% of its initial voltage?

A. An exponential rate of one
B. One time constant
C. One exponential period
D. A time factor of one

E5B01 Answer: B. A time-constant is the time required for the capacitor in an RC circuit to be charged to 63.2% of the applied voltage or to discharge to 36.8% of its initial voltage.

What letter is commonly used to represent susceptance?

A. G
B. X
C. Y
D. B

E5B02 Answer: D. The letter 'B' is commonly used to represent susceptance.

How is impedance in polar form converted to an equivalent admittance?

A. Take the reciprocal of the angle and change the sign of the magnitude
B. Take the reciprocal of the magnitude and change the sign of the angle
C. Take the square root of the magnitude and add 180 degrees to the angle
D. Square the magnitude and subtract 90 degrees from the angle

E5B03 Answer: B. To convert impedance in polar form to an equivalent admittance, take the reciprocal of the magnitude and change the sign of the angle.

What is the time constant of a circuit having two 220-microfarad capacitors and two 1-megohm resistors, all in parallel?

A. 55 seconds
B. 110 seconds
C. 440 seconds
D. 220 seconds

E5B04 Answer: D. The time constant of a circuit having two 220-microfarad capacitors and two 1-megohm resistors, all in parallel, is 220 seconds.

What is the effect on the magnitude of pure reactance when it is converted to susceptance?

A. It is unchanged
B. The sign is reversed
C. It is shifted by 90 degrees
D. It becomes the reciprocal

E5B05 Answer: D. When a pure reactance is converted to a susceptance, the magnitude of the susceptance is the reciprocal of the magnitude of the reactance.

What is susceptance?

A. The magnetic impedance of a circuit
B. The ratio of magnetic field to electric field
C. The imaginary part of admittance
D. A measure of the efficiency of a transformer

E5B06 Answer: C. Susceptance is the imaginary part of admittance.

What is the phase angle between the voltage across and the current through a series RLC circuit if XC is 500 ohms, R is 1 kilohm, and XL is 250 ohms?

A. 68.2 degrees with the voltage leading the current
B. 14.0 degrees with the voltage leading the current
C. 14.0 degrees with the voltage lagging the current
D. 68.2 degrees with the voltage lagging the current

E5B07 Answer: C. The phase angle of a series RLC circuit with XC = 500 ohms, R = 1 kilohm, and XL = 250 ohms is 14.0 degrees with the voltage lagging the current.

What is the phase angle between the voltage across and the current through a series RLC circuit if XC is 300 ohms, R is 100 ohms, and XL is 100 ohms?

A. 63 degrees with the voltage lagging the current
B. 63 degrees with the voltage leading the current
C. 27 degrees with the voltage leading the current
D. 27 degrees with the voltage lagging the current

E5B08 Answer: A. The phase angle of a series RLC circuit with XC = 300 ohms, R = 100 ohms, and XL = 100 ohms is 63 degrees with the voltage lagging the current.

What is the relationship between the AC current through a capacitor and the voltage across a capacitor?

A. Voltage and current are in phase
B. Voltage and current are 180 degrees out of phase
C. Voltage leads current by 90 degrees
D. Current leads voltage by 90 degrees

E5B09 Answer: D. In a capacitor, AC current leads voltage by 90 degrees.

What is the relationship between the AC current through an inductor and the voltage across an inductor?

A. Voltage leads current by 90 degrees
B. Current leads voltage by 90 degrees
C. Voltage and current are 180 degrees out of phase
D. Voltage and current are in phase

E5B10 Answer: A. In an inductor, voltage leads AC current by 90 degrees.

What is the phase angle between the voltage across and the current through a series RLC circuit if XC is 25 ohms, R is 100 ohms, and XL is 75 ohms?

A. 27 degrees with the voltage lagging the current
B. 27 degrees with the voltage leading the current
C. 63 degrees with the voltage lagging the current
D. 63 degrees with the voltage leading the current

E5B11 Answer: B. The phase angle of a series RLC circuit with XC = 25 ohms, R = 100 ohms, and XL = 75 ohms is 27 degrees with the voltage leading the current.

What is admittance?

A. The inverse of impedance
B. The term for the gain of a field effect transistor
C. The inverse of reactance
D. The term for the on-impedance of a field effect transistor

E5B12 Answer: A. Admittance is the inverse of impedance.

E5C – Coordinate systems and phasors in electronics: Rectangular Coordinates; Polar Coordinates; Phasors

Which of the following represents pure capacitive reactance of 100 ohms in rectangular notation?

A. 0 – j100
B. 0 + j100
C. 100 – j0
D. 100 + j0

E5C01 Answer: A. "0 – j100" represents pure capacitive reactance of 100 ohms in rectangular notation.

How are impedances described in polar coordinates?

A. By X and R values
B. By real and imaginary parts
C. By magnitude and phase angle
D. By Y and G values

E5C02 Answer: C. Impedances are described by magnitude and phase angle in polar coordinates.

Which of the following represents an inductive reactance in polar coordinates?

A. A positive 45 degree phase angle
B. A negative 45 degree phase angle
C. A positive 90 degree phase angle
D. A negative90 degree phase angle

E5C03 Answer: C. A positive 90 degree phase angle represents an inductive reactance in polar coordinates.

What type of Y-axis scale is most often used for graphs of circuit frequency response?

A. Linear
B. Scatter
C. Random
D. Logarithmic

E5C04 Answer: D. A logarithmic Y-axis scale is most often used for graphs of circuit frequency response.

What kind of diagram used to show the phase relationship between impedances at a given frequency?

A. Venn diagram
B. Near field diagram
C. Phasor diagram
D. Far field diagram

E5C05 Answer: C. A phasor diagram is used to show the phase relationship between impedances at a given frequency.

What does the impedance 50 – j25 represent?

A. 50 ohms resistance in series with 25 ohms inductive reactance
B. 50 ohms resistance in series with 25 ohms capacitive reactance
C. 25 ohms resistance in series with 50 ohms inductive reactance
D. 25 ohms resistance in series with 50 ohms capacitive reactance

E5C06 Answer: B. The impedance 50–j25 represents 50 ohms resistance in series with 25 ohms capacitive reactance.

Where is the impedance of a pure resistance plotted on rectangular coordinates?

A. On the vertical axis
B. On a line through the origin, slanted at 45 degrees
C. On a horizontal line, offset vertically above the horizontal axis
D. On the horizontal axis

E5C07 Answer: D. The impedance of a pure resistance is plotted on the horizontal axis on rectangular coordinates.

What coordinate system is often used to display the phase angle of a circuit containing resistance, inductive and/or capacitive reactance?

A. Maidenhead grid
B. Faraday grid
C. Elliptical coordinates
D. Polar coordinates

E5C08 Answer: D. Polar coordinates are often used to display the phase angle of a circuit containing resistance, inductive and/or capacitive reactance.

When using rectangular coordinates to graph the impedance of a circuit, what do the axes represent?

A. The X axis represents the resistive component and the Y axis represents the reactive component
B. The X axis represents the reactive component and the Y axis represents the resistive component
C. The X axis represents the phase angle and the Y axis represents the magnitude
D. The X axis represents the magnitude and the Y axis represents the phase angle

E5C09 Answer: A. When using rectangular coordinates to graph the impedance of a circuit, the horizontal axis represents the resistive component.

Figure E5-1

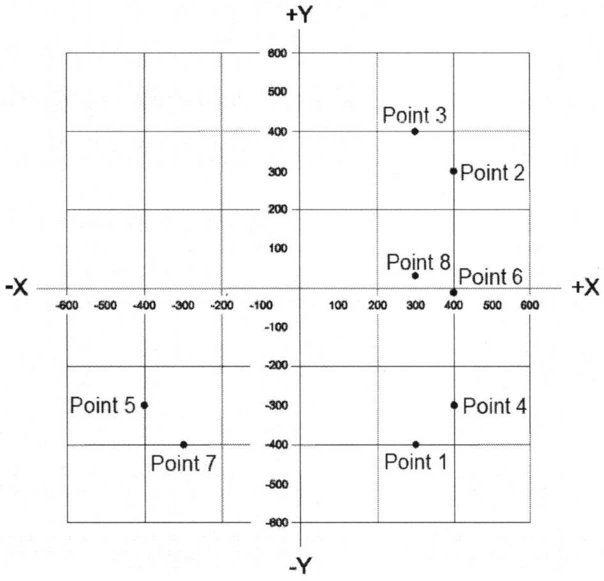

Which point on Figure E5-1 best represents the impedance of a series circuit consisting of a 400-ohm resistor and a 38-picofarad capacitor at 14 MHz?

A. Point 2
B. Point 4
C. Point 5
D. Point 6

E5C10 Answer: B. Point 4 on Figure E5-1 best represents the impedance of a series circuit consisting of a 400 ohm resistor and a 38 picofarad capacitor at 14 MHz.

Which point in Figure E5-1 best represents the impedance of a series circuit consisting of a 300-ohm resistor and an 18-microhenry inductor at 3.505 MHz?

A. Point 1
B. Point 3
C. Point 7
D. Point 8

E5C11 Answer: B. Point 3 on Figure E5-1 best represents the impedance of a series circuit consisting of a 300 ohm resistor and an 18 microhenry inductor at 3.505 MHz.

Which point on Figure E5-1 best represents the impedance of a series circuit consisting of a 300-ohm resistor and a 19-picofarad capacitor at 21.200 MHz?

A. Point 1
B. Point 3
C. Point 7
D. Point 8

E5C12 Answer: A. Point 1 on Figure E5-1 best represents the impedance of a series circuit consisting of a 300 ohm resistor and a 19 picofarad capacitor at 21.200 MHz.

E5D – RF EFFECTS IN COMPONENTS AND CIRCUITS: SKIN EFFECT; REAL AND REACTIVE POWER; ELECTRICAL LENGTH OF CONDUCTORS

What is the result of conductor skin effect?

A. Resistance increases as frequency increases because RF current flows closer to the surface
B. Resistance decreases as frequency increases because electron mobility increases
C. Resistance increases as temperature increases because of the change in thermal coefficient
D. Resistance decreases as temperature increases because of the change in thermal coefficient

E5D01 Answer: A. As a result of conductor skin effect, resistance increases as frequency increases because RF current flows closer to the surface.

Why is it important to keep lead lengths short for components used in circuits for VHF and above?

A. To increase the thermal time constant
B. To minimize inductive reactance
C. To maintain component lifetime
D. All these choices are correct

E5D02 Answer: B. It is important to keep lead lengths short for components used in circuits for VHF and above to minimize inductive reactance.

What is the phase relationship between current and voltage for reactive power?

A. They are out of phase
B. They are in phase
C. They are 90 degrees out of phase
D. They are 45 degrees out of phase

E5D03 Answer: C. Current and voltage are 90 degrees out of phase for reactive power.

Why are short connections used at microwave frequencies?

A. To increase neutralizing resistance
B. To reduce phase shift along the connection
C. To increase compensating capacitance
D. To reduce noise figure

E5D04 Answer: B. Short connections are used at microwave frequencies to reduce phase shift along the connection.

What parasitic characteristic causes electrolytic capacitors to be unsuitable for use at RF?

A. Skin effect
B. Shunt capacitance
C. Inductance
D. Dielectric leakage

E5D05 Answer: C. Inductance is the parasitic characteristic that causes electrolytic capacitors to be unsuitable for use at RF.

What parasitic characteristic creates an inductor's self-resonance?

A. Skin effect
B. Dielectric loss
C. Coupling
D. Inter-turn capacitance

E5D06 Answer: D. Inter-turn capacitance is the parasitic characteristic that creates an inductor's self-resonance.

What combines to create the self-resonance of a component?

A. The component's resistance and reactance
B. The component's nominal and parasitic reactance
C. The component's inductance and capacitance
D. The component's electrical length and impedance

E5D07 Answer: B. The nominal and parasitic reactance combine to create the self-resonance of a component.

What is the primary cause of loss in film capacitors at RF?

A. Inductance
B. Dielectric loss
C. Self-discharge
D. Skin effect

E5D08 Answer: D. Skin effect is the primary cause of loss in film capacitors at RF.

What happens to reactive power in ideal inductors and capacitors?

A. It is dissipated as heat in the circuit
B. Energy is stored in magnetic or electric fields, but power is not dissipated
C. It is canceled by Coulomb forces in the capacity and inductor
D. It is dissipated in the formation of inductive and capacitive fields

E5D09 Answer: B. Reactive power in ideal inductors and capacitors is not dissipated, but energy is stored in magnetic or electric fields.

As a conductor's diameter increases, what is the effect on its electrical length?

A. Thickness has no effect on electrical length
B. It varies randomly
C. It decreases
D. It increases

E5D10 Answer: D. As a conductor's diameter increases, its electrical length also increases.

How many watts are consumed in a circuit consisting of a 100-ohm resistor in series with a 100-ohm inductive reactance drawing 1 ampere?

A. 70.7 watts
B. 100 watts
C. 141.4 watts
D. 200 watts

E5D11 Answer: B. 100 Watts are consumed in a circuit consisting of a 100-ohm resistor in series with a 100-ohm inductive reactance drawing 1 ampere.

What is reactive power?

A. Power consumed in circuit Q
B. Power consumed by an inductor's wire resistance
C. The power consumed in inductors and capacitors
D. Wattless, nonproductive power

E5D12 Answer: D. Reactive power is wattless, nonproductive power.

E6 – Circuit Components

E6A – Semiconductor Materials and Devices: Semiconductor Materials; Bipolar Junction Transistors; Operation and Types of Field-Effect Transistors

In what application is gallium arsenide used as a semiconductor material?

A. In high-current rectifier circuits
B. In high-power audio circuits
C. In microwave circuits
D. In very low-frequency RF circuits

E6A01 Answer: C. Gallium arsenide is used as a semiconductor material in microwave circuits.

Which of the following semiconductor materials contains excess free electrons?

A. N-type
B. P-type
C. Bipolar
D. Insulated gate

E6A02 Answer: A. N-type semiconductor materials contain excess free electrons.

Why does a PN-junction diode not conduct current when reverse biased?

A. Only P-type semiconductor material can conduct current
B. Only N-type semiconductor material can conduct current
C. Holes in P-type material and electrons in the N-type material are separated by the applied voltage, widening the depletion region
D. Excess holes in P-type material combine with the electrons in N-type material, converting the entire diode into an insulator

E6A03 Answer: C. A PN-junction diode does not conduct current when reverse biased because holes in P-type material and electrons in the N-type material are separated by the applied voltage, widening the depletion region.

What is the name given to an impurity atom that adds holes to a semiconductor crystal structure?

A. Insulator impurity
B. N-type impurity
C. Acceptor impurity
D. Donor impurity

E6A04 Answer: C. Acceptor impurities are atoms that add holes to a semiconductor crystal structure.

How does DC input impedance at the gate of a field-effect transistor (FET) compare with that of a bipolar transistor?

A. They are both low impedance
B. An FET has lower input impedance
C. An FET has higher input impedance
D. They are both high impedance

E6A05 Answer: C. An FET has high input impedance; a bipolar transistor has low input impedance.

What is the beta of a bipolar junction transistor?

A. The frequency at which the current gain is reduced to 0.707
B. The change in collector current with respect to the change in base current
C. The breakdown voltage of the base-to-collector junction
D. The switching speed

E6A06 Answer: B. The beta of a bipolar junction transistor is the change in collector current with respect to the change in base current.

Which of the following indicates that a silicon NPN junction transistor is biased on?

A. Base-to-emitter resistance of approximately 6 to 7 ohms
B. Base-to-emitter resistance of approximately 0.6 to 0.7 ohms
C. Base-to-emitter voltage of approximately 6 to 7 volts
D. Base-to-emitter voltage of approximately 0.6 to 0.7 volts

E6A07 Answer: D. A base-to-emitter voltage of approximately 0.6 to 0.7 volts would indicate that a silicon NPN junction transistor is biased on.

What is the term for the frequency at which the grounded-base current gain of a bipolar junction transistor has decreased to 0.7 of the gain obtainable at 1 kHz?

A. Corner frequency
B. Alpha rejection frequency
C. Beta cutoff frequency
D. Alpha cutoff frequency

E6A08 Answer: D. Alpha cutoff frequency is the frequency at which the grounded-base current gain of a transistor has decreased to 0.7 of the gain obtainable at 1 kHz.

What is a depletion-mode field-effect transistor (FET)?

A. An FET that exhibits a current flow between source and drain when no gate voltage is applied
B. An FET that has no current flow between source and drain when no gate voltage is applied
C. Any FET that exhibits very high electron mobility due to a lack of holes in the N-type material
D. Any FET for which holes are the majority carriers

E6A09 Answer: A. A depletion-mode FET is an FET that exhibits a current flow between source and drain when no gate voltage is applied.

Figure E6-1

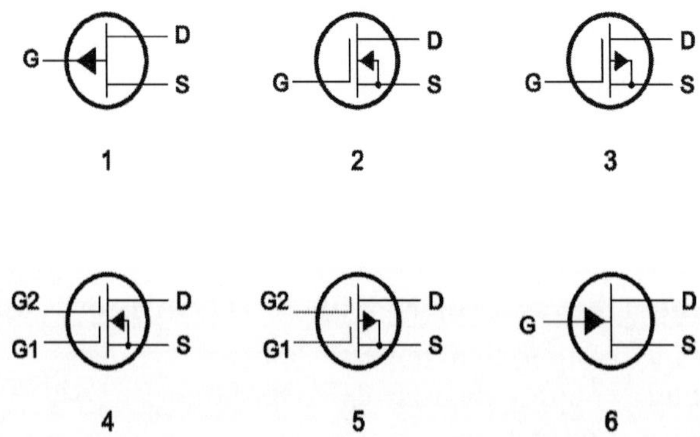

In Figure E6-1, what is the schematic symbol for an N-channel dual-gate MOSFET?

A. 2
B. 4
C. 5
D. 6

E6A10 Answer: B. In Figure E6-1, the schematic symbol for an N-channel dual-gate MOSFET is 4.

In Figure E6-1, what is the schematic symbol for a P-channel junction FET?

A. 1
B. 2
C. 3
D. 6

E6A11 Answer: A. In Figure E6-1, the schematic symbol for a P-channel junction FET is 1.

What is the purpose of connecting Zener diodes between a MOSFET gate and its source or drain?

A. To provide a voltage reference for the correct amount of reverse-bias gate voltage
B. To protect the substrate from excessive voltages
C. To keep the gate voltage within specifications and prevent the device from overheating
D. To protect the gate from static damage

E6A12 Answer: D. The purpose of connecting Zener diodes between a MOSFET gate and its source or drain is to protect the gate from static damage.

E6B – Diodes

What is the most useful characteristic of a Zener diode?

A. A constant current drop under conditions of varying voltage
B. A constant voltage drop under conditions of varying current
C. A negative resistance region
D. An internal capacitance that varies with the applied voltage

E6B01 Answer: B. Zener diodes are most useful because they have a constant voltage drop under conditions of varying current.

Which characteristic of a Schottky diode makes it a better choice than a silicon junction diode for use as a power supply rectifier?

A. Much higher reverse voltage breakdown
B. More constant reverse avalanche voltage
C. Longer carrier retention time
D. Less forward voltage drop

E6B02 Answer: D. Schottky diodes can be more useful than ordinary diodes in some applications because they have less forward voltage drop.

What property of an LED's semiconductor material determines its forward voltage drop?

A. Intrinsic resistance
B. Band gap
C. Junction capacitance
D. Junction depth

E6B03 Answer: B. The forward voltage drop of an LED's semiconductor material is determined by its band gap.

What type of semiconductor device is designed for use as a voltage-controlled capacitor?

A. Varactor diode
B. Tunnel diode
C. Silicon-controlled rectifier
D. Zener diode

E6B04 Answer: A. Varactor diodes are designed for use as voltage-controlled capacitors.

What characteristic of a PIN diode makes it useful as an RF switch?

A. Extremely high reverse breakdown voltage
B. Ability to dissipate large amounts of power
C. Reverse bias controls its forward voltage drop
D. Low junction capacitance

E6B05 Answer: D. The low junction capacitance in a PIN diode makes it useful as an RF switch.

Which of the following is a common use of a Schottky diode?

A. In oscillator circuits as the negative resistance element
B. As a variable capacitance in an automatic frequency control circuit
C. In power supplies as a constant voltage reference
D. As a VHF/UHF mixer or detector

E6B06 Answer: D. A Schottky diode is commonly used as a VHF/UHF mixer or detector.

What causes a junction diode to fail from excessive current?

A. Excessive inverse voltage
B. Excessive junction temperature
C. Insufficient forward voltage
D. Charge carrier depletion

E6B07 Answer: B. Excessive junction temperature causes a junction diode to fail.

Which of the following is a Schottky barrier diode?

A. Metal-semiconductor junction
B. Electrolytic rectifier
C. PIN junction
D. Thermionic emission diode

E6B08 Answer: A. Metal-semiconductor junctions are used to make Schottky barrier diodes.

What is a common use for point-contact diodes?

A. As a constant current source
B. As a constant voltage source
C. As an RF detector
D. As a high-voltage rectifier

E6B09 Answer: C. Point contact diodes are used as RF detectors.

Figure E6-2

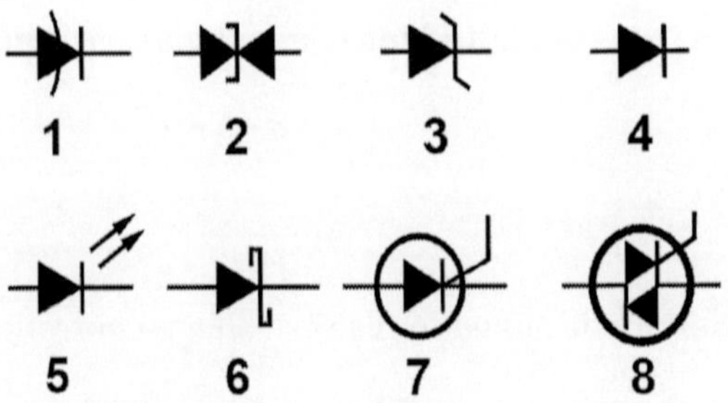

In Figure E6-2, what is the schematic symbol for a Schottky diode?

A. 1
B. 6
C. 2
D. 3

E6B10 Answer: B. In Figure E6-2, the schematic symbol for a Schottky diode is 6.

What is used to control the attenuation of RF signals by a PIN diode?

A. Forward DC bias current
B. A variable RF reference voltage
C. Reverse voltage larger than the RF signal
D. Capacitance of an RF coupling capacitor

E6B11 Answer: A. Forward DC bias current is used to control the attenuation of RF signals by a PIN diode.

E6C – Digital ICs: Families of Digital ICs; Gates; Programmable Logic Devices (PLDs)

What is the function of hysteresis in a comparator?

A. To prevent input noise from causing unstable output signals
B. To allow the comparator to be used with AC input signals
C. To cause the output to change states continually
D. To increase the sensitivity

E6C01 Answer: A. Hysteresis in a comparator prevents input noise from causing unstable output signals.

What happens when the level of a comparator's input signal crosses the threshold voltage?

A. The IC input can be damaged
B. The comparator changes its output state
C. The reference level appears at the output
D. The feedback loop becomes unstable

E6C02 Answer: B. When the level of a comparator's input signal crosses the threshold, the comparator changes its output state.

What is tri-state logic?

A. Logic devices with 0, 1, and high-impedance output states
B. Logic devices that utilize ternary math
C. Logic with three output impedance which can be selected to better match the load impedance
D. A counter with eight states

E6C03 Answer: A. Tri-state logic devices have 0, 1, and high-impedance output states.

Which of the following is an advantage of BiCMOS logic?

A. Its simplicity results in much less expensive devices than standard CMOS
B. It is immune to electrostatic damage
C. It has the high input impedance of CMOS and the low output impedance of bipolar transistors
D. All these choices are correct

E6C04 Answer: C. BiCMOS logic has the advantage of high input impedance and low output impedance.

Which of the following digital logic families has the lowest power consumption?

A. Schottky TTL
B. ECL
C. NMOS
D. CMOS

E6C05 Answer: D. CMOS has a lower power consumption than Schottky TTL, ECL, and NMOS.

Why do CMOS digital integrated circuits have high immunity to noise on the input signal or power supply?

A. Large bypass capacitance is inherent
B. The input switching threshold is about two times the power supply voltage
C. The input switching threshold is about one-half the power supply voltage
D. Bandwidth is very limited

E6C06 Answer: C. CMOS digital integrated circuits have high immunity to noise on the input signal because the input switching threshold is about one-half the power supply voltage.

What best describes a pull-up or pull-down resistor?

A. A resistor in a keying circuit used to reduce key clicks
B. A resistor connected to the positive or negative supply line used to establish a voltage when an input or output is an open circuit
C. A resistor that ensures that an oscillator frequency does not drift
D. A resistor connected to an op-amp output that prevents signals from exceeding the power supply voltage

E6C07 Answer: B. Pull-up or pull-down resistors are connected to the positive or negative supply line and used to establish a voltage when an input or output is an open circuit.

Figure E6-3

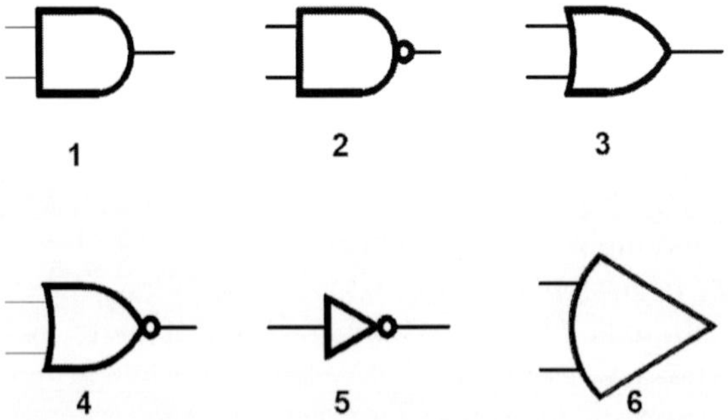

In Figure E6-3, what is the schematic symbol for a NAND gate?

A. 1
B. 2
C. 3
D. 4

E6C08 Answer: B. In Figure E6-3, the schematic symbol for a NAND gate is 2.

What is used to design the configuration of a field-programmable gate array (FPGA)?

A. Karnaugh maps
B. Hardware description language (HDL)
C. An auto-rotator
D. Machine and assembly language

E6C09 Answer: B. Hardware description language (HDL) is used to design the configuration of a field-programmable gate array (FPGA).

In Figure E6-3, what is the schematic symbol for a NOR gate?

A. 1
B. 2
C. 3
D. 4

E6C10 Answer: D. In Figure E6-3, the schematic symbol for a NOR gate is 4.

In Figure E6-3, what is the schematic symbol for the NOT operation (inversion)?

A. 2
B. 4
C. 5
D. 6

E6C11 Answer: C. In Figure E6-3, the schematic symbol for the NOT operation is 5.

E6D – Inductors and Piezoelectricity: Permeability, Core Material, and Configuration; Transformers; Piezoelectric Devices

What is piezoelectricity?

A. The ability of materials to generate electromagnetic waves of a certain frequency when voltage is applied
B. A characteristic of materials that have an index of refraction which depends on the polarization of the electromagnetic wave passing through it
C. A characteristic of materials that generate voltage when stressed and that flex when a voltage is applied
D. The ability of materials to generate voltage when an electromagnetic wave of a certain frequency is applied

E6D01 Answer: C. Piezoelectricity is a characteristic of materials that generate voltage when stressed and that flex when a voltage is applied.

What is the equivalent circuit of a quartz crystal?

A. Series RLC in parallel with a shunt C representing electrode and stray capacitance
B. Parallel RLC, where C is the parallel combination of resonance capacitance of the crystal and electrode and stray capacitance
C. Series RLC, where C is the parallel combination of resonance capacitance of the crystal and electrode and stray capacitance
D. Parallel RLC, where C is the series combination of resonance capacitance of the crystal and electrode and stray capacitance

E6D02 Answer: A. The equivalent circuit of a quartz crystal is series RLC in parallel with a shunt C representing electrode and stray capacitance.

Which of the following is an aspect of the piezoelectric effect?

A. Mechanical deformation of material due to the application of a voltage
B. Mechanical deformation of material due to the application of a magnetic field
C. Generation of electrical energy in the presence of light
D. Increased conductivity in the presence of light

E6D03 Answer: A. The piezoelectric effect is mechanical deformation of material due to the application of a voltage.

Why are cores of inductors and transformers sometimes constructed of thin layers?

A. To simplify assembly during manufacturing
B. To reduce power loss from eddy currents in the core
C. To increase the cutoff frequency by reducing capacitance
D. To save cost by reducing the amount of magnetic material

E6D04 Answer: B. The cores of inductors and transformers are sometimes constructed of thin layers to reduce power loss from eddy currents in the core.

How do ferrite and powdered iron compare for use in an inductor core?

A. Ferrite cores generally have lower initial permeability
B. Ferrite cores generally have better temperature stability
C. Ferrite cores generally require fewer turns to produce a given inductance value
D. Ferrite cores are easier to use with surface mount technology

E6D05 Answer: C. Ferrite cores generally require fewer turns than powdered iron to produce a given inductance value.

What core material property determines the inductance of an inductor?

A. Permittivity
B. Resistance
C. Reactivity
D. Permeability

E6D06 Answer: D. Permeability of the core material determines the inductance of an inductor.

What is the current that flows in the primary winding of a transformer when there is no load on the secondary winding?

A. Stabilizing current
B. Direct current
C. Excitation current
D. Magnetizing current

E6D07 Answer: D. The magnetizing current flows in the primary winding of a transformer when there is no load on the secondary current.

Which of the following materials has the highest temperature stability of its magnetic characteristics?

A. Brass
B. Powdered iron
C. Ferrite
D. Aluminum

E6D08 Answer: B. Powdered iron has higher temperature stability of its magnetic characteristics than brass, ferrite, or aluminum.

What devices are commonly used as VHF and UHF parasitic suppressors at the input and output terminals of a transistor HF amplifier?

A. Electrolytic capacitors
B. Butterworth filters
C. Ferrite beads
D. Steel-core toroids

E6D09 Answer: C. Ferrite beads are commonly used as VHF and UHF parasitic suppressors at the input and output terminals of transistor HF amplifiers.

What is a primary advantage of using a toroidal core instead of a solenoidal core in an inductor?

A. Toroidal cores confine most of the magnetic field within the core material
B. Toroidal cores make it easier to couple the magnetic energy into other components
C. Toroidal cores exhibit greater hysteresis
D. Toroidal cores have lower Q characteristics

E6D10 Answer: A. Toroidal cores confine most of the magnetic field within the core material, while solenoidal cores do not.

Which type of core material decreases inductance when inserted into a coil?

A. Ceramic
B. Brass
C. Ferrite
D. Aluminum

E6D11 Answer: B. Brass as a core material decreases inductance when inserted into a coil.

What causes inductor saturation?

A. Operation at too high a frequency
B. Selecting a core with low permeability
C. Operation at excessive magnetic flux
D. Selecting a core with excessive permittivity

E6D12 Answer: C. Inductor saturation is caused by operation at excessive magnetic flux.

E6E – Semiconductor Materials and Packages for RF Use

Why is gallium arsenide (GaAs) useful for semiconductor devices operating at UHF and higher frequencies?

A. Higher noise figures
B. Higher electron mobility
C. Lower junction voltage drop
D. Lower transconductance

E6E01 Answer: B. Higher electron mobility makes gallium arsenide (GaAs) useful for semiconductor devices operating at UHF and higher frequencies.

Which of the following device packages is a through-hole type?

A. DIP
B. PLCC
C. BGA
D. SOT

E6E02 Answer: A. DIP is a type of through-hole device packaging.

Which of the following materials supports the highest frequency of operation when used in MMICs?

A. Silicon
B. Silicon nitride
C. Silicon dioxide
D. Gallium nitride

E6E03 Answer: D. Gallium nitride supports the highest frequency of operation when used in MMICs.

Which is the most common input and output impedance of MMICs?

A. 50 ohms
B. 300 ohms
C. 450 ohms
D. 75 ohms

E6E04 Answer: A. 50 ohms is the most common input and output impedance of MMICs.

Which of the following noise figure values is typical of a low-noise UHF preamplifier?

A. 0.5 dB
B. -10 dB
C. 44 dBm
D. -20 dBm

E6E05 Answer: A. 0.5 dB is a typical noise value of a low-noise UHF preamplifier.

What characteristics of MMICs make them a popular choice for VHF through microwave circuits?

A. The ability to retrieve information from a single signal even in the presence of other strong signals
B. Extremely high Q factor and high stability over a wide temperature range
C. Nearly infinite gain, very high input impedance, and very low output impedance
D. Controlled gain, low noise figure, and constant input and output impedance over the specified frequency range

E6E06 Answer: D. MMICs have controlled gain, low noise figures, and constant input and output impedances over the specified frequency range, making them popular for VHF through microwave circuits.

What type of transmission line is often used for connections to MMICs?

A. Miniature coax
B. Circular waveguide
C. Parallel wire
D. Microstrip

E6E07 Answer: D. Microstrip is the type of transmission line often used for connections to MMICs.

How is power supplied to the most common type of MMIC?

A. Through a capacitor and RF choke connected to the amplifier input lead
B. MMICs require no operating bias
C. Through a resistor and/or RF choke connected to the amplifier output lead
D. Directly to the bias voltage (Vcc) lead

E6E08 Answer: C. Power supplies are normally connected to MMICs through a resistor and/or RF choke connected to the amplifier output lead.

Which of the following component package types have the least parasitic effects at frequencies above the HF range?

A. TO-220
B. Axial lead
C. Radial lead
D. Surface mount

E6E09 Answer: D. Components in surface mount packaging have the least parasitic effects at frequencies above the HF range.

What advantage does surface-mount technology offer at RF compared to using through-hole components?

A. Smaller circuit area
B. Shorter circuit board traces
C. Components have less parasitic inductance and capacitance
D. All these choices are correct

E6E10 Answer: D. Advantages of surface-mount technology offer at RF compared to using through-hole components include smaller circuit area, shorter circuit board traces, and the components have less parasitic inductance and capacitance.

What is a characteristic of DIP packaging used for integrated circuits?

A. Extremely low stray capacitance (dielectrically isolated package)
B. Extremely high resistance between pins (doubly insulated package)
C. Two chips in each package (dual in package)
D. A total of two rows of connecting pins placed on opposite sides of the package (dual in-line package)

E6E11 Answer: D. DIP packaging for ICs is a total of two rows of connecting pins placed on opposite sides of the package.

Why are DIP through-hole package ICs not typically used at UHF and higher frequencies?

A. Excessive dielectric loss
B. Epoxy coating is conductive above 300 MHz
C. Excessive lead length
D. Unsuitable for combining analog and digital signals

E6E12 Answer: C. DIP through-hole package Ics are not typically used at UHF and higher frequencies due to excessive lead length.

E6F – Electro-optical Technology: Photoconductivity; Photovoltaic Devices; Optical Sensors and Encoders; Optical Isolation Switching

What absorbs the energy from light falling on a photovoltaic cell?

A. Protons
B. Photons
C. Electrons
D. Holes

E6F01 Answer: C. Electrons absorb the energy from light falling on photovoltaic cells.

What happens to photoconductive material when light shines on it?

A. Resistance decreases
B. Resistance increases
C. Reflectivity increases
D. Reflectivity decreases

E6F02 Answer: A. Resistance decreases when light shines on photoconductive material.

What is the most common configuration of an optoisolator or optocoupler?

A. A lens and a photomultiplier
B. A frequency-modulated helium-neon laser
C. An amplitude-modulated helium-neon laser
D. An LED and a phototransistor

E6F03 Answer: D. Optoisolators and optocouplers are most often used as LEDs and phototransistors, respectively.

What is the photovoltaic effect?

A. The conversion of voltage to current when exposed to light
B. The conversion of light to electrical energy
C. The effect that causes a photodiode to emit light when a voltage is applied
D. The effect that causes a phototransistor's beta to decrease when exposed to light

E6F04 Answer: B. The photovoltaic effect is the conversion of light to electrical energy.

Which of the following describes an optical shaft encoder?

A. A device that detects rotation of a control by interrupting a light source with a patterned wheel
B. A device that measures the strength of a beam of light using analog-to-digital conversion
C. An optical computing device in which light is coupled between devices by fiber optics
D. A device for generating RTTY signals by means of a rotating light source

E6F05 Answer: A. An optical shaft encoder is a device that detects rotation of a control by interrupting a light source with a patterned wheel.

Which of these materials is most commonly used to create photoconductive devices?

A. Polyphenol acetate
B. Argon
C. Crystalline semiconductor
D. All these choices are correct

E6F06 Answer: C. Crystalline semiconductors are most commonly used to create photoconductive devices.

What is a solid-state relay?

A. A relay using transistors to drive the relay coil
B. A device that uses semiconductors to implement the functions of an electromechanical relay
C. A mechanical relay that latches in the on or off state each time it is pulsed
D. A semiconductor switch that uses a monostable multivibrator circuit

E6F07 Answer: B. A solid-state relay is a device that uses semiconductors to implement the functions of an electromechanical relay.

Why are optoisolators often used in conjunction with solid-state circuits when switching 120 VAC circuits?

A. Optoisolators provide a low-impedance link between a control circuit and a power circuit
B. Optoisolators provide impedance matching between the control circuit and power circuit
C. Optoisolators provide an electrical isolation between a control circuit and the circuit being switched
D. Optoisolators eliminate the effects of reflected light in the control circuit

E6F08 Answer: C. Optoisolators are often used in conjunction with solid-state circuits when switching 120 VAC because they provide an electrical isolation between a control circuit and the circuit being switched.

What is the efficiency of a photovoltaic cell?

A. The output RF power divided by the input DC power
B. The output of lumens divided by the input power in watts
C. The open-circuit voltage divided by the short-circuit current under full illumination
D. The relative fraction of light that is converted to current

E6F09 Answer: D. The efficiency of a photovoltaic cell is the relative fraction of light that is converted to current.

What is the most common material used in power-generating photovoltaic cells?

A. Selenium
B. Silicon
C. Cadmium Sulfide
D. Copper oxide

E6F10 Answer: B. The most common material used in power-generating photovoltaic cells is silicon.

What is the approximate open-circuit voltage produced by a fully illuminated silicon photovoltaic cell?

A. 0.5 V
B. 0.7 V
C. 1.1 V
D. 1.5 V

E6F11 Answer: A. The approximate open-circuit voltage produced by a fully illuminated silicon photovoltaic cell is 0.5 V.

E7 – Practical Circuits

E7A – Digital Circuits: Digital Circuit Principles and Logic Circuits; Classes of Logic Elements; Positive and Negative Logic; Frequency Dividers; Truth Tables

Which circuit is bistable?

A. An AND gate
B. An OR gate
C. A flip-flop
D. A bipolar amplifier

E7A01 Answer: C. Flip-flops are bi-stable circuits.

What is the function of a decade counter?

A. It produces one output pulse for every 10 input pulses
B. It decodes a decimal number for display on a seven-segment LED display
C. It produces 10 output pulses for every input pulse
D. It decodes a binary number for display on a seven-segment LED display

E7A02 Answer: A. Decade counters produce one output pulse for every ten input pulses.

Which of the following can divide the frequency of a pulse train by 2?

A. An XOR gate
B. A flip-flop
C. An OR gate
D. A multiplexer

E7A03 Answer: B. Flip-flops can divide the frequency of a pulse train by 2.

How many flip-flops are required to divide a signal frequency by 16?

A. 4
B. 6
C. 8
D. 16

E7A04 Answer: A. Four flip-flops are required to divide a signal frequency by 16.

Which of the following circuits continuously alternates between two states without an external clock signal?

A. Monostable multivibrator
B. J-K flip-flop
C. T flip-flop
D. Astable multivibrator

E7A05 Answer: D. Astable multivibrators continuously alternate between two states without an external clock.

What is a characteristic of a monostable multivibrator?

A. It switches temporarily to an alternate state for a set time
B. It produces a continuous square wave
C. It stores one bit of data
D. It maintains a constant output voltage, regardless of variations in the input voltage

E7A06 Answer: A. Monostable multivibrators switch temporarily to an alternate state for a set time.

What logical operation does a NAND gate perform?

A. It produces a 0 at its output only if all inputs are 0
B. It produces a 1 at its output only if all inputs are 1
C. It produces a 0 at its output if some but not all inputs are 1
D. It produces a 0 at its output only if all inputs are 1

E7A07 Answer: D. NAND gates produce a 0 at their output only if all inputs are 1.

What logical operation does an OR gate perform?

A. It produces a 1 at its output if any inputs are 1
B. It produces a 0 at its output if all inputs are 1
C. It produces a 0 at its output if some but not all inputs are 1
D. It produces a 1 at its output if all inputs are 0

E7A08 Answer: A. OR gates produce 1 at their output if any inputs are 1.

What logical operation is performed by an exclusive NOR gate?

A. It produces a 0 at its output only if all inputs are 0
B. It produces a 1 at its output only if all inputs are 1
C. It produces a 0 at its output if one and only one of its inputs is 1
D. It produces a 1 at its output if one and only one input is 1

E7A09 Answer: C. Exclusive NOR gates produce 0 at their output if one and only one of their inputs is 1.

What is a truth table?

A. A list of inputs and corresponding outputs for an op-amp
B. A list of inputs and corresponding outputs for a digital device
C. A diagram showing logic states when the digital device output is true
D. A table of logic symbols that indicate the logic states of an op-amp

E7A10 Answer: B. A truth table is a list of inputs and corresponding outputs for a digital device.

What does "positive logic" mean in reference to logic devices?

A. The logic devices have high noise immunity
B. High voltage represents a 1, low voltage a 0
C. The logic circuit is in the "true" condition
D. 1s and 0s are defined as different positive voltage levels

E7A11 Answer: B. In reference to logic devices, positive logic means that high voltage represents a 1 and low voltage represents a 0.

E7B – Amplifiers: Class of Operation; Vacuum Tube and Solid-State Circuits; Distortion and Intermodulation; Spurious and Parasitic Suppression; Switching-Type Amplifiers

For what portion of the signal cycle does each active element in a push-pull, Class AB amplifier conduct?

A. More than 180 degrees but less than 360 degrees
B. Exactly 180 degrees
C. The entire cycle
D. Less than 180 degrees

E7B01 Answer: A. A class AB amplifier operates on more than 180 degrees but less than 360 degrees of a signal cycle.

What is a Class D amplifier?

A. A type of amplifier that uses switching technology to achieve high efficiency
B. A low power amplifier that uses a differential amplifier for improved linearity
C. An amplifier that uses drift-mode FETs for high efficiency
D. An amplifier biased to be relatively free from distortion

E7B02 Answer: A. A class D amplifier uses switching technology to achieve high efficiency.

What circuit is required at the output of an RF switching amplifier?

A. A filter to remove harmonic content
B. A high-pass filter to compensate for low gain at low frequencies
C. A matched load resistor to prevent damage by switching frequencies
D. A temperature compensating load resistor to improve linearity

E7B03 Answer: A. A filter to remove harmonic content is required at the output of an RF switching amplifier.

What is the operating point of a Class A common emitter amplifier?

A. Approximately halfway between saturation and cutoff
B. Approximately halfway between the emitter voltage and the base voltage
C. At a point where the bias resistor equals the load resistor
D. At a point where the load line intersects the zero bias current curve

E7B04 Answer: A. The operating point of a Class A common emitter amplifier is approximately halfway between saturation and cutoff.

What can be done to prevent unwanted oscillations in an RF power amplifier?

A. Tune the stage for minimum loading
B. Tune both the input and output for maximum power
C. Install parasitic suppressors and/or neutralize the stage
D. Use a phase inverter in the output filter

E7B05 Answer: C. Installing parasitic suppressors and/or neutralizing the stage can prevent unwanted oscillations in an RF power amplifier.

What is a characteristic of a grounded-grid amplifier?

A. High power gain
B. Low input impedance
C. High electrostatic damage protection
D. Low bandwidth

E7B06 Answer: B. A grounded-grid amplifier has low input impedance.

Which of the following is the likely result of using a Class C amplifier to amplify a single-sideband phone signal?

A. Reduced intermodulation products
B. Increased overall intelligibility
C. Reduced third-order intermodulation
D. Signal distortion and excessive bandwidth

E7B07 Answer: D. Signal distortion and excessive bandwidth can result from using a Class C amplifier to amplify a single-sideband phone signal.

Why are switching amplifiers more efficient than linear amplifiers?

A. Switching amplifiers operate at higher voltages
B. The switching device is at saturation or cutoff most of the time
C. Linear amplifiers have high gain resulting in higher harmonic content
D. Switching amplifiers use push-pull circuits

E7B08 Answer: B. Switching amplifiers are more efficient than linear amplifiers because the switching device is at saturation or cutoff most of the time.

What is a characteristic of an emitter follower (or common collector) amplifier?

A. Low input impedance and phase inversion from input to output
B. Differential inputs and single output
C. Acts as an OR circuit if one input is grounded
D. Input and output signals in-phase

E7B09 Answer: D. An emitter follower (or common collector) amplifier has input and output signals in-phase.

Figure E7-1

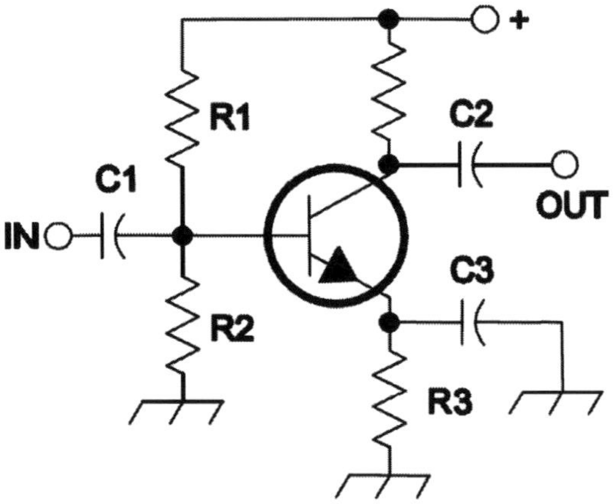

In Figure E7-1, what is the purpose of R1 and R2?

A. Load resistors
B. Voltage divider bias
C. Self bias
D. Feedback

E7B10 Answer: B. In Figure E7-1, R1 and R2 are used as a voltage divider bias.

In Figure E7-1, what is the purpose of R3?

A. Fixed bias
B. Emitter bypass
C. Output load resistor
D. Self bias

E7B11 Answer: D. In Figure E7-1, R3 is a self-bias.

What type of amplifier circuit is shown in Figure E7-1?

A. Common base
B. Common collector
C. Common emitter
D. Emitter follower

E7B12 Answer: C. A common emitter amplifier is shown in Figure E7-1.

E7C – Filters and Matching Networks: Types of Networks; Types of Filters; Filter Applications; Filter Characteristics; Impedance Matching

How are the capacitors and inductors of a low-pass filter Pi-network arranged between the network's input and output?

A. Two inductors are in series between the input and output, and a capacitor is connected between the two inductors and ground
B. Two capacitors are in series between the input and output, and an inductor is connected between the two capacitors and ground
C. An inductor is connected between the input and ground, another inductor is connected between the output and ground, and a capacitor is connected between the input and output
D. A capacitor is connected between the input and ground, another capacitor is connected between the output and ground, and an inductor is connected between input and output

E7C01 Answer: D. In a low-pass filter Pi-network, a capacitor is connected between the input and ground, another capacitor is connected between the output and ground, and an inductor is connected between input and output.

What is the frequency response of a T-network with series capacitors and a shunt inductor?

A. Low-pass
B. High-pass
C. Band-pass
D. Notch

E7C02 Answer: B. The frequency response of a T-network with series capacitors and a shunt inductor is high-pass.

What is the purpose of adding an inductor to a Pi-network to create a Pi-L-network?

A. Greater harmonic suppression
B. Higher efficiency
C. To eliminate one capacitor
D. Greater transformation range

E7C03 Answer: A. The purpose of adding an inductor to a Pi-network to create a Pi-L-network is for greater harmonic suppression.

How does an impedance-matching circuit transform a complex impedance to a resistive impedance?

A. It introduces negative resistance to cancel the resistive part of impedance
B. It introduces transconductance to cancel the reactive part of impedance
C. It cancels the reactive part of the impedance and changes the resistive part to a desired value
D. Reactive currents are dissipated in matched resistances

E7C04 Answer: C. An impedance-matching circuit cancels the reactive part of the impedance and changes the resistive part to a desired value.

Which filter type is described as having ripple in the passband and a sharp cutoff?

A. A Butterworth filter
B. An active LC filter
C. A passive op-amp filter
D. A Chebyshev filter

E7C05 Answer: D. A Chebyshev filter is described as having ripple in the passband and a sharp cutoff.

What are the characteristics of an elliptical filter?

A. Gradual passband rolloff with minimal stop band ripple
B. Extremely flat response over its pass band with gradually rounded stop-band corners
C. Extremely sharp cutoff with one or more notches in the stop band
D. Gradual passband rolloff with extreme stop-band ripple

E7C06 Answer: C. An elliptical filter has an extremely sharp cutoff with one or more notches in the stop band.

Which describes a Pi-L-network?

A. A Phase Inverter Load network
B. A Pi-network with an additional output series inductor
C. A network with only three discrete parts
D. A matching network in which all components are isolated from ground

E7C07 Answer: B. A Pi-network with an additional series inductor on the output could be used to match a vacuum tube final amplifier to a 50 ohm unbalanced output.

Which of the following is most frequently used as a band-pass or notch filter in VHF and UHF transceivers?

A. A Sallen-Key filter
B. A helical filter
C. A swinging choke filter
D. A finite impulse response filter

E7C08 Answer: B. A helical filter is most frequently used as a band-pass or notch filter in VHF and UHF transceivers.

What is a crystal lattice filter?

A. A power supply filter made with interlaced quartz crystals
B. An audio filter made with four quartz crystals that resonate at 1 kHz intervals
C. A filter using lattice-shaped quartz crystals for high-Q performance
D. A filter with narrow bandwidth and steep skirts made using quartz crystals

E7C09 Answer: D. A crystal lattice filter is a filter with narrow bandwidth and steep skirts made using quartz crystals.

Which of the following filters is used in a 2-meter band repeater duplexer?

A. A crystal filter
B. A cavity filter
C. A DSP filter
D. An L-C filter

E7C10 Answer: B. A cavity filter is used in a 2-meter band repeater duplexer.

Which of the following measures a filter's ability to reject signals in adjacent channels?

A. Passband ripple
B. Phase response
C. Shape factor
D. Noise factor

E7C11 Answer: C. Shape factor measures a filter's ability to reject signals in adjacent channels.

E7D – Power Supplies and Voltage Regulators; Solar Array Charge Controllers

How does a linear electronic voltage regulator work?

A. It has a ramp voltage as its output
B. It eliminates the need for a pass transistor
C. The control element duty cycle is proportional to the line or load conditions
D. The conduction of a control element is varied to maintain a constant output voltage

E7D01 Answer: D. A linear electronic voltage regulator varies the conduction of a control element to maintain a constant output voltage.

How does a switchmode voltage regulator work?

A. By alternating the output between positive and negative voltages
B. By varying the duty cycle of pulses input to a filter
C. By varying the conductivity of a pass element
D. By switching between two Zener diode reference voltages

E7D02 Answer: B. A switchmode voltage regulator works by varying the duty cycle of pulses input to a filter.

What device is used as a stable voltage reference?

A. A Zener diode
B. A digital-to-analog converter
C. An SCR
D. An analog-to-digital converter

E7D03 Answer: A. A Zener diode is used as a stable voltage reference.

Which of the following describes a three-terminal voltage regulator?

A. A series current source
B. A series regulator
C. A shunt regulator
D. A shunt current source

E7D04 Answer: B. A series regulator is a three-terminal voltage regulator.

Which of the following types of linear voltage regulator operates by loading the unregulated voltage source?

A. A constant current source
B. A series regulator
C. A shunt current source
D. A shunt regulator

E7D05 Answer: D. A shunt regulator operates by loading the unregulated voltage source.

Figure E7-2

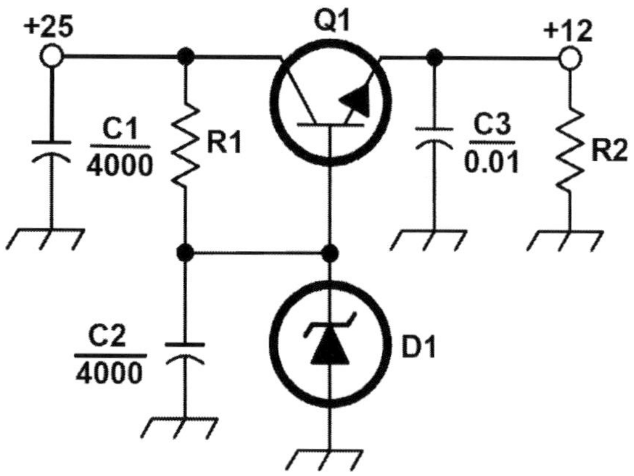

What is the purpose of Q1 in the circuit shown in Figure E7-2?

A. It provides negative feedback to improve regulation
B. It provides a constant load for the voltage source
C. It controls the current to keep the output voltage constant
D. It provides regulation by switching or "chopping" the input DC voltage

E7D06 Answer: C. The purpose of Q1 in the circuit shown in Figure E7-2 is controlling the current to keep the output voltage constant.

What is the purpose of C2 in the circuit shown in Figure E7-2?

A. It bypasses rectifier output ripple around D1
B. It is a brute force filter for the output
C. To prevent self-oscillation
D. To provide fixed DC bias for Q1

E7D07 Answer: A. The purpose of C2 in the circuit shown in Figure E7-2 is bypassing the rectifier output ripple around D1.

What type of circuit is shown in Figure E7-2?

A. Switching voltage regulator
B. Common emitter amplifier
C. Linear voltage regulator
D. Common base amplifier

E7D08 Answer: C. A linear voltage regulator is shown in Figure E7-2.

How is battery operating time calculated?

A. Average current divided by capacity in amp-hours
B. Average current divided by internal resistance
C. Capacity in amp-hours divided by average current
D. Internal resistance divided by average current

E7D09 Answer: C. Battery operating time is calculated by dividing the capacity in amp-hours by the average current.

Why is a switching type power supply less expensive and lighter than an equivalent linear power supply?

A. The inverter design does not require any output filtering
B. The control circuitry uses less current, therefore smaller heat sinks are required
C. The high frequency inverter design uses much smaller transformers and filter components for an equivalent power output
D. It recovers power from the unused portion of the AC cycle, thus using fewer components

E7D10 Answer: C. The primary reason that a switching type power supply is less expensive and light than an equivalent linear power supply is that the high frequency inverter design uses much smaller transformers and filter components for an equivalent power output.

What is the purpose of an inverter connected to a solar panel output?

A. Reduce AC ripple on the output
B. Maintain voltage with varying illumination levels
C. Prevent discharge when panel is not illuminated
D. Convert the panel's output from DC to AC

E7D11 Answer: D. An inverter is connected to a solar panel output to convert the panel's output from DC to AC.

What is the dropout voltage of an analog voltage regulator?

A. Minimum input voltage for rated power dissipation
B. Maximum output voltage drop when the input voltage is varied over its specified range
C. Minimum input-to-output voltage required to maintain regulation
D. Maximum that the output voltage may decrease at rated load

E7D12 Answer: C. The dropout voltage of an analog voltage regulator is the minimum input-to-output voltage required to maintain regulation.

Which of the following calculates power dissipated by a series linear voltage regulator?

A. Input voltage multiplied by input current
B. Input voltage divided by output current
C. Voltage difference from input to output multiplied by output current
D. Output voltage multiplied by output current

E7D13 Answer: C. The equation for calculating power dissipated by a series linear voltage regulator is voltage difference from input to output multiplied by output current.

What is the purpose of connecting equal-value resistors across power supply filter capacitors connected in series?

A. Equalize the voltage across each capacitor
B. Discharge the capacitors when voltage is removed
C. Provide a minimum load on the supply
D. All these choices are correct

E7D14 Answer: D. Connecting equal-value resistors across power supply filter capacitors connected in series serves to equalize the voltage across each capacitor, discharge the capacitors when voltage is removed, and provide a minimum load on the supply.

What is the purpose of a step-start circuit in a high-voltage power supply?

A. To provide a dual-voltage output for reduced power applications
B. To compensate for variations of the incoming line voltage
C. To prevent arcing across the input power switch or relay contacts
D. To allow the filter capacitors to charge gradually

E7D15 Answer: D. A step-start circuit in a high voltage power supply serves to allow the filter capacitors to charge gradually.

E7E – Modulation and Demodulation: Reactance, Phase and Balanced Modulators; Detectors; Mixers

Which of the following can be used to generate FM phone signals?

A. Balanced modulation of the audio amplifier
B. Reactance modulation of a local oscillator
C. Reactance modulation of the final amplifier
D. Balanced modulation of a local oscillator

E7E01 Answer: B. Reactance modulation of a local oscillator can be used to generate FM phone signals.

What is the function of a reactance modulator?

A. To produce PM or FM signals by varying a resistance
B. To produce AM signals by varying an inductance
C. To produce AM signals by varying a resistance
D. To produce PM or FM signals by varying a capacitance

E7E02 Answer: D. A reactance modulator produces PM or FM signals by varying a capacitance.

What is a frequency discriminator?

A. An FM generator circuit
B. A circuit for filtering closely adjacent signals
C. An automatic band-switching circuit
D. A circuit for detecting FM signals

E7E03 Answer: D. A frequency discriminator is a circuit for detecting FM signals.

What is one way to produce a single-sideband phone signal?

A. Use a balanced modulator followed by a filter
B. Use a reactance modulator followed by a mixer
C. Use a loop modulator followed by a mixer
D. Use product detector with a DSB signal

E7E04 Answer: A. A single-sideband phone signal can be produced by using a balanced modulator followed by a filter.

What is added to an FM speech channel to boost the higher audio frequencies?

A. A de-emphasis network
B. A harmonic enhancer
C. A heterodyne enhancer
D. A pre-emphasis network

E7E05 Answer: D. A pre-emphasis network is added to an FM speech channel to boost the higher audio frequencies.

Why is de-emphasis used in FM communications receivers?

A. For compatibility with transmitters using phase modulation
B. To reduce impulse noise reception
C. For higher efficiency
D. To remove third-order distortion products

E7E06 Answer: A. De-emphasis is used in FM communications receivers for compatibility with transmitters using phase modulation.

What is meant by the term "baseband" in radio communications?

A. The lowest frequency band that the transmitter or receiver covers
B. The frequency range occupied by a message signal prior to modulation
C. The unmodulated bandwidth of the transmitted signal
D. The basic oscillator frequency in an FM transmitter that is multiplied to increase the deviation and carrier frequency

E7E07 Answer: B. "Baseband" is the frequency range occupied by a message signal prior to modulation.

What are the principal frequencies that appear at the output of a mixer?

A. Two and four times the original frequency
B. The square root of the product of input frequencies
C. The two input frequencies along with their sum and difference frequencies
D. 1.414 and 0.707 times the input frequency

E7E08 Answer: C. The principal frequencies that appear at the output of a mixer are the two input frequencies along with their sum and difference frequencies.

What occurs when the input signal levels to a mixer are too high?

A. Spurious mixer products are generated
B. Mixer blanking occurs
C. Automatic limiting occurs
D. Excessive AGC voltage levels are generated

E7E09 Answer: A. When the input signal levels to a mixer are too high, spurious mixer products are generated.

How does a diode envelope detector function?

A. By rectification and filtering of RF signals
B. By breakdown of the Zener voltage
C. By mixing signals with noise in the transition region of the diode
D. By sensing the change of reactance in the diode with respect to frequency

E7E10 Answer: A. A diode envelope detector functions by rectifying and filtering of RF signals.

Which type of detector is used for demodulating SSB signals?

A. Discriminator
B. Phase detector
C. Product detector
D. Phase comparator

E7E11 Answer: C. A product detector is used for demodulating SSB signals.

E7F –SOFTWARE DEFINED RADIO FUNDAMENTALS; DIGITAL SIGNAL PROCESSING (DSP) FILTERING, MODULATION, AND DEMODULATION; ANALOG-DIGITAL CONVERSION; DIGITAL FILTERS

What is meant by "direct sampling" in software defined radios?

A. Software is converted from source code to object code during operation of the receiver
B. I and Q signals are generated by digital processing without the use of RF amplification
C. Incoming RF is digitized by an analog-to-digital converter without being mixed with a local oscillator signal
D. A switching mixer is used to generate I and Q signals directly from the RF input

E7F01 Answer: C. Direct sampling in software defined radios is when incoming RF is digitized by an analog-to-digital converter without being mixed with a local oscillator signal.

What kind of digital signal processing audio filter is used to remove unwanted noise from a received SSB signal?

A. An adaptive filter
B. A crystal-lattice filter
C. A Hilbert-transform filter
D. A phase-inverting filter

E7F02 Answer: A. An adaptive filter is used to remove unwanted noise from a received SSB signal.

What type of digital signal processing filter is used to generate an SSB signal?

A. An adaptive filter
B. A notch filter
C. A Hilbert-transform filter
D. An elliptical filter

E7F03 Answer: C. A Hilbert-transform filter is used to generate an SSB signal.

Which method generates an SSB signal using digital signal processing?

A. Mixing products are converted to voltages and subtracted by adder circuits
B. A frequency synthesizer removes unwanted sidebands
C. Varying quartz crystal characteristics emulated in digital form
D. Signals are combined in quadrature phase relationship

E7F04 Answer: D. Signals combined in quadrature phase relationship generate an SSB signal using digital signal processing.

How frequently must an analog signal be sampled to be accurately reproduced?

A. At least half the rate of the highest frequency component of the signal
B. At least twice the rate of the highest frequency component of the signal
C. At the same rate as the highest frequency component of the signal
D. At four times the rate of the highest frequency component of the signal

E7F05 Answer: B. An analog signal must at least be sampled at twice the rate of the highest frequency component of the signal to be accurately reproduced.

What is the minimum number of bits required to sample a signal with a range of 1 volt at a resolution of 1 millivolt?

A. 4 bits
B. 6 bits
C. 8 bits
D. 10 bits

E7F06 Answer: D. The minimum number of bits required to sample a signal with a range of 1 volt at a resolution of 1 millivolt is 10.

What function is performed by a Fast Fourier Transform?

A. Converting analog signals to digital form
B. Converting digital signals to analog form
C. Converting signals from the time domain to the frequency domain
D. Converting signals from the frequency domain to the time domain

E7F07 Answer: C. A Fast Fourier Transform can convert signals from the time domain to the frequency domain.

What is the function of decimation?

A. Converting data to binary-coded decimal form
B. Reducing the effective sample rate by removing samples
C. Attenuating the signal
D. Removing unnecessary significant digits

E7F08 Answer: B. Decimation is reducing the effective sample rate by removing samples.

Why is an anti-aliasing filter required in a decimator?

A. It removes high-frequency signal components that would otherwise be reproduced as lower frequency components
B. It peaks the response of the decimator, improving bandwidth
C. It removes low-frequency signal components to eliminate the need for DC restoration
D. It notches out the sampling frequency to avoid sampling errors

E7F09 Answer: A. An anti-aliasing filter is required in a decimator to remove high-frequency signal components that would otherwise be reproduced as lower frequency components.

What aspect of receiver analog-to-digital conversion determines the maximum receive bandwidth of a direct-sampling software defined radio (SDR)?

A. Sample rate
B. Sample width in bits
C. Integral non-linearity
D. Differential non-linearity

E7F10 Answer: A. Sample rate determines the maximum receive bandwidth of a direct-sampling software defined radio (SDR).

What sets the minimum detectable signal level for a direct-sampling software defined receiver in the absence of atmospheric or thermal noise?

A. Sample clock phase noise
B. Reference voltage level and sample width in bits
C. Data storage transfer rate
D. Missing codes and jitter

E7F11 Answer: B. Reference voltage level and sample width in bits sets the minimum detectable signal level for a direct-sampling software defined receiver in the absence of atmospheric or thermal noise.

Which of the following is generally true of Finite Impulse Response (FIR) filters?

A. FIR filters can delay all frequency components of the signal by the same amount
B. FIR filters are easier to implement for a given set of passband rolloff requirements
C. FIR filters can respond faster to impulses
D. All these choices are correct

E7F12 Answer: A. FIR filters delay all frequency components of the signal by the same amount.

What is the function of taps in a digital signal processing filter?

A. To reduce excess signal pressure levels
B. Provide access for debugging software
C. Select the point at which baseband signals are generated
D. Provide incremental signal delays for filter algorithms

E7F13 Answer: D. Taps in a digital signal processing filter provide incremental signal delays for filter algorithms.

Which of the following would allow a digital signal processing filter to create a sharper filter response?

A. Higher data rate
B. More taps
C. Lower Q
D. Double-precision math routines

E7F14 Answer: B. Having more taps would allow a digital signal processing filter to create a sharper filter response.

E7G – Operational Amplifiers: Characteristics and Applications

What is the typical output impedance of an op-amp?

A. Very low
B. Very high
C. 100 ohms
D. 10,000 ohms

E7G01 Answer: A. The typical output impedance of an op-amp is very low.

What is the frequency response of the circuit in E7-3 if a capacitor is added across the feedback resistor?

A. High-pass filter
B. Low-pass filter
C. Band-pass filter
D. Notch filter

E7G02 Answer: B. If a capacitor is added across the feedback resistor, a low-pass filter is the frequency response of the circuit in E7-3.

What is the typical input impedance of an op-amp?

A. 100 ohms
B. 10,000 ohms
C. Very low
D. Very high

E7G03 Answer: D. The typical input impedance of an op-amp is very high.

What is meant by the term "op-amp input offset voltage"?

A. The output voltage of the op-amp minus its input voltage
B. The difference between the output voltage of the op-amp and the input voltage required in the immediately following stage
C. The differential input voltage needed to bring the open loop output voltage to zero
D. The potential between the amplifier input terminals of the op-amp in an open loop condition

E7G04 Answer: C. "Op-amp input offset voltage" is the differential input voltage needed to bring the open loop output voltage to zero.

How can unwanted ringing and audio instability be prevented in an op-amp audio filter?

A. Restrict both gain and Q
B. Restrict gain but increase Q
C. Restrict Q but increase gain
D. Increase both gain and Q

E7G05 Answer: A. Ringing and audio instability can be prevented in an op-amp audio filter by restricting both gain and Q.

What is the gain-bandwidth of an operational amplifier?

A. The maximum frequency for a filter circuit using that type of amplifier
B. The frequency at which the open-loop gain of the amplifier equals one
C. The gain of the amplifier at a filter's cutoff frequency
D. The frequency at which the amplifier's offset voltage is zero

E7G06 Answer: B. The gain-bandwidth of an operational amplifier is the frequency at which the open-loop gain of the amplifier equals one.

Figure E7-3

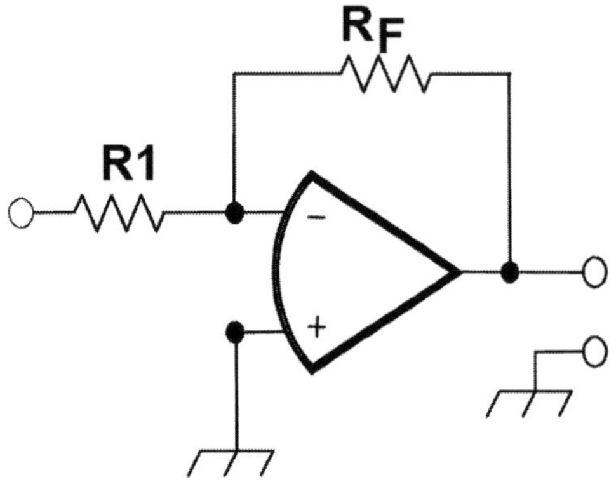

What voltage gain can be expected from the circuit in Figure E7-3 when R1 is 10 ohms and RF is 470 ohms?

A. 0.21
B. 4700
C. 47
D. 24

E7G07 Answer: C. The voltage gain from the circuit in Figure E7-3 when R1 is 10 ohms and RF is 470 ohms should be 47.

How does the gain of an ideal operational amplifier vary with frequency?

A. It increases linearly with increasing frequency
B. It decreases linearly with increasing frequency
C. It decreases logarithmically with increasing frequency
D. It does not vary with frequency

E7G08 Answer: D. The gain of an ideal operational amplifier does not vary with frequency.

What will be the output voltage of the circuit shown in Figure E7-3 if R1 is 1000 ohms, RF is 10,000 ohms, and 0.23 volts DC is applied to the input?

A. 0.23 volts
B. 2.3 volts
C. -0.23 volts
D. -2.3 volts

E7G09 Answer: D. The output voltage of the circuit shown in Figure E7-3 when R1 is 1000 ohms, RF is 10,000 ohms, and 0.23 volts DC is applied to the input is -2.3 volts.

What absolute voltage gain can be expected from the circuit in Figure E7-3 when R1 is 1800 ohms and RF is 68 kilohms?

A. 1
B. 0.03
C. 38
D. 76

E7G10 Answer: C. A voltage gain of 38 can be expected from the circuit in Figure E7-3 when R1 is 1800 ohms and RF is 68 kilohms.

What absolute voltage gain can be expected from the circuit in Figure E7-3 when R1 is 3300 ohms and RF is 47 kilohms?

A. 28
B. 14
C. 7
D. 0.07

E7G11 Answer: B. An absolute voltage gain of 14 can be expected from the circuit in Figure E7-3 when R1 is 3300 ohms and RF is 47 kilohms.

What is an operational amplifier?

A. A high-gain, direct-coupled differential amplifier with very high input impedance and very low output impedance
B. A digital audio amplifier whose characteristics are determined by components external to the amplifier
C. An amplifier used to increase the average output of frequency modulated amateur signals to the legal limit
D. A RF amplifier used in the UHF and microwave regions

E7G12 Answer: A. An operational amplifier is a high-gain, direct-coupled differential amplifier with very high input impedance and very low output impedance.

E7H – Oscillators and Signal Sources: Types of Oscillators; Synthesizers and Phase-Locked Loops; Direct Digital Synthesizers; Stabilizing Thermal Drift; Microphonics; High-Accuracy Oscillators

What are three common oscillator circuits?

A. Taft, Pierce and negative feedback
B. Pierce, Fenner and Beane
C. Taft, Hartley and Pierce
D. Colpitts, Hartley and Pierce

E7H01 Answer: D. Colpitts, Hartley and Pierce are all three common oscillator circuits.

What is a microphonic?

A. An IC used for amplifying microphone signals
B. Distortion caused by RF pickup on the microphone cable
C. Changes in oscillator frequency due to mechanical vibration
D. Excess loading of the microphone by an oscillator

E7H02 Answer: C. A microphonic is a change in oscillator frequency due to mechanical vibration.

What is a phase-locked loop?

A. An electronic servo loop consisting of a ratio detector, reactance modulator, and voltage-controlled oscillator
B. An electronic circuit also known as a monostable multivibrator
C. An electronic servo loop consisting of a phase detector, a low-pass filter, a voltage-controlled oscillator, and a stable reference oscillator
D. An electronic circuit consisting of a precision push-pull amplifier with a differential phase input

E7H03 Answer: C. A phase-locked loop is an electronic servo loop consisting of a phase detector, a low-pass filter, a voltage-controlled oscillator, and a stable reference oscillator.

How is positive feedback supplied in a Colpitts oscillator?

A. Through a tapped coil
B. Through link coupling
C. Through a capacitive divider
D. Through a neutralizing capacitor

E7H04 Answer: C. Positive feedback is supplied through a capacitive divider in a Colpitts oscillator.

How is positive feedback supplied in a Pierce oscillator?

A. Through a tapped coil
B. Through link coupling
C. Through a neutralizing capacitor
D. Through a quartz crystal

E7H05 Answer: D. Positive feedback is supplied through a quartz crystal in a Pierce oscillator.

Which of these functions can be performed by a phase-locked loop?

A. Wide-band AF and RF power amplification
B. Frequency synthesis and FM demodulation
C. Photovoltaic conversion and optical coupling
D. Comparison of two digital input signals and digital pulse counting

E7H06 Answer: B. A phase-locked loop can perform frequency synthesis and FM demodulation.

How can an oscillator's microphonic responses be reduced?

A. Use NP0 capacitors
B. Reduce noise on the oscillator's power supply
C. Increase the gain
D. Mechanically isolate the oscillator circuitry from its enclosure

E7H07 Answer: D. An oscillator's microphonic responses can be reduced by mechanically isolating the oscillator circuitry from its enclosure.

Which of the following components can be used to reduce thermal drift in crystal oscillators?

A. NP0 capacitors
B. Toroidal inductors
C. Wirewound resistors
D. Non-inductive resistors

E7H08 Answer: A. NP0 capacitors can be used to reduce thermal drift in crystal oscillators.

What type of frequency synthesizer circuit uses a phase accumulator, lookup table, digital-to-analog converter, and a low-pass anti-alias filter?

A. A direct digital synthesizer
B. A hybrid synthesizer
C. A phase-locked loop synthesizer
D. A direct conversion synthesizer

E7H09 Answer: A. A direct digital synthesizer uses a phase accumulator, lookup table, digital-to-analog converter, and a low-pass anti-alias filter.

What information is contained in the lookup table of a direct digital synthesizer (DDS)?

A. The phase relationship between a reference oscillator and the output waveform
B. Amplitude values that represent the desired waveform
C. The phase relationship between a voltage-controlled oscillator and the output waveform
D. Frequently used receiver and transmitter frequencies

E7H10 Answer: B. The amplitude values that represent a desired waveform are contained in the lookup table of a direct digital synthesizer.

What are the major spectral impurity components of direct digital synthesizers?

A. Broadband noise
B. Digital conversion noise
C. Spurious signals at discrete frequencies
D. Harmonics of the local oscillator

E7H11 Answer: C. The major spectral impurity components of direct digital synthesizers are spurious signals at discrete frequencies.

Which of the following ensures that a crystal oscillator operates on the frequency specified by the crystal manufacturer?

A. Provide the crystal with a specified parallel inductance
B. Provide the crystal with a specified parallel capacitance
C. Bias the crystal at a specified voltage
D. Bias the crystal at a specified current

E7H12 Answer: B. A crystal oscillator must be provided with a specified parallel capacitance to ensure that it provides the frequency specified by the manufacturer.

Which of the following is a technique for providing highly accurate and stable oscillators needed for microwave transmission and reception?

A. Use a GPS signal reference
B. Use a rubidium stabilized reference oscillator
C. Use a temperature-controlled high Q dielectric resonator
D. All these choices are correct

E7H13 Answer: D. GPS signal references, rubidium stabilized reference oscillators, temperature-controlled high Q dielectric resonators can be used for providing highly accurate and stable oscillators needed for microwave transmission and reception.

E8 – Signals and Emissions

E8A –Fourier Analysis: RMS Measurements; Average RF Power and Peak Envelope Power (PEP); Analog/Digital Conversion

What technique shows that a square wave is made up of a sine wave and its odd harmonics?

A. Fourier analysis
B. Vector analysis
C. Numerical analysis
D. Differential analysis

E8A01 Answer: A. Fourier analysis shows that a square wave is made up of a sine wave and its odd harmonics.

Which of the following is a type of analog-to-digital conversion?

A. Successive approximation
B. Harmonic regeneration
C. Level shifting
D. Phase reversal

E8A02 Answer: A. Successive approximation is a type of analog-to-digital conversion.

Which of the following describes a signal in the time domain?

A. Power at intervals of phase
B. Amplitude at different times
C. Frequency at different times
D. Discrete impulses in time order

E8A03 Answer: B. Amplitude at different times describes a signal in the time domain.

What is "dither" with respect to analog-to-digital converters?

A. An abnormal condition where the converter cannot settle on a value to represent the signal
B. A small amount of noise added to the input signal to reduce quantization noise
C. An error caused by irregular quantization step size
D. A method of decimation by randomly skipping samples

E8A04 Answer: B. "Dither" in analog to digital converters is a small amount of noise added to the input signal to reduce quantization noise.

What is the benefit of making voltage measurements with a true-RMS calculating meter?

A. An inverse Fourier transform can be used
B. The signal's RMS noise factor is also calculated
C. The calculated RMS value can be converted directly into phasor form
D. RMS is measured for both sinusoidal and non-sinusoidal signals

E8A05 Answer: D. Making voltage measurements with a true-RMS calculating meter is beneficial because RMS is measured for both sinusoidal and non-sinusoidal signals.

What is the approximate ratio of PEP-to-average power in an unprocessed single-sideband phone signal?

A. 2.5 to 1
B. 25 to 1
C. 1 to 1
D. 100 to 1

E8A06 Answer: A. The approximate ratio of PEP-to-average power in an unprocessed single-sideband phone signal is 2.5 to 1.

What determines the PEP-to-average power ratio of an unprocessed single-sideband phone signal?

A. The frequency of the modulating signal
B. Speech characteristics
C. The degree of carrier suppression
D. Amplifier gain

E8A07 Answer: B. The speech characteristics determine the PEP-to-average power ratio of an unprocessed single-sideband phone signal.

Why are direct or flash conversion analog-to-digital converters used for a software defined radio?

A. Very low power consumption decreases frequency drift
B. Immunity to out-of-sequence coding reduces spurious responses
C. Very high speed allows digitizing high frequencies
D. All these choices are correct

E8A08 Answer: C. A direct or flash conversion analog-to-digital converter are used for a software defined radio because the very high speed allows digitizing high frequencies.

How many different input levels can be encoded by an analog-to-digital converter with 8-bit resolution?

A. 8
B. 8 multiplied by the gain of the input amplifier
C. 256 divided by the gain of the input amplifier
D. 256

E8A09 Answer: D. An analog-to-digital converter with 8-bit resolution can encode 256 levels.

What is the purpose of a low-pass filter used in conjunction with a digital-to-analog converter?

A. Lower the input bandwidth to increase the effective resolution
B. Improve accuracy by removing out-of-sequence codes from the input
C. Remove harmonics from the output caused by the discrete analog levels generated
D. All these choices are correct

E8A10 Answer: C. A low-pass filter used in conjunction with a digital-to-analog converter serves to remove harmonics from the output caused by the discrete analog levels generated.

Which of the following is a measure of the quality of an analog-to-digital converter?

A. Total harmonic distortion
B. Peak envelope power
C. Reciprocal mixing
D. Power factor

E8A11 Answer: A. Total harmonic distortion is a measure of the quality of an analog-to-digital converter.

E8B – Modulation and Demodulation: Modulation Methods; Modulation Index and Deviation Ratio; Frequency and Time Division Multiplexing; Orthogonal Frequency Division Multiplexing

What is the modulation index of an FM signal?

A. The ratio of frequency deviation to modulating signal frequency
B. The ratio of modulating signal amplitude to frequency deviation
C. The modulating signal frequency divided by the bandwidth of the transmitted signal
D. The bandwidth of the transmitted signal divided by the modulating signal frequency

E8B01 Answer: A. The modulation index of an FM signal is the ratio of frequency deviation to modulating signal frequency.

How does the modulation index of a phase-modulated emission vary with RF carrier frequency?

A. It increases as the RF carrier frequency increases
B. It decreases as the RF carrier frequency increases
C. It varies with the square root of the RF carrier frequency
D. It does not depend on the RF carrier frequency

E8B02 Answer: D. The modulation index of a phase-modulated emission does not depend on the RF carrier frequency.

What is the modulation index of an FM phone signal having a maximum frequency deviation of 3000 Hz either side of the carrier frequency when the modulating frequency is 1000 Hz?

A. 3
B. 0.3
C. 6
D. 0.6

E8B03 Answer: A. The modulation index of an FM phone signal having a maximum frequency deviation of 3000 Hz either side of the carrier frequency when the modulating frequency is 1000 Hz is 3.

What is the modulation index of an FM phone signal having a maximum carrier deviation of plus or minus 6 kHz when modulated with a 2 kHz modulating frequency?

A. 0.3
B. 3
C. 0.6
D. 6

E8B04 Answer: B. The modulation index of an FM phone signal having a maximum carrier deviation of plus or minus 6 kHz when modulated with a 2 kHz modulating frequency is 3.

What is the deviation ratio of an FM phone signal having a maximum frequency swing of plus-or-minus 5 kHz when the maximum modulation frequency is 3 kHz?

A. 60
B. 0.167
C. 0.6
D. 1.67

E8B05 Answer: D. The deviation ratio of an FM phone signal having a maximum frequency swing of plus-or-minus 5 kHz when the maximum modulation frequency is 3 kHz is 1.67.

What is the deviation ratio of an FM phone signal having a maximum frequency swing of plus or minus 7.5 kHz when the maximum modulation frequency is 3.5 kHz?

A. 2.14
B. 0.214
C. 0.47
D. 47

E8B06 Answer: A. The deviation ratio of an FM phone signal having a maximum frequency swing of plus or minus 7.5 kHz when the maximum modulation frequency is 3.5 kHz is 2.14.

Orthogonal frequency-division multiplexing (ODFM) is a technique used for which type of amateur communication?

A. Digital modes
B. Extremely low-power contacts
C. EME
D. OFDM signals are not allowed on amateur bands

E8B07 Answer: A. Orthogonal frequency-division multiplexing (ODFM) is a technique used for digital modes of amateur communication.

What describes orthogonal frequency-division multiplexing (ODFM)?

A. A frequency modulation technique that uses non-harmonically related frequencies
B. A bandwidth compression technique using Fourier transforms
C. A digital mode for narrow-band, slow-speed transmissions
D. A digital modulation technique using subcarriers at frequencies chosen to avoid intersymbol interference

E8B08 Answer: D. Orthogonal frequency-division multiplexing (ODFM) is a digital modulation technique using subcarriers at frequencies chosen to avoid intersymbol interference.

What is deviation ratio?

A. The ratio of the audio modulating frequency to the center carrier frequency
B. The ratio of the maximum carrier frequency deviation to the highest audio modulating frequency
C. The ratio of the carrier center frequency to the audio modulating frequency
D. The ratio of the highest audio modulating frequency to the average audio modulating frequency

E8B09 Answer: B. Deviation ratio is the ratio of the maximum carrier frequency deviation to the highest audio modulating frequency.

What is frequency division multiplexing (FDM)?

A. The transmitted signal jumps from band to band at a predetermined rate
B. Dividing the transmitted signal into separate frequency bands that each carry a different data stream
C. The transmitted signal is divided into packets of information
D. Two or more information streams are merged into a digital combiner, which then pulse position modulates the transmitter

E8B10 Answer: B. Frequency division multiplexing is when the transmitted signal is divided into separate frequency bands that each carry a different data stream.

What is digital time division multiplexing?

A. Two or more data streams are assigned to discrete sub-carriers on an FM transmitter
B. Two or more signals are arranged to share discrete time slots of a data transmission
C. Two or more data streams share the same channel by transmitting time of transmission as the sub-carrier
D. Two or more signals are quadrature modulated to increase bandwidth efficiency

E8B11 Answer: B. Digital time division multiplexing is when two or more signals are arranged to share discrete time slots of a data transmission.

E8C – Digital Signals: Digital Communication Modes; Information Rate vs. Bandwidth; Error Correction; Constellation Diagrams

What is Quadrature Amplitude Modulation or QAM?

A. A technique for digital data compression used in digital television which removes redundancy in the data by comparing bit amplitudes
B. Transmission of data by modulating the amplitude of two carriers of the same frequency but 90 degrees out of phase
C. A method of performing singled sideband modulation by shifting the phase of the carrier and modulation components of the signal
D. A technique for analog modulation of television video signals using phase modulation and compression

E8C01 Answer: B. Quadrature Amplitude Modulation, or QAM, is the transmission of data by modulating the amplitude of two carriers of the same frequency but 90 degrees out of phase.

What is the definition of symbol rate in a digital transmission?

A. The number of control characters in a message packet
B. The maximum rate at which the forward error correction code can make corrections
C. The rate at which the waveform changes to convey information
D. The number of characters carried per second by the station-to-station link

E8C02 Answer: C. Symbol rate in a digital transmission is the rate at which the waveform changes to convey information.

Why should the phase of a PSK signal be changed at the zero crossing of the RF signal?

A. To minimize bandwidth
B. To simplify modulation
C. To improve carrier suppression
D. All these choices are correct

E8C03 Answer: A. The phase of a PSK signal should be changed at the zero crossing of the RF signal in order to minimize bandwidth.

What technique minimizes the bandwidth of a PSK31 signal?

A. Zero-sum character encoding
B. Reed-Solomon character encoding
C. Use of sinusoidal data pulses
D. Use of linear data pulses

E8C04 Answer: C. Use of sinusoidal data pulses helps minimize the bandwidth of a PSK31 signal.

What is the approximate bandwidth of a 13-WPM International Morse Code transmission?

A. 13 Hz
B. 26 Hz
C. 52 Hz
D. 104 Hz

E8C05 Answer: C. The approximate bandwidth of a 13-WPM International Morse Code transmission is 52 Hz.

What is the bandwidth of an FT8 signal?

A. 10 Hz
B. 50 Hz
C. 600 Hz
D. 2.4 kHz

E8C06 Answer: B. An FT8 signal has a bandwidth of 50 Hz.

What is the bandwidth of a 4800-Hz frequency shift, 9600-baud ASCII FM transmission?

A. 15.36 kHz
B. 9.6 kHz
C. 4.8 kHz
D. 5.76 kHz

E8C07 Answer: A. A 4800-Hz frequency shift, 9600-baud ASCII FM transmission requires a bandwidth of 15.36 kHz.

How does ARQ accomplish error correction?

A. Special binary codes provide automatic correction
B. Special polynomial codes provide automatic correction
C. If errors are detected, redundant data is substituted
D. If errors are detected, a retransmission is requested

E8C08 Answer: D. ARQ accomplishes error correction by requesting a retransmission if errors are detected.

Which digital code allows only one bit to change between sequential code values?

A. Binary Coded Decimal Code
B. Extended Binary Coded Decimal Interchange Code
C. Extended ASCII
D. Gray code

E8C09 Answer: D. In Gray code, each preceding or following character changes by only one bit.

How can data rate be increased without increasing bandwidth?

A. It is impossible
B. Increasing analog-to-digital conversion resolution
C. Using a more efficient digital code
D. Using forward error correction

E8C10 Answer: C. Data rate can be increased without increasing bandwidth by using a more efficient digital code.

What is the relationship between symbol rate and baud?

A. They are the same
B. Baud is twice the symbol rate
C. Baud rate is half the symbol rate
D. The relationship depends on the specific code used

E8C11 Answer: A. Symbol rate and baud are the same.

What factors affect the bandwidth of a transmitted CW signal?

A. IF bandwidth and Q
B. Modulation index and output power
C. Keying speed and shape factor (rise and fall time)
D. All these choices are correct

E8C12 Answer: C. Keying speed and shape factor (rise and fall time) affect the bandwidth of a transmitted CW signal.

What is described by the constellation diagram of a QAM or QPSK signal?

A. How many carriers may be present at the same time
B. The possible phase and amplitude states for each symbol
C. Frequency response of the signal stream
D. The number of bits used for error correction in the protocol

E8C13 Answer: B. The constellation diagram of a QAM or QPSK signal describes the possible phase and amplitude states for each symbol.

What type of addresses do nodes have in a mesh network?

A. Email
B. Trust server
C. Internet Protocol (IP)
D. Talk group

E8C14 Answer: C. Nodes in a mesh network have Internet Protocol (IP) addresses.

What technique do individual nodes use to form a mesh network?

A. Forward error correction and Viterbi codes
B. Acting as store-and-forward digipeaters
C. Discovery and link establishment protocols
D. Custom code plugs for the local trunking systems

E8C15 Answer: C. Individual nodes use discovery and link establishment protocols to form a mesh network.

E8D – Keying Defects and Overmodulation of Digital Signals; Digital Codes; Spread Spectrum

Why are received spread spectrum signals resistant to interference?

A. Signals not using the spread spectrum algorithm are suppressed in the receiver
B. The high power used by a spread spectrum transmitter keeps its signal from being easily overpowered
C. Built-in error correction codes minimize interference
D. If interference is detected by the receiver, it will signal the transmitter to change frequencies

E8D01 Answer: A. Received spread spectrum signals are resistant to interference because signals not using the spread spectrum algorithm are suppressed in the receiver.

What spread spectrum communications technique uses a high-speed binary bit stream to shift the phase of an RF carrier?

A. Frequency hopping
B. Direct sequence
C. Binary phase-shift keying
D. Phase compandored spread spectrum

E8D02 Answer: B. Direct sequence uses a high-speed binary bit stream to shift the phase of an RF carrier.

How does the spread spectrum technique of frequency hopping work?

A. If interference is detected by the receiver, it will signal the transmitter to change frequencies
B. RF signals are clipped to generate a wide band of harmonics which provides redundancy to correct errors
C. A binary bit stream is used to shift the phase of an RF carrier very rapidly in a pseudorandom sequence
D. Rapidly varying frequency of the transmitted signal according to a pseudorandom sequence

E8D03 Answer: D. In frequency hopping, the frequency of the transmitted signal is varied rapidly according to a pseudorandom sequence.

What is the primary effect of extremely short rise or fall time on a CW signal?

A. More difficult to copy
B. The generation of RF harmonics
C. The generation of key clicks
D. More difficult to tune

E8D04 Answer: C. Extremely short rise or fall time on a CW signal lead to the generation of key clicks.

What is the most common method of reducing key clicks?

A. Increase keying waveform rise and fall times
B. Insert low-pass filters at the transmitter output
C. Reduce keying waveform rise and fall times
D. Insert high-pass filters at the transmitter output

E8D05 Answer: A. The most common method of reducing key clicks is increasing keying waveform rise and fall times.

What is the advantage of including parity bits in ASCII characters?

A. Faster transmission rate
B. Signal-to-noise ratio is improved
C. A larger character set is available
D. Some types of errors can be detected

E8D06 Answer: D. By including a parity bit with an ASCII character stream, some types of errors can be detected.

What is a common cause of overmodulation of AFSK signals?

A. Excessive numbers of retries
B. Excessive frequency deviation
C. Bit errors in the modem
D. Excessive transmit audio levels

E8D07 Answer: D. A common cause of overmodulation of AFSK signals is excessive transmit audio levels.

What parameter evaluates distortion of an AFSK signal caused by excessive input audio levels?

A. Signal-to-noise ratio
B. Baud error rate
C. Repeat Request Rate (RRR)
D. Intermodulation Distortion (IMD)

E8D08 Answer: D. Intermodulation Distortion (IMD) evaluates distortion of an AFSK signal caused by excessive input audio levels.

What is considered an acceptable maximum IMD level for an idling PSK signal?

A. +5 dB
B. +10 dB
C. +15 dB
D. -30 dB

E8D09 Answer: D. An acceptable maximum IMD level for an idling PSK signal is -30 dB.

What are some of the differences between the Baudot digital code and ASCII?

A. Baudot uses 4 data bits per character, ASCII uses 7 or 8; Baudot uses 1 character as a letters/figures shift code, ASCII has no letters/figures code
B. Baudot uses 5 data bits per character, ASCII uses 7 or 8; Baudot uses 2 characters as letters/figures shift codes, ASCII has no letters/figures shift code
C. Baudot uses 6 data bits per character, ASCII uses 7 or 8; Baudot has no letters/figures shift code, ASCII uses 2 letters/figures shift codes
D. Baudot uses 7 data bits per character, ASCII uses 8; Baudot has no letters/figures shift code, ASCII uses 2 letters/figures shift codes

E8D10 Answer: B. Baudot uses 5 data bits per character, ASCII uses 7 or 8; Baudot uses 2 characters as letters/figures shift codes, ASCII has no letters/figures shift code.

What is one advantage of using ASCII code for data communications?

A. It includes built-in error correction features
B. It contains fewer information bits per character than any other code
C. It is possible to transmit both uppercase and lowercase text
D. It uses one character as a shift code to send numeric and special characters

E8D11 Answer: C. An advantage of using ASCII code for data communications is that it is possible to transmit both uppercase and lowercase text.

E9 – Antennas and Transmission Lines

E9A – Basic Antenna Parameters: Radiation Resistance, Gain, Beamwidth, Efficiency; Effective Radiated Power (ERP) and Effective Isotropic Radiated Power (EIRP)

What is an isotropic radiator?

A. A calibrated, unidirectional antenna used to make precise antenna gain measurements
B. An omnidirectional, horizontally polarized, precisely calibrated antenna used to make field measurements of antenna gain
C. A hypothetical, lossless antenna having equal radiation intensity in all directions used as a reference for antenna gain
D. A spacecraft antenna used to direct signals toward Earth

E9A01 Answer: C. An isotropic radiator is a hypothetical, lossless antenna having equal radiation intensity in all directions used as a reference for antenna gain.

What is the effective radiated power (ERP) of a repeater station with 150 watts transmitter power output, 2 dB feed line loss, 2.2 dB duplexer loss, and 7 dBd antenna gain?

A. 469 watts
B. 78.7 watts
C. 420 watts
D. 286 watts

E9A02 Answer: D. The effective radiated power (ERP) of a repeater station with 150 watts transmitter power output, 2 dB feed line loss, 2.2 dB duplexer loss, and 7 dBd antenna gain is 286 watts.

What term describing total radiated power takes into account all gains and losses?

A. Power factor
B. Half-power bandwidth
C. Effective radiated power
D. Apparent power

E9A03 Answer: C. Effective radiated power takes into account all gains and losses when describing total radiated power.

Which of the following factors affect the feed point impedance of an antenna?

A. Transmission line length
B. Antenna height
C. The settings of an antenna tuner at the transmitter
D. The input power level

E9A04 Answer: B. Antenna height may affect the feed point impedance of an antenna.

What does the term "ground gain" mean?

A. The change in signal strength caused by grounding the antenna
B. The gain of the antenna with respect to a dipole at ground level
C. To force net gain to 0 dB by grounding part of the antenna
D. An increase in signal strength from ground reflections in the environment of the antenna

E9A05 Answer: D. Ground gain refers to an increase in signal strength from ground reflections in the environment of the antenna.

What is the effective radiated power (ERP) of a repeater station with 200 watts transmitter power output, 4 dB feed line loss, 3.2 dB duplexer loss, 0.8 dB circulator loss, and 10 dBd antenna gain?

A. 317 watts
B. 2000 watts
C. 126 watts
D. 300 watts

E9A06 Answer: A. The effective radiated power (ERP) of a repeater station with 200 watts transmitter power output, 4 dB feed line loss, 3.2 dB duplexer loss, 0.8 dB circulator loss, and 10 dBd antenna gain is 317 watts.

What is the effective isotropic radiated power (EIRP) of a repeater station with 200 watts transmitter power output, 2 dB feed line loss, 2.8 dB duplexer loss, 1.2 dB circulator loss, and 7 dBi antenna gain?

A. 159 watts
B. 252 watts
C. 632 watts
D. 63.2 watts

E9A07 Answer: B. The effective isotropic radiated power (EIRP) of a repeater station with 200 watts transmitter power output, 2 dB feed line loss, 2.8 dB duplexer loss, 1.2 dB circulator loss, and 7 dBi antenna gain is 252 watts.

What frequency has the smallest first Fresnel zone?

A. 5.8 GHz
B. 3.4 GHz
C. 2.4 GHz
D. 900 MHz

E9A08 Answer: A. 5.8 GHz has a smaller first Fresnel zone than 3.4 GHz, 2.4 GHz, and 900 MHz.

What is antenna efficiency?

A. Radiation resistance divided by transmission resistance
B. Radiation resistance divided by total resistance
C. Total resistance divided by radiation resistance
D. Effective radiated power divided by transmitter output

E9A09 Answer: B. Antenna efficiency is radiation resistance divided by total resistance.

Which of the following improves the efficiency of a ground-mounted quarter-wave vertical antenna?

A. Installing a radial system
B. Isolating the coax shield from ground
C. Shortening the radiating element
D. All these choices are correct

E9A10 Answer: A. Installing a radial system improves the efficiency of a ground-mounted quarter-wave vertical antenna.

Which of the following determines ground losses for a ground-mounted vertical antenna operating on HF?

A. The standing wave ratio
B. Distance from the transmitter
C. Soil conductivity
D. Take-off angle

E9A11 Answer: C. Soil conductivity determines ground losses for a ground-mounted vertical antenna operating on HF.

How much gain does an antenna have compared to a half-wavelength dipole if it has 6 dB gain over an isotropic radiator?

A. 3.85 dB
B. 6.0 dB
C. 8.15 dB
D. 2.79 dB

E9A12 Answer: A. An antenna has a gain of 3.85 dB compared to a half-wavelength dipole when it has 6 dB gain over an isotropic antenna.

E9B – Antenna Patterns and Designs: E and H Plane Patterns; Gain as a Function of Pattern; Antenna Modeling

Figure E9-1

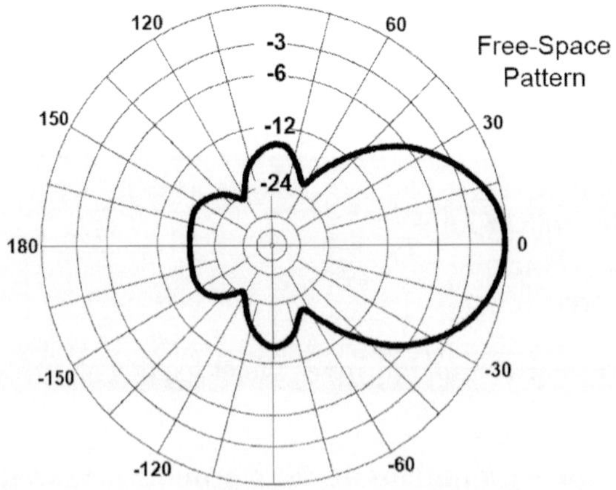

What is the 3 dB beamwidth of the antenna radiation pattern shown in Figure E9-1?

A. 75 degrees
B. 50 degrees
C. 25 degrees
D. 30 degrees

E9B01 Answer: B. In the antenna radiation pattern shown in Figure E9-1, the 3 dB beamwidth is 50 degrees.

In the antenna radiation pattern shown in Figure E9-1, what is the front-to-back ratio?

A. 36 dB
B. 14 dB
C. 24 dB
D. 18 dB

E9B02 Answer: D. In the antenna radiation pattern shown in Figure E9-1, the front-to-back ratio is 18 dB.

In the antenna radiation pattern shown in Figure E9-1, what is the front-to-side ratio?

A. 12 dB
B. 24 dB
C. 18 dB
D. 14 dB

E9B03 Answer: D. In the antenna radiation pattern shown in Figure E9-1, the front-to-side ratio is 14 dB.

Figure E9-2

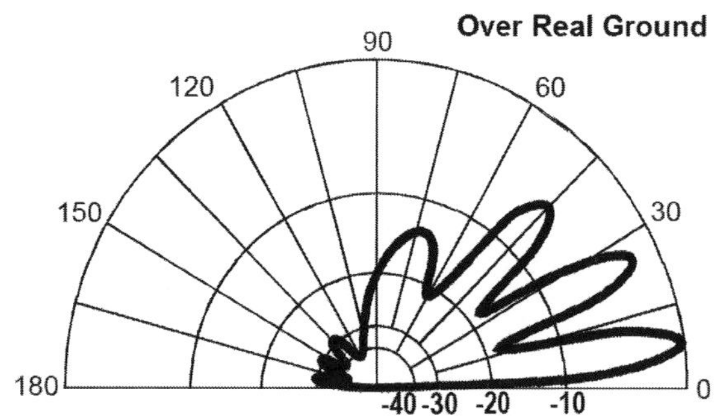

What is the front-to-back ratio of the radiation pattern shown in Figure E9-2?

A. 15 dB
B. 28 dB
C. 3 dB
D. 38 dB

E9B04 Answer: B. The front-to-back ratio of the radiation pattern shown in Figure E9-2 is 28 dB.

What type of antenna pattern is shown in Figure E9-2?

A. Elevation
B. Azimuth
C. Radiation resistance
D. Polarization

E9B05 Answer: A. An elevation antenna pattern over real ground is shown in Figure E9-2.

What is the elevation angle of peak response in the antenna radiation pattern shown in Figure E9-2?

A. 45 degrees
B. 75 degrees
C. 7.5 degrees
D. 25 degrees

E9B06 Answer: C. The elevation angle of peak response in the antenna radiation pattern shown in Figure E9-2 is 7.5 degrees.

What is the difference in radiated power between a lossless antenna with gain and an isotropic radiator driven by the same power?

A. The power radiated from the directional antenna is increased by the gain of the antenna
B. The power radiated from the directional antenna is stronger by its front-to-back ratio
C. They are the same
D. The power radiated from the isotropic radiator is 2.15 dB greater than that from the directional antenna

E9B07 Answer: C. The radiated power of a lossless antenna with gain and an isotropic radiator driven by the same power is the same.

What is the far field of an antenna?

A. The region of the ionosphere where radiated power is not refracted
B. The region where radiated power dissipates over a specified time period
C. The region where radiated field strengths are constant
D. The region where the shape of the radiation pattern no longer varies with distance

E9B08 Answer: D. The far field of an antenna is the region where the shape of the radiation pattern no longer varies with distance.

What type of analysis is commonly used for modeling antennas?

A. Graphical analysis
B. Method of Moments
C. Mutual impedance analysis
D. Calculus differentiation with respect to physical properties

E9B09 Answer: B. Method of Moments is a type of computer program technique commonly used for modeling antennas.

What is the principle of a Method of Moments analysis?

A. A wire is modeled as a series of segments, each having a uniform value of current
B. A wire is modeled as a single sine-wave current generator
C. A wire is modeled as a single sine-wave voltage source
D. A wire is modeled as a series of segments, each having a distinct value of voltage across it

E9B10 Answer: A. In Method of Moments analysis, a wire is modeled as a series of segments, each having a uniform value of current.

What is a disadvantage of decreasing the number of wire segments in an antenna model below 10 segments per half-wavelength?

A. Ground conductivity will not be accurately modeled
B. The resulting design will favor radiation of harmonic energy
C. The computed feed point impedance may be incorrect
D. The antenna will become mechanically unstable

E9B11 Answer: C. Decreasing the number of wire segments in an antenna model below 10 segments per half-wavelength may result in the computed feed point impedance being incorrect.

E9C – Practical Wire Antennas; Folded Dipoles; Phased Arrays; Effects of Ground Near Antennas

What is the radiation pattern of two 1/4-wavelength vertical antennas spaced 1/2-wavelength apart and fed 180 degrees out of phase?

A. Cardioid
B. Omni-directional
C. A figure-8 broadside to the axis of the array
D. A figure-8 oriented along the axis of the array

E9C01 Answer: D. The radiation pattern of two 1/4-wavelength vertical antennas spaced 1/2-wavelength apart and fed 180 degrees out of phase is a figure-8 oriented along the axis of the array.

What is the radiation pattern of two 1/4-wavelength vertical antennas spaced 1/4-wavelength apart and fed 90 degrees out of phase?

A. Cardioid
B. A figure-8 end-fire along the axis of the array
C. A figure-8 broadside to the axis of the array
D. Omni-directional

E9C02 Answer: A. The radiation pattern of two 1/4-wavelength vertical antennas spaced 1/4-wavelength apart and fed 90 degrees out of phase is a cardioid.

What type of radiation pattern is created by two 1/4-wavelength vertical antennas spaced 1/2-wavelength apart and fed in phase?

A. Omni-directional
B. Cardioid
C. A Figure-8 broadside to the axis of the array
D. A Figure-8 end-fire along the axis of the array

E9C03 Answer: C. The radiation pattern of two 1/4-wavelength vertical antennas spaced 1/2-wavelength apart and fed in phase is a figure-8 broadside to the axis of the array.

What happens to the radiation pattern of an unterminated long wire antenna as the wire length is increased?

A. Fewer lobes form with the major lobes increasing closer to broadside to the wire
B. Additional lobes form with major lobes increasingly aligned with the axis of the antenna
C. The elevation angle increases, and the front-to-rear ratio decreases
D. The elevation angle increases, while the front-to-rear ratio is unaffected

E9C04 Answer: B. Additional lobes form with major lobes increasingly aligned with the axis of the antenna length as wire length is increased.

What is the purpose of feeding an off-center-fed dipole (OCFD) between the center and one end instead of at the midpoint?

A. To create a similar feed point impedance on multiple bands
B. To suppress off-center lobes at higher frequencies
C. To resonate the antenna across a wider range of frequencies
D. To reduce common-mode current coupling of the feed line shield

E9C05 Answer: A. An off-center-fed dipole (OCFD) is fed between the center and one end instead of at the midpoint to create a similar feed point impedance on multiple bands.

What is the effect of adding a terminating resistor to a rhombic or long-wire antenna?

A. It reflects the standing waves on the antenna elements back to the transmitter
B. It changes the radiation pattern from bidirectional to unidirectional
C. It changes the radiation pattern from horizontal to vertical polarization
D. It decreases the ground loss

E9C06 Answer: B. Adding a terminating resistor to a rhombic or long-wire antenna changes the radiation pattern from bidirectional to unidirectional.

What is the approximate feed point impedance at the center of a two-wire half-wave folded dipole antenna?

A. 300 ohms
B. 72 ohms
C. 50 ohms
D. 450 ohms

E9C07 Answer: A. The approximate feed point impedance at the center of a two-wire half-wave folded dipole antenna is 300 ohms.

What is a folded dipole antenna?

A. A dipole one-quarter wavelength long
B. A center-fed dipole with the ends folded down 90 degrees at the midpoint of each side
C. A half-wave dipole with an additional parallel wire connecting its two ends
D. A dipole configured to provide forward gain

E9C08 Answer: C. A folded dipole antenna is a half-wave dipole with an additional parallel wire connecting its two ends.

Which of the following describes a G5RV antenna?

A. A wire antenna center-fed through a specific length of open-wire line connected to a balun and coaxial feed line
B. A multi-band trap antenna
C. A phased array antenna consisting of multiple loops
D. A wide band dipole using shorted coaxial cable for the radiating elements and fed with a 4:1 balun

E9C09 Answer: A. A G5RV antenna is a wire antenna center-fed through a specific length of open-wire line connected to a balun and coaxial feed line.

Which of the following describes a Zepp antenna?

A. A horizontal array capable of quickly changing the direction of maximum radiation by changing phasing lines
B. An end-fed half-wavelength dipole
C. An omni-directional antenna commonly used for satellite communications
D. A vertical array capable of quickly changing the direction of maximum radiation by changing phasing lines

E9C10 Answer: B. A Zepp antenna is an end-fed half-wavelength dipole.

How is the far-field elevation pattern of a vertically polarized antenna affected by being mounted over seawater versus soil?

A. Radiation at low angles decreases
B. Additional lobes appear at higher elevation angles
C. Separate elevation lobes will combine into a single lobe
D. Radiation at low angles increases

E9C11 Answer: D. A vertically polarized antenna mounted over seawater would have more low-angle radiation than one mounted over soil.

Which of the following describes an extended double Zepp antenna?

A. An end-fed full-wave dipole antenna
B. A center-fed 1.5-wavelength dipole antenna
C. A center-fed 1.25-wavelength dipole antenna
D. An end-fed 2-wavelength dipole antenna

E9C12 Answer: C. An extended double Zepp antenna is a center-fed 1.25-wavelength antenna.

How does the radiation pattern of a horizontally polarized antenna vary with increasing height above ground?

A. The takeoff angle of the lowest elevation lobe increases
B. The takeoff angle of the lowest elevation lobe decreases
C. The horizontal beamwidth increases
D. The horizontal beamwidth decreases

E9C13 Answer: B. The main lobe takeoff angle of a horizontally polarized antenna decreases with increasing height above ground.

How does the radiation pattern of a horizontally-polarized antenna mounted above a long slope compare with the same antenna mounted above flat ground?

A. The main lobe takeoff angle increases in the downhill direction
B. The main lobe takeoff angle decreases in the downhill direction
C. The horizontal beamwidth decreases in the downhill direction
D. The horizontal beamwidth increases in the uphill direction

E9C14 Answer: B. A horizontally-polarized antenna mounted above a long slope would have a decreased main lobe takeoff angle in the downhill direction compared to same antenna mounted above flat ground.

E9D – Yagi Antennas; Parabolic Reflectors; Feed Point Impedance and Loading of Electrically Short Antennas; Antenna Q; RF Grounding

How much does the gain of an ideal parabolic dish antenna change when the operating frequency is doubled?

A. 2 dB
B. 3 dB
C. 4 dB
D. 6 dB

E9D01 Answer: D. The gain of an ideal parabolic dish antenna changes by 6 dB when the operating frequency is doubled.

How can two linearly polarized Yagi antennas be used to produce circular polarization?

A. Stack two Yagis to form an array with the respective elements in parallel planes fed 90 degrees out of phase
B. Stack two Yagis fed to form an array with the respective elements in parallel planes in phase
C. Arrange two Yagis on the same axis and perpendicular to each other with the driven elements at the same point on the boom fed 90 degrees out of phase
D. Arrange two Yagis collinear to each other with the driven elements fed 180 degrees out of phase

E9D02 Answer: C. Placing two Yagis on the same axis and perpendicular to each other with the driven elements at the same point on the boom fed 90 degrees out of phase would result in circular polarization.

What is the most efficient location for loading coil on an electrically short whip?

A. Near the center of the vertical radiator
B. As low as possible on the vertical radiator
C. At a voltage maximum
D. At a voltage null

E9D03 Answer: A. The most efficient location for loading coil on an electrically short whip is near the center of the vertical radiator.

Why should antenna loading coils have a high ratio of reactance to resistance?

A. To swamp out harmonics
B. To lower the radiation angle
C. To maximize efficiency
D. To minimize the Q

E9D04 Answer: C. Antenna coils should have a high ratio of reactance to resistance to maximize efficiency.

Approximately how long is a Yagi's driven element?

A. 234 divided by frequency in MHz
B. 1005 divided by frequency in MHz
C. ¼ wavelength
D. ½ wavelength

E9D05 Answer: D. A Yagi's driven element is approximately ½ its wavelength.

What happens to the SWR bandwidth when one or more loading coils are used to resonate an electrically short antenna?

A. It is increased
B. It is decreased
C. It is unchanged if the loading coil is located at the feed point
D. It is unchanged if the loading coil is located at a voltage maximum point

E9D06 Answer: B. As one or more loading coils are used to resonate an electrically short antenna, the SWR bandwidth decreases.

What is an advantage of top loading an electrically short HF vertical antenna?

A. Lower Q
B. Greater structural strength
C. Higher losses
D. Improved radiation efficiency

E9D07 Answer: D. An advantage of top loading an electrically short HF vertical antenna is improved radiation efficiency.

What happens as the Q of an antenna increases?

A. SWR bandwidth increases
B. SWR bandwidth decreases
C. Gain is reduced
D. More common-mode current is present on the feed line

E9D08 Answer: B. As the Q of an antenna increases, SWR bandwidth decreases.

What is the function of a loading coil used in an electrically short antenna?

A. To increase the SWR bandwidth by increasing net reactance
B. To lower the losses
C. To lower the Q
D. To resonate the antenna by cancelling the capacitive reactance

E9D09 Answer: D. Loading coils used in an electrically short antenna resonate the antenna by cancelling the capacitive reactance.

How does radiation resistance of a base-fed whip antenna change below its resonant frequency?

A. Radiation resistance increases
B. Radiation resistance decreases
C. Radiation resistance becomes imaginary
D. Radiation resistance does not depend on frequency

E9D10 Answer: B. The radiation resistance of a base-fed whip antenna decreases below its resonant frequency.

Why do most two-element Yagis with normal spacing have a reflector instead of a director?

A. Lower SWR
B. Higher receiving directivity factor
C. Greater front-to-side
D. Higher gain

E9D11 Answer: D. Most two-element Yagis with normal spacing have a reflector instead of a director due to higher gain.

What is the purpose of making a Yagi's parasitic elements either longer or shorter than resonance?

A. Wind torque cancellation
B. Mechanical balance
C. Control of phase shift
D. Minimize losses

E9D12 Answer: C. A Yagi's parasitic elements are made either longer or short than resonance to gain control of phase shift.

E9E – Matching: Matching Antennas to Feed Lines; Phasing Lines; Power Dividers

Which matching system for Yagi antennas requires the driven element to be insulated from the boom?

A. Gamma
B. Beta or hairpin
C. Shunt-fed
D. T-match

E9E01 Answer: B. The shunt-fed system for Yagi antennas requires the driven element to be insulated from the boom.

What antenna matching system matches coaxial cable to an antenna by connecting the shield to the center of the antenna and the conductor a fraction of a wavelength to one side?

A. Gamma match
B. Delta match
C. T-match
D. Sub match

E9E02 Answer: A. The gamma match matches coaxial cable to an antenna by connecting the shield to the center of the antenna and the conductor a fraction of a wavelength to one side.

What matching system uses a short length of transmission line connected in parallel with the feed line at or near the feed point?

A. Gamma match
B. Delta match
C. T-match
D. Stub match

E9E03 Answer: D. The stub match uses a short length of transmission line connected in parallel with the feed line at or near the feed point.

What is the purpose of the series capacitor in a gamma match?

A. To provide DC isolation between the feed line and the antenna
B. To cancel unwanted inductive reactance
C. To provide a rejection notch that prevents the radiation of harmonics
D. To transform the antenna impedance to a higher value

E9E04 Answer: B. The series capacitor in a gamma match cancels unwanted inductive reactance.

What Yagi driven element feed point impedance is required to use a beta or hairpin matching system?

A. Capacitive (driven element electrically shorter than ½ wavelength)
B. Inductive (driven element electrically longer than ½ wavelength)
C. Purely resistive
D. Purely reactive

E9E05 Answer: A. The capacitive (driven element electrically shorter than ½ wavelength) Yagi driven element feed point impedance is required to use a beta or hairpin matching system.

Which of these transmission line impedances would be suitable for constructing a quarter-wave-Q-section for matching a 100-ohm feed point impedance to a 50-ohm transmission line?

A. 50 ohms
B. 62 ohms
C. 75 ohms
D. 90 ohms

E9E06 Answer: C. A feed line impedance of 75 ohms would be suitable for constructing a quarter-wave Q-section for matching a 100-ohm feed point impedance to a 50-ohm transmission line.

What parameter describes the interaction of a load and transmission line?

A. Characteristic impedance
B. Reflection coefficient
C. Velocity factor
D. Dielectric constant

E9E07 Answer: B. Reflection coefficient is the parameter that describes the interaction of a load and transmission line.

What is a use for a Wilkinson divider?

A. To divide the operating frequency of a transmitter signal so it can be used on a lower frequency band
B. To feed high-impedance antennas from a low-impedance source
C. To divide power equally between two 50-ohm loads while maintaining 50-ohm input impedance
D. To divide the frequency of the input to a counter to increase its frequency range

E9E08 Answer: C. A Wilkinson divider is used to divide power equally between two 50-ohm loads while maintaining 50-ohm input impedance.

Which of the following is used to shunt-feed a grounded tower at its base?

A. Double-bazooka match
B. Beta or hairpin
C. Gamma match
D. All these choices are correct

E9E09 Answer: C. Gamma match is used to shunt-feed a grounded tower at its base.

What is the purpose of using multiple driven elements connected through phasing lines?

A. To control the antenna's radiation pattern
B. To prevent harmonic radiation from the transmitter
C. To allow single-band antennas to operate on other bands
D. To create a low-angle radiation pattern

E9E11 Answer: A. Multiple driven elements connected through phasing lines are used to control the antenna's radiation pattern.

E9F – Transmission Lines: Characteristics of Open and Shorted Feed Lines; Coax versus Open-Wire; Velocity Factor; Electrical Length; Coaxial Cable Dielectrics; Microstrip

What is the velocity factor of a transmission line?

A. The ratio of its characteristic impedance to its termination impedance
B. The ratio of its termination impedance to its characteristic impedance
C. The velocity of a wave in the transmission line multiplied by the velocity of light in a vacuum
D. The velocity of a wave in the transmission line divided by the velocity of light in a vacuum

E9F01 Answer: D. The velocity factor of a transmission line is the velocity of a wave in the transmission line divided by the velocity of light in a vacuum.

Which of the following has the biggest effect on the velocity factor of a transmission line?

A. The characteristic impedance
B. The transmission line length
C. The insulating dielectric material
D. The center conductor resistivity

E9F02 Answer: C. The insulating dielectric material has the biggest effect on the velocity factor of a transmission line.

Why is the electrical length of a coaxial cable longer than its physical length?

A. Skin effect is less pronounced in the coaxial cable
B. Skin effect is more pronounced in the coaxial cable
C. Electromagnetic waves move faster in the coaxial cable than in air
D. Electrical signals move more slowly in a coaxial cable than in air

E9F03 Answer: D. The electrical length of a coaxial cable is longer than its physical length because electrical signals move more slowly in a coaxial cable than in air.

What impedance does a 1/2-wavelength transmission line present to an RF generator when the line is shorted at the far end?

A. Very high impedance
B. Very low impedance
C. The same as the characteristic impedance of the line
D. The same as the output impedance of the RF generator

E9F04 Answer: B. A 1/2 wavelength transmission line presents a very low impedance to an RF generator when the line is shorted at the far end.

What is microstrip?

A. Special shielding material designed for microwave frequencies
B. Miniature coax used for low power applications
C. Short lengths of coax mounted on printed circuit boards to minimize time delay between microwave circuits
D. Precision printed circuit conductors above a ground plane that provide constant impedance interconnects at microwave frequencies

E9F05 Answer: D. Microstrip is a precision printed circuit conductor above a ground plane that provides constant impedance interconnects at microwave frequencies.

What is the approximate physical length of an air-insulated, parallel conductor transmission line that is electrically 1/2 wavelength long at 14.10 MHz?

A. 7.0 meters
B. 8.5 meters
C. 10.6 meters
D. 13.3 meters

E9F06 Answer: C. An air-insulated, parallel conductor transmission line that is electrically one-half wavelength long at 14.10 MHz has an approximate physical length of 10.6 meters.

How does parallel conductor transmission line compare to coaxial cable with a plastic dielectric?

A. Lower loss
B. Higher SWR
C. Smaller reflection coefficient
D. Lower velocity factor

E9F07 Answer: A. Parallel conductor transmission line has lower loss than a coaxial cable with a plastic dielectric.

Which of the following is a significant difference between foam dielectric coaxial cable and solid dielectric coaxial cable, assuming all other parameters are the same?

A. Foam dielectric coaxial cable has lower safe maximum operating voltage
B. Foam dielectric coaxial cable has lower loss per unit of length
C. Foam dielectric coaxial cable has higher velocity factor
D. All these choices are correct

E9F08 Answer: D. Foam dielectric coaxial cable has lower safe operating maximum voltage, lower loss per unit of length, and higher velocity factor than solid dielectric coaxial cable, assuming all other parameters are the same.

What impedance does a ¼-wavelength transmission line present to an RF generator when the line is shorted at the far end?

A. Very high impedance
B. Very low impedance
C. The same as the characteristic impedance of the transmission line
D. The same as the generator output impedance

E9F09 Answer: A. A ¼-wavelength transmission line presents very high impedance to an RF generator when the line is shorted at the far end.

What impedance does a 1/8-wavelength transmission line present to an RF generator when the line is shorted at the far end?

A. A capacitive reactance
B. The same as the characteristic impedance of the line
C. An inductive reactance
D. Zero

E9F10 Answer: C. A 1/8-wavelength transmission line presents an inductive reactance to an RF generator when the line is shorted at the far end.

What impedance does a 1/8-wavelength transmission line present to an RF generator when the line is open at the far end?

A. The same as the characteristic impedance of the line
B. An inductive reactance
C. A capacitive reactance
D. Infinite

E9F11 Answer: C. A 1/8-wavelength transmission line presents a capacitive reactance to an RF generator when the line is open at the far end.

What impedance does a 1/4-wavelength transmission line present to an RF generator when the line is open at the far end?

A. The same as the characteristic impedance of the line
B. The same as the input impedance to the generator
C. Very high impedance
D. Very low impedance

E9F12 Answer: D. A 1/4-wavelength transmission line presents a very low impedance to an RF generator when the line is open at the far end.

E9G – The Smith Chart

Which of the following can be calculated using a Smith chart?

A. Impedance along transmission lines
B. Radiation resistance
C. Antenna radiation pattern
D. Radio propagation

E9G01 Answer: A. Impedance along transmission lines can be calculated using a Smith chart.

What type of coordinate system is used in a Smith chart?

A. Voltage circles and current arcs
B. Resistance circles and reactance arcs
C. Voltage lines and current chords
D. Resistance lines and reactance chords

E9G02 Answer: B. Resistance circles and reactance arcs are used in Smith charts.

Which of the following is often determined using a Smith chart?

A. Beam headings and radiation patterns
B. Satellite azimuth and elevation bearings
C. Impedance and SWR values in transmission lines
D. Point-to-point propagation reliability as a function of frequency

E9G03 Answer: C. Impedance and SWR values in transmission lines are often determined using a Smith chart.

What are the two families of circles and arcs that make up a Smith chart?

A. Inductance and capacitance
B. Reactance and voltage
C. Resistance and reactance
D. Voltage and impedance

E9G04 Answer: C. Resistance and reactance are the two families of circles and arcs that make up a Smith chart.

Which of the following is a common use for a Smith chart?

A. Determine the length and position of an impedance matching stub
B. Determine the impedance of a transmission line, given the physical dimensions
C. Determine the gain of an antenna given the physical and electrical parameters
D. Determine the loss/100 feet of a transmission line, given the velocity factor and conductor materials

E9G05 Answer: A. A common use for a Smith chart is to determine the length and position of an impedance matching stub.

Figure E9-3

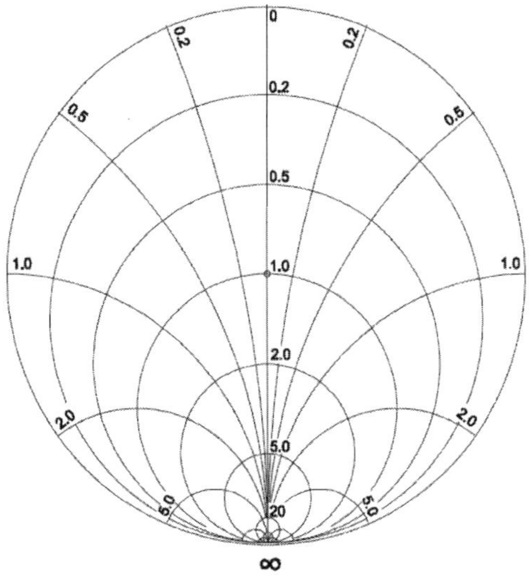

On the Smith chart shown in Figure E9-3, what is the name for the large outer circle on which the reactance arcs terminate?

A. Prime axis
B. Reactance axis
C. Impedance axis
D. Polar axis

E9G06 Answer: B. The large outer circle on which the reactance arcs terminate is the reactance axis in Figure E9-3.

On the Smith chart shown in Figure E9-3, what is the only straight line shown?

A. The reactance axis
B. The current axis
C. The voltage axis
D. The resistance axis

E9G07 Answer: D. On the Smith chart shown in Figure E9-3, the only straight line shown is the resistance axis.

How is a Smith chart normalized?

A. Reassign the reactance axis with resistance values
B. Reassign the resistance axis with reactance values
C. Reassign the prime center's impedance value
D. Reassign the prime center to the reactance axis

E9G08 Answer: C. A Smith chart is normalized by reassigning the prime center to the reactance axis.

What third family of circles is often added to a Smith chart during the process of designing impedance matching networks?

A. Constant-SWR circles
B. Transmission line length circles
C. Coaxial-length circles
D. Radiation-pattern circles

E9G09 Answer: A. Constant-SWR circles are often added to a Smith chart during the process of designing impedance matching networks.

What do the arcs on a Smith chart represent?

A. Frequency
B. SWR
C. Points with constant resistance
D. Points with constant reactance

E9G10 Answer: D. The arcs on a Smith chart represent points with constant reactance.

In what units are the wavelength scales on a Smith chart calibrated?

A. In fractions of transmission line electrical frequency
B. In fractions of transmission line electrical wavelength
C. In fractions of antenna electrical wavelength
D. In fractions of antenna electrical frequency

E9G11 Answer: B. The wavelength scales on a Smith chart are calibrated in fractions of transmission line electrical wavelength.

E9H – Receiving Antennas: Radio Direction Finding (RDF) Techniques; Beverage Antennas; Single- and Multiple-Turn Loops

When constructing a Beverage antenna, which of the following factors should be included in the design to achieve good performance at the desired frequency?

A. Its overall length must not exceed 1/4 wavelength
B. It must be mounted more than 1 wavelength above ground
C. It should be configured as a four-sided loop
D. It should be one or more wavelengths long

E9H01 Answer: D. Beverage antennas should be one or more wavelengths long.

Which is generally true for 160- and 80-meter receiving antennas?

A. Atmospheric noise is so high that directivity is much more important than losses
B. They must be erected at least 1/2 wavelength above the ground to attain good directivity
C. Low loss coax transmission line is essential for good performance
D. All these choices are correct

E9H02 Answer: A. 160- and 80-meter receiving antennas generally have atmospheric noise so high that directivity is much more important than losses.

What is Receiving Directivity Factor (RDF)?

A. Forward gain compared to the gain in the reverse direction
B. Relative directivity compared to isotropic
C. Relative directivity compared to a dipole
D. Peak antenna gain compared to average gain over the hemisphere around and above the antenna

E9H03 Answer: D. Receiving Directivity Factor (RDF) is peak antenna gain compared to average gain over the hemisphere around and above the antenna.

What is the purpose of placing an electrostatic shield around a small-loop direction-finding antenna?

A. It adds capacitive loading, increasing the bandwidth of the antenna
B. It eliminates unbalanced capacitive coupling to the antenna's surroundings, improving the depth of its nulls
C. It eliminates tracking errors caused by strong out-of-band signals
D. It increases signal strength by providing a better match to the feed line

E9H04 Answer: B. The purpose of placing an electrostatic shield around a small-loop direction-finding antenna is to eliminate unbalanced capacitive coupling to the antenna's surroundings, improving the depth of its nulls.

What challenge is presented by a small wire-loop antenna for direction finding?

A. It has a bidirectional pattern
B. It does not have a clearly defined null
C. It is practical for use only on VHF and higher bands
D. All these choices are correct

E9H05 Answer: A. A challenge presented by a small wire-loop antenna for direction finding is that it has a bidirectional pattern.

What indicates the correct value of terminating resistance for a Beverage antenna?

A. Maximum feed point DC resistance at the center of the desired frequency range
B. Minimum low-angle front-to-back ratio at the design frequency range
C. Maximum DC current in the terminating resistor
D. Minimum variation in SWR over the desired frequency range

E9H06 Answer: D. Minimum variation in SWR over the desired frequency range indicates the correct value of terminating resistance for a Beverage antenna.

What is the function of a Beverage antenna's termination resistor?

A. Increase the front-to-side ratio
B. Absorb signals from the reverse direction
C. Decrease SWR bandwidth
D. Eliminate harmonic reception

E9H07 Answer: B. A Beverage antenna's termination resistor absorbs signals from the reverse direction.

What is the function of a sense antenna?

A. It modifies the pattern of a DF antenna array to provide a null in one direction
B. It increases the sensitivity of a DF antenna array
C. It allows DF antennas to receive signals at different vertical angles
D. It provides diversity reception that cancels multipath signals

E9H08 Answer: A. A sense antenna modifies the pattern of a DF antenna array to provide a null in one direction.

What type of radiation pattern is created by a single-turn, terminated loop such as a pennant antenna?

A. Cardioid
B. Bidirectional
C. Omnidirectional
D. Hyperbolic

E9H09 Answer: A. A single-turn, terminated loops such as a pennant antenna creates a cardioid radiation pattern.

How can the output voltage of a multiple-turn receiving loop antenna be increased?

A. By reducing the permeability of the loop shield
B. By utilizing high impedance wire for the coupling loop
C. By increasing the number of turns and/or the area enclosed by the loop
D. All these choices are correct

E9H10 Answer: C. The output voltage of a multiple-turn receiving loop antenna can be increased by increasing either the number of turns and/or the area enclosed by the loop.

What feature of a cardioid pattern antenna makes it useful for direction-finding antennas?

A. A very sharp peak
B. A single null
C. Broadband response
D. High radiation angle

E9H11 Answer: B. The single null part of a cardioid pattern antenna is useful for direction-finding antennas.

E0 – Safety

E0A – Safety: RF radiation hazards; hazardous materials; grounding

What is the primary function of an external earth connection or ground rod?

A. Prevent static build up on power lines
B. Lightning charge dissipation
C. Reduce RF current flow between pieces of equipment
D. Protect break panel from power surges

E0A01 Answer: B. The primary function of an external earth connection or ground rod is lightning charge dissipation.

When evaluating RF exposure levels from your station at a neighbor's home, what must you do?

A. Ensure signals from your station are less than the controlled Maximum Permitted Exposure (MPE) limits
B. Ensure signals from your station are less than the uncontrolled Maximum Permitted Exposure (MPE) limits
C. Ensure signals from your station are less than the controlled Maximum Permitted Emission (MPE) limits
D. Ensure signals from your station are less than the uncontrolled Maximum Permitted Emission (MPE) limits

E0A02 Answer: B. You must make sure signals from your station are less than the uncontrolled MPE limits.

Over what range of frequencies are the FCC human body RF exposure limits most restrictive?

A. 300 kHz to 3 MHz
B. 3 to 30 MHz
C. 30 to 300 MHz
D. 300 to 3000 MHz

E0A03 Answer: C. The FCC human body RF exposure limits are most restrictive over 30 to 300 MHz.

When evaluating a site with multiple transmitters operating at the same time, the operators and licensees of which transmitters are responsible for mitigating over-exposure situations?

A. Each transmitter that produces 20 percent or more of its MPE limit in areas where the total MPE limit is exceeded
B. Each transmitter operating with a duty cycle greater than 25 percent
C. Each transmitter that produces 5 percent or more of its MPE limit in areas where the total MPE limit is exceeded.
D. Each transmitter operating with a duty cycle greater than 50 percent

E0A04 Answer: C. When evaluating a site with multiple transmitters operating at the same time, the operators and licensees of transmitters that produces 5 percent or more of its MPE limit in areas where the total MPE limit is exceeded are responsible for mitigating over-exposure situations.

What hazard is creating by operating at microwave frequencies?

A. Microwaves are ionizing radiation
B. The high gain antennas commonly used can result in high exposure levels
C. Microwaves are in the frequency range where wave velocity is higher
D. The extremely high frequency energy can damage the joints of antenna structures

E0A05 Answer: B. One of the potential hazards of operating at microwave frequencies is that the high gain antennas commonly used can result in high exposure levels.

Why are there separate electric (E) and magnetic (H) MPE limits at frequencies below 300 MHz?

A. The body reacts to electromagnetic radiation from both the E and H fields
B. Ground reflections and scattering make the field strength vary with location
C. E field and H field radiation intensity peaks can occur at different locations
D. All these choices are correct

E0A06 Answer: D. There are multiple reasons why there are separate electric (E) and magnetic (H) field MPE limits at frequencies below 300 MHz, including different body reactions, varying field strength due to ground reflections and scattering, and different radiation intensity peaks.

What is meant by "100% tie-off" regarding tower safety?

A. All loose ropes and guts secured to a fixed structure
B. At least one lanyard attached to the tower at all times
C. All tools secured to the climber's harness
D. All circuit breakers feeding power to the tower must be tied close with tape, cable, or ties

E0A07 Answer: B. In regard to tower safety, "100% tie-off" means that at least one lanyard is attached to the tower at all times.

What does SAR measure?

A. Signal Attenuation Ratio
B. Signal Amplification Rating
C. The rate at which RF energy is absorbed by the body
D. The rate of RF energy reflected from stationary terrain

E0A08 Answer: C. SAR measures the rate at which RF energy is absorbed by the body.

Which of the following types of equipment are exempt from RF exposure evaluations?

A. Transceivers with less than 7 watts of RF output
B. Antennas that radiate only in the near field
C. Hand-held transceivers sold before May 3, 2021
D. Dish antennas less than one meter in diameter

E0A09 Answer: C. Hand-held transceivers sold before May 3, 2021, are exempt from RF exposure evaluations.

When must an RF exposure evaluation be performed on an amateur station operating on 80 meters?

A. An evaluation must always be performed
B. When the ERP of the station is less than 10 watts
C. When the station's operating mode is CW
D. When the output power from the transmitter is less than 100 watts

E0A10 Answer: A. An RF exposure evaluation must always be performed on an amateur station operating on 80 meters.

To what should lanyards be attached while climbing?

A. Antenna mast
B. Guy brackets
C. Tower rungs
D. Tower legs

E0A11 Answer: D. Lanyards should be attached to tower legs while climbing.

Where should a shock-absorbing lanyard be attached to a tower when working above ground?

A. Above the climber's head level
B. To the belt of the fall-arrest harness
C. Even with the climber's waist
D. To the next lowest set of guys

E0A12 Answer: A. Shock-absorbing lanyards should be attached above the climber's head level when working above ground.

Ham Radio Extra Class Practice Tests

Want to take this practice test in an online interactive format?
Check out the online resources page, which includes interactive practice questions and much more: **mometrix.com/resources719/hamradioextra**

Test #1 Practice Questions

1. Why is it not legal to transmit a 3 kHz bandwidth USB signal with a carrier frequency of 14.348 MHz?

a. USB is not used on 20-meter phone
b. The lower 1 kHz of the signal is outside the 20-meter band
c. 14.348 MHz is outside the 20-meter band
d. The upper 1 kHz of the signal is outside the 20-meter band

2. Which of the following constitutes a spurious emission?

a. An amateur station transmission made without the proper call sign identification
b. A signal transmitted to prevent its detection by any station other than the intended recipient
c. Any transmitted signal that unintentionally interferes with another licensed radio station and whose levels exceed 40 dB below the fundamental power level
d. An emission outside the signal's necessary bandwidth that can be reduced or eliminated without affecting the information transmitted

3. What is the maximum bandwidth for a data emission on 60 meters?

a. 60 Hz
b. 170 Hz
c. 1.5 kHz
d. 2.8 kHz

4. What is the definition of telemetry?

a. One-way transmission of measurements at a distance from the measuring instrument
b. Two-way transmissions in excess of 1000 feet
c. Two-way transmissions of data
d. One-way transmission that initiates, modifies, or terminates the functions of a device at a distance

5. For which types of out-of-pocket expenses do the Part 97 rules state that VEs and VECs may be reimbursed?

a. Preparing, processing, administering, and coordinating an examination for an amateur radio operator license
b. Teaching an amateur operator license examination preparation course
c. No expenses are authorized for reimbursement
d. Providing amateur operator license examination preparation training materials

6. On what frequencies are spread spectrum transmissions permitted?

a. Only on amateur frequencies above 50 MHz
b. Only on amateur frequencies above 222 MHz
c. Only on amateur frequencies above 420 MHz
d. Only on amateur frequencies above 144 MHz

7. What is the direction of an ascending pass for an amateur satellite?

a. From west to east
b. From east to west
c. From south to north
d. From north to south

8. In digital television, what does a coding rate of ¾ mean?

a. 25% of the data sent is forward error correction data
b. Data compression reduces data rate by ¾
c. ¼ of the time interval is used as a guard interval
d. Three, four-bit words are used to transmit each pixel

9. What indicator is required to be used by US-licensed operators when operating a station via remote control and the remote transmitter is located in the US?

a. / followed by the USPS two-letter abbreviation for the state in which the remote station is located
b. /R# where # is the district of the remote station
c. / followed by the ARRL Section of the remote station
d. No additional indicator is required

10. Which of the following digital modes is designed for meteor scatter communications?

a. WSPR
b. MSK144
c. Hellschreiber
d. APRS

11. Which of the following types of modulation is common for data emissions below 30 MHz?

a. DTMF tones modulating an FM signal
b. FSK
c. Pulse modulation
d. Spread spectrum

12. What is the approximate maximum separation measured along the surface of the Earth between two stations communicating by EME?

a. 2,000 miles, if the Moon is at perigee
b. 2,000 miles, if the Moon is at apogee
c. 5,000 miles, if the Moon is at perigee
d. 12,000 miles, if the Moon is "visible" by both stations

13. Where is transequatorial propagation (TEP) most likely to occur?

a. Between points separated by 2,000 miles to 3,000 miles over a path perpendicular to the geomagnetic equator
b. Between points located 1,500 miles to 2,000 miles apart on the geomagnetic equator
c. Between points located at each other's antipode
d. Through the region where the terminator crosses the geographic equator

14. What is the cause of short-term radio blackouts?

a. Coronal mass ejections
b. Sunspots on the solar equator
c. North-oriented interplanetary magnetic field
d. Solar flares

15. Which of the following limits the highest frequency signal that can be accurately displayed on a digital oscilloscope?

a. Sampling rate of the analog-to-digital converter
b. Analog-to-digital converter reference frequency
c. Q of the circuit
d. All these choices are correct

16. Which of the following factors most affects the accuracy of a frequency counter?

a. Input attenuator accuracy
b. Time base accuracy
c. Decade divider accuracy
d. Temperature coefficient of the logic

17. What is an effect of excessive phase noise in an SDR receiver's master clock oscillator?

a. It limits the receiver's ability to receive strong signals
b. It can affect the receiver's frequency calibration
c. It decreases the receiver's third-order intercept point
d. It can combine with strong signals on nearby frequencies to generate interference

18. What is meant by the blocking dynamic range of a receiver?

a. The difference in dB between the noise floor and the level of an incoming signal that will cause 1 dB of gain compression
b. The minimum difference in dB between the levels of two FM signals that will cause one signal to block the other
c. The difference in dB between the noise floor and the third-order intercept point
d. The minimum difference in dB between two signals which produce third-order intermodulation products greater than the noise floor

19. What problem can occur when using an automatic notch filter (ANF) to remove interfering carriers while receiving CW signals?

a. Removal of the CW signal as well as the interfering carrier
b. Any nearby signal passing through the DSP system will overwhelm the desired signal
c. Excessive ringing
d. All these choices are correct

20. What can cause the voltage across reactances in a series RLC circuit to be higher than the voltage applied to the entire circuit?

a. Resonance
b. Capacitance
c. Low quality factor (Q)
d. Resistance

21. What is the term for the time required for the capacitor in an RC circuit to be charged to 63.2% of the applied voltage or to discharge to 36.8% of its initial voltage?

a. An exponential rate of one
b. One time constant
c. One exponential period
d. A time factor of one

22. Which of the following represents pure capacitive reactance of 100 ohms in rectangular notation?

a. 0 – j100
b. 0 + j100
c. 100 – j0
d. 100 + j0

23. What is the result of conductor skin effect?

a. Resistance increases as frequency increases because RF current flows closer to the surface
b. Resistance decreases as frequency increases because electron mobility increases
c. Resistance increases as temperature increases because of the change in thermal coefficient
d. Resistance decreases as temperature increases because of the change in thermal coefficient

24. In what application is gallium arsenide used as a semiconductor material?

a. In high-current rectifier circuits
b. In high-power audio circuits
c. In microwave circuits
d. In very low-frequency RF circuits

25. What is the most useful characteristic of a Zener diode?

a. A constant current drop under conditions of varying voltage
b. A constant voltage drop under conditions of varying current
c. A negative resistance region
d. An internal capacitance that varies with the applied voltage

26. What is the function of hysteresis in a comparator?

a. To prevent input noise from causing unstable output signals
b. To allow the comparator to be used with AC input signals
c. To cause the output to change states continually
d. To increase the sensitivity

27. What is piezoelectricity?

a. The ability of materials to generate electromagnetic waves of a certain frequency when voltage is applied
b. A characteristic of materials that have an index of refraction which depends on the polarization of the electromagnetic wave passing through it
c. A characteristic of materials that generate voltage when stressed and that flex when a voltage is applied
d. The ability of materials to generate voltage when an electromagnetic wave of a certain frequency is applied

28. Why is gallium arsenide (GaAs) useful for semiconductor devices operating at UHF and higher frequencies?

a. Higher noise figures
b. Higher electron mobility
c. Lower junction voltage drop
d. Lower transconductance

29. What absorbs the energy from light falling on a photovoltaic cell?

a. Protons
b. Photons
c. Electrons
d. Holes

30. Which circuit is bistable?

a. An AND gate
b. An OR gate
c. A flip-flop
d. A bipolar amplifier

31. For what portion of the signal cycle does each active element in a push-pull, Class AB amplifier conduct?

a. More than 180 degrees but less than 360 degrees
b. Exactly 180 degrees
c. The entire cycle
d. Less than 180 degrees

32. How are the capacitors and inductors of a low-pass filter Pi-network arranged between the network's input and output?

a. Two inductors are in series between the input and output, and a capacitor is connected between the two inductors and ground
b. Two capacitors are in series between the input and output, and an inductor is connected between the two capacitors and ground
c. An inductor is connected between the input and ground, another inductor is connected between the output and ground, and a capacitor is connected between the input and output
d. A capacitor is connected between the input and ground, another capacitor is connected between the output and ground, and an inductor is connected between input and output

33. How does a linear electronic voltage regulator work?

a. It has a ramp voltage as its output
b. It eliminates the need for a pass transistor
c. The control element duty cycle is proportional to the line or load conditions
d. The conduction of a control element is varied to maintain a constant output voltage

34. Which of the following can be used to generate FM phone signals?

a. Balanced modulation of the audio amplifier
b. Reactance modulation of a local oscillator
c. Reactance modulation of the final amplifier
d. Balanced modulation of a local oscillator

35. What is meant by "direct sampling" in software defined radios?

a. Software is converted from source code to object code during operation of the receiver
b. I and Q signals are generated by digital processing without the use of RF amplification
c. Incoming RF is digitized by an analog-to-digital converter without being mixed with a local oscillator signal
d. A switching mixer is used to generate I and Q signals directly from the RF input

36. What is the typical output impedance of an op-amp?

a. Very low
b. Very high
c. 100 ohms
d. 10,000 ohms

37. What are three common oscillator circuits?

a. Taft, Pierce and negative feedback
b. Pierce, Fenner and Beane
c. Taft, Hartley and Pierce
d. Colpitts, Hartley and Pierce

38. What technique shows that a square wave is made up of a sine wave and its odd harmonics?

a. Fourier analysis
b. Vector analysis
c. Numerical analysis
d. Differential analysis

39. What is the modulation index of an FM signal?

a. The ratio of frequency deviation to modulating signal frequency
b. The ratio of modulating signal amplitude to frequency deviation
c. The modulating signal frequency divided by the bandwidth of the transmitted signal
d. The bandwidth of the transmitted signal divided by the modulating signal frequency

40. What is Quadrature Amplitude Modulation or QAM?

a. A technique for digital data compression used in digital television which removes redundancy in the data by comparing bit amplitudes
b. Transmission of data by modulating the amplitude of two carriers of the same frequency but 90 degrees out of phase
c. A method of performing singled sideband modulation by shifting the phase of the carrier and modulation components of the signal
d. A technique for analog modulation of television video signals using phase modulation and compression

41. Why are received spread spectrum signals resistant to interference?

a. Signals not using the spread spectrum algorithm are suppressed in the receiver
b. The high power used by a spread spectrum transmitter keeps its signal from being easily overpowered
c. Built-in error correction codes minimize interference
d. If interference is detected by the receiver it will signal the transmitter to change frequencies

42. What is an isotropic radiator?

a. A calibrated, unidirectional antenna used to make precise antenna gain measurements
b. An omnidirectional, horizontally polarized, precisely calibrated antenna used to make field measurements of antenna gain
c. A hypothetical, lossless antenna having equal radiation intensity in all directions used as a reference for antenna gain
d. A spacecraft antenna used to direct signals toward Earth

Question 43 pertains to the following graphic:

Figure E9-1

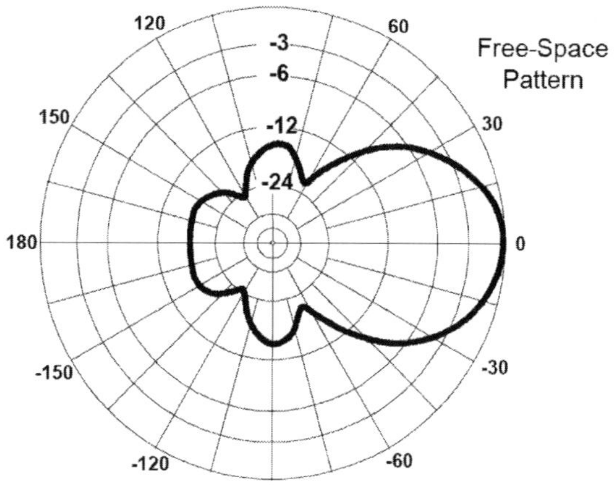

43. What is the 3 dB beamwidth of the antenna radiation pattern shown in Figure E9-1?

a. 75 degrees
b. 50 degrees
c. 25 degrees
d. 30 degrees

44. What is the radiation pattern of two 1/4-wavelength vertical antennas spaced 1/2-wavelength apart and fed 180 degrees out of phase?

a. Cardioid
b. Omni-directional
c. A figure-8 broadside to the axis of the array
d. A figure-8 oriented along the axis of the array

45. How much does the gain of an ideal parabolic dish antenna change when the operating frequency is doubled?

a. 2 dB
b. 3 dB
c. 4 dB
d. 6 dB

46. Which matching system for Yagi antennas requires the driven element to be insulated from the boom?

a. Gamma
b. Beta or hairpin
c. Shunt-fed
d. T-match

47. What is the velocity factor of a transmission line?

a. The ratio of its characteristic impedance to its termination impedance
b. The ratio of its termination impedance to its characteristic impedance
c. The velocity of a wave in the transmission line multiplied by the velocity of light in a vacuum
d. The velocity of a wave in the transmission line divided by the velocity of light in a vacuum

48. Which of the following can be calculated using a Smith chart?

a. Impedance along transmission lines
b. Radiation resistance
c. Antenna radiation pattern
d. Radio propagation

49. When constructing a Beverage antenna, which of the following factors should be included in the design to achieve good performance at the desired frequency?

a. Its overall length must not exceed 1/4 wavelength
b. It must be mounted more than 1 wavelength above ground
c. It should be configured as a four-sided loop
d. It should be one or more wavelengths long

50. What is the primary function of an external earth connection or ground rod?

a. Prevent static build up on power lines
b. Lightning charge dissipation
c. Reduce RF current flow between pieces of equipment
d. Protect break panel from power surges

Test #1 Answer Key and Explanations

1. D: It is not legal to transmit a 3 kHz bandwidth USB signal with a carrier frequency of 14.348 MHz because the upper 1 kHz of the signal is outside the 20-meter band.

2. D: A spurious emission is an emission outside the signal's necessary bandwidth that can be reduced or eliminated without affecting the information transmitted.

3. D: The maximum bandwidth for a data emission on 60 meters is 2.8 kHz.

4. A: Telemetry is one-way transmission of measurements at a distance from the measuring instrument.

5. A: The Part 97 rules state that VEs and VECs may be reimbursed for preparing, processing, administering and coordinating an examination for an amateur radio license.

6. B: Spread spectrum transmissions are permitted only on amateur frequencies above 222 MHz.

7. C: An amateur satellite goes from south to north in an ascending pass.

8. A: In digital television, a coding rate of ¾ means that 25% of the data sent is forward error correction data.

9. D: No additional indicator is required when US-licensed operators operate a station via remote control where the transmitter is located in the US

10. B: The MSK144 digital mode is designed for meteor scatter communications.

11. B: FSK modulation is common for data emissions below 30 MHz.

12. D: The approximate maximum separation measured along the surface of the Earth between two stations communicating by EME is 12,000 miles, if the Moon is "visible" by both stations.

13. A: Transequatorial propagation (TEP) is most likely to occur between points separated by 2,000 miles to 3,000 miles over a path perpendicular to the geomagnetic equator.

14. D: Solar flares cause short-term radio blackouts.

15. A: The sampling rate of the analog-to-digital converter limits the highest frequency signal that can be accurately displayed on a digital oscilloscope.

16. B: Time base accuracy most affects the overall accuracy of a frequency counter.

17. D: Excessive phase noise in an SDR receiver's master clock oscillator can combine with strong signals on nearby frequencies to generate interference.

18. A: The blocking dynamic range of a receiver is the difference in dB between the noise floor and the level of an incoming signal which will cause 1 dB of gain compression.

19. A: Using an automatic notch filter (ANF) to remove interfering carriers while receiving CW signals can remove the CW signal as well as the interfering carrier.

20. A: Resonance can cause the voltage across reactances in a series RLC circuit to be higher than the voltage applied to the entire circuit.

21. B: A time-constant is the time required for the capacitor in an RC circuit to be charged to 63.2% of the applied voltage or to discharge to 36.8% of its initial voltage.

22. A: "0 – j100" represents pure capacitive reactance of 100 ohms in rectangular notation.

23. A: As a result of conductor skin effect, resistance increases as frequency increases because RF current flows closer to the surface.

24. C: Gallium arsenide is used as a semiconductor material in microwave circuits.

25. B: Zener diodes are most useful because they have a constant voltage drop under conditions of varying current.

26. A: Hysteresis in a comparator prevents input noise from causing unstable output signals.

27. C: Piezoelectricity is a characteristic of materials that generate voltage when stressed and that flex when a voltage is applied.

28. B: Higher electron mobility makes gallium arsenide (GaAs) useful for semiconductor devices operating at UHF and higher frequencies.

29. C: Electrons absorb the energy from light falling on photovoltaic cells.

30. C: Flip-flops are bi-stable circuits.

31. A: A class AB amplifier operates on more than 180 degrees but less than 360 degrees of a signal cycle.

32. D: In a low-pass filter Pi-network, a capacitor is connected between the input and ground, another capacitor is connected between the output and ground, and an inductor is connected between input and output.

33. D: A linear electronic voltage regulator varies the conduction of a control element to maintain a constant output voltage.

34. B: Reactance modulation of a local oscillator can be used to generate FM phone signals.

35. C: Direct sampling in software defined radios is when incoming RF is digitized by an analog-to-digital converter without being mixed with a local oscillator signal.

36. A: The typical output impedance of an op-amp is very low.

37. D: Colpitts, Hartley and Pierce are all three common oscillator circuits.

38. A: Fourier analysis shows that a square wave is made up of a sine wave plus all of its odd harmonics.

39. A: The modulation index of an FM signal is the ratio of frequency deviation to modulating signal frequency.

40. B: Quadrature Amplitude Modulation, or QAM, is the transmission of data by modulating the amplitude of two carriers of the same frequency but 90 degrees out of phase.

41. A: Received spread spectrum signals are resistant to interference because signals not using the spread spectrum algorithm are suppressed in the receiver.

42. C: An isotropic radiator is a hypothetical, lossless antenna having equal radiation intensity in all directions used as a reference for antenna gain.

43. B: In the antenna radiation pattern shown in Figure E9-1, the 3 dB beamwidth is 50 degrees.

44. D: The radiation pattern of two 1/4-wavelength vertical antennas spaced 1/2-wavelength apart and fed 180 degrees out of phase is a figure-8 oriented along the axis of the array.

45. D: The gain of an ideal parabolic dish antenna changes by 6 dB when the operating frequency is doubled.

46. B: The shunt-fed system for Yagi antennas requires the driven element to be insulated from the boom.

47. D: The velocity factor of a transmission line is the velocity of the wave in the transmission line divided by the velocity of light in a vacuum.

48. A: Impedance along transmission lines can be calculated using a Smith chart.

49. D: Beverage antennas should be one or more wavelengths long.

50. B: The primary function of an external earth connection or ground rod is lightning charge dissipation.

Test #2 Practice Questions

1. When using a transceiver that displays the carrier frequency of phone signals, which of the following displayed frequencies represents the lowest frequency at which a properly adjusted LSB emission will be totally within the band?

a. The exact lower band edge
b. 300 Hz above the lower band edge
c. 1 kHz above the lower band edge
d. 3 kHz above the lower band edge

2. Which of the following is an acceptable bandwidth for digital voice or slow-scan TV transmissions made on the HF amateur bands?

a. 3 kHz
b. 10 kHz
c. 15 kHz
d. 20 kHz

3. Which of the following apply to communications transmitted to amateur foreign stations in foreign countries?

a. Third party traffic must be limited to that intended for the exclusive use of government and non-Government Organization (NGOs) involved in emergency relief activities
b. All transmissions must be in English
c. Communications must be limited to those incidental to the purpose of the amateur service and remarks of a personal nature
d. All these choices are correct

4. Which of the following may transmit encrypted messages?

a. Telecommand signals to terrestrial repeaters
b. Telecommand signals from a space telecommand station
c. Auxiliary relay links carrying repeater audio
d. Mesh network backbone nodes

5. Who does Part 97 task with maintaining the pools of questions for all US amateur license examinations?

a. The VEs
b. The FCC
c. The VECs
d. The ARRL

6. What privileges are authorized in the US to persons holding an amateur service license granted by the government of Canada?

a. None, they must obtain a US license
b. Full privileges of the General class license on the 80-, 40-, 20-, and 10-meter bands
c. The operating terms and conditions of the Canadian amateur service license, not to exceed US Amateur Extra class license privileges
d. Full privileges, up to and including those of the Amateur Extra class license, on the 80, 40, 20, 15, and 10 meter bands

7. Which of the following is a characteristic of an inverting linear transponder?

a. Doppler shift is reduced because the uplink and downlink shifts are in opposite directions
b. Signal position in the band is reversed
c. Upper sideband on the uplink becomes lower sideband on the downlink, and vice versa
d. All these choices are correct

8. How many horizontal lines make up a fast-scan (NTSC) television frame?

a. 30
b. 60
c. 525
d. 1080

9. Which of the following file formats is used for exchanging amateur radio log data?

a. NEC
b. ARLD
c. ADIF
d. OCF

10. What information replaces signal-to-noise ratio when using the FT8 or FT4 modes in a VHF contest?

a. RST report
b. State abbreviation
c. Serial number
d. Grid square

11. Which of the following synchronizes WSJT-X digital mode transmit/receive timing?

a. Alignment of frequency shifts
b. Synchronization of computer clocks
c. Sync-field transmission
d. Sync-pulse timing

12. What characterizes libration fading of an EME signal?

a. A slow change in the pitch of the CW signal
b. A fluttery, irregular fading
c. A gradual loss of signal as the sun rises
d. The returning echo is several hertz lower in frequency than the transmitted signal

13. What is the approximate maximum range for signals using transequatorial propagation?

a. 1,000 miles
b. 2,500 miles
c. 5,000 miles
d. 7,500 miles

14. What is indicated by a rising A- or K-index?

a. Increasing disturbance of the geomagnetic field
b. Decreasing disturbance of the geomagnetic field
c. Higher levels of solar UV radiation
d. An increase in the critical frequency

15. Which of the following parameters does a spectrum analyzer display on the vertical and horizontal axes?

a. Signal amplitude and time
b. Signal amplitude and frequency
c. SWR and frequency
d. SWR and time

16. What is the significance of voltmeter sensitivity expressed in ohms per volt?

a. The full scale reading of the voltmeter multiplied by its ohms per volt rating is the input impedance of the voltmeter
b. The reading in volts multiplied by the ohms per volt rating will determine the power drawn by the device under test
c. The reading in ohms divided by the ohms per volt rating will determine the voltage applied to the circuit
d. The full scale reading in amps divided by ohms per volt rating will determine the size of shunt needed

17. Which of the following receiver circuits can be effective in eliminating interference from strong out-of-band signals?

a. A front-end filter or pre-selector
b. A narrow IF filter
c. A notch filter
d. A properly adjusted product detector

18. Which of the following describes problems caused by poor dynamic range in a receiver?

a. Spurious signals caused by cross-modulation and desensitization from strong adjacent signals
b. Oscillator instability requiring frequent retuning and loss of ability to recover the opposite sideband
c. Poor weak signal reception caused by insufficient local oscillator injection
d. Oscillator instability and severe audio distortion of all but the strongest received signals

19. Which of the following types of noise can often be reduced by a digital noise reduction?

a. Broadband white noise
b. Ignition noise
c. Power line noise
d. All these choices are correct

20. What is the resonant frequency of an RLC circuit if R is 22 ohms, L is 50 microhenries, and C is 40 picofarads?

a. 44.72 MHz
b. 22.36 MHz
c. 3.56 MHz
d. 1.78 MHz

21. What letter is commonly used to represent susceptance?

a. G
b. X
c. Y
d. B

22. How are impedances described in polar coordinates?

a. By X and R values
b. By real and imaginary parts
c. By phase angle and magnitude
d. By Y and G values

23. Why is it important to keep lead lengths short for components used in circuits for VHF and above?

a. To increase the thermal time constant
b. To minimize inductive reactance
c. To maintain component lifetime
d. All these choices are correct

24. Which of the following semiconductor materials contains excess free electrons?

a. N-type
b. P-type
c. Bipolar
d. Insulated gate

25. Which characteristic of a Schottky diode makes it a better choice than a silicon junction diode for use as a power supply rectifier?

a. Much higher reverse voltage breakdown
b. More constant reverse avalanche voltage
c. Longer carrier retention time
d. Less forward voltage drop

26. What happens when the level of a comparator's input signal crosses the threshold?

a. The IC input can be damaged
b. The comparator changes its output state
c. The reference level appears at the output
d. The feedback loop becomes unstable

27. What is the equivalent circuit of a quartz crystal?

a. Series RLC in parallel with a shunt C representing electrode and stray capacitance
b. Parallel RLC, where C is the parallel combination of resonance capacitance of the crystal and electrode and stray capacitance
c. Series RLC, where C is the parallel combination of resonance capacitance of the crystal and electrode and stray capacitance
d. Parallel RLC, where C is the series combination of resonance capacitance of the crystal and electrode and stray capacitance

28. Which of the following device packages is a through-hole type?

a. DIP
b. PLCC
c. BGA
d. SOT

29. What happens to photoconductive material when light shines on it?

a. Resistance decreases
b. Resistance increases
c. Reflectivity increases
d. Reflectivity decreases

30. What is the function of a decade counter?

a. It produces one output pulse for every 10 input pulses
b. It decodes a decimal number for display on a seven-segment LED display
c. It produces 10 output pulses for every input pulse
d. It decodes a binary number for display on a seven-segment LED display

31. What is a Class D amplifier?

a. A type of amplifier that uses switching technology to achieve high efficiency
b. A low power amplifier that uses a differential amplifier for improved linearity
c. An amplifier that uses drift-mode FETs for high efficiency
d. An amplifier biased to be relatively free from distortion

32. What is the frequency response of a T-network with series capacitors and a shunt inductor?

a. Low-pass
b. High-pass
c. Band-pass
d. Notch

33. How does a switchmode voltage regulator work?

a. By alternating the output between positive and negative voltages
b. By varying the duty cycle of pulses input to a filter
c. By varying the conductivity of a pass element
d. By switching between two Zener diode reference voltages

34. What is the function of a reactance modulator?

a. To produce PM or FM signals by varying a resistance
b. To produce AM signals by varying an inductance
c. To produce AM signals by varying a resistance
d. To produce PM or FM signals by varying a capacitance

35. What kind of digital signal processing audio filter is used to remove unwanted noise from a received SSB signal?

a. An adaptive filter
b. A crystal-lattice filter
c. A Hilbert-transform filter
d. A phase-inverting filter

36. What is the frequency response of the circuit in E7-3 if a capacitor is added across the feedback resistor?

a. High-pass filter
b. Low-pass filter
c. Band-pass filter
d. Notch filter

37. What is a microphonic?

a. An IC used for amplifying microphone signals
b. Distortion caused by RF pickup on the microphone cable
c. Changes in oscillator frequency due to mechanical vibration
d. Excess loading of the microphone by an oscillator

38. Which of the following is a type of analog-to-digital conversion?

a. Successive approximation
b. Harmonic regeneration
c. Level shifting
d. Phase reversal

39. How does the modulation index of a phase-modulated emission vary with RF carrier frequency?

a. It increases as the RF carrier frequency increases
b. It decreases as the RF carrier frequency increases
c. It varies with the square root of the RF carrier frequency
d. It does not depend on the RF carrier frequency

40. What is the definition of symbol rate in a digital transmission?

a. The number of control characters in a message packet
b. The maximum rate at which the forward error correction code can make corrections
c. The rate at which the waveform changes to convey information
d. The number of characters carried per second by the station-to-station link

41. What spread spectrum communications technique uses a high-speed binary bit stream to shift the phase of an RF carrier?

a. Frequency hopping
b. Direct sequence
c. Binary phase-shift keying
d. Phase compandored spread spectrum

42. What is the effective radiated power (ERP) of a repeater station with 150 watts transmitter power output, 2 dB feed line loss, 2.2 dB duplexer loss, and 7 dBd antenna gain?

a. 469 watts
b. 78.7 watts
c. 420 watts
d. 286 watts

Question 43 pertains to the following graphic:

Figure E9-1

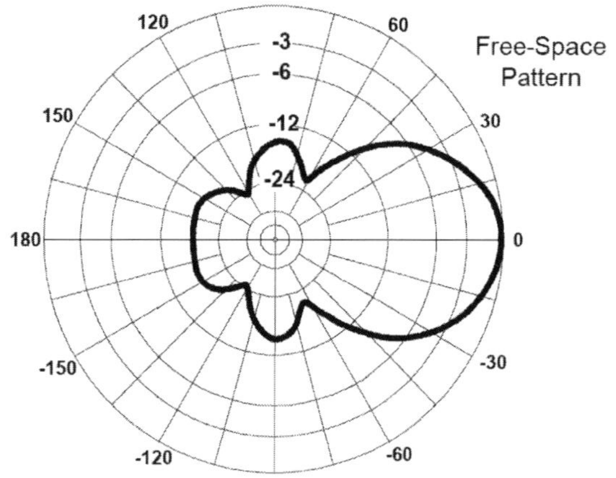

43. In the antenna radiation pattern shown in Figure E9-1, what is the front-to-back ratio?

a. 36 dB
b. 14 dB
c. 24 dB
d. 18 dB

44. What is the radiation pattern of two ¼-wavelength vertical antennas spaced ¼-wavelength apart and fed 90 degrees out of phase?

a. Cardioid
b. A figure-8 end-fire along the axis of the array
c. A figure-8 broadside to the axis of the array
d. Omni-directional

45. How can two linearly polarized Yagi antennas be used to produce circular polarization?

a. Stack two Yagis to form an array with the respective elements in parallel planes fed 90 degrees out of phase
b. Stack two Yagis fed to form an array with the respective elements in parallel planes in phase
c. Arrange two Yagis on the same axis and perpendicular to each other with the driven elements at the same point on the boom fed 90 degrees out of phase
d. Arrange two Yagis collinear to each other with the driven elements fed 180 degrees out of phase

46. What antenna matching system matches coaxial cable to an antenna by connecting the shield to the center of the antenna and the conductor a fraction of a wavelength to one side?

a. Gamma match
b. Delta match
c. T-match
d. Sub match

47. Which of the following has the biggest effect on the velocity factor of a transmission line?

a. The characteristic impedance
b. The transmission line length
c. The insulating dielectric material
d. The center conductor resistivity

48. What type of coordinate system is used in a Smith chart?

a. Voltage circles and current arcs
b. Resistance circles and reactance arcs
c. Voltage lines and current chords
d. Resistance lines and reactance chords

49. Which is generally true for 160- and 80-meter receiving antennas?

a. Atmospheric noise is so high that directivity is much more important than losses
b. They must be erected at least 1/2 wavelength above the ground to attain good directivity
c. Low loss coax transmission line is essential for good performance
d. All these choices are correct

50. When evaluating RF exposure levels from your station at a neighbor's home, what must you do?

a. Ensure signals from your station are less than the controlled Maximum Permitted Exposure (MPE) limits
b. Ensure signals from your station are less than the uncontrolled Maximum Permitted Exposure (MPE) limits
c. Ensure signals from your station are less than the controlled Maximum Permitted Emission (MPE) limits
d. Ensure signals from your station are less than the uncontrolled Maximum Permitted Emission (MPE) limits

Test #2 Answer Key and Explanations

1. D: The lowest frequency at which a properly adjusted LSB emission will be totally within the band is 3 kHz above the lower band edge.

2. A: 3 KHz is an acceptable bandwidth for digital voice or slow-scan TV transmissions made on the HF amateur bands.

3. C: Communications transmitted to amateur foreign stations in foreign countries must be limited to those incidental to the purpose of the amateur service and remarks of a personal nature.

4. B: Telecommand signals from a space telecommand station may transmit encrypted messages.

5. C: The VECs are tasked by Part 97 with maintaining the pools of questions for all US amateur license examinations.

6. C: Persons in the US holding an amateur service license granted by the Government of Canada are granted the operating terms and conditions of the Canadian amateur service license, not to exceed US Amateur Extra class privileges.

7. D: Characteristics of an inverting linear transponder are that the doppler shift is reduced because the uplink and downlink shifts are in opposite directions, the signal position in the band is reversed, and the upper sideband on the uplink becomes lower sideband on the downlink, and vice versa.

8. C: There are 525 horizontal lines in a fast-scan (NTSC) television frame.

9. C: The ADIF file format is used for exchanging amateur radio log data.

10. D: The grid square replaces the signal-to-noise ration when using the FT8 or FT4 modes in a VHF contest.

11. B: The synchronization of computer clocks synchronizes WSJT-X digital mode transmit/receive timing.

12. B: A fluttery, irregular fading characterizes libration fading of an EME signal.

13. C: The approximate maximum range for signals using transequatorial propagation is 5,000 miles.

14. A: A rising A- or K-index indicates increasing disturbance of the geomagnetic field.

15. B: A spectrum analyzer displays the signal amplitude and frequency on the vertical and horizontal axes, respectively.

16. A: Voltmeter sensitivity is expressed in ohms per volt because the full scale reading of the voltmeter multiplied by its ohms per volt rating is the input impedance of the voltmeter.

17. A: A front-end filter or pre-selector can be effective in eliminating interference from strong out-of-band signals.

18. A: Spurious signals caused by cross-modulation and desensitization from strong adjacent signals are both problems caused by poor dynamic range in a receiver.

19. D: Broadband white noise, ignition noise, and power line noise can often be reduced by a digital noise reduction.

20. C: The resonant frequency of an RLC circuit where R is 22 ohms, L is 50 microhenries, and C is 40 picofarads is 3.56 MHz.

21. D: The letter 'B' is commonly used to represent susceptance.

22. C: Impedances are described by magnitude and phase angle in polar coordinates.

23. B: It is important to keep lead lengths short for components used in circuits for VHF and above to minimize inductive reactance.

24. A: N-type semiconductor materials contain excess free electrons.

25. D: Schottky diodes can be more useful than ordinary diodes in some applications because they have less forward voltage drop.

26. B: When the level of a comparator's input signal crosses the threshold, the comparator changes its output state.

27. A: The equivalent circuit of a quartz crystal is series RLC in parallel with a shunt C representing electrode and stray capacitance.

28. A: DIP is a type of through-hole device packaging.

29. A: Resistance decreases when light shines on photoconductive material.

30. A: Decade counters produce one output pulse for every ten input pulses.

31. A: A class D amplifier uses switching technology to achieve high efficiency.

32. B: The frequency response of a T-network with series capacitors and a shunt inductor is high-pass.

33. B: A switchmode voltage regulator works by varying the duty cycle of pulses input to a filter.

34. D: A reactance modulator produces PM or FM signals by varying a capacitance.

35. A: An adaptive filter is used to remove unwanted noise from a received SSB signal.

36. B: If a capacitor is added across the feedback resistor, a low-pass filter is the frequency response of the circuit in E7-3.

37. C: A microphonic is a change in oscillator frequency due to mechanical vibration.

38. A: Successive approximation is a type of analog-to-digital conversion.

39. D: The modulation index of a phase-modulated emission does not depend on the RF carrier frequency.

40. C: Symbol rate in a digital transmission is the rate at which the waveform changes to convey information.

41. B: Direct sequence uses a high-speed binary bit stream to shift the phase of an RF carrier.

42. D: The effective radiated power (ERP) of a repeater station with 150 watts transmitter power output, 2 dB feed line loss, 2.2 dB duplexer loss, and 7 dBd antenna gain is 286 watts.

43. D: In the antenna radiation pattern shown in Figure E9-1, the front-to-back ratio is 18 dB.

44. A: The radiation pattern of two ¼-wavelength vertical antennas spaced ¼-wavelength apart and fed 90 degrees out of phase is a cardioid.

45. C: Placing two Yagis on the same axis and perpendicular to each other with the driven elements at the same point on the boom fed 90 degrees out of phase would result in circular polarization.

46. A: The gamma match matches coaxial cable to an antenna by connecting the shield to the center of the antenna and the conductor a fraction of a wavelength to one side.

47. C: The insulating dielectric material has the biggest effect on the velocity factor of a transmission line.

48. B: Resistance circles and reactance arcs are used in Smith charts.

49. A: 160- and 80-meter receiving antennas generally have atmospheric noise so high that directivity is much more important than losses.

50. B: You must make sure signals from your station are less than the uncontrolled MPE limits.

Test #3 Practice Questions

1. What is the highest legal carrier frequency on the 20-meter band for transmitting a 2.8 kHz wide USB digital signal?

a. 14.0708 MHz
b. 14.1002 MHz
c. 14.1472 MHz
d. 14.3490 MHz

2. Within what distance must an amateur station protect an FCC monitoring facility from harmful interference?

a. 1 mile
b. 3 miles
c. 10 miles
d. 30 miles

3. How long must an operator wait after filing a notification with the Utilities Technology Council (UTC) before operating on the 2200-meter or 630-meter band?

a. Operators must not operate until approval is received
b. Operators may operate after 30 days, providing they have not been told that their station is within 1 kilometer of PLC systems using those frequencies
c. Operators may not operate until a test signal has been transmitted in coordination with the local power company
d. Operations may commence immediately, and may continue unless interference is reported by the UTC

4. What is a space telecommand station?

a. An amateur station located on the surface of the Earth for communication with other Earth stations by means of Earth satellites
b. An amateur station that transmits communications to initiate, modify or terminate functions of a space station
c. An amateur station located in a satellite or a balloon more than 50 kilometers above the surface of the Earth
d. An amateur station that receives telemetry from a satellite or balloon more than 50 kilometers above the surface of the Earth

5. What is a Volunteer Examiner Coordinator?

a. A person who has volunteered to administer amateur operator license examinations
b. An organization paid by the volunteer examiner team to publicize and schedule examinations
c. An organization that has entered into an agreement with the FCC to coordinate, prepare, and administer amateur operator license examinations
d. The person who has entered into an agreement with the FCC to be the VE session manager

6. Under what circumstances may a dealer sell an external RF power amplifier capable of operation below 144 MHz if it has not been granted FCC certification?

a. Gain is less than 23 dB when driven by power of 10 watts or less
b. The equipment dealer assembled it from a kit
c. It was manufactured and certificated in a country which has a reciprocal certification agreement with the FCC
d. The amplifier is constructed or modified by an amateur radio operator for use at an amateur station

7. How is an upload signal processed by an inverting linear transponder?

a. The signal is detected and remodulated on the reverse sideband
b. The signal is passed through a nonlinear filter
c. The signal is reduced to I and Q components and the Q component is filtered out
d. The signal is mixed with a local oscillator signal and the difference product is transmitted

8. How is an interlaced scanning pattern generated in a fast-scan (NTSC) television system?

a. By scanning two fields simultaneously
b. By scanning each field from bottom to top
c. By scanning lines from left to right in one field and right to left in the next
d. By scanning odd numbered lines in one field and even numbered lines in the next

9. From which of the following bands is amateur radio contesting generally excluded?

a. 30 meters
b. 6 meters
c. 70 centimeters
d. 33 centimeters

10. Which of the following digital modes is designed for EME communications?

a. MSK144
b. PACTOR III
c. WSPR
d. Q65

11. To what does the "4" in FT4 refer?

a. Multiples of 4 bits of user information
b. Four-tone continuous-phase frequency shift keying
c. Four transmit/receive cycles per minute
d. All these choices are correct

12. When scheduling EME contacts, which of these conditions will generally result in the least path loss?

a. When the moon is at perigee
b. When the moon is full
c. When the moon is at apogee
d. When the MUF is above 30 MHz

13. At what time of day is transequatorial propagation most likely to occur?

a. Morning
b. Noon
c. Afternoon or early evening
d. Late at night

14. Which of the following signal paths is most likely to experience high levels of absorption when the A-index or K-index is elevated?

a. Transequatorial
b. Through the auroral oval
c. Sporadic-E
d. NVIS

15. Which of the following test instruments is used to display spurious signals and/or intermodulation distortion products generated by an SSB transmitter?

a. A differential resolver
b. A spectrum analyzer
c. A logic analyzer
d. A network analyzer

16. Which S parameter is equivalent to forward gain?

a. S11
b. S12
c. S21
d. S22

17. What is the term for the suppression in an FM receiver of one signal by another stronger signal on the same frequency?

a. Desensitization
b. Cross-modulation interference
c. Capture effect
d. Frequency discrimination

18. What creates intermodulation interference between two repeaters in close proximity?

a. The output signals cause feedback in the final amplifier of one or both transmitters
b. The output signals mix in the final amplifier of one or both transmitters
c. The input frequencies are harmonically related
d. The output frequencies are harmonically related

19. Which of the following types of noise are removed by a noise blanker?

a. Broadband white noise
b. Impulse noise
c. Hum and buzz
d. All these choices are correct

20. What is the magnitude of the impedance of a series RLC circuit at resonance?

a. High, as compared to the circuit resistance
b. Approximately equal to capacitive reactance
c. Approximately equal to inductive reactance
d. Approximately equal to circuit resistance

21. How is impedance in polar form converted to an equivalent admittance?

a. Take the reciprocal of the angle and change the sign of the magnitude
b. Take the reciprocal of the magnitude and change the sign of the angle
c. Take the square root of the magnitude and add 180 degrees to the angle
d. Square the magnitude and subtract 90 degrees from the angle

22. Which of the following represents an inductive reactance in polar coordinates?

a. A positive 45 degree phase angle
b. A negative 45 degree phase angle
c. A positive 90 degree phase angle
d. A negative90 degree phase angle

23. What is the phase relationship between current and voltage for reactive power?

a. They are out of phase
b. They are in phase
c. They are 90 degrees out of phase
d. They are 45 degrees out of phase

24. Why does a PN-junction diode not conduct current when reverse biased?

a. Only P-type semiconductor material can conduct current
b. Only N-type semiconductor material can conduct current
c. Holes in P-type material and electrons in the N-type material are separated by the applied voltage, widening the depletion region
d. Excess holes in P-type material combine with the electrons in N-type material, converting the entire diode into an insulator

25. What property of an LED's semiconductor material determines its forward voltage drop?

a. Intrinsic resistance
b. Band gap
c. Junction capacitance
d. Junction depth

26. What is tri-state logic?

a. Logic devices with 0, 1, and high-impedance output states
b. Logic devices that utilize ternary math
c. Logic with three output impedance which can be selected to better match the load impedance
d. A counter with eight states

27. Which of the following is an aspect of the piezoelectric effect?

a. Mechanical deformation of material by the application of a voltage
b. Mechanical deformation of material by the application of a magnetic field
c. Generation of electrical energy in the presence of light
d. Increased conductivity in the presence of light

28. Which of the following materials supports the highest frequency of operation when used in MMICs?

a. Silicon
b. Silicon nitride
c. Silicon dioxide
d. Gallium nitride

29. What is the most common configuration of an optoisolator or optocoupler?

a. A lens and a photomultiplier
b. A frequency-modulated helium-neon laser
c. An amplitude-modulated helium-neon laser
d. An LED and a phototransistor

30. Which of the following can divide the frequency of a pulse train by 2?

a. An XOR gate
b. A flip-flop
c. An OR gate
d. A multiplexer

31. What circuit is required at the output of an RF switching amplifier?

a. A filter to remove harmonic content
b. A high-pass filter to compensate for low gain at low frequencies
c. A matched load resistor to prevent damage by switching frequencies
d. A temperature compensating load resistor to improve linearity

32. What is the purpose of adding an inductor to a Pi-network to create a Pi-L-network?

a. Greater harmonic suppression
b. Higher efficiency
c. Does not require a capacitor
d. Greater transformation range

33. What device is used as a stable voltage reference?

a. A Zener diode
b. A digital-to-analog converter
c. An SCR
d. An analog-to-digital converter

34. What is a frequency discriminator?

a. An FM generator circuit
b. A circuit for filtering two closely adjacent signals
c. An automatic band-switching circuit
d. A circuit for detecting FM signals

35. What type of digital signal processing filter is used to generate an SSB signal?

a. An adaptive filter
b. A notch filter
c. A Hilbert-transform filter
d. An elliptical filter

36. What is the typical input impedance of an op-amp?

a. 100 ohms
b. 10,000 ohms
c. Very low
d. Very high

37. What is a phase-locked loop?

a. An electronic servo loop consisting of a ratio detector, reactance modulator, and voltage-controlled oscillator
b. An electronic circuit also known as a monostable multivibrator
c. An electronic servo loop consisting of a phase detector, a low-pass filter, a voltage-controlled oscillator, and a stable reference oscillator
d. An electronic circuit consisting of a precision push-pull amplifier with a differential phase input

38. Which of the following describes a signal in the time domain?

a. Power at intervals of phase
b. Amplitude at different times
c. Frequency at different times
d. Discrete impulses in time order

39. What is the modulation index of an FM phone signal having a maximum frequency deviation of 3000 Hz either side of the carrier frequency when the modulating frequency is 1000 Hz?

a. 3
b. 0.3
c. 6
d. 0.6

40. Why should phase-shifting of a PSK signal be done at the zero crossing of the RF signal?

a. To minimize bandwidth
b. To simplify modulation
c. To improve carrier suppression
d. All these choices are correct

41. How does the spread spectrum technique of frequency hopping work?

a. If interference is detected by the receiver, it will signal the transmitter to change frequencies
b. RF signals are clipped to generate a wide band of harmonics which provides redundancy to correct errors
c. A binary bit stream is used to shift the phase of an RF carrier very rapidly in a pseudorandom sequence
d. Rapidly varying frequency of the transmitted signal according to a pseudorandom sequence

42 What term describing total radiated power takes into account all gains and losses?

a. Power factor
b. Half-power bandwidth
c. Effective radiated power
d. Apparent power

Question 43 pertains to the following graphic:

Figure E9-1

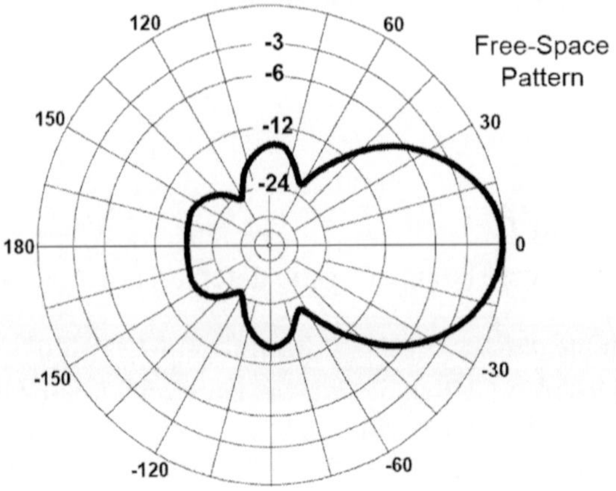

43 In the antenna radiation pattern shown in Figure E9-1, what is the front-to-side ratio?

a. 12 dB
b. 24 dB
c. 18 dB
d. 14 dB

44. What type of radiation pattern is created by two 1/4-wavelength vertical antennas spaced 1/2-wavelength apart and fed in phase?

a. Omni-directional
b. Cardioid
c. A Figure-8 broadside to the axis of the array
d. A Figure-8 end-fire along the axis of the array

45. What is the most efficient location for loading coil on an electrically short whip?

a. Near the center of the vertical radiator
b. As low as possible on the vertical radiator
c. At a voltage maximum
d. At a voltage null

46. What matching system uses a short length of transmission line connected in parallel with the feed line at or near the feed point?

a. Gamma match
b. Delta match
c. T-match
d. Stub match

47. Why is the electrical length of a coaxial cable longer than its physical length?

a. Skin effect is less pronounced in the coaxial cable
b. Skin effect is more pronounced in the coaxial cable
c. Electromagnetic waves move faster in the coaxial cable than in air
d. Electrical signals move more slowly in a coaxial cable than in air

48. Which of the following is often determined using a Smith chart?

a. Beam headings and radiation patterns
b. Satellite azimuth and elevation bearings
c. Impedance and SWR values in transmission lines
d. Point-to-point propagation reliability as a function of frequency

49. What is Receiving Directivity Factor (RDF)?

a. Forward gain compared to the gain in the reverse direction
b. Relative directivity compared to isotropic
c. Relative directivity compared to a dipole
d. Peak antenna gain compared to average gain over the hemisphere around and above the antenna

50. Over what range of frequencies are the FCC human body RF exposure limits most restrictive?

a. 300 kHz to 3 MHz
b. 3 to 30 MHz
c. 30 to 300 MHz
d. 300 to 3000 MHz

Test #3 Answer Key and Explanations

1. C: 14.1472 MHz is the maximum legal carrier frequency on the 20-meter band for transmitting a 2.8 kHz wide USB data signal.

2. A: An amateur station located within 1 mile (1600 m) of an FCC monitoring facility must protect it from harmful interference.

3. B: Operators may operate on the 2200-meter or 630-meter band after 30 days, providing they have not been told that their station is within 1 kilometer of PLC systems using those frequencies, after filing a notification with the Utilities Technology Council (UTC).

4. B: A space telecommand station is an amateur station that transmits communications to initiate, modify, or terminate functions of a space station.

5. C: A Volunteer Examiner Coordinator is an organization that has entered into an agreement with the FCC to coordinate, prepare, and administer amateur operator license examinations.

6. D: A dealer may sell an external RF power amplifier capable of operation below 144 MHz if the amplified has been constructed or modified by an amateur radio operator for use at an amateur station.

7. D: In an inverting linear transponder, an upload signal is processed by mixing the signal with a local oscillator signal and transmitting the difference product.

8. D: In a fast-scan (NTSC) television system, an interlaced scanning pattern is generated by scanning odd-numbered lines in one field and even-numbered lines in the next.

9. A: Amateur radio contesting is generally excluded from the 30-meter band.

10. D: The Q65 digital mode is designed for EME communications.

11. B: The "4" in FT4 refers to four-tone continuous-phase frequency shift keying.

12. A: Scheduling EME contacts when the Moon is at perigee will generally result in the least path loss.

13. C: Transequatorial propagation is most likely to occur in the afternoon or early evening.

14. B: Paths through the auroral oval are more likely to experience high levels of absorption when the A-index or K-index is elevated than transequatorial, sporadic-E, or NVIS propagation.

15. B: A spectrum analyzer is used to display spurious signals and/or intermodulation distortion products generated by an SSB transmitter.

16. C: The S21 parameter is equivalent to forward gain.

17. C: Capture effect is the term for the suppression in an FM receiver of one signal by another stronger signal on the same frequency.

18. B: Intermodulation interference between two repeaters in close proximity is created when the output signals mix in the final amplifier of one or both transmitters.

19. B: Impulse noise is removed by a noise blanker.

20. D: The magnitude of the impedance of a series RLC circuit at resonance is approximately equal to circuit resistance.

21. B: To convert impedance in polar form to an equivalent admittance, take the reciprocal of the magnitude and change the sign of the angle.

22. C: A positive 90 degree phase angle represents an inductive reactance in polar coordinates.

23. C: Current and voltage are 90 degrees out of phase for reactive power.

24. C: A PN-junction diode does not conduct current when reverse biased because holes in P-type material and electrons in the N-type material are separated by the applied voltage, widening the depletion region.

25. B: The forward voltage drop of an LED's semiconductor material is determined by its band gap.

26. A: Tri-state logic devices have 0, 1, and high-impedance output states.

27. A: The piezoelectric effect is mechanical deformation of material by the application of a voltage.

28. D: Gallium nitride supports the highest frequency of operation when used in MMICs.

29. D: Optoisolators and optocouplers are most often used as LEDs and phototransistors, respectively.

30. B: Flip-flops can divide the frequency of a pulse train by 2.

31. A: A filter to remove harmonic content is required at the output of an RF switching amplifier.

32. A: The purpose of adding an inductor to a Pi-network to create a Pi-L-network is for greater harmonic suppression.

33. A: A Zener diode is used as a stable voltage reference.

34. D: A frequency discriminator is a circuit for detecting FM signals.

35. C: A Hilbert-transform filter is used to generate an SSB signal.

36. D: The typical input impedance of an op-amp is very high.

37. C: A phase-locked loop is an electronic servo loop consisting of a phase detector, a low-pass filter, a voltage-controlled oscillator, and a stable reference oscillator.

38. B: Amplitude at different times describes a signal in the time domain.

39. A: The modulation index of an FM-phone signal having a maximum frequency deviation of 3000 Hz either side of the carrier frequency when the modulating frequency is 1000 Hz is 3.

40. A: Phase-shifting of a PSK signal should be done at the zero crossing of the RF signal in order to minimize bandwidth.

41. D: In frequency hopping, the frequency of the transmitted signal is varied rapidly according to a pseudorandom sequence.

42. C: Effective radiated power takes into account all gains and losses when describing total radiated power.

43. D: In the antenna radiation pattern shown in Figure E9-1, the front-to-side ratio is 14 dB.

44. C: The radiation pattern of two 1/4-wavelength vertical antennas spaced 1/2-wavelength apart and fed in phase is a figure-8 broadside to the axis of the array.

45. A: The most efficient location for loading coil on an electrically short whip is near the center of the vertical radiator.

46. D: The stub match uses a short length of transmission line connected in parallel with the feed line at or near the feed point.

47. D: The electrical length of a coaxial cable is longer than its physical length because electrical signals move more slowly in a coaxial cable than in air.

48. C: Impedance and SWR values in transmission lines are often determined using a Smith chart.

49. D: Receiving Directivity Factor (RDF) is forward gain compared to average gain over the entire hemisphere.

50. C: The FCC human body RF exposure limits are most restrictive over 30 to 300 MHz.

Seven Additional Ham Radio Extra Class Practice Tests

To take these additional practice tests, visit the online resources page:
mometrix.com/resources719/hamradioextra

How to Overcome Test Anxiety

Just the thought of taking a test is enough to make most people a little nervous. A test is an important event that can have a long-term impact on your future, so it's important to take it seriously and it's natural to feel anxious about performing well. But just because anxiety is normal, that doesn't mean that it's helpful in test taking, or that you should simply accept it as part of your life. Anxiety can have a variety of effects. These effects can be mild, like making you feel slightly nervous, or severe, like blocking your ability to focus or remember even a simple detail.

If you experience test anxiety—whether severe or mild—it's important to know how to beat it. To discover this, first you need to understand what causes test anxiety.

Causes of Test Anxiety

While we often think of anxiety as an uncontrollable emotional state, it can actually be caused by simple, practical things. One of the most common causes of test anxiety is that a person does not feel adequately prepared for their test. This feeling can be the result of many different issues such as poor study habits or lack of organization, but the most common culprit is time management. Starting to study too late, failing to organize your study time to cover all of the material, or being distracted while you study will mean that you're not well prepared for the test. This may lead to cramming the night before, which will cause you to be physically and mentally exhausted for the test. Poor time management also contributes to feelings of stress, fear, and hopelessness as you realize you are not well prepared but don't know what to do about it.

Other times, test anxiety is not related to your preparation for the test but comes from unresolved fear. This may be a past failure on a test, or poor performance on tests in general. It may come from comparing yourself to others who seem to be performing better or from the stress of living up to expectations. Anxiety may be driven by fears of the future—how failure on this test would affect your educational and career goals. These fears are often completely irrational, but they can still negatively impact your test performance.

Elements of Test Anxiety

As mentioned earlier, test anxiety is considered to be an emotional state, but it has physical and mental components as well. Sometimes you may not even realize that you are suffering from test anxiety until you notice the physical symptoms. These can include trembling hands, rapid heartbeat, sweating, nausea, and tense muscles. Extreme anxiety may lead to fainting or vomiting. Obviously, any of these symptoms can have a negative impact on testing. It is important to recognize them as soon as they begin to occur so that you can address the problem before it damages your performance.

The mental components of test anxiety include trouble focusing and inability to remember learned information. During a test, your mind is on high alert, which can help you recall information and stay focused for an extended period of time. However, anxiety interferes with your mind's natural processes, causing you to blank out, even on the questions you know well. The strain of testing during anxiety makes it difficult to stay focused, especially on a test that may take several hours. Extreme anxiety can take a huge mental toll, making it difficult not only to recall test information but even to understand the test questions or pull your thoughts together.

Effects of Test Anxiety

Test anxiety is like a disease—if left untreated, it will get progressively worse. Anxiety leads to poor performance, and this reinforces the feelings of fear and failure, which in turn lead to poor performances on subsequent tests. It can grow from a mild nervousness to a crippling condition. If allowed to progress, test anxiety can have a big impact on your schooling, and consequently on your future.

Test anxiety can spread to other parts of your life. Anxiety on tests can become anxiety in any stressful situation, and blanking on a test can turn into panicking in a job situation. But fortunately, you don't have to let anxiety rule your testing and determine your grades. There are a number of relatively simple steps you can take to move past anxiety and function normally on a test and in the rest of life.

Physical Steps for Beating Test Anxiety

While test anxiety is a serious problem, the good news is that it can be overcome. It doesn't have to control your ability to think and remember information. While it may take time, you can begin taking steps today to beat anxiety.

Just as your first hint that you may be struggling with anxiety comes from the physical symptoms, the first step to treating it is also physical. Rest is crucial for having a clear, strong mind. If you are tired, it is much easier to give in to anxiety. But if you establish good sleep habits, your body and mind will be ready to perform optimally, without the strain of exhaustion. Additionally, sleeping well helps you to retain information better, so you're more likely to recall the answers when you see the test questions.

Getting good sleep means more than going to bed on time. It's important to allow your brain time to relax. Take study breaks from time to time so it doesn't get overworked, and don't study right before bed. Take time to rest your mind before trying to rest your body, or you may find it difficult to fall asleep.

Along with sleep, other aspects of physical health are important in preparing for a test. Good nutrition is vital for good brain function. Sugary foods and drinks may give a burst of energy but this burst is followed by a crash, both physically and emotionally. Instead, fuel your body with protein and vitamin-rich foods.

Also, drink plenty of water. Dehydration can lead to headaches and exhaustion, especially if your brain is already under stress from the rigors of the test. Particularly if your test is a long one, drink water during the breaks. And if possible, take an energy-boosting snack to eat between sections.

Along with sleep and diet, a third important part of physical health is exercise. Maintaining a steady workout schedule is helpful, but even taking 5-minute study breaks to walk can help get your blood pumping faster and clear your head. Exercise also releases endorphins, which contribute to a positive feeling and can help combat test anxiety.

When you nurture your physical health, you are also contributing to your mental health. If your body is healthy, your mind is much more likely to be healthy as well. So take time to rest, nourish your body with healthy food and water, and get moving as much as possible. Taking these physical steps will make you stronger and more able to take the mental steps necessary to overcome test anxiety.

Mental Steps for Beating Test Anxiety

Working on the mental side of test anxiety can be more challenging, but as with the physical side, there are clear steps you can take to overcome it. As mentioned earlier, test anxiety often stems from lack of preparation, so the obvious solution is to prepare for the test. Effective studying may be the most important weapon you have for beating test anxiety, but you can and should employ several other mental tools to combat fear.

First, boost your confidence by reminding yourself of past success—tests or projects that you aced. If you're putting as much effort into preparing for this test as you did for those, there's no reason you should expect to fail here. Work hard to prepare; then trust your preparation.

Second, surround yourself with encouraging people. It can be helpful to find a study group, but be sure that the people you're around will encourage a positive attitude. If you spend time with others who are anxious or cynical, this will only contribute to your own anxiety. Look for others who are motivated to study hard from a desire to succeed, not from a fear of failure.

Third, reward yourself. A test is physically and mentally tiring, even without anxiety, and it can be helpful to have something to look forward to. Plan an activity following the test, regardless of the outcome, such as going to a movie or getting ice cream.

When you are taking the test, if you find yourself beginning to feel anxious, remind yourself that you know the material. Visualize successfully completing the test. Then take a few deep, relaxing breaths and return to it. Work through the questions carefully but with confidence, knowing that you are capable of succeeding.

Developing a healthy mental approach to test taking will also aid in other areas of life. Test anxiety affects more than just the actual test—it can be damaging to your mental health and even contribute to depression. It's important to beat test anxiety before it becomes a problem for more than testing.

Study Strategy

Being prepared for the test is necessary to combat anxiety, but what does being prepared look like? You may study for hours on end and still not feel prepared. What you need is a strategy for test prep. The next few pages outline our recommended steps to help you plan out and conquer the challenge of preparation.

Step 1: Scope Out the Test

Learn everything you can about the format (multiple choice, essay, etc.) and what will be on the test. Gather any study materials, course outlines, or sample exams that may be available. Not only will this help you to prepare, but knowing what to expect can help to alleviate test anxiety.

Step 2: Map Out the Material

Look through the textbook or study guide and make note of how many chapters or sections it has. Then divide these over the time you have. For example, if a book has 15 chapters and you have five days to study, you need to cover three chapters each day. Even better, if you have the time, leave an extra day at the end for overall review after you have gone through the material in depth.

If time is limited, you may need to prioritize the material. Look through it and make note of which sections you think you already have a good grasp on, and which need review. While you are studying, skim quickly through the familiar sections and take more time on the challenging parts. Write out your plan so you don't get lost as you go. Having a written plan also helps you feel more in control of the study, so anxiety is less likely to arise from feeling overwhelmed at the amount to cover.

Step 3: Gather Your Tools

Decide what study method works best for you. Do you prefer to highlight in the book as you study and then go back over the highlighted portions? Or do you type out notes of the important information? Or is it helpful to make flashcards that you can carry with you? Assemble the pens, index cards, highlighters, post-it notes, and any other materials you may need so you won't be distracted by getting up to find things while you study.

If you're having a hard time retaining the information or organizing your notes, experiment with different methods. For example, try color-coding by subject with colored pens, highlighters, or post-it notes. If you learn better by hearing, try recording yourself reading your notes so you can listen while in the car, working out, or simply sitting at your desk. Ask a friend to quiz you from your flashcards, or try teaching someone the material to solidify it in your mind.

Step 4: Create Your Environment

It's important to avoid distractions while you study. This includes both the obvious distractions like visitors and the subtle distractions like an uncomfortable chair (or a too-comfortable couch that makes you want to fall asleep). Set up the best study environment possible: good lighting and a comfortable work area. If background music helps you focus, you may want to turn it on, but otherwise keep the room quiet. If you are using a computer to take notes, be sure you don't have any other windows open, especially applications like social media, games, or anything else that could distract you. Silence your phone and turn off notifications. Be sure to keep water close by so you stay hydrated while you study (but avoid unhealthy drinks and snacks).

Also, take into account the best time of day to study. Are you freshest first thing in the morning? Try to set aside some time then to work through the material. Is your mind clearer in the afternoon or evening? Schedule your study session then. Another method is to study at the same time of day that you will take the test, so that your brain gets used to working on the material at that time and will be ready to focus at test time.

Step 5: Study!

Once you have done all the study preparation, it's time to settle into the actual studying. Sit down, take a few moments to settle your mind so you can focus, and begin to follow your study plan. Don't give in to distractions or let yourself procrastinate. This is your time to prepare so you'll be ready to fearlessly approach the test. Make the most of the time and stay focused.

Of course, you don't want to burn out. If you study too long you may find that you're not retaining the information very well. Take regular study breaks. For example, taking five minutes out of every hour to walk briskly, breathing deeply and swinging your arms, can help your mind stay fresh.

As you get to the end of each chapter or section, it's a good idea to do a quick review. Remind yourself of what you learned and work on any difficult parts. When you feel that you've mastered the material, move on to the next part. At the end of your study session, briefly skim through your notes again.

But while review is helpful, cramming last minute is NOT. If at all possible, work ahead so that you won't need to fit all your study into the last day. Cramming overloads your brain with more information than it can process and retain, and your tired mind may struggle to recall even previously learned information when it is overwhelmed with last-minute study. Also, the urgent nature of cramming and the stress placed on your brain contribute to anxiety. You'll be more likely to go to the test feeling unprepared and having trouble thinking clearly.

So don't cram, and don't stay up late before the test, even just to review your notes at a leisurely pace. Your brain needs rest more than it needs to go over the information again. In fact, plan to finish your studies by noon or early afternoon the day before the test. Give your brain the rest of the day to relax or focus on other things, and get a good night's sleep. Then you will be fresh for the test and better able to recall what you've studied.

Step 6: Take a Practice Test

Many courses offer sample tests, either online or in the study materials. This is an excellent resource to check whether you have mastered the material, as well as to prepare for the test format and environment.

Check the test format ahead of time: the number of questions, the type (multiple choice, free response, etc.), and the time limit. Then create a plan for working through them. For example, if you have 30 minutes to take a 60-question test, your limit is 30 seconds per question. Spend less time on the questions you know well so that you can take more time on the difficult ones.

If you have time to take several practice tests, take the first one open book, with no time limit. Work through the questions at your own pace and make sure you fully understand them. Gradually work up to taking a test under test conditions: sit at a desk with all study materials put away and set a timer. Pace yourself to make sure you finish the test with time to spare and go back to check your answers if you have time.

After each test, check your answers. On the questions you missed, be sure you understand why you missed them. Did you misread the question (tests can use tricky wording)? Did you forget the information? Or was it something you hadn't learned? Go back and study any shaky areas that the practice tests reveal.

Taking these tests not only helps with your grade, but also aids in combating test anxiety. If you're already used to the test conditions, you're less likely to worry about it, and working through tests until you're scoring well gives you a confidence boost. Go through the practice tests until you feel comfortable, and then you can go into the test knowing that you're ready for it.

Test Tips

On test day, you should be confident, knowing that you've prepared well and are ready to answer the questions. But aside from preparation, there are several test day strategies you can employ to maximize your performance.

First, as stated before, get a good night's sleep the night before the test (and for several nights before that, if possible). Go into the test with a fresh, alert mind rather than staying up late to study.

Try not to change too much about your normal routine on the day of the test. It's important to eat a nutritious breakfast, but if you normally don't eat breakfast at all, consider eating just a protein bar. If you're a coffee drinker, go ahead and have your normal coffee. Just make sure you time it so that the caffeine doesn't wear off right in the middle of your test. Avoid sugary beverages, and drink enough water to stay hydrated but not so much that you need a restroom break 10 minutes into the test. If your test isn't first thing in the morning, consider going for a walk or doing a light workout before the test to get your blood flowing.

Allow yourself enough time to get ready, and leave for the test with plenty of time to spare so you won't have the anxiety of scrambling to arrive in time. Another reason to be early is to select a good seat. It's helpful to sit away from doors and windows, which can be distracting. Find a good seat, get out your supplies, and settle your mind before the test begins.

When the test begins, start by going over the instructions carefully, even if you already know what to expect. Make sure you avoid any careless mistakes by following the directions.

Then begin working through the questions, pacing yourself as you've practiced. If you're not sure on an answer, don't spend too much time on it, and don't let it shake your confidence. Either skip it and come back later, or eliminate as many wrong answers as possible and guess among the remaining ones. Don't dwell on these questions as you continue—put them out of your mind and focus on what lies ahead.

Be sure to read all of the answer choices, even if you're sure the first one is the right answer. Sometimes you'll find a better one if you keep reading. But don't second-guess yourself if you do immediately know the answer. Your gut instinct is usually right. Don't let test anxiety rob you of the information you know.

If you have time at the end of the test (and if the test format allows), go back and review your answers. Be cautious about changing any, since your first instinct tends to be correct, but make sure you didn't misread any of the questions or accidentally mark the wrong answer choice. Look over any you skipped and make an educated guess.

At the end, leave the test feeling confident. You've done your best, so don't waste time worrying about your performance or wishing you could change anything. Instead, celebrate the successful completion of this test. And finally, use this test to learn how to deal with anxiety even better next time.

Review Video: Test Anxiety
Visit mometrix.com/academy and enter code: 100340

Important Qualification

Not all anxiety is created equal. If your test anxiety is causing major issues in your life beyond the classroom or testing center, or if you are experiencing troubling physical symptoms related to your anxiety, it may be a sign of a serious physiological or psychological condition. If this sounds like your situation, we strongly encourage you to seek professional help.

Online Resources

Due to our efforts to try to keep this book to a manageable length, we've created a link that will give you access to all of your online resources:

mometrix.com/resource719/hamradiotech

mometrix.com/resource719/hamradiogen

mometrix.com/resource719/hamradioextra